So <u>THAT'S</u> What It Means!

So <u>THAT'S</u> What It Means!

By
Don Campbell ✳ **Wendell Johnston**
John Walvoord ✳ **John Witmer**

Charles R. Swindoll, General Editor
Roy B. Zuck, Managing Editor

NELSON REFERENCE & ELECTRONIC
A Division of Thomas Nelson Publishers
Since 1798

www.thomasnelson.com

Library of Congress Cataloging-in-Publication Data

So that's what it means! / Donald K. Campbell . . . [et al.]; Charles R. Swindoll, general editor; Roy B. Zuck, managing editor
   p.   cm.—

ISBN 0-7852-5252-5 (adapted from 0-8499-1381-0, The theological wordbook)
   1. Theology—Terminology.   2. Bible—Theology.
   I. Campbell, Donald K.   II. Swindoll, Charles R.   III. Zuck, Roy B.
   BR96.5 .T442000   00–026807
                                                       CIP

Printed in the United States of America

1 2 3 4 5 6 7 — 10 09 08 07 06 05 04

CONTENTS

FOREWORD

In this tremendous reference tool, *So That's What It Means!* four Dallas Theological Seminary stalwarts and theological statesmen—Donald K. Campbell, Wendell G. Johnston, John F. Walvoord, and John A. Witmer—discuss numerous terms that you will encounter as you read and study the Scriptures. These men have devoted their lives to theological education—studying and teaching the Bible and theology, and each one has served for many years as an adminstrator at Dallas Seminary. You will realize the seasoned years of study these men have invested as soon as you scan the first few entries.

One of the distinctives of Dallas Theological Seminary has been our strong emphasis on theology. After all, it's our middle name! From the beginning, our theological curriculum has been based on the Scriptures. The school's founder and first president, Lewis Sperry Chafer, placed strong emphasis on a biblical theology derived from a thorough study of God's inerrant Word. This legacy continues in this popular adaptation of *The Theological Wordbook.*

Each of the two hundred terms discussed in this volume focuses on what the Scriptures say on that topic. And at the end of each topic is a brief, one-sentence application, suggesting one way that doctrinal truth should impact our thoughts, attitudes, or actions. These short admonitions demonstrate that every aspect of theology is relevant to our lives.

The two hundred terms discussed in *So That's What It Means!* cover the gamut of the Scriptures, ranging from Angels to Antichrist, from Depravity to Demons, Babylon to Baptism, and Suffering to Worship—words pertaining to all the major doctrines in God's precious Word.

Our authors have done the body of Christ an outstanding service by shedding light on terms that are frequently used within the Christian community but that have special meaning within the Christian context.

I suggest you place this volume in a special, easy-to-find spot in your personal library. You will be reaching for it often!

—CHARLES R. SWINDOLL
General Editor

PREFACE

You are reading the Bible in your devotions, and you run across a word or phrase in the Scriptures that puzzles you. For example, you read of apostasy, the laying on of hands, the Transfiguration, or firstfruits.

Or you are preparing a sermon, and you want to know what the rest of Scripture says about a certain subject, such as fasting, hope, prayer, rewards, or temptations.

Perhaps you are preparing a Bible lesson on a topic such as angels, assurance, forgiveness, the Trinity, or wisdom.

Where can you find a succinct yet thorough discussion of these and many other doctrinal topics that are mentioned in Scripture and elsewhere? *So That's What It Means!* is the answer!

This volume gives you a concise summary of what the Bible teaches on exactly two hundred theological and biblical topics. And every essay is packed with an abundance of Bible references so that you can check the Scriptures themselves.

The Bible's doctrinal themes are far from irrelevant. And that's why each article in *So That's What It Means!* concludes with a one-sentence application, a pithy exhortation or statement to help drive home the relevance of that theological subject to life.

The initials at the end of each article designate the person who wrote the article.

DKC—Donald K. Campbell
WGJ—Wendell G. Johnston
JAW—John A. Witmer
JFW—John F. Walvoord

These men, each one a skilled Bible expositor and theologian, formerly served as faculty members of Dallas Theological Seminary. Each author contributed fifty topics in this compilation of two hundred topics. Editor Joseph Snider worked with their manuscripts to make them even easier for lay Christians to understand.

We trust you will find this book helpful as you study—and share—God's precious Word.

—ROY B. ZUCK
Managing Editor

ABIDING

In His teaching on abiding Jesus took a well-known word meaning "to dwell" or "to remain" and gave it a spiritual significance. The Greek word for abide (*menō*) occurs over one hundred times in the New Testament, with more than half of these occurrences in John's Gospel and 1 John. This word describes the intimate relationship to Christ of all those who belong to Him.

Some Old Testament verses use the word *abide* or *dwell* to express a believer's relationship with God the Father. Examples include Psalms 15:1 ("LORD, who may *dwell* in your sanctuary?") and 91:1 ("He who *dwells* in the shelter of the Most High will rest in the shadow of the Almighty"). These instances suggest safety, rest, and nearness to God, but they lack the intimacy of the connection we have with Christ in the New Testament teaching on abiding.

In John 6:56 Christ first taught about the relationship He wanted to have with His disciples. "Whoever eats my flesh and drinks my blood remains [*menō*] in me, and I in him." The disciples found these words hard to grasp. Jesus explained them in His Upper Room Discourse the night before He was crucified. He told them He was leaving to go back to God the Father, but that they would not understand this until He was resurrected. "On that day you will realize that I am in my Father, and you are in me, and I am in you" (14:20).

The disciples would then have the same kind of relationship with Christ that He had with the Father (17:20–23).

The disciples were used to seeing Jesus and conversing with Him face to face. The idea of having a spiritual connection to Him seemed strange. How could they abide in Him when He would not be there? He explained that after His ascension into heaven He would abide in them through His Word (15:7). The Holy Spirit, whom He would send to guide them into all truth (16:13), would teach them, reminding them of everything Jesus had taught them (14:26). From their side, the disciples would abide in Him by obeying His Word. "If you obey my commands, you will remain [abide] in my love" (15:10). He compared "abiding" in Him to the connection between a grapevine and its branches. They could readily understand that comparison.

Abiding in Christ, like branches "abiding" in a vine, produces several results for us. Abiding leads to a vital prayer life. It results in a productive spiritual life; that is, we bear fruit just as a branch of the vine bears grapes. Jesus did not identify the nature of the fruit we will bear. Apparently whatever we do while depending on Him qualifies as "fruit." In fact, because of abiding in Christ, we will bear "much fruit" (15:8) and do greater works than He did (14:12).

In 1 John 2—4 the apostle John expanded on Jesus' teaching about abiding. In these three chapters John refers to "abiding" twenty-six times. Such emphasis makes "abiding" a major theme of the epistle. Abiding in Christ affects our conduct. John wrote, "Whoever claims to live [*menō*] in him must walk as Jesus did" (2:6). Abiding "in the light" leads us to love other believers (2:9–11). Abiding in God's Word enables us to overcome the evil one (2:14), and it guards us from being deceived by his false teachers (2:26–27; see also 4:6). Abiding in fellowship with Christ gives us confidence about the future (2:28; 4:17). When we abide we will be characterized by righteous living (3:6), and the Holy Spirit's indwelling will assure us that we are abiding in Christ (4:13).

There is one other New Testament passage that indirectly teaches about abiding in Christ. It was written by another disciple who had also been in the Upper Room with John and Christ. Peter did not use the term *abiding*, but there are several similarities between 2 Peter 1:1–11 and John 15:1–11. First, Jesus told His disciples that fruitfulness would result from abiding in Him (15:5). Peter said fruitfulness depends on possessing Christ's character qualities (1 Pet. 1:8). Second, Jesus said He would abide in His disciples through His Word (John 15:7). Peter wrote that the Lord has given us "his very great and precious promises" (His Word) so that through these promises we may share in His divine nature (2 Pet. 1:4). Third, Jesus said obedience to His Word was the way for the disciples to abide in Him (John 15:10). Peter said, "If you *do* these things, you will never fall" (2 Pet. 1:10). Fourth, when a believer is abiding, the fruit produced will last (John 15:16). Peter wrote that believers will receive a rich welcome into the eternal kingdom of the Lord (2 Pet. 1:11).

Day-by-day abiding in Christ should be the goal of every believer, and the way to abide is clearly laid out in Scripture. **—WGJ**

***

Nothing can be compared to the joy of abiding in an intimate loving relationship with Jesus Christ.

ABOMINATION

The Old Testament translates four Hebrew words "abomination" to describe what is detestable, hateful, or unethical. Heathen rites of worship in Old Testament times were especially detestable to God. In the New Testament the Greek word *bdelygma* is translated "abomination" (Matt. 24:15; Mark 13:14; Rev. 17:4–5), "detestable" (Luke 16:15), and "shameful" (Rev. 21:27). It is clear that God hates sins of all kinds, and they are a basis for divine judgment.

In biblical prophecy the most important appearance of this term is "the abomination that causes desolation," spoken of by Daniel. The phrase first occurs in Daniel 8:13, where Daniel asked, "How long will it take for the vision to be fulfilled—the vision concerning the daily sacrifice, the rebellion that causes desolation, and the surrender of the sanctuary and of the host that will be trampled underfoot?" The phrase also occurs in Daniel 9:27; 11:31; and 12:11. Daniel 8 and 11 predict the efforts of Antiochus Epiphanes IV, ruler of Syria from 175 to 164 B.C., to stamp out the Jewish religion and replace it with pagan worship.

After the death of Alexander the Great, his empire had been divided among his four generals. Seleucus received the Middle East, and Antiochus was one of his successors. In 168 B.C. Antiochus built a pagan altar in the Jerusalem temple as a place to offer sacrifices to Zeus, the supreme god of the Greek pantheon. Among the sacrifices offered was a sow, which was an abomination to the Jews.

First and Second Maccabbees record that thousands of Jewish men, women, and children were killed in this attempt to stamp out the Jewish religion. But before Antiochus's death by natural causes in 164 B.C., the Jewish temple had been cleansed and the Jewish sacrificial system restored. Daniel 11:21–33 describes this sequence of events. Daniel emphasized the desecration of the temple and the temporary abolition of the daily sacrifices.

Daniel 12:11 predicts, "From the time that the daily sacrifice is abolished and the abomination that causes desolation is set up, there will be 1,290 days." Bible scholars who don't believe in a literal millennium say this happened in the time of Antiochus Epiphanes. Premillennarians say this abomination is a different one, the one spoken of by Christ in Matthew 24:15. This abomination causing desolation will occur in the seven-year period of Tribulation immediately preceding the Second Coming of Christ. It will follow the pattern of Antiochus Epiphanes's outrage during the second century B.C. The abomination of Matthew 24:15 refers to the setting up of an image of the Antichrist in the Jerusalem temple, an image that the false prophet will miraculously cause to speak (Rev. 13:14–15; see also 2 Thess. 2:9). This will occur for three and a half years or forty-two months, the second half of the seven-year period indicated in Daniel 9:27 (see Rev. 13:5).   **—JFW**

***

In a world of confusing and competing values, believers should call detestable and abominable what God calls detestable and abominable, and love what God loves and hate what He hates.

ADAM

God gave the name "Adam" to the first human being He created. The word most likely comes from the Hebrew verb "to be red" and is also related to the noun for "earth" or "ground." Besides being the name of the first man, *adam* also is the common word "man," "human being," or "humankind" (see Gen. 1:26–27; 2:7; 3:8). Adam fathered all of humanity. Therefore, differences of skin color, culture, customs, and language are incidental. No subgroup of Adam's descendants is better than any other.

God created Adam "in his own image" (Gen. 1:27). However, at every point of comparison God is infinite and humans are finite. While people have intellect, God is omniscient, that is, infinitely knowledgeable and wise (Ps. 139:1–6). People have emotions. God can be said to *be* love (1 John 4:8, 16). His anger leads to eternal judgment (Pss. 30:5; 103:8–9). While people possess will so they can make choices and plans, God is the sovereign Creator and Ruler of the universe (Dan. 4:34–35). Human beings also share imperfectly and finitely in other attributes of God such as life, wisdom, and justice. In addition God delegated to people the responsibility to "rule over" the earth as His representatives (Gen. 1:26).

The Bible suggests that God created Adam physically full-grown and mentally mature. He immediately placed Adam in the Garden of Eden to take care of it, and He brought Adam all the birds and animals to name (2:19–20). Since "no suitable helper was found"

for Adam among the animals, God created a woman out of a rib taken from Adam (2:21–25).

Adam and Eve were created innocent, unfamiliar with and untested by temptation or sin. They were also spiritually alive, as shown by the following facts. They bore "the image of God" (1:27). God freely talked with Adam (2:16–17) and fellowshipped with both Adam and Eve in the Garden of Eden. God's warning not to eat "from the tree of the knowledge of good and evil, for when you eat of it you will surely die" (2:17) assumes they were spiritually alive. However, when Adam and Eve ate of that tree, they instantaneously died spiritually (3:7–8). The process of physical death started immediately and reached its conclusion for Adam after 930 years (5:5).

When the serpent approached Eve, she gave in to temptation, ate of the fruit, and gave some to Adam and he ate (3:6). God spoke to Adam as the responsible party in the first couple (3:9–11, 17–19). Romans 5:12 identifies Adam as the head of the human race.

How did God's judgment of physical and spiritual death pass from Adam to all of his descendants? Two major views try to answer this question. One is called "the federal theory." It arose out of covenant theology. This theory looks at Adam as the representative of the human race with whom God had established a covenant of works for all humanity. When Adam sinned and violated the covenant of works, God's judgment of both physical and spiritual death was applied not only to him but also to the entire human race that he represented.

The second view is called "the seminal headship" view. This theory says every human being resided seminally (in "seed" form) in Adam and thus participated in his sin and judgment. The writer of Hebrews employed this kind of reasoning when he said, "Levi, who collects the tenth, paid the tenth through Abraham, because when Melchizedek met Abraham, Levi was still in the body of his ancestor" (Heb. 7:9–10). Paul implied universal participation in Adam's sin when he wrote that "sin entered the world through one man, and death through sin, and in this way death came to all men, because all sinned" (Rom. 5:12).

The biblical account that God personally and immediately created Adam "in the image of God" opposes the theory of modern science that mankind evolved from primates over a very long period of time. Even though there are gaps in the genealogical records of Genesis 5 and 11 prior to Abram, the elapsed time since the creation of Adam and Eve has to be much less than the seven hundred thousand years suggested by many anthropologists for human evolution. Genesis presents Adam as a historical person whom God created comparatively recently.

The New Testament regards Adam as the first human being and head of the human race. Luke traced the Lord Jesus' physical ancestry back to "Adam, the son of God" (Luke 3:23–38). And Jude wrote of "Enoch, the seventh from Adam" (Jude 14). Even Jesus spoke of the creation of Adam and Eve (Matt. 19:4–5; Mark 10:6–8, quoting Gen. 1:27 and 2:24). Paul spoke of Adam more frequently than any other Old Testament person (see, for example, 1 Cor. 15:22, 45; 1 Tim. 2:13–14).

Paul treated Adam and Jesus as pivotal historical figures. He contrasted Adam and Christ as the great troublemaker and the great problem-solver. Adam sinned and introduced death to the human race. Jesus conquered death and made a way for all of us to conquer it with Him (1 Cor. 15:21–22). This contrast between Adam and Christ continues in Paul's discussion of the nature of the resurrection body. The resurrection body given by Christ, "the last Adam" (15:45), transforms the physical body inherited from Adam, "the first man" (15:45, 47).   —**JAW**

* * *

Since we are all related in some way to every living human being, we should hold no prejudice in our hearts against others.

ADOPTION

"Adoption" is one of "the riches of God's grace" (Eph. 1:5, 7). We receive those "riches" as benefits of God's redemption made possible through the death of Christ. When we believe in the Lord Jesus Christ for salvation, we are placed at that moment into the family of God with all the rights and privileges of an adult child (Rom. 8:15). We becomes heirs of everything God makes available for His children (8:17). Our inheritance is not limited to the blessings of this life; complete fulfillment will be ours in heaven throughout eternity (8:23).

Why does the Bible refer to salvation as both new birth and adoption? The birth image communicates the new beginning associated with regeneration. The adoption metaphor speaks to the family rights of a child of God. New believers may be babes in Christ in terms of spiritual maturity, but they are not minor children as far as inheritance rights are concerned. The adoption language makes clear we don't have to "grow up" to be heirs with Christ.

Adoption is a common practice in many cultures. In biblical times couples who had no son could adopt one, and that son would become a full family member and the heir of the family estate. Unlike Greek, biblical Hebrew had no term for adoption. However, the Old Testament records some examples. Abraham was willing to consider his servant Eliezer as his heir (Gen. 15:3). Archaeological evidence from the time of the patriarchs indicates that it was not uncommon for a wealthy, childless man to will his estate to his most trusted servant. Pharaoh's daughter adopted Moses, and he grew up in her home (Ex. 2:10).

Paul alone among New Testament writers developed the theological significance of adoption in relation to salvation in Christ. Galatians is the earliest of his epistles to mention adoption. He affirmed that faith in Jesus Christ, not obedience to the Law, brings justification (Gal. 2:16). Christ redeems those who were under the Law (4:5), and one of the results of that gracious act of God is adoption. In Galatians 4:5 the New American Standard Bible reads literally "adoption as sons," and the New International Version interprets the phrase as "the full rights of sons." The indwelling Spirit of God serves as evidence of this adoption. He helps us understand and enjoy the privileges of sonship (4:6).

Paul later expanded the concept of adoption in the Book of Romans. He stated that those who are in Christ have been placed under the control of the Holy Spirit (8:9) and have received "a spirit of adoption" (8:15, NASB). God's adopted children are heirs of all that He has for them. They are coheirs with Christ (8:17). Part of that inheritance consists of spiritual privileges enjoyed now on earth. Most of their glorious inheritance awaits the day when all the promises of God will be fulfilled (8:23).

Returning to where this article started, Ephesians 1:5 adds another dimension to adoption. It declares that this marvelous and gracious privilege of adoption was in the heart and plans of God before the creation of the world. God chose His children for adoption so He could lavish His love on them. This results in praise and adoration to God and enhances His glory (1:6). Being adopted as a child of God is a great spiritual privilege, stemming from the riches of His grace.

—**WGJ**

***

Count the specific blessings you have because you have been graciously received into the family of God.

ADULTERY

Adultery is voluntary sexual relations between a man and woman of whom at least one is married to someone else. The seventh commandment in the Mosaic Law forbids this specific form of sexual immorality (Ex. 20:14; Deut. 5:18; Luke 18:20). The Law punished adulterers with death by stoning (Lev. 20:10–12; Deut. 22:20–27).

God views adultery seriously and punishes it severely because marriage is a sacred relationship established when He created Eve as a "helper suitable" for Adam (Gen. 2:18, 20–23). In addition, marriage is the most intimate union two people can share and must be protected (2:23–24; Matt. 19:4–6; 1 Cor. 6:16). In the sexual union of marriage a man and a woman "become one flesh" (Gen. 2:24; Matt. 19:5; 1 Cor. 6:16). For this reason Jesus listed adultery as a sin as serious as murder and theft (Matt. 15:19).

Old Testament writers used adultery as a word picture to describe the spiritual unfaithfulness of Israel to God. The Bible compares Israel's covenantal relationship to God (Ex. 19:3–8; 24:3–8) to a marriage. God is the "husband" (Is. 54:5; Jer. 31:32) and Israel is the "wife" (Is. 54:6). Israel's unfaithfulness in forsaking the Lord to worship false gods was described as adultery (Jer. 3:6, 8–9, 20), and Israel was called an "adulterous wife" (Ezek. 16:32). Because of Israel's spiritual adultery, God would forsake and punish her (16:38), but only temporarily (Is. 54:6–7; Ezek. 16:59–60). The way the prophet Hosea pursued and forgave his unfaithful wife Gomer illustrated God's dealings with Israel in her spiritual adultery (Hos. 1:2; 2:2; 3:1). Any time a believer forsakes the Lord to give primary allegiance and devotion to something else, that person commits spiritual adultery (James 4:4).

—**JAW**

***

Christ calls us all not only to physical faithfulness but also to faithfulness in every passing thought and glance.

ADVOCATE

In the Old Testament, Satan tested Job, whose life was the epitome of righteous living. Job suffered great loss through this severe experience. In his struggles he sought an advocate, someone to stand in his defense (Job 16:19–21). This is the only place where the New International Version uses the word *advocate*. In 1 John 2:1 both the New American Standard Bible and the New King James Version translate *paraklētos* as *advocate*. The New International Version translates it as "one who speaks to the Father in our defense."

An advocate is someone who argues for a cause or pleads on behalf of another person. In Job's case he wanted someone who could defend him before God because he thought what had happened to him was unjust. Job desperately *sought* an advocate, while the apostle John declared that believers *already have* an advocate.

When we place our faith in Christ, the penalty of our sin is paid. Yet we still have the capacity to sin (1 John 1:8). Though we are not characterized by a life of sin (3:9), we still occasionally commit sin (1:9). However, when we sin, we are not condemned, because we have an Advocate, Jesus Christ, who pleads our case before the Father.

In His Upper Room Discourse Jesus used the word *paraklētos* four times in reference to the Holy Spirit (John 14:16, 26; 15:26; 16:7). The New International Version translates this word as "Counselor." Jesus asked the Father to give His disciples someone like Himself to be in them since He would no longer physically be with them (14:17). As the indwelling Counselor (literally, "one called alongside to help"), the Holy Spirit would be the disciples' Teacher (14:26) and a witness to the character of Christ (15:26). The Holy Spirit would also convict the world of guilt (16:7–8). Yet in relation to sin in our lives, the Lord has retained the responsibility of being our Advocate Himself. **—WGJ**

***

Knowing that the risen Christ defends you before God the Father, don't allow Satan to intimidate you because of your sins.

AGE

The principal Old Testament word for "age" is *'ôlam,* which indicates an indefinite (usually lengthy) period of time. Sometimes it is used in the sense of everlasting, with a past or future point of view. For instance, looking back God is said to be "from all eternity" (Ps. 93:2). In Micah 5:2 the future messianic Ruler is described as "one who will be ruler over Israel, whose origins are from of old, from ancient times." The expression "ancient times" can be translated "as from days of eternity [ʿôlam].'' This points to the Messiah's existence from eternity past.

On the other hand, ʿôlam is also used of an indefinite future time. In this sense the word may refer to the unknown length of a person's life (Deut. 15:17; Ps. 61:7). The earth is said to exist for an indefinite time. It is in this sense that Genesis 13:15 used ʿôlam in the Lord's promise to Abraham: ''All the land that you see I will give to you and your offspring forever'' (Gen. 13:15). Since the earth will ultimately be destroyed, including the Promised Land (Rev. 20:11; 21:1), Genesis 13:15 refers to the land existing not into eternity but rather for an indefinite period of time into the future.

In Isaiah 45:17 the word ''ages'' (ʿôlam in the plural) is used of Israel's ongoing future: ''You [Israel] will never be put to shame or disgraced, to ages everlasting.''

Frequently in Scripture the word ʿôlam ascribes eternity to God. ''The LORD is the everlasting God'' (Is. 40:28). ''I live forever'' (Deut. 32:40). ''From everlasting to everlasting you are God'' (Ps. 90:2). ''The God of Israel, [is] from everlasting to everlasting'' (106:48; see also Neh. 9:5). God ''lives forever'' (Dan. 12:7). Also God's love is ''from everlasting to everlasting'' (Ps. 103:17).

In the New Testament the Greek word aiōn is similar in meaning to ʿôlam. Aiōn indicates an indefinite period of time, either in the past or

the future. God s promises were made in the past (''long ago,'' Luke 1:70; Acts 3:21) and His saving of Gentiles has been known in the past (''known for ages,'' Acts 15:18). The plural ''ages'' is a comprehensive expression of all past ages, as in 1 Corinthians 2:7 (''before time began''), Ephesians 3:9 (''for ages past''), and Colossians 1:26 (''the mystery that has been kept hidden for ages and generations''). Also Ephesians 3:11 refers to God's ''eternal purpose'' (literally, ''the purpose of the ages'').

The future ages are in view in the angel's promise to Mary that her son ''will reign over the house of Jacob forever ['unto the ages,' aiōnas]'' (Luke 1:33). Age (singular) is often used in the sense of forever, that is, eternity, as in John 6:51, 58; 1 Peter 1:25; 1 John 2:17; and 2 John 2. The plural ages also means eternity, as in, for example, Romans 1:25; 9:5; 11:36; and 2 Corinthians 11:31. The unusual expression ''unto the age of the age'' in Hebrews 1:8 means ''for ever and ever.'' The phrase ''unto the ages of ages,'' meaning ''for ever,'' occurs a dozen times, often in doxologies, the formal statements of praise that conclude some sections of New Testament books (for example, Rom. 16:27; Rev. 7:12). This phrase is also used of God's eternal existence (Rev. 4:9–10; 10:6; 15:7).

An important use of aiōn is in reference to a long period of time in the present or the future. Jesus distinguished these two when He said that the blasphemy of the Holy Spirit "will not be forgiven, either in this age or in the age to come" (Matt. 12:32).

Often the return of Christ is described as beginning a new age and consummating the present age. The disciples asked Him, "What will be the sign of your coming and of the end of the age?" (Matt. 24:3).

It is important to note that the present age contrasts with both the past Old Testament era and the future yet-to-come age. In the present age we enjoy many spiritual blessings, blessings that will continue on for eternity. We now have eternal life (John 3:16, 36; 5:24; 6:47), spiritual life that will continue after death for all eternity. If we sacrifice possessions and family for Christ "in this present age," we will be richly rewarded, receiving "a hundred times as much . . . in the age to come" (Mark 10:30). The present age is a time of burdens; the phrase "the worries of this life" (Matt. 13:22; Mark 4:19) is literally "the cares of this age." We are not to be conformed to or to love the sinful ways of the present age ("world," Rom. 12:2; 2 Tim. 4:10; cf. Titus 2:12).

The present age is a time characterized by evil (Gal. 1:4). Satan is the ruler of "this age" (2 Cor. 4:4). The future Millennium, when Satan will be bound, will introduce a totally new age in which Christ will rule from Jerusalem. Following the millennial kingdom, God will usher in the eternal age in which all things will be brought to their consummation. God's redemptive program, which we now enjoy, will be fully displayed in the Millennium and in the eternal state. "In the coming ages [God will] show the incomparable riches of his grace, expressed in his kindness to us in Christ Jesus" (Eph. 2:7).   —JFW

* * *

Do not be conformed to or love the sinful ways of this present age.

ANGELS

At least thirty-three books of the Bible mention angels, with more than 100 references in the Old Testament and more than 160 in the New Testament. Angels are referred to as "sons of God" (Job 1:6, NASB; 38:7, NASB); "holy ones" (Ps. 89:7); and "the host" (1 Sam. 17:45; Ps. 89:8, NASB). Several times Christ affirmed the existence of angels (Matt. 18:10; 22:29–30; 25:31–32, 41). Some argue that Christ talked about angels and demons only to teach lessons to an audience that believed in them or that He shared the superstitions of His contemporaries. But the first view implies that Christ was intellectually dishonest, and the second makes Him subject to error. The biblical evidence says Christ truly believed in and testified to the existence of angels. To deny their reality is to say He was wrong.

God created angels by His Word (Ps. 148:5). We don't know when He created them, but they were present when the earth was created and sang praises to the Lord (Job 38:7). We know angels were created by and for Christ (Col. 1:16). They were created holy (Mark 8:38; Acts 10:22) and are innumerable (Dan. 7:10; Matt. 26:53; Heb. 12:22; Rev. 5:11). Their numbers neither increase nor decrease, for they do not have children (Matt. 22:30) nor do they die (Luke 20:36).

On occasion angels appeared to people looking as though they possessed solid human bodies (Gen. 18:2; Matt. 28:3). Yet they are called spirits (Heb. 1:14). As spirit beings they may perhaps possess bodies of a spiritual order (1 Cor. 15:44).

Angels possess the essential elements of personality—intelligence (1 Pet. 1:12), emotions (Luke 2:13; 15:10), and will (Jude 6). Their knowledge, while greater than that of humans, is limited. They are not omniscient. Angels have greater power than humans, but they are not omnipotent. They can appear and disappear, but they are not omnipresent. Angels were not created in God's image and do not participate in the redemption provided by Christ. In the age to come, redeemed humanity will be exalted above the angels and will judge the fallen among them (1 Cor. 6:3).

These fallen angels are called demons. Some are bound (2 Pet. 2:4; Jude 6) but most are free. Demons are referred to as Satan's "angels" (Rev. 12:7, 9). The unfallen angels, called "elect angels" (1 Tim. 5:21), may be described as follows: (1) Michael, the only angel called the archangel, is the defender of Israel (Dan. 10:13, 21; 12:1; Jude 9; Rev. 12:7). (2) Gabriel, an angel of high rank, was entrusted with delivering important messages from God to individuals such as Daniel (Dan. 8:16; 9:21), Zechariah (Luke 1:19), and Mary (Luke 1:26). (3) "Rulers," "principalities," "authorities," and "powers," referred to frequently in the Scriptures, seem to be good and evil angels who engage in an unending struggle to control human beings and governments (Dan. 10:13; Eph. 1:21; 3:10; 6:12; Col. 2:15). (4) Cherubim are the guardians of the holiness and presence of God (Gen. 3:24; Ex. 25:17–22; Pss. 80:1; 99:1; Is. 37:16; Ezek. 10:4–5). (5) Seraphim are mentioned only in Isaiah 6:2–6, where they are described as praising God and extolling His holiness. (6) The Angel of the Lord, a term found frequently in the Old Testament often refers to the preincarnate Christ (Gen. 16:7, 9, 11; 22:11, 15; Ex. 3:2; Judg. 2:1, 4; 6:11–12, 21–22; 13:3, 13, 15–17, 20–21; 2 Sam. 24:16; Zech. 1:11–12; 3:1, 5–6; 12:8).

As God's messengers or ambassadors, unfallen angels minister in a variety of ways. They were involved when God created the world, when He gave the Mosaic Law (Acts 7:38, 53; Gal. 3:19; Heb. 2:2), during Christ's First

Advent (Matt. 2:13–15, 19–20; 4:11; 28:2, 5; Luke 2:13; 22:43; Acts 1:10), and during the early days of the church (Acts 8:26; 12:7; 27:23–24; 1 Cor. 4:9). They will also be involved in announcing judgments in the Tribulation (Rev. 8—10; 14—16). They will accompany Christ at His Second Coming (Matt. 24:31; 25:31). They will be engaged in events following His return (Matt. 13:39; Rev. 19:17–18; 20:1–3).

Angels come and go before God (Job 1:6; 2:1), worship God (Pss. 103:20; 148:20; Luke 2:13; Heb. 1:6; Rev. 5:11–12; 7:11–12), and obey God (Ps. 103:20–21).

Some verses suggest that angels protect and guard believers (Ex. 23:20; Pss. 34:7; 91:11–12; Matt. 4:6; 18:10). Angels minister to Christians (Heb. 1:14); and they deliver believers from harm, as in the case of Lot (Gen. 19:15–17), Joseph (48:16), the Israelites (Num. 20:16), Daniel's three friends (Dan. 3:28), Daniel himself (6:22), the apostles as a group (Acts 5:19), and Peter as an individual (12:7). Apparently angels know what happens on the earth (Luke 15:10; 1 Cor. 4:9; 11:10). Angels can guide (Acts 8:26), give strength (1 Kin. 19:5, 7; Dan. 10:18–19; Luke 22:43), and comfort (Luke 1:30; 2:10; Matt. 28:5; Acts 27:23–24).

Popular interest in angels is sometimes carried to an unbalanced extreme. When heretics at Colosse worshiped angels as divine intermediaries, Paul sent a strong warning (Col. 2:18) and affirmed that angels are under Jesus, "who is the Head over all power and authority" (2:10). The object of our faith is Jesus, not angels.

—DKC

***

Thank God for the protective care of angels.

ANOINTING

The practice of anointing with oil was widespread in Bible times. Anointing could be a simple rubbing of oil onto someone's body for medicinal or cosmetic purposes. Anointing also could refer to a religious or political ritual in which oil was poured on someone or something to indicate the person or object was set apart for a special purpose.

In the everyday sense of anointing, olive oil in particular was applied after bathing (Ruth 3:3), to wounds (Luke 10:34), on dead bodies (John 19:39), or on released prisoners (2 Chr. 28:15). The head and feet of honored individuals were sometimes anointed with special oils or perfumes (Ps. 23:5; John 12:3).

The first reference in Scripture to the ritual sense of anointing is when Jacob anointed a pillar he had set up at Bethel as a memorial of his encounter with God (Gen. 31:13). In Old Testament times anointing often had a religious significance, setting objects and persons apart for God's service. Specially prepared oils were used to anoint the tabernacle, its furniture, and Aaron and his sons (Ex. 28:40–42; 29:1–46; 30:22–33; 40:10–11). These persons and objects were thus sanctified or set apart for religious purposes.

The Old Testament occasionally mentions the anointing of prophets (1 Kin. 19:16). It frequently refers to the anointing of kings, dating from the beginning of the monarchy. Samuel, sometimes called "the king-maker," anointed both Saul and David (1 Sam. 10:1; 16:13). It's of special significance that when David was anointed, the Spirit of the Lord departed from Saul and came on him. Thus the anointing not only set rulers aside to serve God, but it also symbolized the coming of the Holy Spirit to enable God's servants to do their work for Him. In this connection the Messiah declared, "The Spirit of the Sovereign Lord is on me, because the Lord has anointed me to preach good news to the poor" (Is. 61:1).

The Hebrew word for anointed gives us the term "messiah," which means the "anointed one." A range of individuals who were appointed to special tasks, even the Persian king Cyrus (Is. 45:1), could be called "anointed ones." The term came to be applied to the coming King from the line of David, *the* Messiah, who will one day rule over the restored Davidic kingdom. Messianic prophecies abound in the Old Testament. The New Testament identified Jesus as the ultimate Anointed One, the Messiah (John 1:41; 4:25).

The practice of anointing continued in New Testament times, but not for induction into leadership. Everyday anointing with oil or perfume is mentioned (Mark 14:8; Luke 7:46; John 12:3). What the New Testament adds to the range of meaning of anointing is the figurative way that God anoints believers (2 Cor. 1:21; 1 John 2:20, 27). This anointing at the moment one believes in Christ involves the gift of the Holy Spirit. It brings to mind the anointing of the Old Testament priests with oil.

The Roman Catholic Church uses James 5:14 to support their sacrament of extreme unction. But, as verses 14–15 show, the elders, not priests, were to pray for the sick person and anoint him with oil. The anointing did not prepare the individual for death but anticipated his restoration to health. The Greek word translated "anoint" means "to rub with oil," not "to anoint ceremonially." In the ancient world "doctors" rubbed a patient's body with olive oil much as a modern nurse would rub a patient's body with lotion. It was not a ceremonial anointing but a means of refreshment, comfort, and grooming in anticipation of the patient being healed, leaving the sickbed, and facing the world.   **—DKC**

***

Consider the fact that every true believer has been anointed by God for His service.

ANTICHRIST

The word *antichrist* refers to anyone who opposes Christ, for the prefix "anti" means "against." But since the prefix can also mean "instead of," the word sometime refers to *the* one who in the future Tribulation will seek to be a substitute for Christ, that is, a pseudo-Christ.

Only four verses (1 John 2:18, 22; 4:3; 2 John 7) include the word *antichrist,* but the idea of an antichrist pervades the Old and New Testaments. The key to the doctrine is found in 1 John 2:18. "Dear children, this is the last hour; and as you have heard that the antichrist is coming, even now many antichrists have come. This is how we know it is the last hour." In contrast to the many antichrists present in John's day, a specific antichrist, who epitomizes the evil of all earlier antichrists, will dominate the second half of the Great Tribulation.

John defined the antichrists of the church age as anyone who "denies the Father and the Son" (2:22). However, the antichrist idea is much broader, covering any person or movement that is contrary to God, whether in the Old or New Testaments. Thus the concept of antichrist in the Old Testament includes those who were guilty of idolatry (Deut. 13:13), rape or sexual sins (Judg. 19:22–25; 20:53), disregard or disrespect of God (1 Sam. 2:12), and lying or evil expressions (1 Kin. 21:10, 13; Prov. 6:12; 16:27).

The concept of a specific antichrist first emerges in the prophecies related to Antiochus Epiphanes IV, a king of Syria (175–164 B.C.). Daniel 11:21–36 describes how this ruler proved to be an antichrist. He persecuted Israel, desecrated the temple, and abolished Israel's daily sacrifices. In these ways he prefigured the Antichrist of the end times.

Daniel 7:7–8 anticipates a revival of the Roman Empire in the end times in the form of ten kingdoms. The little horn mentioned in 7:8 depicts a ruler who will uproot three of the ten horns. That means he will subdue three kingdoms (7:24) and then rule over all ten countries of the revived Roman Empire. He will become a world ruler (Rev. 13:8). Called "Antichrist" in 1 John 2:18, he will be against Christ and will be His principal opponent in the end times. He will attempt to be a substitute for Christ, the King of kings. Satan will enable the Antichrist to have a world government in the last three and a half years before the Second Coming.

The Antichrist will sit in the future temple (which Israel will build to restore the Mosaic system of sacrifices) to be worshiped (Dan. 11:36–37; Matt. 24:15; 2 Thess. 2:4). Daniel called him "the ruler who will come" (Dan. 9:26) and "the king who will do as he pleases" (11:36). Paul dubbed him "the man of lawlessness" and "the lawless one" (2 Thess. 2:3, 9). This situation is called an "abomination" because Jewish sacrifices will be stopped and sacrifices of a pagan character will be substituted (Dan. 9:27; 12:11).

The revived Roman Empire will be like a beast out of the sea, having seven heads and ten horns (Rev. 13:1; see also Dan. 7:7). Besides being presented as an eleventh horn, the Antichrist is depicted as the eighth head on the beast (Rev. 17:11). This points to his leadership of the revived Roman Empire.

The Anitichrist will recover from what is called "a fatal wound" (13:3, 12). Some interpreters say this wound suggests that someone from the past will be resurrected to fulfill this role. Many individuals have been suggested, including Nero. But no one from the past has fulfilled the function of the future Antichrist. The view that the Antichrist will die from the wound and be resurrected is supported by the fact that the word "slain" (13:3, literal translation) is also used of Christ (5:6; 13:8). However, it may be preferable to say that Satan will heal the Antichrist from a serious wound, because one of his heads, not his entire body, will have a mortal wound. In any case he will come on the scene as a supernatural person empowered by Satan. He will gain worldwide acceptance and exercise authority over the entire world for forty-two months (13:5–8).

The Antichrist's number 666 (Rev. 13:18) has been interpreted in many ways. Perhaps the number simply means that just as six is one less than seven, the "perfect" number, so the super number 666 falls short of the perfection of 777. No matter how hard the Antichrist tries, and no matter how much satanic help he has, he will fall short in his divine pretensions.

At the Second Coming of Christ, the Antichrist will be captured and "thrown alive into the fiery lake of burning sulfur" (19:20). Paul referred to this event when he called the Antichrist "the man doomed to destruction" (2 Thess. 2:3), and Daniel wrote that this future world ruler "will come to his end" (Dan. 11:45).

In the Reformation the church identified the Roman Catholic Church as the Antichrist, and in more recent times prominent individuals who have opposed the church and Christ have been said to be the Antichrist. The Roman Church retaliated by saying Protestants were antichrists. However, those who believe in a future fulfillment of many of the prophecies in Daniel and Revelation believe a personal Antichrist will dominate the world for three and a half years of terrible tribulation and then, as stated, will be destroyed by Christ at His Second Coming.   **—JFW**

APOSTASY

The Greek word *apostasia* is found only twice in the New Testament (Acts 21:21; 2 Thess. 2:3), but the concept appears many times throughout Scripture. "Apostasy" means "a falling away from," a deserting or turning from a position or view formerly held. In a political sense the concept of apostasy meant a defection from authority (Acts 5:37). In a religious sense it is a defection from truth (Acts 21:21; 1 Tim. 4:1).

Spiritual apostasy occurs when someone who claimed to be a believer denies what he or she formerly professed to believe. An apostate is not one who was saved and then lost his or her salvation. An apostate, though once claiming to be a believer, never was saved in the first place. Relatively minor differences in doctrine are not referred to as apostasy; instead apostasy is a departure from major components of Christian truth.

The New Testament identifies the following characteristics of apostates: embracing doctrines of demons, having a seared conscience, lying, forbidding marriage, and prohibiting the eating of certain foods (1 Tim. 4:1–3). Apostates may have a form of godliness but they don't experience its power or reality (2 Tim. 3:5). Apostasy is denounced in Hebrews 10:26–29; 2 Peter 2:15–21; and Jude 3–4.

Apostasy is a departure from truth not simply because of ignorance. Apostasy is deliberate and therefore merits divine judgment. The only cure for apostasy is for the apostate to turn to Christ for salvation, to become a true believer in Christ. The New International Version does not use the word *apostasy* but renders *apostasia* as "to turn away" from Moses (Acts 21:21) or as "rebellion" (2 Thess. 2:3). The latter reference speaks of the extensive apostasy that will occur in the seven-year period immediately preceding the Second Coming of Christ.

—JFW

APOSTLESHIP

An apostle was someone sent on a mission as a representative of the sender. Early in His ministry Jesus chose twelve men from among His followers and named them apostles (Luke 6:13). He gave them authority to represent Him in His mission (Matt. 10:2; Mark 3:16). Interestingly Jesus Himself is called "the apostle" by the author of the Book of Hebrews (Heb. 3:1). The pattern of apostleship was established when God sent His Son to this earth on a stated mission (John 17:23).

Immediately after Jesus' ascension Peter declared it was necessary to choose someone to take the place of Judas and maintain the number of twelve apostles. The qualifications were restrictive. Candidates must have been with Jesus and the disciples from the time of John's baptism and have witnessed the Resurrection (Acts 1:21–22). At least two men were qualified, but the final decision rested with the Lord and was discovered by drawing lots (1:24–26). This was the first apostolic decision made after the Ascension, so it's likely that Christ instructed His disciples about the unusual procedure during the forty days before He left them (1:3). Peter also drew on the authority of the Old Testament Scriptures (1:16, 20). The uniqueness of the twelve apostles will continue for eternity, for in the New Jerusalem their names are inscribed on the city's twelve foundations (Rev. 21:14).

The Book of Acts gives glimpses of the ministry of the Twelve. Their activity laid the foundation of the church (Eph. 2:20; 4:11). They provided leadership for the early believers and explained the work of the Spirit in their midst (Acts 2:14–36; 3:11–26). These men were in the forefront of the proclamation of the gospel. They focused on the ministry of evangelism (4:2, 8–12; 5:42). The apostles emphasized worship as they led the church in prayer and praise (5:23–31).

God entrusted the overall care of the early believers to the apostles. They cared for physical (4:35, 37) as well as spiritual needs (6:4). In protecting the purity of the church, the apostles exercised discernment and discipline (5:1–11). They performed miraculous signs and wonders to authenticate the work of the Lord among the people and to convince unbelievers to come to Christ (5:12; 9:32–35). Apostolic miracles validated the work of the Holy Spirit, especially as the gospel spread beyond Jerusalem (8:14–17; 2 Cor. 12:12). Important doctrinal teachings were approved or rejected in the early church based on the testimony of the apostles (Acts 15:6–11).

Apostleship extended beyond the Twelve, but in a sense that was distinct from that group. Paul is an example of an apostle who was not one of the Twelve. His apostleship is well attested in Scripture. In his introductions to nine of his letters he referred to himself as an apostle (see, for example, 1 Cor. 1:1; Gal. 1:1). He was *the* apostle to the Gentiles just as Peter was to the Jews (Gal. 2:8–9). Paul himself recognized the uniqueness of his apostleship (1 Cor. 15:8–10).

The New Testament refers to three others as apostles: Barnabas (Acts 14:14), Andronicus, and Junias (Rom. 16:7). We don't know how and when they received this designation, but like the Twelve, they were sent with delegated authority to minister for the Lord. They were sent on their missions by local churches. No biblical evidence exists to suggest that there are apostles today, in the sense that the gift of apostleship is defined in the New Testament.   **—WGJ**

***

Give thanks to the Lord for the faithful work of the apostles and especially the apostles' letters of instruction recorded in the Bible.

ARK OF THE COVENANT

The ark of the covenant was one of the items of furniture for the tabernacle. "Ark" is an old-fashioned English term for a container. This ark contained the covenant, the stone tablets on which the finger of God wrote the Ten Commandments (along with Aaron's rod that budded and a pot of manna) (Ex. 31:18; Heb. 9:4). Gifted craftsmen appointed by Moses made the ark and the rest of the tabernacle at Mount Sinai during the year Israel camped there following the revelation of the Law of God (Ex. 31:1–11; Num. 1:1; 10:11). The ark was the only piece of furniture in the Most Holy Place of the tabernacle (and later of Solomon's temple)

The ark was an acacia wood chest three and a half feet in length and two and a half feet in both width and height, overlaid with gold inside and out. It had a lid of solid gold topped with figures of two cherubim. Some English versions call this lid "the mercy seat"

(Ex. 25:17, 21–22, NASB; 1 Chr. 28:11, NASB). The New International Version calls it "an atonement cover" (Ex. 25:17). Once a year on the Day of Atonement the high priest sprinkled blood on the mercy seat of the ark to cover Israel's sins committed during the previous twelve months (Lev. 16).

The mercy seat also was where the presence of God was "localized" and revealed (Ex. 25:22; Lev. 16:2). Two beaten-gold cherubim faced one another on the lid of the ark. The wings of the cherubim spread over the middle of the lid (Ex. 25:20). Between the cherubim, the presence of God in some mysterious sense was evident. The Israelites could not portray the likeness of God (Deut. 4:15–19), so the mercy seat was the strongest visible symbol of God's presence among His people. During the wilderness wandering a pillar of cloud by day and a pillar of fire by night hovered over the tabernacle where the ark was (Num. 9:15).

The ark of the covenant accompanied Israel from Sinai to Canaan and served as a constant reminder of God's presence with His people. The ark played a significant role when Israel entered Canaan (Josh. 3—4), conquered Jericho (6:6–11), and renewed the covenant at Mount Ebal (8:33).

In the time of the judges, however, the people began to assign magical powers to the ark. The Israelites rushed the ark of the covenant into the battle of Aphek when they started losing to the Philistines. They expected the ark to unleash God's power on the enemy (1 Sam. 4:1–10). But God let the Philistines defeat Israel and capture the ark (4:19–11). Later the Philistines returned the ark, but Samuel, the last and best of the judges, left it at a private residence in a village near Jerusalem (6:21—7:2). He feared popular superstition about the ark would distract Israel from its need for repentance, faith, and godly living.

King David brought the ark to his newly established capital, Jerusalem (2 Sam. 6). His son, Solomon, built the temple David had dreamed of. When that magnificent structure was completed, the ark was installed behind the curtain in the Most Holy Place and the glory cloud filled the temple (1 Kin. 8:1–11). Throughout the remainder of the kingdom period, the ark remained in the temple, except for its temporary removal during the reign of the apostate King Manasseh (2 Chr. 35:3). No one knows for certain what happened to the ark when Nebuchadnezzar destroyed Jerusalem in 586 B.C. Some say the ark was destroyed along with the temple. Others suggest Jeremiah hid the ark in a cave on Mount Nebo (2 Maccabees 2:4–8). Still others say the ark remains concealed under Jerusalem's temple mount, and some suggest that the ark was taken to heaven where heavenly worshipers view it (Rev. 11:19).

Ezekiel graphically described the departure of God's glorious presence from above the mercy seat at the time of the Exile (Ezek. 10:4, 18; 11:23). Isaiah had already declared that because of Israel's sin God no longer accepted their sacrifices at the temple (Is. 1:11–14). When Jesus Christ entered history, He eliminated the need for the Old Testament worship system. The ark of the covenant, and particularly the mercy seat, had pointed forward to Jesus Christ whom God presented as a "sacrifice of atonement" (Rom. 3:25).

In the Greek Old Testament the term *hilastērion* translated the Hebrew word for mercy seat. In the New Testament *hilastērion* is rendered "propitiation" in some Bible versions and "atoning sacrifice" in the New International Version. The sacrifice of Jesus fulfilled for all time what had been predicted annually by the sacrifices of the Day of Atonement. The guilt and penalty of sin were removed, and God's wrath was forever turned away from those who believe (Rom. 3:23–26).

—**DKC**

***

Thank God that the purpose and function of the ark of the covenant were fulfilled in the person and work of Jesus Christ.

ASCENSION

The Ascension of Christ refers to when Jesus visibly returned to heaven forty days after His resurrection from the dead (Acts 1:3). The Ascension occurred on the Mount of Olives outside the eastern walls of Jerusalem and was witnessed by many of Jesus' disciples (vv. 9–11). Today a church (converted into a mosque) marks the supposed site. As Jesus went up into heaven before the astonished eyes of the disciples, a cloud hid Him from their sight. They stared in wonder into the sky until two angels appeared with the promise that "this same Jesus" would one day "come back in the same way you have seen Him go into heaven."

The Old Testament prophesied the Ascension (Pss. 68:18; 110:1). The New Testament mentions it or assumes it many times. Jesus often spoke generally of returning to His Father. Occasionally He specifically predicted His ascension (John 6:62; 20:17). Luke reported the event briefly in Luke 24:51 and more completely in Acts 1:6–11. Paul wrote of Christ ascending "higher than all the heavens" (Eph. 4:10) and as having been "taken up in glory" (1 Tim. 3:16). Other passages state that the Lord "has gone into heaven" (1 Pet. 3:22) and "through the heavens" (Heb. 4:14). All New Testament passages about Christ's present activity at the right hand of the Father presuppose the Ascension.

A few theologians interpret John 20:17 to mean Christ ascended privately to the Most Holy Place in heaven before His public ascension. At this first ascension, Jesus supposedly presented the blood of His sacrifice to the Father as the high priest presented blood on the Day of Atonement. However, when Jesus told Mary Magdalene, "I ascend" (NASB), He didn't have in mind that very moment. His present tense verb looked the short distance into the future to His ascension from the Mount of Olives. The passage in Hebrews that declares, "he entered the Most Holy Place once for all by his own blood" (Heb. 9:12), refers to the overall fact of His completed atonement rather than to a trip to heaven with a container of His blood.

The Ascension of Jesus ended the earthly ministry of God's Son. No longer would He live with self-limitations, humiliations, sufferings, and the veiling of His glory. When Jesus entered heaven, He received the answer to His prayer, "And now, Father, glorify me in your presence with the glory I had with you before the world began" (John 17:5). He also became the first resurrected and glorified human to set foot in heaven. Christ's presence in glory triggered the descent of the Holy Spirit (16:7). Jesus took His place at the Father's right hand. From there He intercedes for believers as their High Priest (Heb. 7:23—8:2). He also serves as the all-powerful "head over everything for the church" (Eph. 1:22).

Along with Jesus' incarnation, atoning death, and resurrection, His ascension forms a vital part of the foundation of our Christian faith.   **—DKC**

***

Focus on the ascended Christ who intercedes for us and who will come for us.

ASSURANCE

The rich young ruler came to Jesus with everything except the assurance of eternal life. He showed his lack of assurance when he asked Jesus, "What must I do to inherit eternal life?" (Mark 10:17; Luke 18:18). That was an honest question. It contains no hint of insincerity. He wasn't trying to trap Jesus with a loaded question. Mark reported, "Jesus looked at him and loved him" (Mark 10:21).

The man had done everything he could think of to earn eternal life, but he wanted to be sure he hadn't overlooked something. Jesus challenged him to face a much deeper problem: His trust was in his money. His faith was defective. He could only have assurance of eternal life by taking the step of faith needed to give away his money and follow Jesus.

Salvation is a gift of God and cannot be earned by any amount of well-intentioned human effort. It must be received by faith. Assurance of salvation is our confidence that the death and resurrection of Christ has paid the price for our sins and gained us God's full forgiveness. Assurance knows

that God has declared us righteous and imparted eternal life to us. This transaction can never be rescinded.

Assurance is our subjective response to the objective promises of the Bible. We believe what God's Word says about God's character, about the saving work of Jesus, and about justification by faith. Lack of assurance is someone's subjective response to troubled thinking or troubled emotions. It is possible to be a genuine believer and yet lack a sense of assurance. Sometimes a persistent pattern of sin causes us to doubt our salvation. Often lack of assurance stems from our failure to take into account all the Bible teaches about our salvation.

We can trust God and His Word regardless of the circumstances or issues of our lives. Jesus said that anyone who believes on Him has eternal life (John 3:16, 36; 5:24; 6:47). On the basis of His promises we can believe in Jesus and be assured immediately that we possess eternal life. Assurance of salvation doesn't come later on the basis of our character and good works.

The apostle Paul wrote that God remains true and His Word certain, even if people are false and unfaithful (Rom. 3:3–4). Salvation is of the Lord, available only through the supernatural work of Jesus Christ on the Cross. Because God does the saving, the forgiving, and the imparting of eternal life, salvation is much more objective than subjective. Accordingly, the entire

Godhead is involved in assurance. God the Father sent His Son and His Spirit to do their works. The Son died for our sins to purchase our forgiveness. The Spirit dwelling in our lives testifies to the truth that we are God's children (Rom. 8:16; Gal. 4:6).

The writer of the Book of Hebrews declared that Jesus by His once-for-all sacrifice for our sins "has made perfect forever those who are being made holy" (Heb. 10:14). This objective truth has subjective implications. We are encouraged to draw near to God with sincere hearts with full assurance because God has provided relief from our guilty consciences (10:22).

Assurance is an important theme of 1 John. The apostle explained the objective reality of this assurance with the words, "God has given us eternal life, and this life is in his Son. He who has the Son has life; he who does not have the Son of God does not have life" (1 John 5:11–12). John then declared that these things were written so that we who believe in Christ may know that we have eternal life (5:13).

This objective fact has practical ramifications. The love we have for other believers witnesses to the reality that we belong to the truth. It "sets our hearts at rest in his presence whenever our hearts condemn us" (3:18–19). We do not always know the motive of our hearts, so John wrote that "God is greater than our hearts, and he knows everything" (3:20). God, who knows the inner depths of our hearts, offers us emotional and practical assurance of our salvation. **—WGJ**

***

Live each day with the reality that your sins have been forgiven and that nothing can separate you from the love of God.

ATONEMENT

The English verb "to atone" has an old-fashioned, historical meaning. It once meant to reconcile estranged parties. In the Bible *atonement* is specialized. The estranged parties are God and humanity, and the estrangement is one-sided, having been caused by our sin. The word *atonement* appears mainly in the Old Testament with reference to various Levitical animal sacrifices. "To atone" translates the Hebrew word *kāpar*, "to cover." Past sins could be "covered" by the blood of sacrificial animals. *Atonement* satisfied God's anger provoked by the sins committed in a segment of time. Future sins weren't affected. The atoning sacrifices Israel offered anticipated God's final and permanent solution for human sin through the death of Jesus Christ on the cross.

The Day of Atonement was an annual observance when the high priest sacrificed a young bull as a "sin offering to make atonement for himself and his household" (Lev. 16:6) and a goat as a "sin offering for the people"

(16:15). Then he was to "lay both hands on the head of [another] goat and confess over it all the wickedness and rebellion of the Israelites—all their sins—and put them on the goat's head." Then the goat was sent "away into the desert" (16:21), symbolically carrying "on itself all their sins to a solitary place" (16:22). The sacrifices of the Day of Atonement "covered" the sins of the past year. The next year it all had to be repeated (16:29, 34).

In addition to the national sacrifices on the Day of Atonement, individual Israelites offered countless burnt offerings and sin offerings as the circumstances of life required them. The offerer identified with the offering by laying his hands on its head (Lev. 4:13–35). Hebrews declares that "it is impossible for the blood of bulls and goats to take away sins" (Heb. 10:4), for "again and again" the priests offered "the same sacrifices, which can never take away sins" (10:11). Earlier the writer of Hebrews reasoned that if "the same sacrifices repeated endlessly year after year" could "make perfect those who draw near to worship . . . would they not have stopped being offered?" (10:1–2).

In contrast to the Old Testament animal sacrifices, the Lord Jesus was "the Lamb of God, who takes away the sin of the world" (John 1:29). As the complete, final sacrifice for sin, Christ "appeared once for all at the end of the ages to do away with sin by the sacrifice of himself" (Heb. 9:26). Because He "was sacrificed once to take away the sins of many people" (9:28), we who believe in Jesus Christ "have been made holy through the sacrifice of the body of Jesus Christ once for all" (10:10; see also 10:12, 14, 17–18).

God covered and forgave the sins of people in past ages on the basis of animal sacrifices offered in faith and obedience to His commands (9:13, 22). It's important to recognize that forgiveness wasn't the result of the bare ritual of animal sacrifice. God expected to look into the hearts of worshipers and find faith in Him and His promises (Gen. 15:6; Rom. 3:3). All of the Old Testament sacrifices anticipated Christ's death, which served "as a ransom to set [Old Testament believers] free from the sins committed under the first covenant" (9:15). Jesus was "the Lamb that was slain from the creation of the world" (Rev. 13:8; see also 1 Pet. 1:20). He paid the penalty for all sins, including those that had been "covered" by the blood of the Old Testament animal sacrifices.

Since the word *atonement* describes the temporary covering of sins in the Old Testament, it isn't the usual term the New Testament uses to refer to Christ's finished work of redemption. The New Testament emphasizes that Christ's death on the Cross was a substitutionary death in the place of sinners. This idea of substitution was foreshadowed in the Old Testament when the priests or worshipers laid their hands on the heads of the sacrificial animals (Lev. 1:4; 4:4, 15, 24, 29, 33) or on the head of the goat sent into the desert on the Day of Atonement (16:21–22).

One of the clearest statements of the substitutionary nature of Jesus' sacrificial death occurs in 1 Peter 2:24: "He himself bore our sins in his body on the tree." Other verses that state this truth are Romans 4:25; 2 Corinthians 5:21; Galatians 1:4; 3:13; Colossians 2:14; 1 Thessalonians 5:10; 1 Timothy 2:6; and Titus 2:14. The most detailed statement of Christ's death in our place, however, occurs in the Old Testament passage Isaiah 53:4–6. In His death Jesus took the place of the sinner (Heb. 2:9) and bore the curse of God's judgment (Gal. 3:13; 2 Cor. 5:21). In this way He satisfied God's just demands (Rom. 3:25–26) and provided to all believers forgiveness (Matt. 26:28; Luke 24:47), reconciliation with God (Rom. 5:11; Col. 1:20), and eternal life (Rom. 6:23; 1 John 5:11–12).

There have been some interesting historical theories about the Atonement of Christ. In the third century, Origen theorized that the death of Jesus was a ransom paid by God to Satan to buy back repentant sinners. In the twelfth century Abelard popularized the moral influence theory of the Atonement. This view taught that Jesus' death demonstrated His loyalty to God and to His mission to draw people to God. We should respond gratefully to His example by living righteous lives devoted to God. Such a view still appeals to liberal theologians who ignore the reality of sin and the price associated with divine forgiveness. At the same time Abelard lived in Italy, an English archbishop named Anselm taught that human sin was an insult to the majesty of God. Accordingly, God became a man and died to satisfy His offended honor.

During the sixteenth century, the Reformers turned from philosophy to biblical exegesis to define Christ's atoning work on the cross. They identified sin as the violation of God's Law. They viewed Christ's death as a substitutionary atonement, meaning He took the punishment deserved by sinners who broke God's Law.

For whom did Jesus die? Theologians have long debated whether Christ died for all humanity or only for the elect, those chosen by God. The view that Christ died only for the elect draws its conclusions from the logic of election. It says that believers were chosen by God "before the creation of the world" (Eph. 1:4) and were predestined "to be adopted as his sons through Jesus Christ" (1:5). All unbelievers are spiritually dead and incapable of responding to God unless He enables them to through

His grace (Eph. 2:1–5). All whom God enables to respond do so because His grace is irresistible. All that Christ did, He did for the elect (Rom. 8:28–39). Therefore, He died only for the elect.

The more generally accepted view among evangelical Christians is that the death of Christ paid the price for all human sin and provides forgiveness sufficient for everyone. However, it is applied only to those who believe. Advocates of this view refer to John 3:16 ("God so loved the world that he gave his one and only Son, that whoever believes in him shall not perish but have eternal life") and many other passages, such as John 1:29; 3:15, 17; 4:42; 2 Corinthians 5:19; 1 Timothy 4:10; Hebrews 2:9; 1 John 2:2; 4:14.

In this view Christ died for the sake of all people. The Synod of Dort (1618–1619) concluded that Jesus' death is "sufficient for all but efficient for the elect." "Everyone who calls on the name of the Lord will be saved" (Joel 2:32; Acts 2:21; Rom. 10:13), but only those chosen by God, the elect, will respond. Jesus said, "All that the Father gives me will come to me, and whoever comes to me I will never drive away" (John 6:37). The gospel message is "whoever will may come," but only those chosen by God the Father and given to Christ will come to Him.

—**JAW**

***

In the power of the indwelling Holy Spirit, live as a person freed from the slave market of sin by Christ's atoning death.

Bb

BABYLON

Babylon is both a place name and a powerful metaphor for evil in the Bible. As a place name it refers either to a city or the empire that spread out from it. As a metaphor for evil, Babylon may refer to the religion centered there, or the name "Babylon" may represent another evil empire or evil religious system that threatens the people of God.

The Tower of Babel gave birth to the name for the city that surrounded it (Gen. 11:9, margin). The site of this ancient city lies about fifty miles south of Baghdad in present-day Iraq. For centuries Babylon was the center of economic and political life in the lower Tigris-Euphrates valley. In the seventh and sixth centuries B.C., a resurgent form of the Babylonian Empire replaced Assyria as the power in the Middle East and appears in the pages of the Old Testament. Under Nebuchadnezzar, this new Babylon conquered Jerusalem, destroyed the temple, and deported much of the population of Judah to Babylonian towns (2 Kin. 25). Because Babylon was a mighty oppressor of the people of God for several generations, the name became a symbol for religious or political evil on a worldwide scope. "Babylon" is frequently mentioned in the prophetic Scriptures, usually with reference to political Babylon, but sometimes as a symbol for another present or future world power.

Daniel 2 and 7 predict that the Babylonian Empire would be conquered by another empire, that of the Medes and the Persians (Dan. 8:20). The downfall of the city of Babylon, recorded in Daniel 5, took place on October 12, 539 B.C. The empire ceased at that moment, but the city endured. It is the subject of extensive biblical prophecies. Beginning in chapter 13, the Book of Isaiah includes a number of prophecies concerning the fall of and God's judgment on Babylon. The Book of Jeremiah contains more than 160 references to Babylon. Jeremiah 51—52 describe particular details of judgment on Babylon, including the statement that Babylon would be completely destroyed and uninhabited. For example, "Babylon will be a heap of ruins, a haunt of jackals, an object of horror and scorn, a place where no one lives" (Jer. 51:37). Her total destruction is also mentioned in 51:43–44. "Her towns will be desolate, a dry and desert land, a land where no one lives, through which no man travels. I will punish Bel in Babylon and make him spew out what he has swallowed.

The nations will no longer stream to him. And the wall of Babylon will fall."

Interpreters dispute whether Jeremiah's prophecies have been fulfilled or await future fulfillment. Babylon, though largely in ruins through the centuries, has always been inhabited. So its final destruction is yet to be fulfilled. Also the vision recorded in Zechariah 5:5–11 points to a yet-future Babylon.

In Revelation 17, Babylon is personified as a harlot astride a scarlet-colored beast. The woman represents false religions, and the beast she rides, with its seven heads and ten horns, represents the revived Roman Empire. "Babylon" foreshadows a world church movement whose influence on Christianity will be felt everywhere (17:15, 18). The ten nations of the revived Roman Empire will destroy the woman called "Babylon." "They will bring her to ruin and leave her naked; they will eat her flesh and burn her with fire" (17:16). This apparently will happen three and a half years before the Second Coming of Christ because the world religion of the end time will consist of the worship of the Antichrist (Dan. 11:36–37; 2 Thess. 2:4).

Revelation 18 records a further prophecy about Babylon. This time Babylon is a gigantic commercial city, which will be destroyed by earthquake and fire at the Second Coming (18:21–24). Scholars differ as to whether this reference to Babylon should be interpreted literally or symbolically. To be the capital of the world empire of the last half of the Tribulation, Babylon would have to be extensively rebuilt. It would take all the influence of the Antichrist to make Babylon a leading economic center of the world. Another view of Revelation 17 and 18 is that Babylon refers to Rome. This is supported by Revelation 17:9, where the woman bearing the title "Babylon the Great" (17:5) is said to sit on seven hills. The city of Rome was built on seven hills. In John's day Rome was "the great city that rules over the kings of the earth" (17:18). Yet a third view is that the Babylon/Rome imagery represents all earthly political power structures.

When you read the prophets of the Old Testament and the Book of Revelation in the New Testament, it's important to distinguish whether Babylon refers to the city, the empire, or another godless religious or political system. Many prophecies about Babylon have been fulfilled historically, but much remains to be fulfilled in connection with the Second Coming.

—**JFW**

***

Rejoice that God will bring judgment on every stronghold of Satan.

BAPTISM

Baptism is a church ritual in which water is applied to a person to indi-cate he or she is a believer in Christ and a member of His church. Throughout church history theologians have argued about almost every detail of doctrine and practice concerning baptism. Most churches, however, regard baptism as a sacrament or an ordinance. It is a sacred ceremony that acknowledges God's provision of salvation.

There are two primary Protestant views of baptism. According to the Baptist view, baptism means immersion in water, and it is administered in the name of the Father, the Son, and the Holy Spirit (Matt. 28:19). The act of baptism is a recognition that one's sins have been forgiven (Acts 2:38; 22:16). It also represents union with Christ (Gal. 3:26–28) and the indwelling of the Holy Spirit (1 Cor. 6:19). The act of baptism acknowledges that the church is the body of Christ, formed by the baptism of the Spirit (1 Cor. 12:13). The Baptist view is that baptism is only for older children, youth, and adults who are believers and that there is no validity to infant baptism.

In contrast, the Reformed view is that baptism may be administered by sprinkling or pouring, and that infants as well as adults may be baptized. Various views of infant baptism are held within the Reformed interpretation. Some regard infant baptism as little more than a dedication of infants. Others believe baptism imparts grace to the infant, connecting it in a way short of salvation to the covenant community. These Reformed thinkers view baptism as an initiation rite into a covenant of grace similar to the rite of circumcision in the Old Testament (Col. 2:11–12). The Reformed view regards baptism as representing union with Christ, a concept also present in the Baptist view. Both the Baptist and Reformed traditions say baptism pictures washing from sin.

Immersionists claim Jesus was immersed in the Jordan River. They point to the verse "He went up out of the water" (Matt. 3:16) and say Jesus must have been immersed. They like to point out that the Greek verb translated "to baptize," *baptizō*, comes from the root word *baptō* that means "to dip." Those who do not practice immersion, however, point out that *baptō* never appears in the New Testament and that *baptizō*, whatever its origin, means "to wash or to purify with water." The main idea in baptism, they claim, is cleansing, not immersion. Baptists respond that *rantizō*, "to sprinkle," is never used of this Christian ordinance.

Some church groups teach that baptism is necessary for salvation. They say new birth occurs at the moment of water baptism. Some Lutheran theologians hold that when children are baptized they are regenerated. They say this means that grace is imparted to the children, but that they must confirm their faith as adults to receive salvation. While many churches practice infant baptism, the Bible does not clearly record any such instance. Some maintain that the baptism of the Philippian jailer's household could have included small children(Acts 16:33).

In addition to water baptism, the New Testament refers eleven times to the baptism of the Holy Spirit (Matt. 3:11; Mark 1:8; Luke 3:16; John 1:30–33; Acts 1:5; 11:16; Rom. 6:1–4; 1 Cor. 12:13; Gal. 3:27; Eph. 4:5; Col. 2:12). The baptism of the Spirit is distinct from His regenerating, indwelling, and sealing ministries. Spirit baptism is the work of the Holy Spirit in which He places a person into the body of Christ at the moment he believes in Christ for salvaiton. The Pentecostal and Holiness traditions assert that it takes place at a time subsequent to conversion, but other evangelicals believe that it takes place at the same time.

In 1 Corinthians 15:29 Paul referred to the custom some people followed in being "baptized for the dead." Of the dozens of explanations of this confusing phrase, the best alternative seems to be that some new converts were baptized to replace on the church roles those who had died ("for" meaning "in place of"). The Mormon practice of "proxy baptism" (the living being baptized on behalf of dead ones to bring them into the fold of Mormonism) conflicts with the rest of Scripture. After death, there is no hope of salvation for the unsaved (Heb. 9:27).
—**JFW**

***

*Realize that being baptized
is a testimony of your faith
in Christ.*

BLASPHEMY

Blasphemy is a specific verbal sin. Someone who blasphemes speaks of God with contempt or makes fun of Him. Some blasphemy is intentional. The speaker hates God and spews bitter words about Him. Other blasphemy is unintentional. The speaker disbelieves in God and mocks Him casually. Both kinds of blasphemy are increasingly common in the modern world.

The Bible takes a hard line against blasphemy. The Old Testament prescribed death as the penalty for blasphemy (Lev. 24:10–16; Num 15:30–31). Israel was a theocracy. That means that God was its ultimate ruler, not some human judge or king. So religious offenses like blasphemy could result in civil penalties, such as capital punishment.

The Old Testament records instances of blasphemy by God's people. Ezra said Israel committed "awful blasphemies" (Neh. 9:18) when at Sinai they referred to the golden calf as "the god who brought you up out of Egypt." The Law defined a deliberate, defiant sin as blasphemy because it arrogantly challenges God's lordship (Num. 15:30–31).

Other Old Testament incidents of blasphemy involved unbelievers. Na-than told David his sin with Bathsheba had "given occasion to the enemies of the LORD to blaspheme" (2 Sam. 12:14, NASB). Isaiah insisted the Assyrians blasphemed God when they said He was no better than the gods of the other nations they had conquered (2 Kin. 19:4, 6, 22). The Babylonians blasphemed God during Israel's captivity (Is. 52:5). Edom mocked God, charging He didn't take very good care of His people (Pss. 44:14; 74:10; Ezek. 35:12, NKJV).

In the time between the Old and New Testaments, Jewish religious leaders displayed serious concern that people might accidentally blaspheme God. They took the position that the name of God was too sacred to say out loud. So they substiuted *'ădōnāy* ("my Lord") for *Yahweh* when they spoke or read about Him. Matthew always wrote "kingdom of heaven" in his Gospel where Mark and Luke wrote "kingdom of God." He may have done that to reverence God's name.

The New Testament treats blasphemy as hostile, contemptuous words aimed at God. The Synoptic Gospel writers all say the Jews blasphemed when they insulted, reviled, and mocked Christ (Matt. 27:39; Mark 15:29; Luke 23:39). The Jews "resisted and blasphemed" God when they rejected Paul's message that Jesus is the Messiah. Luke recorded that the Jews "resisted and blasphemed" (Acts 18:6, NASB). Perhaps they cursed Christ when Paul said He was God manifest in the flesh. Gentiles blaspheme God's name because of the hypocrisy of the Jews (Rom. 2:24).

On their part, the Jewish religious leaders had consistently accused Christ of blasphemy (Matt. 26:65; Mark 2:7; 14:64; Luke 5:21; John 10:33). Jesus forgave sins. He assumed authority in the temple. He applied messianic Scripture to Himself. The religious establishment recognized that Jesus taught and acted in a way that elevated Himself to divine status. They had to either worship Him or charge Him with blasphemy.

On one occasion the Pharisees charged that Jesus did His miracles by Satan's power rather than God's. Jesus responded with strong words: "I tell you the truth, all the sins and blasphemies of men will be forgiven them. But whoever blasphemes against the Holy Spirit will never be forgiven; he is guilty of an eternal sin" (Mark 3:28–29). Historically we've called this "the unpardonable sin."

The death of Christ makes possible the forgiveness of every sin. Theoretically a person who blasphemed against the Holy Spirit would be forgiven if he came to faith in Christ. Jesus' point is that some people become so hardened against Him that they will never come to faith in Him. This heinous sin may therefore be described as "the unpardoned sin" rather than "the unpardonable sin."

Blasphemy abounds in popular cul-ture where entertainers and media gurus have discovered that secular audiences like to make fun of things holy. God's name peppers most television and movie scripts. It's possible to become desensitized to such nonstop, thoughtless blasphemy. It would not be wise to do so. Blasphemy, even mindless blasphemy, cheapens what is holy and divine. Blasphemy, after all, is the language of false teachers (2 Pet. 2:12). Ultimately it will be the native tongue of the Antichrist (Rev. 13:1, 5–6).   **—DKC**

***

Realize the seriousness of mocking or insulting God, and be sensitive to the holiness of His name and person.

BLESSING

"Blessing" is a rich biblical term that means much more than wishing someone well. We might say, "Bless you" and mean little more than "Have a good day!" The Bible uses the term *blessing* to speak of God's special favor upon someone.

The concept of blessing shifts as we move from the Old to the New Testaments. In the Old Testament *blessing* is a concrete term for enriching someone or something. In the New Testament *blessing* means to speak well of someone. *Blessed* may mean "fortunate" or "happy."

Let's first look at the Old Testament

concept of *blessing*. God blessed all sorts of things during creation. He blessed the sea and the birds (Gen. 1:22). He blessed the man and woman He created in His own image (1:28). He set apart the seventh day and blessed it (2:2–3). As stated earlier, the Hebrew term translated *blessing* implies enrichment. Enrichment can relate to material things such as land and food (Gen. 28:4; Deut. 12:15; 16:15), or it can be spiritual (Num. 6:24–27; Is. 19:25). Blessing always springs ultimately from God, for He alone has the power to enrich.

God blessed individuals like Noah (Gen. 9:1), Abraham (24:1), and Isaac (26:3). Sometimes worshipers blessed God in the form of praise and worship (Gen. 24:48, NASB; Ps. 103:1, NASB). To bless God was to want to see His reputation enriched by praise. Someone might bless another person: Jacob blessed Joseph (Gen. 48:15), and Rebekah's family blessed her (24:60). David ascribed praise to God for sending Abigail and then blessed her for restraining his anger (1 Sam. 25:32–33). Jacob blessed his sons and foretold their future (Gen. 49:28). An Old Testament blessing had great significance and was not to be treated lightly. For instance, when Esau learned Jacob had cheated him of his blessing, he wept and begged his father Isaac to find a blessing for him too (27:38; Heb. 12:17).

You too could mark stages in your children's growth by naming their strengths, pointing out where they might grow spiritually, giving them opportunities and resources for personal growth, and cheering them on to success. We should make it our goal to bless—to enrich—our children.

God is the source of blessing or enrichment. No legitimate blessing can be made or withheld in His name without His authorization. The story of Balak and Balaam in the Book of Numbers illustrates this. Balak, king of Moab, hired the prophet Balaam to curse the Israelites. Balaam, however, could not curse them because God had blessed them (Num. 22:12).

The prophets spoke a good deal about the blessings of God. The one who trusted in God would prosper and have no fears (Jer. 17:7–9). God desired to bless all those who waited for Him (Is. 30:18) and were obedient to Him (56:1–2). God withheld blessing from the disobedient (Jer. 18:10, NASB). In the Millennium, when God will restore Israel to her land, He will bless her with security and an abundant harvest (Is. 32:18–20; Ezek. 34:25–29). Though Israel has been an object of cursing among the nations, she will be blessed when God delivers her (Zech. 8:13).

In the New Testament the concept of *blessing* becomes more abstract and spiritual. The New Testament does not promise material prosperity to believers in Christ as the Old Testament does for Israel. The Greek word used to translate the Hebrew word for "blessing" is *eulogia,* which means to speak well of someone or to praise and extol that person. We get the English term "eulogy" from this word. "To bless" then came to mean to speak well of someone.

Another New Testament term for "blessing" is *makarios,* which means "happy" or "fortunate." In Jesus' Beatitudes (Matt. 5:3–11) He used the word *makarios* to emphasize inner qualities of immediate benefit to those whose hearts were turned to the Lord. The sermon also anticipated a future time when the meek will truly inherit the earth (5:5), as spoken of by the prophets. The Pharisees were not blessed by God, for while they emphasized an outward display of piety they lacked inner reality (5:20).

The idea of enrichment in *makarios* is primarily spiritual—a deep abiding joy and satisfaction that comes from receiving and enjoying the God's resources for living the Christian life (Eph. 1:3; 2 Pet. 1:3–4).

In this sense the New Testament epistles speak of our blessing as the inner delight that stems from our personal, intimate relationship with the risen Christ. Paul described the blessedness of being justified by faith (Rom. 4). The blessing given to Abraham (salvation by faith) is also available to the Gentiles (Gal. 3:13–14). James called the man blessed who is able to stand up under trials and testing, because he will receive a reward from the Lord (James 1:12). Peter admonished people who follow Christ to seek a blessing by behaving in a way that reflects the graciousness of Christ, even when pressured or insulted (1 Pet. 3:9).

The New Testament fittingly closes with Christ in heaven seated next to the Father and receiving blessing (praise) from angels and every creature from heaven and earth (Rev. 5:11–14). Truly He is worthy! Those who trust Christ are called "blessed and holy" and will reign with Him for a thousand years (20:6). **—WGJ**

***

Write down all the blessings that come from your being in the body of Christ, and regularly give thanks for them.

BLINDNESS

Blindness is inability to see. In the Bible blindness can be physical or spiritual. Physical blindness may be lifelong or the result of injury, illness, or divine intervention. Spiritual blindness may be the lifelong result of the sin nature, or it may result from the activity of the devil to dull a person's spiritual perception in a given situation.

The Gospels record a number of times when Jesus healed blind people (Matt. 9:27–30; 11:5; 12:22; 15:31–32; 20:29–34; 21:14; Luke 4:18; John 5:3; 9:1–12). Healing blindness was a spectacular miracle, and it always suggested Jesus could give spiritual sight. Additionally, Jesus' ability to heal blindness (as well as many other serious illnesses) helped demonstrate that He is the Son of God.

The Bible says a lot about spiritual blindness in the Old and New Testaments. It results from sin (Zeph. 1:17). Isaiah announced that Israel's sinful leaders were blind (Is. 43:8; 56:10). Several times Jesus told the Pharisees they were blind. They lacked spiritual insight, so they were unable and unwilling to "see" who Jesus was (Matt. 23:16–17, 19, 24, 26; John 9:39–41). Many people who heard Jesus' parables did not comprehend their meaning because they were spiritually blind (Matt. 13:14–15). In fact they could not believe because of their blindness to God's ways (John 12:39–40).

Those who are blind (*typhlos*) to spiritual things are also said to have heart-hardness (*pōrōsis*). The New International Version renders this word "stubborn" (Mark 3:5), "darkened" in understanding (Eph. 4:18), and "hardening" (Rom. 11:25). The verb *pōroō* is rendered "deadened" (John 12:40), "hardened" (Rom. 11:7), and "dull" (2 Cor. 3:14). Spiritual "sight" occurs in the heart. When someone's heart is hard, that person loses the insight necessary to respond to God's Word and Spirit.

Paul wrote, "The man without the Spirit does not accept the things that come from the Spirit of God, for they are foolishness to him, and he cannot understand them, because they are spiritually discerned" (1 Cor. 2:14). "The minds of unbelievers" are blinded by Satan, "the god of this age" (2 Cor. 4:4). Theology is a rational science that organizes biblical data into doctrinal form. Reasonably intelligent unsaved people can understand theology as a system of propositions, but they cannot grasp the supernatural dimension of spiritual truth that imparts and empowers life.

Even people who know Christ as Savior may stumble around like blind people because they resist the truth and Spirit of God. (2 Pet. 1:9; 1 John 2:11; Rev. 3:17). When blinded by sin, we need to yield once again to the Holy Spirit. The "spiritual man" (1 Cor. 2:15) is able to understand the things of God. Someone walking in the light of God's revelation (1 John 1:7) has his spiritual eyes opened so he can comprehend the truth of God.

In the present age Israel as a whole is hardened to the truth of the gospel (Rom. 11:7, 25). The people's spiritual eyes are darkened (11:10) because they rejected Jesus as their Messiah. This blindness won't last forever; it is "a hardening in part" (11:25) until the church age (in which many Gentiles are coming to Christ) is complete. Many Jews in the Tribulation will come to Christ. And after Israel's Messiah-Deliverer comes at the Rapture, many

Israelites will have their spiritual eyes opened and will recognize Jesus as their Messiah and Savior (11:26–27).

—**JFW**

***

Pray daily that the Holy Spirit will open your eyes to comprehend what God has revealed in His Word.

BLOOD

Blood is the red fluid pumped by the heart through the arteries, capillaries, and veins in the body of a human or vertebrate animal. Blood is composed of a straw-colored fluid called plasma, red and white blood cells, and platelets that enable clotting. Blood carries nourishment and oxygen to the cells of the body and carbon dioxide and other waste products from them.

Scripture often uses the term *blood* in this normal sense with reference to both animals and humans. *Blood* is also employed as a synonym for life itself. The theological significance of *blood* is in this metaphorical portion of the word's meaning. The Bible, therefore, associates loss of blood with violence, death of humans, and the death of animals in religious sacrifices.

Several Old Testament passages also associate *blood* with life. Genesis 9:4 states, "Only you shall not eat flesh with its life, that is, its blood" (NASB). Leviticus 17:11 declares, "For the life of a creature is in the blood, and I have given it to you to make atonement for yourselves on the altar; it is the blood that makes atonement for one's life." Deuteronomy 12:23 exhorts, "But be sure you do not eat the blood, because the blood is the life, and you must not eat the life with the meat."

In recent years some scholars have debated whether biblical sacrifices shed their blood as a symbol of death or life. Some claim that in the offering of bloody sacrifices the life of the animal was released from the body and presented to God. The death of the animal was the means of freeing its life. They also contend that references to the blood of Christ should be understood to mean Christ's life was set free to provide salvation.

This view removes punishment for sin from the meaning of biblical sacrifices. If the *blood* of animals and the *blood* of Jesus paid a penalty that sinners otherwise would have been required to pay, that *blood* represents death. Sin in the Old Testament was considered so serious that it was punished by death: "The person who sins will die" (Ezek. 18:20, NASB). The sacrificial death of an animal was accepted in the place of the human sinner. In the New Testament, salvation is provided, not by the life of Christ set free on behalf of sinners, but by the death of Christ (for example, Col. 1:20, "by making peace through his blood, shed on the cross").

The Greek word *haima,* "blood," occurs 99 times in the New Testament. More than three dozen of these occurrences refer to the blood of Christ. Most of them deal with His death on the cross. Paul called the blood of Jesus "a sacrifice of atonement" (Rom. 3:25; see Lev. 17:11). Paul wrote that by the blood of Christ we are justified (Rom. 5:9), reconciled to God (5:10), redeemed (Eph. 1:7), brought near to God (2:13), forgiven (1:7), and given peace with God (Col. 1:20). Peter affirmed that we have been redeemed from our old and empty way of life "with the precious blood of Christ" (1 Pet. 1:18–19). John declared that Christ's blood provides continual cleansing for sin in the life of the believer (1 John 1:7). The writer of Hebrews emphasized that the Old Testament system of sacrifices and offerings found its final fulfillment in the blood of Christ, that is, in His sacrificial death (Heb. 9:7–28; 13:11–12).

At the Last Supper, Jesus spoke of the cup as "the new covenant in my blood, which is poured out for you" (Luke 22:20). We are exhorted to remember and proclaim His death by participating in the Lord's Supper, that is, by eating the bread and drinking the cup (1 Cor. 11:25–27). The blood of Christ is the "once-for-all" means of redemption. We must never forget or take for granted the suffering and death of Jesus on our behalf and in our place.　　　**—DKC**

***

In His love for us Christ did not hold back His own lifeblood, thus calling us to a sacrificial pouring out of ourselves in service to others.

BODY

Everyone has a human body, given by God, much as He gave a body to Adam, the first man, in the Garden of Eden. Of course our mother and father have an important part—working with God—to produce our bodies. Since Adam was an original creation, something new, God formed him (fully developed) from the dust of the ground. Then the Bible says God breathed life into Adam's body and he "became a living being." Thus being a person involves more than having a physical body.

When God finished creating Adam, He called His handiwork "very good" (Gen. 1:31). Much later, when Jesus came into the world, He came in a human body. That tells us there was still nothing wrong with the body itself, because Jesus was perfect and without sin. He could not have lived in a body that was sinful. Some people have insisted that our bodies, like the rest of the world, are contaminated by sin. That view forced them to conclude that Jesus was not really present in a body, but only "appeared" to be. The church has rejected this as a heresy (a teaching that goes against God's truth) because living in a body was part of what made Jesus "fully human."

Certainly the Bible teaches that sin had a negative effect on Adam's body. He began to experience pain and even death because of sin (Gen. 3:17–19). When the Old Testament refers to *body* it almost always is talking about the physical body. At the same time Adam's spirit was affected too. He found himself separated from fellowship with God—no more intimate walks and talks together in the Garden.

Jesus used two words to refer to humanity's physical side: *sōma* ("body") and *sarχ* ("flesh"). Both words speak of our whole person (see Matt. 6:23 and 19:5). He used *flesh* to describe physical birth as something different from spiritual birth (John 3:6). He also used *flesh* when talking about marriage (Matt. 19:5; Mark 10:8). When He was talking about how to have eternal life, He used *flesh* in a figurative way (John 6:51–56). On the other hand, at the Lord's Supper He used *body* to refer to Himself (Matt. 26:26), and *body* is how the Scriptures speak of Jesus' crucified body (Matt. 27:58; Mark 15:45; Luke 24:3). After the Resurrection, though, Jesus spoke of His *flesh* to emphasize that He was really present and not just a ghost (Luke 24:39).

The apostle Paul draws a clearer line between the two words in his teaching. He speaks of body (*sōma*) in referring to that part of us that serves as the temple of the Holy Spirit (Rom. 6:13; 8:11; 1 Cor. 6:19–20). Living for Jesus in a sinful world requires that our bodies be committed to Him (Rom. 12:1–2). We need to exercise control of our bodies as part of a consistent Christian witness in this life (1 Cor. 9:27). When we ourselves are resurrected, our bodies (*sōma*) will be changed and will last forever (Rom. 8:23; 1 Cor. 15:52–53).

Paul describes the *flesh* as the enemy of God (Rom. 8:7). People who live in the *flesh* are focused on the things of this world rather than the values and principles of God. Their end will be spiritual death and separation from God.

Paul also makes a distinction between the natural body and the spiritual body (1 Cor. 15:42–49). The natural body is our physical body that will die and decay and then be raised up when our Lord returns. The spiritual body, he says, is something immortal, that exists throughout eternity (1 Cor. 15:53–54).

The New Testament uses "body" in yet another way: to picture the church. Jesus is the Head of this body (Col. 1:18). All believers work together, each performing the function of one of the parts of a human body (1 Cor. 12:12–26). Under the guidance and leadership of the Head, we who are hands, feet, skin, bones, heart, etc., carry out the critical functions of the church from day to day. And together under Christ's direction we continually grow in the Spirit (Eph. 4:15–16). **—WGJ**

***

Our physical bodies are a gift from God, to be accepted from Him as His creation. One day every believer will receive a new resurrected body in which he or she will serve Him.

BRIDE

The noun "bride" applies to a woman as she is being married and as she celebrates her wedding. The Bible uses *bride* in this literal sense in many narratives. The theological meanings attached to the word *bride* arise from its symbolic uses. These metaphorical usages depend on connotations associated with the term. A *bride* is thought of as beautiful, virginal, joyous, deeply in love with her bridegroom, committed to him, eager to care for him, and expecting to live happily ever after as his only beloved.

In the Old Testament, Israel is described as a nation that started out as the bride and wife of the Lord. Sadly, Israel was regularly unfaithful to her marriage vows. As we read these passages, we're expected to think, "When Israel was a bride, she never expected to act like this. What happened to her love for her Husband as the years of marriage piled up?"

Gomer, the adulterous wife of the prophet Hosea, illustrated Israel's spiritual adultery. Though Gomer was unfaithful, Hosea loved her and took her back (Hos. 1:2–3; 3:1–3). Similarly after God chastises Israel for her unfaithfulness (2:1–13), He will restore her to Himself in the millennial kingdom (2:14–23; see also 3:5; 14:4).

In the New Testament, the church is the future bride of Christ. The church is betrothed to Him. Through the centuries of the church age, she is preparing herself to marry her Lord. Though the Scriptures acknowledge the frequent unfaithfulness of the church, the ideal is described in 2 Corinthians 11:2, which speaks of the church as a pure virgin to be presented to Christ. This relationship is detailed in Ephesians 5:22–33.

In New Testament times, Jewish marriages had three stages: (a) the payment of a dowry by the parents of the bridegroom (which confirmed the couple's commitment to each other), (b) the bridegroom's claiming of the bride, sometimes up to a year later, and (c) the wedding feast. The parable of the ten virgins in Matthew 25:1–13 depicts a bridegroom with his friends parading through the streets at midnight to the home of the bride. When they arrive, she joins the procession with her girlfriends and goes to the home of the bridegroom, where there is a wedding banquet.

We need to use this model to understand the future marriage of the church to Christ. At the Rapture, Christ will appear like the bridegroom claiming His bride for Himself. He will take her to the Father's house.

At the Second Coming of Christ, guests will be invited to His wedding banquet (Rev. 19:7). In New Testament times there was no marriage ceremony in Jewish weddings. The "wedding" was the wedding feast (see also 19:9; Matt. 22:2; 25:10). First, the Groom claims His bride and brings her to His Father's house. Then comes the wedding feast. This sequence confirms that the Rapture will take place before the Second Coming.

Betrothal in New Testament times indicated a formal alliance. The groom had paid a dowry, and it took a legal divorce to dissolve the union (Matt. 1:19). Christ has paid the price for the church, like a dowry, on the Cross. We should not be unfaithful to our "betrothal vows" by loving the world or the things of the world (1 John 2:15). We must center our affections on Christ (Col. 3:1–3).

In the Old Testament, Israel was the unfaithful wife of the Lord. In the New Testament, the church is a virgin bride waiting for Christ's return. This contrast is rooted in the different purposes of God for Israel and the church. The church will be raptured at the beginning of the end-time events and taken to heaven. Israel will be restored after the Second Coming of Christ at the beginning of the millennial kingdom. At that time believing Israel will enter into the millennial kingdom related to Christ as a restored spouse (Ezek. 20:32–38).

The figure of the bride emphasizes the central importance of our love for the Lord. Christ Himself declared in Matthew 22:37–38: "'Love the Lord your God with all your heart and with all your soul and with all your mind.' This is the first and greatest commandment."

The New Jerusalem, the habitat of all saints in the eternal state, is also called a bride. This imagery does not mean, as some suggest, that the New Jerusalem is to be inhabited only by the church. John was depicting the city as a beautiful place, as beautiful as a bride. All believers—Old Testament and New Testament—will reside there.

—JFW

***

In heaven we will experience the sweet joy of being claimed as His own by the One for whom we have been watching.

BUILDING

"Building" can mean either the act of erecting a structure or the structure itself. Further, the Bible uses the word *building* in both its literal sense and in metaphorical senses. In the Old Testament, certain buildings were theologically important. In the New Testament, *building* tends to be used symbolically.

The tabernacle and the temple were the most significant buildings in the Old Testament. The tabernacle was an elaborate tent built according to the instructions God gave Moses at Mount Sinai. The tabernacle was where God dwelt among His people (Ex. 25:8). It was Israel's first place of worship, and its importance can be seen by the number of references to it in Exodus and Leviticus.

The temple was equally significant. David spent many years preparing for this building (2 Sam. 7:1–2; 1 Chr. 17:1). God did not let David build the temple because he was a warrior who had shed a lot of blood. God directed that David's son Solomon build the "house" (28:6). This temple was a magnificent building, but it was God's presence that set it apart from all other structures.

While David planned a "house" for God of stone and precious metals, the Lord promised David He would build a "house" for him (17:10). The term "house" pictured the dynasty God would build through David and his descendants. Solomon's temple was destroyed by the Babylonians in 586 B.C., but the prophet Amos had already predicted God would rebuild it (Amos 9:11–12).

Zechariah described another "house" to be built in opposition to the house of God (Zech. 5:11), a place where wickedness would reside (5:8). The angel who revealed this to the prophet identified the location of this place as Babylonia (5:11; see also Rev. 17—18).

In New Testament times local con-gregations did not construct build-ings for worship. Jesus had taught that worshiping God "in spirit and truth" was more important than any building constructed for worship (John 4:21–24). Just as God promised to build a "house" for David, so Jesus said He would build a church that would be invincible (Matt. 16:18). He built His church on the foundation of the apostles and prophets, with Himself as the cornerstone (Eph. 2:20).

The building blocks of the church of Jesus Christ are believers from every national and ethnic group, all who have professed faith in Jesus Christ as their Savior (1:11–13; 2:22). Paul also described this unique group as the temple of the Holy Spirit (1 Cor. 3:9, 16). This church *building* has universal dimensions. It has visible expressions on every continent of the world as believers meet together for worship and ministry. Peter used a similar figure to describe this building. Christ, he wrote, is the living Stone, and believers are living stones who are built into a spiritual house (1 Pet. 2:4–5).

The term *building* also refers figuratively to the spiritual growth of believers. God gave gifted people to the church so that Christians could be "built up" and reach spiritual maturity and be more like Christ (Eph. 4:11–13). People are built up as they apply the truth they have been taught (Col. 2:6–7). Believers also build each other up by encouraging one another (1 Thess. 5:11).

Paul used a building analogy to contrast the flimsiness of our physical bodies to the permanence of our future glorified bodies. He called our present bodies "tents" (2 Cor. 5:1, 4). He said that when the "tent" of a believer collapses in death, he or she will receive a new body, an eternal house in heaven, called a "building from God" (5:1). **—WGJ**

***

Be careful how you build your life, and make sure the quality of your deeds reflects your yieldedness to the Spirit.

Cc

CALLING

When God focuses His attention on a person or group to direct them to follow His will, He is *calling* them. Early in the Old Testament God called Abraham to follow Him and become the channel of His blessing to the world (Gen. 12:1–3). Much of the rest of the Old Testament tells about God's call of Abraham's descendants, the nation of Israel. God chose Israel "out of all the peoples on the face of the earth to be his people, his treasured possession" (Deut. 7:6; 14:2; see also Pss. 132:13; 135:4). Israel is the nation God called (Is. 48:12) and chose (44:1; see 45:4; Amos 3:2; Hag. 2:23) to be a channel of blessing to the world. He called kings and prophets to guide Israel.

In the New Testament, divine calling occurs at three levels. The first and primary calling is to salvation (Rom. 8:28, 30; 1 Cor. 1:9, 24; Gal. 1:6, 15; 2 Thess. 2:13–15; Heb. 3:1; 9:15; 1 Pet. 1:15; 2:9; 5:10; 2 Pet. 1:3–6; Jude 1). The second level of calling extends to all believers. God calls us to lead holy and peaceful lives (1 Cor. 1:2; 7:15; Eph. 4:1; Col. 3:15; 2 Tim. 1:9; 1 Pet. 3:9). A third kind of calling in the New Testament is restricted to certain individuals. God calls some to special service, such as being an apostle (Rom. 1:1; 1 Cor. 1:1; 15:9; Gal. 1:15) or a missionary (Acts 13:2; 16:10).

Christians disagree about certain aspects of God's calling to salvation. When a gospel appeal is made to a general audience, how does God *call* everyone in the group and how does He *call* those who respond in faith? Calvinists say God calls them differently. They refer to God's general call of everyone and His effectual call of the elect (Rom. 8:28–30; 9:23–26). They describe God's effectual calling to salvation as "irresistible." God's call is part of His work of salvation.

Arminians say God calls everyone in the same way. He extends the same (common) grace to all who hear the Good News of Jesus' death for them on the Cross. Everyone there receives sufficient grace to believe. The responsibility for belief or unbelief is entirely in the will of the hearer and not in the call of God.

The Bible often speaks of grace (for example, Rom. 5:2; Eph. 2:5, 8), but the terms "irresistible grace" and "sufficient grace" are not biblical expressions. They arise out of attempts to systematize biblical teaching about salvation. For instance, *calling* to salvation is associated with predestination (Rom. 8:30). On that basis, the idea of an effectual call of the elect makes good sense. Jesus said people can be under conviction by the Holy Spirit and fully aware of their need to receive Christ as Savior but still reject Christ (John 16:8–11). Conviction, then, is related to God's general calling but is antecedent to an effectual calling to salvation. The call to salvation is initiated by God the Father, is made effective by the Holy Spirit, and results in a proper relationship with Jesus Christ as the Savior.

—**JFW**

***

Each believer is a "called" one,
summoned to escape the
darkness and live in the light.

CANONICITY

Canonicity is a non-biblical term used to describe the Bible's inherent authority as the God-breathed, infallible Word of God written by divinely chosen messengers. It also indicates that the people of God throughout the centuries have accepted the books of the Bible as their sole rule of faith and practice—the canon of Scripture. People don't bestow canonicity on the books of the Bible. They recognize and respond to their inherent authority.

The word *canonicity* builds on the Greek word *kanōn*, which originally meant "a rod" and then by extension "a measuring rod," "a rule," or "a standard" (Gal. 6:16). Various historic church groups also use the word *canon* to identify their sets of rules for worship and government.

The Old Testament books were written largely by divinely appointed leaders in Israel—Moses, Joshua, Samuel, David, Solomon, the prophets. They were accepted as canonical almost immediately. God Himself authenticated Moses' writings to Joshua (Josh. 1:7–8), who passed them on to Israel (23:6). David told Solomon to revere the Law of Moses (1 Kin. 2:3). The authority of Moses' writings was affirmed numerous times later in the Old Testament (2 Kin. 14:6; 23:25; Ezra 6:18; Neh. 8; Dan. 9:11–14; Mal. 4:4).

New Testament writers accepted the divine authority of the Old Testament and quoted from it approximately 250 times. The New Testament quotes every Old Testament book except Esther, Ecclesiastes, and the Song of Solomon. The New Testament phrase "the Law or the Prophets" (Matt. 5:17) was shorthand for the Old Testament. The Jewish Council of Jamnia (A.D. 90) officially confirmed the traditionally recognized Old Testament books. In A.D. 170 Melito of Sardis produced the first Christian list of thirty-nine Old Testament books.

The New Testament books were written either by apostles appointed by the Lord Jesus or by individuals intimately associated with the apostles. Two of the latter were James and Jude, the half-brothers of Jesus and leaders in the first-generation church. As a result, the authoritative character of those books was often quickly recognized. Some New Testament books claim authority (see Col. 4:16; 1 Thess. 5:20; 1 Tim. 5:18; 2 Pet. 3:16).

The early church fathers debated the canonicity of a few New Testament books for quite some time. It took nearly four hundred years to clarify which writings did not reflect the character of true Scripture and which did. The Council of Carthage (A.D. 397) designated the New Testament as the twenty-seven books we now have.

Many liberal theologians don't hesitate to question the worth of various Old Testament and New Testament books, but no church body has seriously considered removing any from the canon of Scripture. Various cults hold up their own so-called sacred writings, but they are not of the same character as the God-breathed writings.

—JAW

***

Receive and obey the words of the Bible, whether spoken or written, as God's authoritative message.

CARNALITY

This word comes from a cluster of Greek words composed of a basic noun (*sarx*, "flesh") and two adjectives (*sarkikos*, "carnal, fleshly," and *sarkinos*, "of flesh, fleshy"). Our English word comes from the Latin *carnalis*. *Carnality* in its simplest dictionary definition means that humans, as well as animals, birds, and fish, live in bodies of flesh (Luke 24:39; 1 Cor. 15:39, 50; 2 Cor. 12:7). It can also refer to the normal appetites, desires, and sensations of the physical body (Rom. 7:14–15, NASB; 1 Cor. 3:1, NASB; 2 Cor. 3:3–5, NASB).

In theological usage, however, *carnality* normally has negative ethical, moral, and spiritual connotations. In this sense Paul confessed, "I am carnal, sold under sin" (Rom. 7:14, NKJV). So are all human beings: "for all have sinned and fall short of the glory of God" (3:23; see also 5:12). Paul said unregenerate people follow "the ways of this world and of the ruler of the kingdom of the air" (Eph. 2:2) and seek to gratify "the cravings of [the] sinful nature [*sarx*] and [follow] its desires and thoughts" (2:3). Even highly ethical and moral people are spiritually "dead in . . . transgressions and sins" (2:1). Therefore they are in the basic state of carnality.

Christians also struggle with carnality, even though they are new creations in Christ (2 Cor. 5:17; Gal. 6:15). The old sin nature is not eradicated by trusting Christ as Savior. It tries to influence our actions whenever possible. Paul told the Corinthian Christians, "I could not speak to you as to spiritual people but as to carnal" (1 Cor. 3:1, NKJV). His complaint was that when, by reason of time, they should be spiritually mature, they were "still carnal," characterized by "envy [and] strife," and "behaving like [unregenerate] men" (3:3, NKJV).

We struggle all our lives as Christians to eliminate our residual sin nature and yield to the indwelling Holy Spirit. Paul observed, "For the sinful nature desires what is contrary to the Spirit, and the Spirit what is contrary to the sinful nature. They are in conflict with each other, so that you do not do what you want" (Gal. 5:17). John encouraged us not to "claim to be without sin" (1 John 1:8), but to "confess our sins" because God will forgive us (1:9). He assured us that "if anybody does sin, we have one who speaks to the Father in our defense—Jesus Christ, the Righteous One" (2:1).

The secret to victory over carnality is "to offer your bodies as living sacrifices, holy and pleasing to God" (Rom. 12:1) and to "live by the Spirit" (Gal. 5:16; see also Rom. 8:5). "Since we live by the Spirit, let us keep in step with the Spirit" (Gal. 5:25), "because those who are led by the Spirit of God are sons of God" (Rom. 8:14).   —JAW

***

Though you cannot eradicate or outgrow carnality in this life, you can control it by being submissive to the indwelling Holy Spirit.

CHASTISEMENT

The word "chastisement" in the King James Version of the Bible translates both the Hebrew noun *mûsār* and the Greek noun *paideia.* Newer English versions (for example, NASB, NIV) prefer the reading "discipline." The basic meanings of "discipline" or "chastisement" are education, guidance, correction, and (sometimes) punishment.

Discipline sounds more positive to modern ears than *chastisment.* That's good because, as Paul declared, "there is now no condemnation for those who are in Christ Jesus" (Rom. 8:1). However, if we persist in sin, God, the perfect disciplinarian, will chastise us. He chastises to correct and train us.

We can avoid chastisement. The Bible counsels: "For if we would judge ourselves, we would not be judged. But when we are judged, we are chastened by the Lord, that we may not be condemned with the world" (1 Cor. 11:31–32, NKJV). If we will bring our sins out into the light, confess them, and correct our ways, God won't have to do it for us (Luke 12:1–2, 1 John 1:5–9). If we hide our sins and try to appear self-righteous, God will discipline us for our own good.

God disciplines His people (the nation Israel in the Old Testament and individual believers in the New Testament) as a father treats his children. That's the basic idea of the concept of chastisement. God trains us, guides us, corrects us, and—if resisted over a long time—punishes us.

The primary New Testament passage about *chastisement* (discipline) is Hebrews 12:5–11. In these verses "discipline" (*paideia*) carries the added sense of correction through suffering. These Hebrew Christians were suffering persecution. The author reminded them that God can use affliction to instruct and train. He shook his finger at his readers for forgetting that Proverbs 3:11–12 says divine discipline is proof of divine love. We also need to remember this in times of suffering.

The writer of Hebrews said divine discipline is an evidence of sonship (Heb. 12:7). Every child of God experiences the Father's chastening hand at some point. Our earthly fathers were responsible to discipline us when we were children. God has the same responsibility for us spiritually. We submitted to our earthly fathers' discipline, even though we didn't enjoy it. How much more should we accept the discipline of our heavenly Father? God wants us to "share in his holiness"

(12:10), that is, reflect His holy character in our lives. In other words, God disciplines us for our own spiritual good.

—**DKC**

***

Thank God for His hand of discipline in our lives because it proves that we are His children and that He loves us.

CHILDREN

The Bible is an adult book. It wasn't written to children, but it says a good deal about them. Generally the Bible speaks positively about children. They are a blessing and a gift from God (Pss. 127:3–5; 113:9; Gen. 33:5; 48:4). Jesus commended childlike humility and faith (Matt. 18:3–4; Luke 18:16–17).

God commanded Adam and Eve to "be fruitful and increase in number" (Gen. 1:28). Sexual relations, conception, and childbirth are part of what God called "very good" at the end of day six of creation (v. 31). At times in its history, the church has been so uncomfortable with human sexuality that it has treated sexual relations and childbirth as though they were sinful.

Conception of a child is a natural physical process, but Scripture states that ultimately God is in control of it. After the very first childbirth, Eve said, "With the help of the LORD I have brought forth a man" (4:1). Several times in Scripture God gave children to barren women—Sarah (18:10;

21:1–2), Rebekah (25:21), Rachel (30:22–23), Hannah (1 Sam. 1:19–20), and Elizabeth (Luke 1:7, 13, 24, 36–37)—and He withheld children from others, such as Leah (Gen. 30:9). It's appropriate for a husband and wife to prayerfully commit to the Lord their desire for a family.

God holds both parents responsible for the physical, mental, and spiritual development of their children (Prov. 22:6). Both the Old and New Testaments expect the father to take the lead in childrearing (Deut. 6:7; 4:9; 11:19; Eph. 6:4; Col. 3:21). To qualify as an elder or a deacon in a local church, a man must demonstrate control of his children and management of his household (1 Tim. 3:4–5, 12; Titus 1:6). Fathers are warned neither to "exasperate" their children (Eph. 6:4) nor to "embitter" them so that they "become discouraged" (Col. 3:21). Constant criticism and correction of a child without corresponding approval and praise lead to rebellion or low self-esteem.

Some people question whether young children need to be converted. The Scriptures, however, assert that everyone is born with a sinful nature (Pss. 51:5; 58:3; Rom. 3:9–12, 23). The possibility of early childhood conversion is supported by Jesus' words that "little ones . . . believe in me" (Matt. 18:6) and "of such is the kingdom of heaven" (19:14, NKJV).

The Bible does not state specifically that children who die as infants or toddlers go to heaven. When his one-week-old son died, David said, "I will go to him, but he will not return to me" (2 Sam. 12:23). This suggests the infant had entered the presence of God when he died. It would be consistent with God's gracious love for Him to provide heaven to very young children who die.

The Bible uses the word *children* metaphorically too. In one sense all human beings are God's children by creation and providential control. At Athens the apostle Paul quoted with approval the Greek poet Aratus's statement that we all are God's "offspring" (Acts 17:28–29). But in a special spiritual sense, people become children of God through faith in the Lord Jesus Christ (John 1:12–13). They are thus "born again" into God's family (Rom. 8:16–17, 19, 21, 23; Eph. 5:8; Phil. 2:15). Since believers in Christ are "dearly loved children," Paul commanded believers to "be imitators of God" (Eph. 5:1). As the heavenly Father of believers, God sets the example for human fathers of how to discipline and train their children (Heb. 12:5–11). —**JAW**

***

Each day be a model of Christlike living, both to your children and to other young persons you contact.

CHRIST

The English word *Christ* reproduces the first syllable of the Greek *christos*.

Christos translates the Old Testament word *māšîah* meaning "anointed one. *Māšîah* comes into English as Messiah.

In the Old Testament, several things or people were ceremonially anointed with oil to indicate they had God's approval. Priests (Ex. 28:41; Lev. 8:12), the tabernacle and its furniture (Lev. 8:10–11; Num. 7:1), and kings (1 Sam. 9:15–16; 10:1; 15:1; 16:12–13; 2 Sam. 2:4; 1 Kin. 1:39; Ps. 89:20) were anointed with oil. Christ was God's "Anointed One" (Ps. 2:2; Acts 4:26). The prophet Daniel related the first advent of the "Anointed One" to the passage of sixty-nine "weeks" (Dan. 9:25–26).

The people of Jesus' day anticipated the Messiah. Andrew told his brother Simon, " 'We have found the Messiah' (that is, the Christ)" (John 1:41). And the Samaritan woman told Jesus, " 'I know that Messiah' (called Christ) 'is coming' " (4:25).

The New Testament gives several other titles to Jesus besides *Christ.* He is called Lord (Mark 7:28), Son of God (Matt. 14:33), Son of Man (20:28), the Word (John 1:1; Rev. 19:13), Savior (John 4:42; 1 John 4:14), High Priest (Heb. 2:17), and Prophet (Luke 24:19). He is referred to by compound titles, such as Jesus Christ, Christ Jesus, and the Lord Jesus Christ. He was also called Jesus Christ our Lord (Rom. 7:25), the Christ of God (Luke 23:35), and our Lord and Savior Jesus Christ (2 Pet. 3:18).

Jesus was the Messiah because He was the descendant of David. His anointing was royal. Jesus did not use the term "Messiah" (or "Christ") of Himself, but He accepted it from His disciples. For example, Peter said, "You are the Christ, the Son of the living God" (Matt. 16:16; see also 16:20). When the high priest Caiaphas asked Jesus at His trial whether He was the Messiah, He answered, "It is as you say" (26:64).

On the Day of Pentecost Peter proclaimed to the Jews "the resurrection of the Christ" and the fact that God "made this Jesus . . . both Lord and Christ" (Acts 2:31, 36). When Paul preached in the synagogue at Thessalonica, he reasoned with the Jews from the Scriptures that Jesus "is the Christ" (17:3). He did the same in Corinth (18:5), as did Apollos (18:27–28).

The Jews viewed the Messiah as a deliverer, whereas Jesus related His messiahship to His sacrifice on the cross (Matt. 16:21; Luke 24:26, 46). This difference in expectation became a stumbling block to Jews (1 Cor. 1:23). The concept of a crucified Messiah, though difficult for the Jews to comprehend, was foundational in the teaching of the early church. Both Peter and Paul emphasized that the Messiah had to suffer (Acts 3:18; 17:3; 26:23).

At His return to earth, Jesus will reign over Israel as her promised Messiah, her Deliverer and King. **—JFW**

***

Honor the Lord Jesus Christ and worship Him wholeheartedly.

CHURCH

The English word *church* derives from the Greek *kyriakon,* "belonging to the Lord." In German the word for church is *kirche.* In Scottish it's *kirk.* In the New Testament, however, *church* translates the Greek noun *ekklēsia,* "an assembly."

In the democratic city-states of Greece the citizens were called out to a local assembly to vote. This assembly (*ekklēsia*) was a group "called out," the literal meaning of *ekklēsia.* In Acts 19:39 *ekklēsia* is translated "a legal assembly."

Jesus used the term only twice. In Matthew 16:18 He said to Peter, "And I tell you that you are Peter, and on this rock I will build my *church,* and the gates of Hades will not overcome it." In Matthew 18:17, in connection with disputes between brothers, Christ said, "If he refuses to listen to them, tell it to the *church;* and if he refuses to listen even to the *church,* treat him as you would a pagan or a tax collector." The assembly or church referred to in the second verse was probably a Jewish assembly, rather than a local Christian church.

Elsewhere in the New Testament the word *ekklēsia* occurs many times with various meanings. Sometimes an *ekklēsia* is a local church (for example, Antioch, Acts 13:1). Sometimes it's all local churches in an area (for example, "to the churches in Galatia," Gal. 1:2). Other times it's the church as the body of Christ (for example, Eph.

1:23 refers to true believers united spiritually to Christ similar to the way parts of a physical body are united to its head). This body of Christ is called the temple of the Holy Spirit (2:21) and "a spiritual house" (1 Pet. 2:5).

The word *church* can be used (a) of the professing church, that is, those gathered geographically in a certain location, whether they are all actually saved or not, and (b) of the body of Christ composed of true believers who are not necessarily all assembled in one locality. Christ referred to the unity of believers in the body of Christ in John 17:1–26. The word *church* may be used in a universal sense to include all true believers of all times whether they are on earth or in heaven.

Why do we need local churches? It seems that God ordained them because He knew our needs: fellowship, worship with others, joint prayer, the teaching and study of scriptural truth, and service to each other's needs. The ordinances of the church, as outlined in Scripture, consist of water baptism and the Lord's Supper (Matt. 28:19; 1 Cor. 11:23–26). Ministers of the church are called elders or overseers (Acts 11:30; 20:17). Qualifications of elders are stated in 1 Timothy 3:2–7 and Titus 1:6–9.

According to Acts 6:1–6 deacons were appointed to care for various ministries such as the distribution of food, care for the widows, and similar matters. Qualifications for deacons are mentioned in 1 Timothy 3:8–12. Some leaders were distinguished as prophets by spiritual gifts (1 Cor. 12:28), but like teachers and those who have other gifts they were not considered officers with formal appointments. The gift of evangelism is recognized in Acts 21:8, but it too is not a formal classification.

Three forms of church government are followed today: (a) episcopal, in which a bishop is the governing authority over a group of churches; (b) presbyterian, in which elders govern the local church; and (c) congregational, in which the congregation acts as a whole on various matters.

For centuries some theologians have given the church the title "the new Israel," implying that Israel has forfeited its right to be called the people of God. The Reformed view sees much continuity between the Old and New Testaments and emphasizes the unity of the people of God in one covenant. The dispensationalist view is that there is more discontinuity, with Israel maintaining its separate promises and destiny. The church should not be referred to as "the new Israel." In this view the church, the body of Christ, began on the Day of Pentecost and will maintain a distinctive identity throughout eternity.   **—JFW**

***

Become involved in a local
church for the purpose of
fellowship, worship, prayer,
study, and service.

CIRCUMCISION

Circumcision is the process of cutting off all or part of the foreskin of the male genital organ. Jews perform circumcision at a religious rite on the eighth day of a boy's life (Lev. 12:3; Luke 1:59; 2:21; Phil. 3:5). Ancient Egypt circumcised for hygienic reasons, Herodotus said. Anthropologists have found circumcision practiced by various people groups in Africa, America, Malaysia, and Polynesia. Today it is routinely performed in developed nations as a hygienic measure, usually shortly after birth. Some tribal peoples perform circumcision as a rite of passage from childhood to adulthood, usually at puberty.

God told Abraham that circumcision was "the sign of the covenant" He was making with him (Gen. 17:11–14). "Abraham was ninety-nine years old when he was circumcised" (17:24). The fact that Ishmael was thirteen years old when he was circumcised (17:25) explains why Muslim boys are circumcised at age thirteen.

The Bible doesn't explain why God chose circumcision as the sign of His covenant with Abraham and his descendants. It involves the shedding of blood, which may signify the ratification of the covenant relationship. It's more likely that circumcision represented dependence on God, dedication to Him, and separation to Him from the world and its practices. Abraham's circumstances at the time God commanded his circumcision suggest these meanings for the ritual. God changed Abram's name to Abraham. He promised to make this old man "very fruitful" (17:6) and "the father of many nations" (17:4). Specifically He promised Abraham a son by Sarah (17:16, 19).

The Old Testament reveals that Israel in its early history didn't always obey God's commands to circumcise boy babies (Ex. 4:25–26; Josh. 5:2–5). Circumcision eventually became a routine external religious rite. By New Testament times it had become a classic mark of Jewish ethnic and religious pride. Jews sometimes looked on the uncircumcised with contempt.

The apostle Paul confronted traditional attitudes toward circumcision when certain Jewish Christians from Judea came to Antioch in Syria and insisted that Gentile believers had to be circumcised to be saved (Acts 15:1). The Council of Jerusalem discussed this dilemma and rejected circumcision as a condition for salvation (15:5–29). But Paul continued to face conflict with "the circumcision group" (Gal. 2:11–13; Titus 1:10).

God never intended circumcision to become merely an external badge of ethnic and religious identity. Circumcision was supposed to cause God's people to reflect on what it meant to belong to Him. Moses told Israel in his farewell address on the east side of the Jordan River, "Circumcise your hearts, therefore, and do not be stiff-necked any longer" (Deut. 10:16). Similarly, just before the Babylonian captivity, Jeremiah told the people of Judah and Jerusalem, "Circumcise yourselves to the LORD, circumcise your hearts" (Jer. 4:4). These were calls to self-denial, separation from the world, and dedication to God as His covenant people.

The apostle Paul, who had been "circumcised the eighth day" (Phil. 3:5), recognized circumcision's spiritual significance. He wrote, "Circumcision has value if you observe the law" (Rom. 2:25), and "A man is not a Jew if he is only one outwardly, nor is circumcision merely outward and physical. No, a man is a Jew if he is one inwardly; and circumcision is circumcision of the heart, by the Spirit" (2:28–29). Paul also recognized that the advantage "in being a Jew" and the value "in circumcision" was that circumcised Jews "have been entrusted with the very words of God" (3:1–2).

In the future God will redeem and restore His chosen people, Israel, and fulfill His covenantal promises to Abraham (Rom. 11:26–27). Then, as Moses said, "The LORD your God will circumcise your hearts and the hearts of your descendants, so that you may love him with all your heart and with all your soul, and live" (Deut. 30:6). In this present church age, however, "Neither circumcision nor uncircumcision means anything; what counts is a new creation" (Gal. 6:15). "For in

Christ Jesus neither circumcision nor uncircumcision has any value. The only thing that counts is faith expressing itself through love" (5:6). As a result of our faith in Jesus Christ and our position in Him, we are "circumcised, in the putting off of the sinful nature, not with a circumcision done by the hands of men but with the circumcision done by Christ" (Col. 2:11).

—**JAW**

* * *

Acknowledge the Holy Spirit's spiritual surgery of circumcising your heart to separate you from the world to Christ.

CITIZENSHIP

The English word "citizen" comes from the same source as "city." Similarly in the Greek of the New Testament *politēs* ("citizenship") derives from *polis* ("city"). The history of the words reflects a time when city-states formed the basic unit of social organization. People who held *citizenship* in the *city* possessed both rights and responsibilities as full-fledged members of a larger group. Citizenship gave people identity in the ancient world as Athenians or Spartans and in the Middle Ages as Londoners or Parisians.

The apostle Paul wrote a letter to the church in Philippi, a Roman colony whose residents held Roman citizenship by virtue of service as mercenaries in the Roman army. Philippians held their citizenship with fierce pride. Paul reminded them, "Our citizenship is in heaven. And we eagerly await a Savior from there, the Lord Jesus Christ" (Phil. 3:20). Earlier he had urged, "Conduct yourselves in a manner worthy of the gospel of Christ" (1:27). The verb translated "conduct yourselves" literally means "live as citizens." We need to feel intense spiritual patriotism about our heavenly citizenship. It gives us wonderful privileges, and it brings with it sobering responsibilities.

The New Testament—especially the Book of Acts—refers frequently to ordinary country-of-origin citizenship. One of the themes of Acts is that God used Roman law to protect the fledgling church. When the apostle Paul was arrested in Jerusalem, he told the commander, "I am a Jew, from Tarsus in Cilicia, a citizen of no ordinary city" (21:39). Later, when he was about to be flogged, he asked the centurion, "Is it legal for you to flog a Roman citizen who hasn't even been found guilty?" (22:25). When Paul, in response to the commander's question, confirmed that he was a Roman citizen, the commander said, "I had to pay a big price for my citizenship" (22:28), to which Paul responded, "I was born a citizen." Still later, when Festus would have sent Paul from Caesarea to Jerusalem to be tried, Paul appealed to Caesar (25:11), which was his right as a Roman citizen.

Earlier, when Paul and Silas were flogged and imprisoned in Philippi without a trial, the magistrates ordered them released the next morning and directed Paul and Silas to leave quietly in peace. Paul demanded that the magistrates come and escort them from the prison because their rights as Roman citizens had been violated by the public beating and imprisonment (16:37). When the magistrates "heard that Paul and Silas were Roman citizens, they were alarmed [and] came to appease them and escorted them from the prison" (16:38–39). Paul knew his rights as a Roman citizen and demanded that they be properly recognized.

In the Epistles, Christians are urged to be good citizens as part of their duty to lead orderly lives. Paul wrote, "Everyone must submit himself to the governing authorities" because they have been established by God (Rom. 13:1). Submission is necessary "not only because of possible punishment but also because of conscience" (13:5). Paul directed Titus to "remind the people to be subject to rulers and authorities" (Titus 3:1) Peter likewise wrote, "Submit yourselves for the Lord's sake to every authority instituted among men" (1 Pet. 2:13). Paul directed that "requests, prayers, intercession and thanksgiving be made for everyone—for kings and all those in authority" (1 Tim. 2:1–2; see also Ezra 6:10).

In the Old Testament, Israel enjoyed a spiritual citizenship by virtue of the God's covenants with Abraham, Moses, and David. Gentiles were "excluded from citizenship in Israel" (Eph. 2:12), but when they placed their faith in Christ they were "no longer foreigners and aliens, but fellow citizens with God's people" (2:19). So Christians have dual citizenship. They are citizens of their country of origin and citizens of heaven. Together with Abraham and other patriarchs, we "are looking for a country of their own" (Heb. 11:14) and "longing for a better country—a heavenly one" (11:16). We recognize that "here we do not have an enduring city, but we are looking for the city that is to come" (13:14). —**JAW**

***

Remember that believers are aliens in a foreign land, living here as ambassadors of our heavenly King and Lord.

CLEANNESS

The Levitical system stressed cleanness as an aspect of holiness before God. Laws about cleanness have two dimensions: one is ceremonial and the other moral. The ceremonial aspect of cleanness qualified Israelites to participate in worship ceremonies. Ceremonial uncleanness, on the other hand, barred them from worship. The moral aspect of cleanness reflected the presence or absence of sin.

The two dimensions of cleanness fit

together in Old Testament thought as shown in Psalm 24:3–4: "Who may ascend the hill of the LORD? Who may stand in his holy place? He who has clean hands [ceremonial] and a pure heart [moral], who does not lift up his soul to an idol or swear by what is false." Only morally and ceremonially clean people could approach the holy God, and then only in the way He prescribed. God pointedly called Israel to cleanness and holiness. Pagan gods, on the other hand, cared little about the morals of their worshipers. Pagan mythology portrayed gods that expected to be served and pampered by worshipers who hoped to be the highest bidders in a corrupt contest to win divine favors. The God of the Bible, however, declared, "I am the LORD your God; consecrate yourselves and be holy, because I am holy" (Lev. 11:44).

The Mosaic Law approached ceremonial cleanness negatively. It described at length all sorts of things that could make someone unclean. Various sexual matters made a person unclean—childbirth (Lev. 12), menstruation (15:19–24), unlawful intercourse (20:10–21), seminal emission (15:16–18; Deut. 23:10), and any unnatural discharge (Lev. 15:1–15). Animals and their meat were classified as clean or unclean. The clean could be eaten but not the unclean (Lev. 11). Kosher practices in modern Judaism arise from these laws. Certain diseases left one unclean. For instance, the uncleanness of leprosy extended to anything the leper touched (Lev. 13—14). And touching a dead person made an Israelite unclean (Num. 19).

Why would God lay down such a complicated series of rules that made it hard for His people to engage in worship? What did many of these things have to do with true holiness? Various theories have been offered to explain why God gave these laws. The principal ones are these: (1) Israel needed to demonstrate within the community of faith and to the watching world that the people of God are distinct. (2) The laws of cleanness protected Israel's health by promoting good hygiene and outlawing food sources that often transmitted disease and parasites. (3) The use of blood for atonement made it off limits for use as a food (Lev. 17:10–14). (4) Animals associated with pagan religions or with witchcraft were prohibited, such as swine, dogs, snakes, and others.

Once the Law outlined the many things that could make someone unclean, it had to prescribe solutions so public worship of God could resume. Here are four solutions to different kinds of uncleanness. (1) The *passage of time* canceled contaminations from a dead body (Num. 19:11), menstruation (Lev. 15:19), or childbirth (Lev. 12). (2) *Water* cleansed a person after contact with various unclean things, such as bodily discharges (15:5–11; see also

Num. 8:7—19:9, 13; 19:17). (3) Sometimes serious defilement could be purged only by *fire,* as in cases of incest (Lev. 20:14) and idolatry (Ex. 32:20). (4) *Sacrificial blood* was the supreme purifier from both ceremonial and moral defilements (Lev. 12:8; 14:21–32; 15:14–15, 29–30; 17:11). A worshiper transferred the uncleanness caused by sin or disease to the sacrificial victim by the laying on of hands.

In the New Testament the Gospels refer several times to people following the cleanness rituals of the Mosaic Law. Mary and Joseph took the infant Jesus to the temple in Jerusalem for the rites of purification (Luke 2:22; see Lev. 12:2–8). The disciples of John the Baptist discussed purification issues with some fellow Jews (John 3:25). Jesus made wine for the wedding at Cana in the pots that held water for cleansing rituals (2:6). When Jesus healed some lepers, He sent them to the priests in Jerusalem to "offer the sacrifices that Moses commanded" (Luke 5:14; Lev. 14:2–32).

However, Jesus disagreed sharply with the Pharisees about the importance of ceremonial cleanness. He rejected all external ceremony that ignored matters of the heart. He accused the Pharisees of scrubbing the outside of cups and plates while ignoring their own inner corruption (Matt. 23:25–26). Uncleanness, Jesus taught, comes from a sinful heart, not from unwashed hands (Mark 7:14–23).

The Book of Acts and the Epistles also emphasize inward purity. Acts 10 records how God taught Peter that people were not unclean simply because they were Gentiles. That lesson was not an academic one. God immediately sent Peter to share the gospel with a Gentile centurion named Cornelius. To Peter's amazement, Cornelius believed the gospel and received the Holy Spirit.

In Romans 14:14 Paul wrote that "no food is unclean in itself." Yet we should not violate our conscience by eating something we regard as unclean. Neither should we use our freedom in a way that tempts other Christians to do something they regard as wrong. The statements that "all food is clean" (14:20) and that "everything is permissible" (1 Cor. 6:12) are a rejection of ceremonialism, not a call to gluttony or hedonism.

The Book of Hebrews was written to explain to Christians with a Jewish background that the rites and ceremonies of the Old Testament had foreshadowed the realities of Jesus' New Covenant. The Old Testament system provided for outward cleansing, whereas the blood of Christ cleanses the conscience (Heb. 9:10–14; 10:22). Thus ceremonial cleanness or uncleanness plays no part in the Christian era because "the blood of Jesus, his Son, purifies us from all sin" (1 John 1:7). **—DKC**

***

Pray with David, "Wash away all my iniquity and cleanse me from my sin" (Ps. 51:2).

COMMANDMENTS

A "commandment" is a written or spoken order. Whoever issues a commandment has authority and expects to be obeyed. God's commandments form the moral framework of the Bible. The term *commandment* represents an important part of both the Mosaic and Christian systems. Various words in the Hebrew Old Testament and the Greek New Testament are translated "commandments," and together they occur about nine hundred times in Scripture.

In the Old Testament God gave most of His commandments in the Mosaic Law. As a legal code they reveal His moral character. Moses told Israel, "Keep his decrees and commands, which I am giving you today, so that it may go well with you and your children after you and that you may live long in the land the LORD your God gives you for all time" (Deut. 4:40). God's commandments in the Mosaic Law regulated Israel's way of life. The commandments of God served the Jews as a tutor (child-discipliner) until Christ came (Gal. 3:24). They were never intended to impart salvation. Salvation comes only by God's grace and human faith in what God reveals to us. Scripture makes it clear that the

law justified no one (Rom. 3:20). Obedience to the commandments does not produce righteousness or life (Gal. 3:21). Instead, disobedience to the commandments proved the innate sinfulness of our human nature (Rom. 7:11–13). Our inability to keep the commandments means we must exercise faith in God's provision for our sins (Gal. 3:23).

Most people assume Israel needed great self-discipline to keep God's commandments. What they actually needed was love. Moses charged, "Hear O Israel: the LORD our God, the LORD is one. Love the LORD your God with all your heart and with all your soul and with all your strength. These commandments that I give you today are to be upon your hearts" (Deut. 6:4–6). The Ten Commandments are usually divided into two groups: the first four pointing vertically to God and the last six pointing horizontally to other people. So Jesus could sum up the Law by saying, " 'Love the Lord your God with all your heart and with all your soul and with all your mind.' This is the first and greatest commandment. And the second is like it: 'Love your neighbor as yourself.' All the Law and the Prophets hang on these two commandments" (Matt. 22:37–40).

The Ten Commandments comprise one small section of the Mosaic Law, but they expressed the heart of God's righteous will for the moral life of Israel (Ex. 20:1–26). Following the Ten

C

Commandments are the judgments that governed the social life of the nation (21:1—24:11). Then came the laws regulating Israel's worship (25:1—31:17). We can analyze the Law and break it into sections, but the Scriptures view all these commandments as a unit. James declared that breaking any one commandment made a person guilty of violating the entire Law (James 2:10).

The New Testament emphasizes that the Law no longer serves the purpose it did before the death of Christ inaugurated the New Covenant. Paul stated, "Christ is the end of the law so that there may be righteousness for everyone who believes" (Rom. 10:4). The leaders of the Jerusalem Council gave an emphatic "No" in answer to the question of whether circumcision was required for salvation (Acts 15:1–35). They knew the Law had ended, and they made no attempt to make Gentile believers keep its many commandments.

Paul affirmed that the Ten Commandments—that which "was engraved in letters on stone"—were done away with (2 Cor. 3:7–11). The writer of Hebrews claimed the Levitical priesthood had ended and been replaced by an eternal Priest, one after the order of Melchizedek. Thus since "there is a change of the priesthood, there must also be a change of the law" (Heb. 7:12).

If the sacrifice of Christ brought an end to the Mosaic Law, why are some of the commandments still binding on Christians? Does the moral law, the Ten Commandments, remain in force while the ceremonial law has been abolished? This could be an acceptable solution had all ten of the commandments been repeated in the New Testament, but the Law regarding the Sabbath is not. Ryrie offers a reasonable solution to this question. He proposes that the Mosaic Law as a code of ethical conduct has been replaced in its entirety by the law of Christ. The law of Christ contains many new commands along with some of the old ones. As children in a family mature from infants to adolescents, they live under different codes of conduct imposed by the parents. Some rules carry over from earlier family codes to later ones, but each old code is abandoned when a new one is adopted. So it is when some of the commandments of the Mosaic Law—including nine of the Ten Commandments—carry over into the new code of the church age (Charles C. Ryrie, *Basic Theology* [Wheaton, Ill.: Victor, 1986], 305). The commandments of the law of Christ operate as grace principles. We obey them out of gratitude to Christ for the salvation He graciously gave us.

The night before His crucifixion, Jesus spoke to His disciples about the New Covenant to be instituted by His death (Matt. 26:17–30). Since the New Covenant replaced the old Mosaic

Covenant, new commandments—the law of Christ—were needed to guide believers. Jesus announced the chief commandment when He told His followers, "A new commandment I give you: Love one another" (John 13:34; see also 1 John 4:21). We are to obey Jesus' commands (2:3) because we love Him (John 14:15, 21). "His commands are not burdensome" (1 John 5:3), and obeying them pleases Him (3:22) and results in experiencing more of His love (John 15:10). He also commands us to be His witnesses (Acts 1:8) and to carry each other's burdens (Gal. 6:2). **—DKC**

***

With God's help keep Christ's commandments, because He said, "Whoever has my commandments and obeys them, he is the one who loves me" (John 14:21).

CONDEMNATION

Condemnation involves treating someone as guilty of an offense. Condemnation may be formal, as when a judge passes sentence on a criminal. It may be personal, as when one spouse severely criticizes or denounces the other.

In the Old Testament the Hebrew word *rāšāʿ* is almost always translated "to condemn." It is a legal term employed with regard to civil matters (Deut. 25:1; Job 34:17; Ps. 94:21) and religious issues (Job 9:20; 10:2; Ps. 37:33;

Prov. 12:2; Is. 50:9; 54:17). Condemnation consists of a verdict of guilt against a person and a sentence of punishment. The Old Testament reports cases when the innocent were condemned and God stepped in to reverse the verdict (1 Kin. 8:32; Ps. 109:31; Is. 50:9). In the New Testament, Christ warned against false judgments at the interpersonal level. "Do not condemn, and you will not be condemned" (Luke 6:37).

In the New Testament the Greek word *katakrinō* means "to give judgment against" or "to condemn." God condemned Sodom and Gomorrah for their sin (2 Pet. 2:6). The whole human race stands condemned because of the sin of Adam (Rom. 5:16, 18). Jesus did not come to condemn the world but to save it (John 3:17–18). Romans 8:1 indicates He succeeded admirably: "Therefore, there is now no condemnation for those who are in Christ Jesus." Sadly, those who reject the Savior and His payment for sin continue under God's condemnation.

The New Testament uses *condemnation* to speak of other kinds of guilt besides the guilt of sin. The writer of Hebrews said one man's godly life can condemn the ungodly (Heb. 11:7). Paul wrote that a person is self-condemned when his unrighteous words and deeds reveal his true character (Titus 3:11). Human judges are expected to condemn justly when the evidence supports a guilty verdict (Luke 23:40–41, NASB).

Other Greek words besides *katakrinō* carry the idea of condemnation. James used one of them to describe rich landlords punishing innocent laborers (James 5:6). Matthew used the same term when he said we must give an account for our words on the day of judgment and be acquitted or condemned (Matt. 12:36–37).

John used still a different word to describe the self-condemnation of an uneasy conscience (1 John 3:20–21). John observed that our consciences are not infallible. He urged us to live in love for our Christian brothers and sisters and trust God's opinion of us more than our condemning consciences.

—**DKC**

* * *

Thank God for His promise that as a believer you will never face condemnation (Rom. 8:1).

CONFESSION

Confession involves speaking the truth. Criminals confess by admitting their guilt for their crimes. Liars confess by acknowledging their lies and telling the truth. Worshipers confess their faith by affirming the Word of God.

In the Old Testament, the Hebrew word for *confession* carries the sense of "acknowledgment," recognition by God's people of their offense against His holiness (Lev. 16:21). Once a year, on the Day of Atonement, the high priest offered a special blood sacrifice to atone for the sins of Israel. The high priest then *confessed* the sins of the people while he laid his hands on the head of a goat. The goat then symbolically carried those acknowledged sins into the desert to show that God had banished them from His sight on the basis of the sacrifice (vv. 20–22).

When Solomon dedicated the temple, he prayed that Israel would recognize it as the dwelling of God and regularly confess their sins to receive forgiveness from Him (2 Chr. 6:36–39). Israel's covenant with the Lord promised the nation prosperity and success for keeping its terms. Israel could recognize its need to confess sin when its army suffered defeat (1 Kin. 8:33; 2 Chr. 6:24) or when it experienced a drought (1 Kin. 8:35; 2 Chr. 6:26).

The end of the Babylonian captivity coincides with the careers of three heroes who confessed Israel's past and present sins. They were Daniel, Ezra, and Nehemiah. In Babylon, Daniel prayed for insight concerning the future of Israel. Before asking God for anything, however, Daniel confessed the sins of God's people that had provoked His judgment on them and pleaded for forgiveness (Dan. 9:3–16). God heard his prayer and told him when to expect Jerusalem and the people to be free from sin (9:20–24). Ezra persuaded and prodded the people to confess their sins, especially the sin of intermarrying with unbelievers from surrounding nations (Ezra 10:1, 11–12).

Nehemiah, with Ezra's help, led the people resettling Jerusalem and Judah in an entire day of Scripture reading and confession of their sins (Neh. 8:1–8; 9:1–3).

The Old Testament also recognizes the importance of individual confession of sin. After David committed adultery with Bathsheba and had her husband killed, he tried to hide his guilt and go on as though nothing had happened. He experienced terrible private anguish because of his guilt and shame (Ps. 32:3–4), but he kept on guarding his public image. Then Nathan the prophet exposed David's sin, and he confessed it fully. God accepted his confession, and his sin was forgiven (2 Sam. 12:13). However, David suffered many consequences of his sin in his personal and family life. Confession brings God's forgiveness, but it doesn't cancel sin's consequences.

In the New Testament, the Greek verb translated "to confess" (*homologeō*) means "to say the same thing" as a way of acknowledging the truth. So does the Latin participle *confessus* from which our English word *confess* comes. The New International Version often uses the word "acknowledge" instead of "confess" to translate *homologeō*. Often this occurs when confession involves a positive affirmation of Christian doctrine and personal faith.

When *confession* involves sin, it means to agree wholeheartedly with God about the guilt of what we have said or done. To confess is to grasp fully that our sin is exactly as bad as God said it is. Genuine confession has nothing to do with reciting a prescribed religious formula. Confession springs from a deep conviction within the heart.

The New Testament uses the word *confession* many ways. It means acknowledging the truth about Christ. Jesus Himself said true disciples must acknowledge (*confess*) Him before men (Matt. 10:32). John the Baptist confessed that Jesus was the promised Messiah (John 1:20–23). Paul taught us to confess Jesus as Lord because God raised Him from the dead (Rom. 10:9). No one receives salvation who has not *confessed* (acknowledged) the death of Christ and the need for deliverance from sin (1 Cor. 15:3–4). The apostle John said every believer should confess both the incarnation and the deity of Christ (1 John 4:2, 15). Someday every person, whether saved or unsaved, will acknowledge that Jesus is all He claimed to be and will confess this to the glory of the Father (Phil. 2:11).

Believers in Jesus as their Savior are not immune to sin (1 John 1:8, 10). When we sin, we need forgiveness and restoration to fellowship with our heavenly Father. We need to confess our sins—to admit the fact of them and the evil character of them. God, who is faithful and just, promises to forgive our confessed sins (1 John 1:9). Continually praying for forgiveness of some specific sin is unnecessary because He promised to forgive sin once it is confessed. Confession restores fellowship with God and with others in the family of God as well (1:3). **—WGJ**

***

Don't fail to confess each sin to the Lord because He will forgive.

CONSCIENCE

In the New Testament the Greek word translated *conscience* comes from a root that means "to see." *Conscience,* therefore, has a basic sense of insight. The earliest uses of the noun—long before the New Testament—had the idea of looking back on one's past and evaluating it. Over time *conscience* developed into the notion of an innate moral sense that approves or disapproves of one's personal actions and thoughts. The New Testament references to *conscience* occur primarily in the letters to Paul. Four others appear in Hebrews (9:9, 14; 10:22; 13:18), and three in 1 Peter (1 Pet. 2:19, NKJV; 3:16, 21).

Paul envisioned *conscience* as an inborn moral standard common to everyone. He wrote that "Gentiles, who do not have the law [the Ten Commandments], do by nature things required by the law" (Rom. 2:14). They "show that the requirements of the law are written on their hearts, their consciences also bearing witness" (2:15). What happens when people consistently disobey or disregard their consciences? Consciences can be "seared as with a hot iron" (1 Tim. 4:2) so they no longer respond strongly to what is wrong, or their consciences can be "corrupted" (Titus 1:15) to the point that they no longer disapprove of wrong.

Paul did not equate the approval of his conscience with the approval of God. He wanted to have a "good conscience" (Acts 23:1), a "conscience clear before God and man" (24:16; see also 2 Tim. 1:3). In fact his conscience testified that he had conducted himself "in the world . . . in the holiness and sincerity that are from God" (2 Cor. 1:12). Nonetheless Paul stated, "I do not judge myself. My conscience is clear, but that does not make me innocent. It is the Lord who judges me" (1 Cor. 4:3–4). He felt it best that the Holy Spirit confirmed the impressions of his conscience (Rom. 9:1).

The conscience plays a role as people hear and consider the gospel of Christ. Both the message and the messenger make impressions on listeners' consciences (2 Cor. 4:2; see also 5:11). It may be that troubles and distorted consciences interfere with positive response to the gospel.

The letters of Paul speak about the problems "weak" consciences can cause among believers. A "weak conscience" is one damaged by long-standing sin patterns of the past. In New Testament days the issue that troubled many weak consciences was meat offered to idols. Most of the meat sold in Gentile butcher shops came from animals sacrificed in pagan temples. Many converts to Christianity from paganism found it hard to eat such meat without associating it with their former immoral worship.

The New Testament says those with weak consciences should not eat meat that had been offered to idols if doing so stirred sinful thoughts and tempted them to sinful actions (1 Cor. 8:4–8). At the same time, Christians with freedom to eat food offered to idols should be careful not to let their freedom "become a stumbling block to the weak" (8:9) and "wound their weak conscience" (8:12). To do so would be to sin against them and against Christ. Today food offered to idols is not an issue, but other debatable practices fall under the same guidelines.

Paul urged Timothy to hold "on to faith and a good conscience" (1 Tim. 1:19; see also 1:5), and the qualifications for a deacon include holding "the deep truths of the faith with a clear conscience" (3:9). The quality of our faith affects the quality of our conscience. Saturate yourself with God's Word, pray regularly, and walk in the Holy Spirit and you will see your conscience become more sensitive and reliable.   **—JAW**

***

Gauge God's approval of your thoughts and actions by His indwelling Holy Spirit and His Word, not by your conscience alone.

CONVERSION

"Conversion" is a word that plays a bigger role in modern evangelical language than it does in the Bible. Certainly the concept of change is a major biblical idea, but *conversion* was not as important a term as "salvation," for example.

In the Old Testament, the idea of *conversion* lies in the Hebrew verb *šûb*, which means "to return." In its spiritual uses *šûb* always implies that God's people had left Him and needed to return to Him (1 Kin. 8:35; Jer. 4:1; Mal. 3:7). This does not sound like *conversion* in the evangelistic sense. These uses of *šûb* occur in the community of Israel. Often the generation that returned to God was not the generation that had left Him. At the personal level, many individual Israelites exercised faith for the first time when the nation returned.

Those who disobeyed God's laws and steadfastly refused to return to the Lord were promised various forms of punishment, including ultimate banishment from the land in captivity (Deut.

28). Conversely, those who did return were promised forgiveness (Is. 55:7), exemption from divine punishment (Jon. 3:9), and productive service (Ps. 51:13).

In the New Testament the Greek verb *epistrephō* similarly means "to return." Twice it is used in the negative sense of turning from right to wrong (Gal. 4:9; 2 Pet. 2:21). Usually it describes turning from the wrong pathway to the right one. Both believers and unbelievers can *epistrephō*. In the case of believers it describes a return to a right relationship with God after fellowship has been interrupted by sin (Luke 22:32) or wrong belief (James 5:19–20).

When "conversion" is used with reference to unbelievers, we've arrived at the sense of the term we're most familiar with. This use of *conversion* relates to the turning of a person from sin to God. Paul wrote that the Thessalonian believers "turned to God from idols to serve the living and true God" (1 Thess. 1:9). *Conversion* differs from regeneration and justification. They are acts of God. *Conversion* is considered an act of the individual in response to the work of the Holy Spirit.

The New Testament links the conversion of an unbeliever with repentance. John the Baptist preached the need for Israel to convert or repent (Matt. 3:2; Mark 1:4; Luke 3:3). He called for a change in actions to show the reality of their conversion (Matt.

3:8; Luke 3:8). Jesus also linked conversion and repentance (Matt. 4:17; Mark 1:15).

The most famous and dramatic biblical conversion belongs to Saul of Tarsus (Acts 9). The Book of Acts reports that apostolic preaching called for people to turn from sin to God (Acts 26:20). The result was the conversion of many people (9:35).   **—DKC**

***

Pray that the consistency of your walk will testify to the reality of your conversion.

CONVICTION

"Conviction" is another commom term in evangelical churches that is uncommon in the New Testament. "Conviction" translates a Greek word that appears only eighteen times in the New Testament. Many of those occurrences have nothing to do with conviction of sin. But in this sense *conviction* means "to bring someone to a realization of his guilt." Conviction is a work of the Holy Spirit that precedes repentance and faith. The Holy Spirit removes the satanic blindness from people's eyes so they can see themselves as God sees them (2 Cor. 4:3–4).

The central passage on conviction is John 16:7–11. Jesus had explained to His disciples that after His death, resurrection, and ascension He would send the Comforter (the Holy Spirit).

The Holy Spirit, Jesus said, would confront human beings regarding sin, righteousness, and judgment (16:8). These three elements constitute the substance of the Spirit's revelation to the unsaved. Jesus went on to describe what He meant by sin, righteousness, and judgment (16:9–11).

First, the Spirit convicts people of "guilt in regard to sin" (16:8). When Jesus expanded on what He meant, He restricted this aspect of conviction to "sin, because men do not believe in me" (16:9; see 3:18; 15:22, 24). Jesus didn't mean that lying, stealing, murder, and other sinful acts didn't matter any more. He meant that all other sins are offshoots from the root sin of unbelief.

Second, the Holy Spirit convicts the lost regarding righteousness (16:10). The Spirit doesn't convict unbelievers that they *lack* righteousness. He convicts them that Jesus *has* righteousness. Concerning this aspect of the Spirit's conviction, Jesus said, "In regard to righteousness, because I am going to the Father." But how is the Ascension related to righteousness?

Jesus was crucified by people who despised Him and considered Him cursed by God (Deut. 21:23; Gal. 3:13). Jesus' resurrection and ascension demonstrated convincingly that He was God's righteous servant (Acts 3:14–15; Is. 53:11). The Spirit bears witness to Jesus' resurrection and ascension. The unsaved who accept the witness of the Spirit find in Jesus Christ all the merit and righteousness they need (2 Cor. 5:21).

Third, the Holy Spirit convicts the lost regarding judgment (16:11). The content of this witness is that "the prince of this world now stands condemned." On the Cross Jesus sealed Satan's fate (see also John 14:30; Col. 2:15). The unsaved should also contemplate the future judgment from which the only escape is found in Jesus Christ (Acts 17:30–31).

In addition to describing the convicting work of God's Spirit, the Greek word also refers to the practice of reproving, rebuking, or correcting within the Christian community. This theme is frequently seen in the Pastoral Epistles (1 Tim. 5:20; 2 Tim. 4:2; Titus 1:9, 13; 2:15). The procedure believers are to follow in this ministry of reproof is spelled out in Matthew 18:15–17.

—DKC

***

Pray that the Holy Spirit will convict your lost friends and relatives regarding sin, righteousness, and judgment.

COVENANTS

The Old and New Testaments both refer to many covenants. Some are normal contracts between people or treaties between nations. Others spell out the terms of relationships between God and His people. In the Old Testament the most prominent word is *berît*, and the most prominent New Testament term is *diathēkē*.

A covenant is an agreement between two parties that involves promises and commitments each makes to the other. Most covenants, therefore have a conditional character. "If you do this, then I promise to do that." An exception is marriage, a two-way commitment between husband and wife that should be neither conditioned or broken (Mal. 2:14). Of the covenants between God and His people, only the Mosaic Covenant carries this distinctly conditional character. The other divine covenants with people are unilateral promises of God. These covenants, made with either Israel or the church, are enjoyed by individuals on the conditions of faith and obedience.

The Old Testament reports a number of covenants in which God promised to accomplish certain things for people. The Edenic Covenant consists of God's promise to Adam and Eve in the Garden of Eden (Gen. 2:16–17). His covenant with Noah includes the promises He made after the Flood (8:21—9:17). The Abrahamic covenant promised Abraham a land, a seed, and a blessing (12:1–3). The Davidic Covenant established David's dynasty and anticipated the Messiah (2 Sam. 7:4–17). The New Covenant establishes peace between God and believers (Jer. 31:31–37). These were not negotiated; they were introduced by God Himself. The

Mosaic Covenant, however, was a conditional covenant. The death of Christ fulfilled and abolished it (Heb. 8:6–7, 13; 9:15).

The New Testament uses the word *covenant* for the testament (will) of a person that becomes effective when he or she dies. The Epistle to the Hebrews especially uses *covenant* in this way. Hebrews contains more than half of the New Testament references to covenants. The covenant of Jesus Christ is said to be better than the Mosaic Covenant (Heb. 7:22). He is the Mediator of this New Covenant (9:15; 12:24). At the Lord's Supper Jesus pointed out that His shed blood constituted the basis for His New Covenant (Matt. 26:28; 1 Cor. 11:25).

The way someone interprets the fulfillment of God's covenants with His people depends on the interpreter's view of the Millennium as variously held by amillenarians, postmillenarians, and premillenarians. This is especially true when you consider how the New Covenant (Jer. 31:31–37) relates to Israel and to the church. Some regard the church as the "new Israel" and apply the New Covenant to the church alone.

Premillennialists prefer to see the New Covenant as the basis for the church age and Israel's future. The New Covenant is based on God's grace, secured by Jesus' death on the Cross. This grace provides salvation for Christians in the church age. It also is the basis for Israel's future restoration. **—JFW**

***

Enjoy the personal benefits God has given every Christian through the New Covenant, which was made possible by the death of Christ.

CREATION

Nothing describes the beginning of all things with more finality, logic, and truth than the opening sentence of the Bible: "In the beginning God created the heavens and the earth" (Gen. 1:1). It affirms that the universe is personal and purposeful. Any quest—whether to understand the scope of the universe or the meaning of one human life—begins and ends with God.

From Genesis through Revelation the Bible consistently says God created everything from nothing (Gen. 14:19, 22; Job 38:4–7; Pss. 33:6–8; 148:1–6; Is. 42:5; 45:12, 18; Mark 13:19; Rom. 1:25; Eph. 3:9; Rev. 4:11; 10:6). In Psalms, one of God's titles is "the LORD, the Maker of heaven and earth" (Pss. 115:15; 121:2; 124:8; 134:3; see 146:6). Elsewhere He is called "the Maker of all things" (Eccl. 11:5). Solomon instructed his readers, "Remember your Creator in the days of your youth" (12:1).

The Bible indicates that all three persons of the Trinity were involved in creation. Genesis introduces stages of creation with the phrase "And God said . . ." (Gen. 1:3, 6, 9, 14, 20, 24).

The apostle John introduced the Son of God as that creative "Word" of God from Genesis. "In the beginning was the Word. . . . Through him all things were made; without him nothing was made that has been made" (1:1, 3). The apostle Paul also wrote of Christ that "by him all things were created: things in heaven and on earth, visible and invisible, whether thrones or powers or rulers or authorities; all things were created by him and for him" (Col. 1:16). The writer of Hebrews states that God "made the universe" through the Son (Heb. 1:2).

God the Father was the architect of creation. The Son implemented the plans and purposes of the Father in creation, even as He later did in redemption. One passage refers to "the Father, from whom all things came" (1 Cor. 8:6). That same verse also speaks of "Jesus Christ, through whom all things came." The Holy Spirit, too, played a role in creation (Gen. 1:2; Job 33:4; Ps. 104:30). In Genesis 1:2 He hovered over the waters of the primordial earth. Perhaps His role was to oversee and superintend, as He did in the process of the inspiration of the Scripture.

The triune God may be in view when "God said, 'Let *us* make man in *our* image, in *our* likeness'" (Gen. 1:26). In attempting to describe the order of the Godhead in creation, theologians speak of creation being from the will of the Father through the agency of the Son by the power of the Spirit.

Genesis 1 narrates the order of creation for the solar system, planet earth, and its life forms, culminating in humans. God probably created the angels before this (Ps. 148:2–5; Col. 1:16), including the "guardian cherub" (Ezek. 28:14–16), elsewhere called Satan. The statement in Genesis 1:2 that "the earth was formless and empty" may suggest that the original complete creation of Genesis 1:1 had been judged by God in conjunction with angelic sin (Is. 14:12–15). But God "did not create" the earth "to be empty" (45:18). The creation of Adam on the sixth day (Gen. 1:26–31) was the capstone of God's creative work (2:1).

The time involved in God's total work of creation cannot be determined from Scripture. The original cosmic creation may have been millions of years ago. Furthermore, although the six creative days were most probably literal days (1:5, 8, 13, 19, 23, 31), large periods of time could have expired between them. The only thing Scripture does indicate is that the creation of humankind is comparatively recent. Gaps exist in the genealogies of Genesis, but they are meaningful records of the ancestry of the human race. Bishop Ussher took the genealogies of Genesis as complete and calculated the date for the creation of Adam to be 4004 B.C. It is difficult to reconcile the biblical evidence with a date for the creation of Adam and Eve of more than ten thousand years ago.

On the seventh day God "rested from all the work of creating that he had done" (2:3). Some time after that, the entrance of sin into human experience marred the physical creation (Rom. 8:19–22) as well as introducing death to humanity (5:12). One of the ways the Bible speaks about salvation through Jesus is to call it "a new creation." Paul said, "Therefore, if anyone is in Christ, he is a new creation" (2 Cor. 5:17; see also Eph. 4:24). Elsewhere he wrote, "What counts is a new creation" (Gal. 6:15), "for we are God's workmanship, created in Christ Jesus to do good works" (Eph. 2:10).

God's salvation through Christ will ultimately extend to the restoration of the universe (Is. 11:6–9; Rom. 8:18–22). Then, after the destruction of the present heavens and earth (2 Pet. 3:7, 10–12), God will create "a new heaven and a new earth, the home of righteousness" (2 Pet. 3:13; see also Is. 65:17; 66:22; Rev. 21:1).   **—JAW**

***

Rejoice in and care for God's beautiful creation, which glorifies Him (Ps. 19:1).

CROSS

The cross symbolizes Christianity to the whole world. It may be the most recognizable emblem of all time. In the Roman Empire the cross, two sturdy but crude intersecting wooden beams, was an instrument of execution. Jesus endured an ignominious death reserved for criminals, though He had committed no crime. As Isaiah the prophet had said, the Messiah would be "numbered with the transgressors" (Is. 53:12). The Gospels record no crucifixions other than those of Jesus and the two robbers with Him. The Crucifixion accounts in the four Gospels are powerfully simple. They say essentially the same thing: "They crucified Him." Crucifixion was common, so no additional words were needed to convey the shame, agony, and devastation of death on a cross.

Jesus gave new meaning to the term *cross* in His teachings. Even before His crucifixion He used the word to convey the concept of discipleship. On at least three occasions Jesus spoke about the cross. First, during His third tour of Galilee, He selected twelve disciples and challenged each one to take up his cross and follow Him. The disciples understood Jesus to be asking for total commitment to Him even at the risk of their lives (Matt. 10:37–39).

Second, Jesus announced His death and resurrection to His disciples in Caesarea Philippi. The message stunned His friends, and Peter rebuked Him for thinking those thoughts. Once again Jesus used the cross to explain discipleship (Matt. 16:21–26; Mark 8:31–37, Luke 9:22–25). Third, just a few months before His crucifixion in Jerusalem, Jesus challenged His followers once more about the cost of following Him

(14:22–35). He said they needed to choose Him over closest family members. They needed to carry their cross (14:26–27), that is, to be so committed to Him that they would die to everything and everyone near and dear in order to follow Him.

As Jesus died on the cross, He said, "It is finished" (John 19:30). He had completed the work for which He was sent by God (Matt. 26:39, 42). His death on the cross satisfied the demands of God's righteousness and brought redemption for humankind (1 Pet. 3:18).

The Cross stands at the center of Paul's theology (1 Cor. 1:23). Paul's emphasis probably is responsible for the emergence of the cross as the symbol for Christian belief. He saw this humiliating and cruel instrument in a new light. He chose to boast about Jesus and the death He died for mankind (Gal. 6:14). The shameful cross stood for everything the world despised—humiliation, suffering, and death. Paul said those qualities are evidence of Christ's love for the world.

Paul also adopted the Cross as his own standard for sacrifice as He followed the example of Christ (Col. 1:24). Jesus' death acted like a magnet drawing the outcasts of the world to Christ (John 12:32). The Cross makes human wisdom foolish (1 Cor. 1:27) and weak people strong (1:25), and it breaks the spirit of the proud and lifts up the meek and humble (1:28). Because of His death Jesus breaks the shackles of those in bondage who believe in Him. The Cross brings peace to those in fear (Heb. 2:14–15), and it unites Jews and Gentiles into one body (Eph. 2:16). The Cross brought complete fulfillment to the system of the Mosaic Law and did away with all the regulations standing against humanity (Col. 2:14–18). Because of the Cross, God gives eternal life to those who believe (Rom. 5:18). The Cross, which to the world seemed proof of defeat, became the means of triumph (Col. 2:15).

Paul wanted to be like Christ in His death (Phil. 3:10). Comprehending the meaning of the Cross enables us to reflect Christ's humility and deep concern for others (2:3–8).

The author of the Epistle to the Hebrews also exhorted us to stay focused on the Cross (Heb. 12:2) in order to avoid losing heart or growing weary. No one of us will face adversity worse than that of the Lord Jesus Christ on the cross (12:3).   **—WGJ**

***

Realize daily the significance of the death of Christ in your life, and find ways to tell others about the Savior's death for them.

CRUCIFY

The Romans executed criminals by crucifixion. Crucifixion involved suspending a convicted felon by his arms from a cross in such a way that he slowly suffocated. Death by crucifix-

ion took hours, if not days, unless the criminal had suffered a great loss of blood during flogging. Executioners could speed death by breaking the legs of the victims so they could no longer support their weight on their feet to gasp for breath (John 19:31–32).

Early in His ministry Jesus anticipated His crucifixion by saying He would be "lifted up" as Moses had lifted up the brass snake in the wilderness (3:14). At the time no one understood what He meant. Even when He clearly stated that He would be killed in Jerusalem and raised on the third day (Matt. 16:21; Mark 8:31; Luke 9:22), His disciples refused to admit the possibility. Some time later Jesus was tried by the Jewish leaders and turned over to the Romans because the Jews were not permitted to carry out a death sentence (John 18:31). Roman soldiers crucified Jesus in Jerusalem, and He died the same day. Secular historical records chronicle the gruesome details of death by crucifixion and the suffering its victims endured. Though the Bible records only sketchy details of the actual event, the Scriptures thoroughly discuss the significance of the crucifixion of Christ. His death was not by accident; He was destined for the cross by the Father to become the Savior of the world (Is. 53:10; Luke 22:42; 1 Pet. 1:19–20).

On several occasions Jesus challenged His followers to take up their crosses and follow Him (Matt. 16:24–25; Luke 14:25–33). Jesus wasn't predicting mass martyrdom or challenging them to mortify their flesh. Jesus used the cross as a symbol for total commitment to God and His mission, regardless of the potential danger.

After His crucifixion and resurrection, Jesus spent forty days with His disciples explaining the kingdom of God (Acts 1:3). During that time He opened their understanding to the significance of His crucifixion (Luke 24:45–47). Not surprisingly, the apostles' preaching centered on Jesus' crucifixion and resurrection. Peter emphasized that the death of Christ is the basis of forgiveness of sins (Acts 3:18–19; 10:43), available to both Jews and Gentiles (11:18). Years later when Peter wrote to scattered believers, he frequently mentioned the crucifixion of Christ (1 Pet. 1:18–21; 2:24; 3:18; 4:1). He clearly stated that Jesus' death on the cross was the payment for sin.

The crucifixion of Christ furnishes the foundation for the doctrine of salvation. In Paul's letter to the Galatians he wrote that Jesus was crucified to free us from the curse of the Law (Gal. 3:13). Each believer is identified with the crucifixion of Christ ("I have been crucified with Christ," 2:20). The apostle looked back to Calvary as the source of freedom from the Law and the source of power to live by faith (2:20). He also claimed that the crucifixion of Christ separated him from the world

system (6:14). What took place at Calvary brought him to his knees, and from the moment of his conversion Paul's preaching focused on Jesus and His death (1 Cor. 1:23; 2:2).

The message of Christ's crucifixion is the power of God to save those who believe (1:18, 24). The gospel Paul proclaimed consisted of the message of the death and resurrection of Jesus (15:3–4). The crucifixion reconciled sinners to God. It also reconciled Gentile believers and Jewish believers (2 Cor. 5:18–19). Those who believe experience justification, redemption, and reconciliation because of the crucifixion of Christ (Rom. 3:24–25; 5:10). Apart from His crucifixion and resurrection we would be lost forever, separated from God and without hope (3:23; Eph. 2:12).

The Christian life also centers around the crucifixion of Christ. Our sanctification has its basis in the Crucifixion (Rom. 6:1–14). We have been united to Christ in His death and resurrection. This identification and union with Christ breaks the power of sin in our lives. We have new life in Christ, and sin need no longer rule over us (6:5–7). We need not be defeated or dominated by sin, because of what Christ accomplished on the cross and because of the power of His resurrection. We must recognize this truth and live in light of it (6:11).

The New Testament does not tell us to crucify ourselves or our sinful nature. Rather, we need to recognize that this has already been accomplished through the crucifixion of Christ (6:6). Therefore, because of what Christ has done, we are to put off the old self and its practices (Eph. 4:22; Col. 3:5; see also Rom. 6:11).   **—WGJ**

***

Realize at the beginning of each day that you died with Christ and that you are free to live for Him and not be a slave to sin.

CURSE

To curse someone means to call on God or occult powers to do harm to that person. A *curse,* then, is a prayer or incantation meant to bring harm or evil to an enemy. In occult practices such things as hexes, evil eyes, and spells are thought to be means of cursing someone. The Bible does not use the word *curse* in the casual sense of profanity or vulgarity. It's a very serious term.

The Bible refers to people cursing other people, people cursing God, and God cursing people. When people curse people, their curse takes the form of a prayer called an "imprecation." Imprecation means calling down the judgment of God (or some false deity) on an enemy. For example, Balak, king of Moab, was afraid of the advancing Israelites. So he summoned the prophet Balaam, saying, "Now come and put a curse on these people" (Num. 22:6). Similarly, Goliath the Philistine "cursed David by his gods" (1 Sam. 17:43).

The Bible also reports how angry, frustrated people can reach the point where they curse God. To curse God is to charge Him with injustice and wrongdoing because of one's afflictions and trials. Satan told God that if He destroyed Job's possessions and struck him with a disease, he would "surely curse you to your face" (Job 1:11; 2:5). After Job lost his possessions and all his children and was physically afflicted, even his wife advised him, "Curse God and die!" (2:9). To Job's great credit, he refused to charge God with wrongdoing (1:22; 2:10).

The first curses in the Bible occur as a result of the sin of Adam and Eve in the Garden of Eden. They are curses spoken by God. When the Bible speaks of God cursing a person, a place, or a thing, it indicates God is imposing a special and severe judgment on something or someone. The curse may take effect immediately, in the future, or both. As an example of the last category, the serpent in Eden was cursed by God to crawl on his belly (Gen. 3:14). That happened immediately. The serpent's curse also indicated the woman's offspring would crush its head (3:15). That happened far in the future when Jesus defeated Satan on the Cross. A further, final execution of that curse will happen when Satan is cast into the lake of fire.

God told Adam, "Cursed is the ground because of you" (3:17), and later God told Cain, "Now you are under a curse" (4:11). After God's judgment on the human race and the earth with the Flood, He told Noah, "Never again will I curse the ground because of man" (8:21).

When God called Abram to leave his country, people, and father's household for a land He would show him, He promised that "whosoever curses you I will curse" (12:3). When Israel entered the Promised Land, Joshua positioned the people of Israel in two groups on Mount Gerizim and Mount Ebal and ratified their covenant with God by reciting to one another all its curses and blessings (Josh. 8:30–35). The Old Testament ends ominously (and appropriately) with God threatening curses on both priests (Mal. 2:2) and people (3:9) because Israel would not keep its covenant with Him.

In the New Testament the concept of *curse* takes on a more individual sense. Paul wrote, "All who rely on observing the law are under a curse, for it is written: 'Cursed is everyone who does not continue to do everything written in the Book of the Law'" (Gal. 3:10; see also Deut. 27:26). He added, however, that "Christ redeemed us from the curse of the law by becoming a curse for us, for it is written: 'Cursed is everyone who is hung on a tree'" (Gal. 3:13; see also Deut. 21:23; Acts 5:30). When He was crucified, Jesus prayed for the people and priests who taunted Him and hurled insults at Him (Matt. 27:39–44), saying, "Father, forgive them, for they do not know what they are doing" (Luke 23:34). Not surprisingly He also calls on us to "bless those who curse you" (6:28).

—**JAW**

***

Be grateful that the hardships and trials God permits to enter your life are not curses from an angry deity but are blessings from the heavenly Father.

Dd

DARKNESS

Darkness is the absence of light. In a physical sense, darkness is a negative thing, a nothing, a lack. But the absence of light carries all sorts of emotional connotations from the time we were children. Darkness symbolizes fear, dread, the unknown, and evil. In the Bible darkness is the antithesis of God and light. The apostle John wrote, "God is light; in him there is no darkness at all" (1 John 1:5). James described God as "the Father of the heavenly lights, who does not change like shifting shadows" (James 1:17). Darkness represents everything opposed to God. It is identified with Satan (Acts 26:18) and his demonic forces (Eph. 6:11–12).

Some religions and philosophies treat

light and darkness as equal forces. Such a system is called dualism because it recognizes two equal powers of contrasting nature. Some Christians wrongly think and act as if God (light) and Satan (darkness) are equal in power. They fear that in some way Satan may defeat God in the daily affairs of their lives. Such belief is unbiblical. It produces anxiety and fear. Since those are spiritual states Satan rejoices in, it seems safe to assume dualism is an idea whose source is darkness rather than light.

The Bible calls unsaved people controlled by Satan (2:1–3) "darkness" (5:8). They are under "the dominion of darkness" (Col. 1:13). They "sat in darkness" (Ps. 107:10), are "living in darkness" (Matt. 4:16; Luke 1:79), and are "walking in darkness" (Is. 9:2). They love "darkness instead of light because their deeds [are] evil" (John 3:19). In fact, "the way of the wicked is like deep darkness" (Prov. 4:19).

Scripture says God controls both physical and spiritual darkness (2 Sam. 22:29; Pss. 18:28; 107:14; Is. 42:16; 49:9). God said, "I form the light and create darkness" (Is. 45:7), a claim demonstrated on the first day of creation (Gen. 1:3–5). Darkness describes the chaotic condition of the waters covering the newly created earth (1:2). Darkness is coupled with distress (Is. 5:30; 8:22), drought and desert (Jer. 2:31; see also 2:6), gloom (Joel 2:2; Zeph. 1:15), and terror (Job 24:17).

God can dispel darkness physically (Gen. 1:3; Josh. 10:12–14) and spiritually (Is. 58:10; 1 Cor. 4:5; 2 Cor. 4:6). In salvation He calls believers "out of darkness into his wonderful light" (1 Pet. 2:9) so that they no longer are "in darkness" (John 12:46). Furthermore He can see in the dark and knows people's hearts and thoughts (Job 34:21–22; Ps. 139:11–12; Dan. 2:22).

God sometimes produces darkness, as He did when He made a covenant with Abram (Gen. 15:7–21) and judged Egypt with a plague of darkness (Ex. 10:21–23). He separated the pursuing Egyptian army from the fleeing Israelites at the Red Sea with a wall of darkness (14:19–20; Josh. 24:7). "Darkness came over all the land" for three hours while Jesus bore God's judgment for the sins of humanity on the Cross (Matt. 27:45–46).

Darkness can represent God's power to judge sin. When God descended on Mount Sinai to deliver the Ten Commandments to Israel through Moses, it was covered with fire and smoke (Ex. 19:16, 18; 20:18), and "Moses approached the thick darkness where God was" (20:21; see also Deut. 4:11; 5:22–23). Moses explained that this display of God's glory and power was designed "to test you, so that the fear of God will be with you to keep you from sinning" (Ex. 20:20). God's judgment of Israel was called darkness (Jer. 13:16; 23:12), as was His judgment of Egypt (Ezek. 32:7–8).

God's final time of judgment—"the day of the LORD" (Amos 5:18)—is called "darkness, not light" (5:20; see Ezek. 34:12; Joel 2:2, 31; Acts 2:20; Rev. 16:10). The ultimate destiny of lost men and women is eternal separation from God. It is described as darkness (Matt. 8:12; 22:13; 25:30), even "pitch darkness" (Prov. 20:20) and "blackest darkness" (2 Pet. 2:17; Jude 13).   **—JAW**

***

In the darkness of this world let your light for Christ shine to point others to faith in Him and thus glorify God the Father.

DAY, DAYS

In the ancient Near East, different cultures began and ended days at different hours. Israel measured days from sunset to sunset. The Babylonians on the other hand began their day at sunrise. Egyptians and Romans viewed a day as the period from one midnight to the next.

According to the Old Testament the daylight hours of a day were divided into morning, noon, and evening (Ps. 55:17). The only day of the week given a name was the Sabbath. By New Testament times the day before the Sabbath was called the Preparation Day (Matt. 27:62).

The plural expression "days" could mean "in the time of," as "in the days of Abraham" (Gen. 26:18, KJV) and in "the days of Noah" (Matt. 24:37). The plural noun also describes a lifetime as in Genesis 5:5, "So all the days that Adam lived were nine hundred and thirty years" (NASB). God the Father is named "the Ancient of Days" (Dan. 7:9, 13).

The word *day* is found over two thousand times in the Old Testament and over 350 times in the New Testament. It has both everyday and special theological meanings in different contexts. It usually isn't too difficult to tell when *day* has a normal meaning or a theological one.

Israel set aside special days on which to worship God, including the Sabbath (Gen. 2:3; Ex. 20:8–11), the Passover (Ex. 12:14), and the Day of Atonement (Lev. 16:29–31). Each day had its own rituals, and ordinary work was banned.

Frequently, especially in the New Testament, the word *day* is used in a figurative sense. Jesus said, "As long as it is day, we must do the work of him who sent me. Night is coming, when no one can work" (John 9:4). Similarly, Paul wrote, "The night is nearly over; the day is almost here. So let us put aside the deeds of darkness and put on the armor of light" (Rom. 13:12).

The days of creation present special interpretive challenges. Some understand the days of creation to be twenty-four-hour or solar days. Others support the day-age view, which theorizes that the creation days were long ages during which the geologic features of the earth developed. A middle view holds to solar days of creative activity by God separated by long periods of geologic time. Still another view is that the days of creation were "revelatory days." Moses received revelation about different aspects of creation on seven consecutive days.

Advocates of the day-age view note that Genesis 2:4 (NASB) indicates all of God's creative activity occurred in a *day* (Hebrew *yôm*). Since *yôm* has an indefinite meaning right within the creation account, might not the other *days* also be of indefinite length? They also point out that since the sun was not created until the fourth day, the first three days could have been of any duration.

The expression in Genesis 2:4 is *yôm* with a preposition of time. This phrase typically means "at the time when." The New International Version translates it "when." The phrase is an idiom that has no bearing on the other uses of *yôm* in the passage. When numbers are attached to *yôm* in a series of days, they are solar days. With regard to the three days before the creation of the sun, no one knows whether the light created on day one radiated from a source that would have caused day and night on a spinning earth. Of course, if God wanted to create in day-length segments, He didn't need the sun to inform Him of the passage of time.

Solar-day advocates also argue that the reference to day and night in Genesis 1:18 makes sense only in reference to solar days. What would be the meaning of day and night if the creative days were ages? Also Exodus 20:11 and 31:17 declare that God created everything in six days and rested on the seventh day. This analogy to mankind's cycle of work and rest suggests that Israelites would have understood the days of creation to be twenty-four hours.

The word *day* has several uses in prophetic portions of the Bible. *The Day of the Lord* occurs frequently in both Old and New Testaments. The Day of the Lord can denote (a) a time of intense divine judgment, (b) the awful judgments of the Great Tribulation, or even (c) the blessings of the millennial kingdom. The outcome of the Day of the Lord is described in Isaiah 2:17, "The arrogance of man will be brought low and the pride of men humbled; the LORD alone will be exalted in that day."

The Day of Christ refers to the coming of Christ for His church. It is the time when the dead in Christ will be raised and living saints will be raptured and taken to be with Christ in heaven (1 Thess. 4:13–17). There saints will appear before the judgment seat of Christ and receive rewards (2 Cor. 5:10). The Day of Christ is referred to in 1 Corinthians 1:8; 2 Corinthians 1:14; and Philippians 1:6, 10; 2:16. It will end when believers return to the earth to reign with Christ.

The Day of God (2 Pet. 3:12) refers to the time when the present creation will pass away and the new heavens and new earth will appear. "*The great day of God Almighty*" (Rev. 16:14), refers to the battle of Armageddon at the time of Christ's return to the earth.

The Bible applies the term *last days* at different places to either the future of Israel or the future of the church. With respect to Israel, *the last days* often describes the days of her kingdom glory (Is. 2:2–5). In Zechariah 12—14 the frequent expression "*on that day*" refers to the return of Christ and the millennial kingdom as they relate to Israel.

The final days of the church before the Rapture will be evil in character (1 Tim. 4:1–5; 2 Tim. 3:1–5; Heb. 1:1–2; James 5:3; 2 Pet. 3:1–9; 1 John 2:15–19; Jude 17–19). New Testament readers are often said to be living in the "last days." In a sense "the last days" began with the First Advent of Christ. The New Testament writers saw that evil will be especially prominent in the final days. They warned against any signs of apostasy or moral degeneration as foreshadowings of the last days. We live in the last historical era before God intervenes to carry out His ultimate plans and purposes.

Other uses of the word *day* in the New Testament Epistles refer to the day of redemption (Eph. 4:30), the day of salvation (2 Cor. 6:2), the day of wrath (Rom. 2:5; Rev. 6:17), and the day of judgment (2 Pet. 2:9; 3:7).   —**DKC**

***

Thank God that this is still the day of salvation.

DEATH

Death is a mystery. No one can know from experience or firsthand report what happens after the cessation of physical life. Death is an enemy (1 Cor. 15:26). It strikes fear and dread into our hearts (Heb. 2:15).

It seems wrong that humans, the crown of God's creation, have a briefer lifespan than many trees and some animals. In fact, since men and women were made in the image of God, why should they die at all? The scriptural answer is that human death is a consequence of sin. Genesis 2:17, the Bible's first reference to death, records God's warning to Adam: "But you must not eat from the tree of the knowledge of good and evil, for when you eat of it you will surely die."

Paul in his Roman epistle describes death as the penalty for sin. He traced the entrance of sin and death to Adam: "Therefore, just as sin entered the world through one man, and death through sin, and in this way death came to all men, because all sinned" (Rom. 5:12). Some theologians read the words "all sinned" and conclude they mean each person sins and therefore dies.

But we must understand the words "all sinned" in connection to our relationship to Adam. We all sinned at the same time Adam sinned. Adam contained the seed of all humanity so that when he sinned, everybody who would ever live sinned.

The writer of Hebrews expressed a similar idea when he said that Levi paid tithes to Melchizedek (Heb. 7:9–10). Levi was born two centuries after the time of Melchizedek, but "Levi . . . paid the tenth through Abraham" (7:9). Abraham, in a sense, contained Levi his great-grandson, as Adam likewise contained his descendants, namely, the entire human race. We universally participated in Adam's sin, so we universally suffer the penalty—human death.

When we scan the Bible to see how it discusses death, we find it can be very matter-of-fact about the subject. The Old Testament views death as a common human experience (see, for example, Gen. 5, with its monotonous repetition of the doleful expression "and he died"). The happy exception of Enoch (5:24) introduces a glimmer of hope that death can be overcome. Still death was feared (Pss. 6:1–5; 88:1–14), especially an early death (2 Kin. 21:1–11). On the other hand, Psalm 90 teaches that even a long lifespan is brief. God, nevertheless, is in control of death. He sometimes granted escape from death (Ps. 68:20); restored dead persons to life (1 Kin. 17:22, 2 Kin. 4:34;

13:21); and promised that death will be overcome by resurrection (Is. 25:8; 26:19; Ezek. 37:11–12; Dan. 12:2; Hos. 13:14).

In the New Testament the death and resurrection of Christ dominates all other mentions of death. His death "has destroyed death and has brought life and immortality to light through the gospel" (2 Tim. 1:10). Through Christ we receive spiritual (eternal) life, even though we remain subject to physical death. It will be the last enemy Christ destroys (1 Cor. 15:26). Christ will banish death from our experience when He returns for us. He will raise the believing dead in imperishable bodies (15:52). Death will be swallowed up in victory (15:54).

The unbelieving dead will be raised to stand before the Great White Throne for judgment. John described the end of that grim scene this way: "Then death and Hades were thrown into the lake of fire. The lake of fire is the second death. If anyone's name was not found written in the book of life, he was thrown into the lake of fire" (Rev. 20:14–15). Thus the second death—eternal death—consists of the separation of the soul and spirit from God. The second death has no power over believers (20:6), for we are heirs of eternal life.

The New Testament distinguishes between physical death and spiritual death. Everyone dies physically (Heb. 9:27) except for the generation who will be alive when the Lord comes for His church (1 Thess. 4:16–17). The writer to the Hebrews said the death of Christ destroyed the one who held the power of death—the devil—and freed those "who all their lives were held in slavery by their fear of death" (Heb. 2:14–15).

Physical death is the separation of the soul and spirit from the body, and spiritual death is the separation of the soul and spirit from God. We were all born spiritually dead (Eph. 2:1–3; Col. 2:13). Spiritual death resulted from the sin of Adam. Each generation inherits it from their parents. The only remedy for spiritual death is regeneration.

The ancient world held dark, depressing views of death. Theocritus, a third-century B.C. Greek poet, wrote, "Hopes are among the living. The dead are without hope." Likewise, Lucretius, a first-century B.C. Roman philosopher, stated, "No one awakes and arises who has once been overtaken by the chilling end of life." In bold contrast, the New Testament proclaims that Christ's redemptive work replaces the fear of death with joyous hope. The sting of death is removed. Departure from this life by death blesses us with all sorts of positive gains in Christ (Phil. 1:21).   **—DKC**

***

The Resurrection of Christ gives us confidence that death has been defeated and we too will be raised.

DECREES

The term "decree" needs to be considered biblically and theologically. Biblically, a decree is a command or a statement of certainty. Usually a decree in the Bible is the work of some king or military ruler who issues a law (Ezra 5:13; Dan. 3:10; Luke 2:1; Acts 17:7). Occasionally a command of God is called a decree. Synonyms for *decree* include "proclamation" (2 Chr. 30:5) and "edict" (Ezra 6:11; Esth. 1:20; Dan. 6:7). The Council of Jerusalem issued "decisions" (Greek, *dogmata;* Acts 16:4).

The decrees of God refer either to His long-range plans (Job 23:14; Jer. 40:2) or to the commands and statutes of His law (Deut. 4:5; 1 Kin. 9:4, 6; Ezra 7:11). In the second sense *decrees* occurs twenty-two times in Psalm 119. The divine decree in Psalm 2:7 pertains to God the Son. "I will proclaim the decree of the LORD: He said to me, 'You are my Son; today I have become your father.'"

In theology the term *decree* (used in the singular) plays an important role in describing God's sovereign rule. God's *decree* includes all of His individual plans and purposes for the future. *Decree* embraces all things, including God's direct actions and His indirect control of the entire universe. *Decree* includes election and predestination of those who are saved.

Some people think election and predestination equal fatalism. This isn't so.

A fatalist views events as inevitable and purposeless. He or she can do nothing to change the course of events. Within God's decree, individuals acts as moral creatures who choose to obey or disobey. There is a dynamic interaction between the will of God and the wills of the people involved. Ultimately it is impossible to understand how human freedom remains intact while it serves the decree of God. It is one more mystery that illustrates that God's ways are higher than ours (Is. 55:9).

The supreme illustration of the decree of God accompanied by human responsibility is the death of Christ. It was decreed by God, because His death was absolutely essential to fulfill God's purposes. At the same time its accomplishment depended on the decisions of individuals. "This man was handed over to you by God's set purpose and foreknowledge; and you, with the help of wicked men, put him to death by nailing him to the cross" (Acts 2:23). Peter and John said that those who crucified Jesus "did what [God's] power and will had decided beforehand should happen" (4:28). —**JFW**

***

Accept the fact that God is in control of every aspect of life, remembering that He will fulfill His purposes for your life.

DEMONS

The English word *demon* reproduces the Greek noun *daimōn,* which appears only once in the New Testament (Matt. 8:31). The usual word for demon in the New Testament is *daimōnion,* the diminutive form of *daimōn.* The New Testament also calls demons "deceiving spirits" (1 Tim. 4:1) and "evil spirits" (Luke 8:2). In some verses the word translated "evil" literally means "unclean" (Matt. 10:1; Mark 1:23; Luke 4:33; Acts 5:16). Most of the biblical references to demons occur in the Gospels in connection with the ministry of Jesus. A few occur in the rest of the New Testament. The Old Testament uses the word "demon" twice in reference to pagan deities (Deut. 32:17; Ps. 106:37).

In early Greek philosophy, *demons* referred to both positive and negative spirit forces in the world. As time passed, the word increasingly meant evil spirits who opposed people. In the Bible demons oppose God, the Lord Jesus Christ, and believers. They could indwell men (Matt. 9:32), women (Luke 8:2), and children (Matt. 17:17–18; Mark 7:25–30), and they could inflict physical and mental harm on those they indwell (Matt. 8:28; 9:32–33; 12:22; Luke 9:42).

Demons are spirit beings, but they obviously desire to indwell and control the bodies of people (Mark 5:12–13). More than one demon can indwell the same person (Luke 11:24–26). A legion of demons had indwelt one man Jesus healed (8:30). If that number was meant literally, six thousand or more evil spirits controlled him. Because demons desire embodiment, some claim they are disembodied spirits of the dead, especially the wicked or unburied. The Bible does not support this view.

Like everything else, demons are under God's control. The Bible does not directly say where demons came from. It does say demons are Satan's agents (Matt. 12:24, 26). The Bible describes demons as rulers, authorities, powers, and spiritual forces of evil (Eph. 6:12). As a result demons are assumed to be the angels created by God who joined Satan in his rebellion against their Creator (Is. 14:12–15; Ezek. 28:12–17; 2 Pet. 3:4).

Like Satan, the demons are unalterably fixed in their opposition to God and His program of salvation among humankind. They cannot repent and receive forgiveness. Their destiny is punishment forever in "the eternal fire" (Matt. 25:41; see Rev. 20:10). Some fallen angels are already confined, awaiting judgment (2 Pet. 2:4; Jude 6). The rest are free to carry out Satan's program.

Demons are more powerful than human beings, but they are no match for God. They are finite, limited, and localized. Though they are spirit beings, they can take on visible forms (Rev. 9:1–11; 16:13). They possess great strength, so that a demon-possessed man could break his chains when "chained hand and foot" (Luke 8:29). Another over-

powered and beat the "seven sons of Sceva" (Acts 19:14–16).

Demons have greater intelligent than human beings, both innately and because they have been accumulating experience since before the creation of Adam and Eve. They knew who Jesus was (Mark 1:24). They knew all about Paul (Acts 19:15). They know God and His plan of salvation (James 2:19). They're aware of the judgment awaiting them (Matt. 8:29). They develop and promote false teachings (1 Tim. 4:1–3).

The Bible says demons may be the spiritual forces behind Gentile nations (Dan. 10:12, 20). When a pagan god displays real power, that power comes from a demon (Deut. 32:17; Ps. 106:28; 1 Cor. 10:20–21).

The primary period of demonic activity in the Bible occurred during the earthly life and ministry of the Lord Jesus Christ (Matt. 4:24; 8:16, 28–33; 9:32–33; 12:22; 17:18; Mark 7:26–30; Luke 4:33–35). Jesus gave His disciples authority and power to cast out demons (Mark 3:15). They used that power (6:13; Luke 10:17) successfully most of the time (Matt. 17:14–21).

The Pharisees liked to accuse Jesus of casting out demons "by Beelzebub, the prince of demons" (Matt. 12:24; see 9:34) and of being demon-possessed (John 7:20; 8:48, 52; 10:20). They had used the same tactic to discredit John the Baptist (Matt. 11:18). Jesus pointed out the illogic of their accusation, stating, "Every kingdom divided against itself will be ruined" (12:25). He turned the charge back on them by asking, "And if I drive out demons by Beelzebub, by whom do your people drive them out?" (12:27).

In the early church the apostles had power over demons (Acts 5:16). Philip (8:7) and Paul (16:16–18) exercised this power too. This authority and power belong to Christians throughout church history (Mark 16:17). The activity of demons apparently will increase in the end times (1 Tim. 4:1; Rev. 9:20). Along with their leader Satan, they undoubtedly will realize that their time of judgment is near. They will have greater freedom to unleash the evil schemes after the removal of the Holy Spirit's work of restraining sin (2 Thess. 2:7).

—JAW

* * *

In view of the demonic forces all around us, "be strong in the Lord and in his mighty power" (Eph. 6:10).

DEPRAVITY

"Depravity" is a biblical concept, but it is not a common word in the Bible. The New International Version contains the word *depravity* twice (Rom. 1:29; 2 Pet. 2:19) and *depraved* five times (Ezek. 16:47; 23:11; Rom. 1:28; Phil. 2:15; 2 Tim. 3:8). The New American Standard Bible uses *depraved* twice (Rom. 1:28; 2 Tim. 3:8). Neither word appears in the King James Bible. Older trans-

lations used words such as *corrupt, perverse,* and *reprobate* to represent the idea of depravity.

Theologians boil down the biblical information about our sin nature and conclude we are depraved. They talk about the total depravity of mankind. Total depravity refers to people in their unregenerate condition of spiritual death and separation from God. Spiritually dead people can't do anything to make themselves acceptable to God. They are totally dependent on God's gracious provision of salvation through Jesus Christ's death on the cross. The word "total" in the phrase "total depravity" means sin affects every aspect of human personality. It does not mean unsaved people behave as perversely as possible all the time.

Total depravity became a fact of the human condition when Adam and Eve disobeyed God's command by eating "from the tree of the knowledge of good and evil" (Gen. 2:17; see 3:6–7). They immediately died spiritually. They demonstrated their separation from God by hiding "from the Lord God among the trees of the garden" (3:8). They transmitted this depravity to their offspring, and Cain murdered his brother Abel (4:8). The next few chapters of Genesis report the mushrooming effects of depravity on succeeding generations. Genesis 6:5, 11–12 describe the inner corruption and outward violence that compelled God to destroy everyone, except for righteous Noah and his family, with a flood (6:7–10, 13). Centuries later David confessed, "Surely I was sinful at birth, sinful from the time my mother conceived me" (Ps. 51:5).

The classic New Testament description of human depravity is in Romans 1:18–32. Paul described the moral and spiritual depths to which the human race sank because they refused to glorify God and to give Him thanks. "Their thinking became futile and their foolish hearts were darkened" (1:21). People became idolaters (1:23) and God "gave them over" (1:24, 26, 28) to practice "every kind of wickedness" (1:29). Such a process of moral decay led up to the Flood all those centuries before. The same cycle of depravity has operated in every age since. It certainly operates today.

Not all unregenerate people behave wickedly. Individual unbelievers often exhibit honesty and kindness in response to social conventions and conscience. Depravity ultimately refers to spiritual death and separation from God. Jesus told the righteous but unbelieving Pharisee, Nicodemus, "No one can see the kingdom of God unless he is born again" (John 3:3). The prophet Isaiah stated, "All our righteous acts are like filthy rags" (Is. 64:6).

Because of their depravity—separation from God—unsaved people cannot save themselves. In addition, "The god of this age has blinded the minds of unbelievers, so that they cannot see the light of the gospel of the glory of Christ" (2 Cor. 4:4). The Holy Spirit has to convict (John 16:7–11) and enlighten depraved individuals before they can respond in faith to the gospel. Salvation is totally by the grace of God.

Regeneration solves the issue of depravity by making us spiritually alive and giving us access to God. When we respond by faith to the gospel of Jesus Christ, the Holy Spirit takes up permanent residence in our hearts and lives (2 Cor. 1:22; Eph. 1:13–14). However, our sin nature is not eradicated (Rom. 7:14—8:14). Fortunately the indwelling Holy Spirit wars against our sin nature (Gal. 5:17), so that we can have victory over sin by living in His power (Rom. 8:4; Gal. 5:25).   **—JAW**

***

When witnessing for Christ, be aware of the depraved hearts of unbelievers and trust the Holy Spirit to convict and save.

DISCIPLE

The English word *disciple* comes from the Latin noun *discipulus*. In the New Testament the Greek word translated "disciple" is *mathētēs*. Both the Latin and the Greek words meant "a pupil" or "learner." Greek culture called both the student of a philosophers and the apprentice of a plumber "disciples." The Old Testament contains a handful of references to teachers and students (1 Chr. 25:8; Is. 8:16; 50:4). "The sons of the prophets" who studied with Samuel, Elijah, and Elisha, come closest to the New Testament concept of disciple.

In the New Testament the term *disciple* is found exclusively in the Gospels and Acts. In Acts the sense of the term changes. Generally the term *disciple* referred to the followers of some teacher. The Gospels refer to the disciples of the Pharisees (Matt. 22:16; Luke 5:33) and of John the Baptist (Matt. 11:2; Mark 2:18; Luke 5:33; John 1:35–37). In one instance observant Jews called themselves "disciples of Moses" (John 9:28).

The primary use of the term *disciples* in the Gospels describes the Twelve: Simon Peter, Andrew, James of Zebedee, John, Philip, Nathanael (also known as Bartholomew), Thomas, Matthew (called Levi), James son of Alphaeus, Simon the Zealot or Canaanite, Judas the brother of James (sometimes called Thaddaeus), and Judas Iscariot. Jesus placed radical demands on these men since He, as an itinerant Teacher, was constantly on the move. His disciples literally were His "followers" (a word used some eighty times in the Gospels to describe the relationship between Jesus and His companions).

The word *follower,* in fact, became a synonym for *disciple.* As a literal follower of Jesus, each disciple had to give up his occupation (Mark 1:18–19), his parents (10:29), and "everything" (10:28). Thus the disciples of Jesus not only benefited from His teachings but also witnessed the unfolding drama of redemption.

The Gospels also use *disciple* to include the multitudes who believed Jesus' words (John 8:30–31) and came regularly to learn from Him (Matt. 5:1–2). These masses (Luke 6:17) represented a cross-section of society from sinners to scribes (Matt. 8:18–22; Mark 1:16–20; Luke 6:14–16; John 19:38). Most of these disciples, who were attracted to Jesus by miracles and authoritative teaching, did not make a firm commitment to Him. When they found His teachings hard to grasp or too challenging, they faded away (John 6:60–66). The true disciples who stuck with Jesus through thick and thin followed Him wholeheartedly and made disciples of others (Matt. 28:19).

In the Book of Acts the word *disciple* shifts in meaning. Acts calls the Twelve "apostles" and uses the word "disciples" as a general term for believers in Christ (Acts 9:25 and 19:1 are exceptions). Acts 11:26 declares, "The disciples were first called Christians at Antioch." This marks the beginning point of the change in the designation of believers.

The writers of the Epistles did not use the word *disciple* a single time. The Gospels and Acts seem to reserve it for those who physically followed Jesus and witnessed the Resurrection. The Epistles stress the role of the Holy Spirit (2 Cor. 3:18), the indwelling Christ (Gal. 2:20), and the fellowship of believers in transforming us into the likeness of Jesus.

Christlikeness was the goal of discipleship in the Gospels (Luke 6:40). Christlikeness still is the goal of our Christian walk. We'll reach that goal when Jesus returns for "we know that when he appears, we shall be like him" (1 John 3:2). **—DKC**

***

Strive to be a true disciple of Jesus, depending on the Holy Spirit to help make you more Christlike.

DISCIPLINE

Discipline sounds like a negative word involving punishment. Actually it is a positive one. *Discipline* is correction and training that produces personal and spiritual growth and maturity. The words translated *discipline* in both Old and New Testaments involve attaining wisdom and doing what is right and proper (for example, Deut. 8:5; Heb.12:5–11). Solomon told his son not to despise the Lord's discipline, "because the LORD disciplines those he loves, as a father the son he delights in" (Prov. 3:11–12).

Chastisement often is an element of discipline, but it's never an end in itself. Rather chastening should bring out the best in us and ultimately cause us to glorify God. The Bible discusses four kinds of discipline: discipline of Israel as a nation, discipline of individual believers, discipline by local churches; and parental discipline of their children.

First, God frequently had to discipline the nation of Israel. While Israel journeyed from Egypt to the Promised Land, God disciplined them through awesome displays of His power. He was teaching them to reverence and obey Him. He spoke audibly from heaven and performed great and awesome deeds (Deut. 4:32–36). The Book of Numbers records several acts of chastening God imposed on Israel in the wilderness. The New Testament says those experiences should discipline and train us to reverence and obey God (1 Cor. 10:11; Heb. 4:11). Sometimes God's discipline of Israel may seem severe, but it came from His love for them (Deut. 4:37). God never asks His people to do things without enabling them to obey Him. God's discipline of Israel always prodded them to rely on Him.

Second, the Book of Proverbs contains the heart of biblical teaching about individual discipline. Given initially to Israel, these instructions apply to believers in any age. We may experience individual discipline at the hands of parents, leaders, and God. According to Solomon those who respond positively to discipline are good examples for others (Prov. 6:23; 10:17). Ignoring discipline results in poverty and shame and reveals that people don't care about themselves (13:18; 15:32).

The person who loves discipline

loves knowledge (12:1), but the one who rejects instruction is a fool (15:5). Fools, Solomon said, are undisciplined and lack knowledge. Folly—the mind-set of fools—is the opposite of wisdom (9:13). Because God disciplines in love, we should not resent His corrections (3:11).

The New Testament instruction on individual discipline builds directly on that of the Old Testament. Hebrews 12 points to Jesus, who willingly endured the Cross, as the perfect example of how to accept the discipline contained in the difficult experiences of our lives. Hardships will discipline and train us if we receive them in the right spirit. These episodes of discipline provide evidence that we have a close relationship with God (Heb. 12:7). Just as our earthly fathers disciplined us, so our heavenly Father disciplines us for our good. None of us likes to be disciplined. It is painful and distressing (12:11). Yet it is God's way of making our lives productive in holiness, righteousness, and peace. We respected our earthly fathers who disciplined us imperfectly and inconsistently. How much more should our hearts respond in love and gratitude to our heavenly Father whose discipline is always fair and results in eternal benefits.

The third kind of discipline discussed in the Bible is church discipline. The first incident of church discipline in the New Testament is startling. Ananias and Sapphira pretended to give all the proceeds from a property sale to the Lord, but they secretly kept part of it for themselves. Peter, guided by the Holy Spirit, challenged them about lying. When they persisted in lying to the Holy Spirit, God struck them dead (Acts 5:1–11). That incident underlines how seriously God regards the integrity of the church.

Discipline becomes necessary when church members sin openly and unrepentantly so that it affects the life and reputation of the congregation (5:4; 1 Cor. 11:27–31). The leadership of the church is responsible to deal with discipline issues within the congregation (5:12). If someone continues in sin after being confronted, then consequences should result (5:11). Disciplinary action should aim at restoring the offender and protecting the congregation (5:5). When offenders respond properly to church discipline, they should be forgiven so Satan cannot take advantage of the situation.

The fourth kind of discipline discussed in the Bible occurs in families. Solomon urged parents to discipline their children even if it means using a rod (Prov. 22:15). Improper or inadequate discipline can contribute to a child's ruin (19:18). Parental neglect of discipline demonstrates hatred instead of love (13:24). In the New Testament, Paul exhorted fathers to bring up their children "in the training and instruction [literally, 'discipline'] of the Lord" (Eph. 6:4). Church leaders need to manage their families well. Child discipline is an important aspect of family management (1 Tim. 3:4, 12; Titus 1:6). Bringing up children in the way of the Lord is a good deed (1 Tim. 5:10).

—**WGJ**

* * *

When God disciplines you, don't lose heart; instead respond positively and learn from those experiences.

DISOBEDIENCE

Disobedience is failure to do something that was commanded. Theologically it means failure to hear and do what God requires. Disobedience may result from simply neglecting God's commands (Heb. 2:1–2) or it may spring from active, outright refusal to do what He requires (Ps. 95:7–11; Heb. 3:16–18). At the root of disobedience lurks a hardened heart, as was true of the people of Israel in the wilderness. A hard heart produces sin and unbelief (3:12). Unbelief and disobedience are linked, because failure to trust the Lord leads directly to failure to do what He commands.

Examples of disobedience abound in the Bible. Even before God created Adam, some of the angels rebelled. Satan led the rebellion. He was a chief angel who proudly aspired to rival God. His disobedience resulted in expulsion from heaven for himself and his fallen angelic cohorts (Is. 14:12, 15). Those

angels live their disobedient existences under a sentence of judgment (2 Pet. 2:4; Jude 6).

Adam and Eve disobeyed God's one prohibition and led the world into the condemnation of sin (Gen. 3:6–11; Rom. 5:12, 18). Moses disregarded God's command to speak to the rock and dishonored the Lord before all Israel (Num. 20:12, 24). Israel failed to believe God would give them the land He promised (Deut. 1:26–27), so they wandered in the wilderness for forty years. One man's secret defiance spelled disaster for Israel after an overwhelming victory over Jericho (Josh. 7:15–26). King Saul failed to obey instructions and offered a sacrifice that displeased the Lord (1 Sam. 15:1–27). Samuel told Saul that God wants obedience far more than He wants sacrifices (15:22). The prophet Jonah rebelled against the Lord's orders and spent three days in the gullet of a great fish before God used him to spark a revival at Nineveh.

The New Testament also takes disobedience very seriously. Ananias and Sapphira lied to the Holy Spirit and took credit for something they didn't do (Acts 5:1–11). They disobeyed the command not to lie. Paul indicated disobedience would characterize the last days (2 Tim. 3:1–2). He said that in the present age disobedience indicates the spirit of the adversary is at work (Eph. 2:2). Church history testifies eloquently that disobeying God brings devastating consequences.

Human disobedience necessitated the death of Christ. Through the disobedience of one man, Paul wrote, many were made sinners (Rom. 5:19). This one trespass condemned all (5:18). Adam's sin was a blatant act, a deliberate disobedience of a command (5:14). Christ's obedience, however, stands in sharp contrast to this one man's sin (5:19). Peter called Jesus the precious Stone for believers and a stumbling stone for those who disobey the message (1 Pet. 2:7–8). Peter treated disobedience as a synonym for unbelief in that case.

The Bible admonishes us several times about disobedience. Church leaders must have obedient children (Titus 1:6). Christians are to submit to people in authority, both in society and in the church, because disobedience is a mark of unbelievers (3:1, 3). Believers should not associate with those who disobey God's Word (2 Thess. 3:14). The gracious conduct of a believing wife can win over a husband who is disobedient to the Word of God (1 Pet. 3:1).   **—WGJ**

***

Learn God's commands in the Scriptures and determine, with the Holy Spirit's help, to obey them.

DISPENSATION

The word *dispensation* has a biblical usage and a theological usage. *Dispensation* translates the Greek word *oikonomia,* which means an administration. *Oikonomia* is a compound word made by adding together *oikos* ("house") and *nomos* ("a law"). It envisioned the way a large estate was managed by a steward, called an *oikonomos.* Paul used *dispensation* three times (Eph. 1:10; 3:2; Col. 1:25, KJV) to refer to the way God is administering the church age.

Theologically, dispensationalism is a way of understanding God's developing relationship with people through history. The term *dispensation* does not in itself involve the concept of an era of time. It's a system by which God administers His grace to people. However, since one dispensation replaces another, the idea of a period of time inevitably enters the picture. Dispensationalism is the view that God has administered the world in various stages of revelation and according to various principles or standards.

The dispensations build on the idea that in Scripture there is progressive revelation, beginning in the Garden of Eden and culminating in the millennial kingdom. In each dispensation the "rule of life" for humanity involved certain obligations, and in each past dispensation mankind failed to live up to God's standards. A number of dispensations can be identified in the Bible. Each built on God's revelation in previous dispensations, but each involved new revelation that dramatically changed the situation.

In Eden the obligation was not to eat of the forbidden fruit. After the Fall, the rule of life was what human conscience indicated was right or wrong. This in turn was succeeded by human government at the time of Noah. Following the failure of human government at the Tower of Babel, God chose a new direction by making a covenant with one man, Abraham, and his descendants. God promised to bless Abraham personally, to bless his descendants after him, and to bless the whole world through his descendants (Gen. 12:1–3).

The Mosaic Law introduced the most dramatic change in the dispensations of the Old Testament. The Mosaic Law concerned only Israel, but it shows us God's concern for the details of human life. The children of Israel showed whether they possessed saving faith by obeying or disobeying the Law. The Mosaic Law did not provide salvation. "No one is justified before God by the law" (Gal. 3:11). Works are never the basis of salvation (Eph. 2:8–9), but they can give evidence of it.

The present church-age dispensation began on the Day of Pentecost (Acts 2; see 11:15) and will end at the Rapture. The final dispensation will be the Millennium, when Christ will reign on the earth. Paul called this "the dispensation [*oikonomia*] of the fullness of the times" (Eph. 1:10, KJV). The Scriptures give extended revelation about three of these divine "economies"—the Mosaic Law, the present church age, and Christ's future reign on earth.

Christ's death abolished the Law of Moses as a way of life, but many of its moral commands are repeated in the New Testament. No one is under the Law of Moses (Gal. 3:25). Believers are not slaves to the Law. Instead, living under the rule of grace, they are sons and heirs of Christ (4:7).

God's rules of life change for mankind under subsequent revelation. But in every dispensation people are saved only by grace through the death of Christ.

All schools of theology recognize the existence of dispensations to some extent. Even nondispensational theologians recognize at least two dispensations—law and grace. Some theologians see the dispensations as divisions of an over-arching "covenant of grace." A branch of dispensationalism known as ultradispensationalism attempts to divide the present age into two divisions, one Jewish and one church-related.

Dispensationalists hold that Scripture maintains a clear distinction between God's program for Israel and His program for the church. This distinctive sets them apart from many mainline churches that believe the church, in some sense, replaces Israel in God's redemptive purposes. **—JFW**

***

List the provisions God has made for you in this present age, as revealed in the New Testament, and appropriate these in your daily life.

DREAMS AND VISIONS

Dreams are images and impressions in the mind of a sleeping person. Most dreams relate to problems and anxieties the sleeper was troubled by while awake. Most of our dreams have some amount of psychological significance, but in the Bible God often used a dream as a means of divine revelation. For example, God revealed to Jacob in a dream that his descendants would inherit all the land around him (Gen. 28:12–15).

These Old Testament characters all had dreams in which God revealed something: Joseph (Gen. 37:5–11), two prisoners of Pharaoh (40:5–22), Pharaoh himself (41:1–32), a Midianite soldier (Judg. 7:13–15), Nebuchadnezzar (Dan. 2:1–45; 4:4–28), and Daniel (7:1–28). Other Old Testament dreams, however, were entirely natural and non-revelatory (Job 20:8; Pss. 73:1–20; 126:1; Eccl. 5:3; Is. 29:7–8). Sometimes false prophets claimed to convey God's message by their dreams (Deut. 13:1–3). They either made up their dreams or channeled the messages of evil spirits (Zech. 10:2).

In the New Testament God gave dreams as a means of revelation to Joseph (Matt. 1:20–23; 2:12–13, 19–20, 22) and Pilate's wife (27:19). In Acts 2:17 Peter quoted the prediction of Joel 2:28, "Your old men will dream dreams," indicating that people will experience dreams and visions in the last days. These may be bona fide revelations.

A dream involved symbolic images or scenarios seen by someone while asleep. In a vision God Himself appears and reveals a message to someone. People in the Bible often saw their visions while they slept, but some saw visions while awake.

Individuals who received visions from God include Abraham (Gen. 15:1; 17:3), Jacob (46:2), Samuel (1 Sam. 3:15), Iddo (2 Chr. 9:29), Isaiah (Is. 1:1), Ezekiel (Ezek. 1:1; 8:3–4; 11:24; 40:2; 43:3), Daniel (Dan. 1:17; 2:19, 49; 7:1–2, 7, 13, 15; 8:1–2, 13–19, 26–27; 9:21, 23–24; 10:1, 7–8, 14, 16), Obadiah (Obad. 1), Micah (Mic. 1:1), Nahum (Nah. 1:1), Zechariah the prophet (Zech. 1:8; 13:4), Zechariah the father of John the Baptist (Luke 1:22), Cornelius (Acts 10:3), Peter (10:17–20), Paul (9:10, 12; 16:9–10; 18:9; 26:19; 2 Cor. 12:1), and John (Rev. 9:17). Nathan and Habakkuk each received information from God in visions.

The New International Version translates "vision" in 2 Samuel 7:17 and Habakkuk 2:2–3 by the word *revelation,* thereby conveying the point that visions communicate information. Usually those seeing visions realized they were receiving supernatural communication. Since the completion of the New Testament, God no longer communicates new revelation by means of visions. **—JFW**

***

Guard against any inclination to equate any dream or personal experience with the revealed Word of God.

Ee

ELECTION

The theological meaning of election is that God chooses people for certain purposes. God may elect a group, such as Israel or the church. He may elect individuals, either in the sense of choosing them to receive eternal life or in the sense of choosing them to perform a special act of service.

God chose the nation Israel and set her apart as a special people among the nations of the world. The Old Testament makes frequent mention of God's election of Israel (Deut. 4:37; 7:6–7; 10:15; 14:2; 1 Kin. 3:8; Pss. 33:12; 105:6, 43; 135:4; Is. 41:8–9; 43:20; 44:1; 45:4; Ezek. 20:5).

God sovereignly chose Israel, without any conditions. His election was not based on Israel's superiority or inferiority to any other nation. God selected Israel for a purpose. She was to be a channel of revelation to others about God's person, work, and will.

God's election gave Israel a special relationship to Him. She became a holy people (Ex. 19:6; 22:31), that is, a people set apart to Him. Israel is God's possession (Deut. 14:2; Pss. 33:12; 135:4).

Therefore she is to praise Him (Is. 43:21). God revealed His nature, perfections, and love through the way He treated His chosen people Israel (Ex. 9:16; 32:9–14; Ps. 106:8, 47; Is. 43:25; 48:9–11; 63:12–14; Ezek. 36:21–24).

Certain individuals and tribes within Israel were elected to do special things in God's plan (Num. 16:5; Deut. 18:1–5; 1 Sam. 10:24; 2 Sam. 6:21; 2 Chr. 6:6; Ps. 78:68). It's important to note at this point that just because Israel was God's chosen people, no individual Israelite automatically had a personal relationship with God (Rom. 9:8). They could only be saved through faith in God's provision for their sins. Nevertheless, God showed His marvelous grace to the world through His dealings with His chosen people Israel (Gen. 12:3).

In the New Testament we see that God elected Christ to save the world from sin. The Son is God's "chosen One" in whom God the Father delights (Is. 42:1). At the Transfiguration God the Father said, "This is my Son, whom I have chosen; listen to him" (Luke 9:35). Though rejected by men,

He was chosen by God the Father to be "the living Stone" and "a chosen and precious cornerstone" (1 Pet. 2:4, 6; see also 1:20), that is, the foundation of the church and of our faith.

Not only did God elect Israel and the Lord Jesus; He also elected those who should be saved. This is the controversial aspect of election in the Bible. Arminian theologians believe a strong definition of election destroys human will. God's choices, however precede creation and time. They lay out the playing field on which we live and make our free moral choices. Our choices made inside of time end up serving His choices made outside of time in ways we cannot comprehend.

God's election to salvation is an unconditional act of His sovereign grace. In eternity past God chose some individuals to salvation, as indicated in Ephesians 1:4 ("before the creation of the world"), 2 Thessalonians 2:13 ("from the beginning"), and 2 Timothy 1:9 ("before the beginning of time"). Election and predestination are two sides of the same coin. Election describes the act of God's choice. Predestination concerns the benefits that result for the chosen one (Eph. 1:4–5, 11). Election is a gracious act of God since no one merits salvation (Rom. 11:5; Eph. 1:7; 2:8–9). God chose to give new birth to those who believe in Him (James 1:18). Church-age believers, God's elect (2 Tim. 2:10; Titus 1:1; 1 Pet. 1:1), are His "chosen people" (1 Pet. 2:9).

He expects us to lead Christ-honoring lives (Col. 3:12) and to bear spiritual fruit (John 15:16).

In Matthew 24:22, 24, and 31 the "elect" refers to those who will be saved during the Tribulation. This represents a special usage of the word, because the elect of the church age will already have been raptured before the Tribulation.

God's election is different from the philosophical attitude called fatalism. Fatalism is the belief that events are fixed without any intelligent end or motivation. Election is part of the purposeful warp and woof of the very fabric of God's creation.

It is also important to distinguish between the omniscience of God and His foreknowledge. Omniscience is a passive characteristic. God is aware of everything that is or possibly could be. Foreknowledge is an active characteristic. He knows how His decreed purposes will work themselves out inside history.

The death of Christ was predetermined by God. It too was woven into the fabric of creation. The wicked men who crucified Him did what they willfully chose to do (Acts 2:23; 4:28). Free human choice accomplished an end result that was absolutely certain. Similarly, God has elected some to salvation and not elected others in accord with His purpose. But individuals must believe in order to be saved. Luke described the ministry of Paul and

Barnabas this way: "All who were appointed [by God] for eternal life believed" (13:48).

Interestingly, Peter exhorts us to make our election "sure" (2 Pet. 1:10). In the preceding verses (1:5–7), Peter described how our faith should express itself in a life "that will keep you from being ineffective and unproductive in your knowledge of the Lord Jesus Christ" (1:8). His point is that it is possible to slip into a false sense of security and think one is a believer when one has never trusted in Christ.

The Bible uses *election* in one other way. In both Testaments God chose some individuals for special ministries. Some of these were David (Ps. 78:70), the twelve apostles (Luke 6:13; John 6:70; Acts 1:2), Stephen (6:9), and Paul (9:15; 22:14). The holy angels who did not follow Satan in his rebellion against God are called elect (1 Tim. 5:21). Their election had nothing to do with salvation from sin. Within God's creative design before He made the angels was the intent that most of them would serve Him eternally. **—JFW**

***

Recognize that being chosen by God is an act of grace, and respond to Him in gratitude and worship.

ENDURANCE

"Endurance" has two basic meanings—permanence and perseverance.

When you speak of God's endurance, you mean He will exist forever. When you speak of human endurance, you mean we will hang in there when the going gets tough.

Creation and the work of His hands may perish, but God will remain. His years never end (Ps. 102:25, 27). Also God's Word (19:9; 1 Pet. 1:23–25), His name (Pss. 72:17; 135:13), and His kingdom (Heb. 12:28) will endure forever. Since God endures, His qualities will also endure forever (for example, His love, Ps. 136:1–25).

Most biblical references to endurance refer to perseverance by people. At least eight Hebrew words express endurance in the Old Testament and seven Greek ones in the New. They all reflect various facets of the concept of holding up or being strong under pressure and adversity. Human endurance is closely related to perseverance. English Bible translators render the Greek word *hypomonē* by both "perseverance" and "endurance."

Faith is the basis of endurance. Moses endured the hostility of Pharaoh because he trusted in the Lord (Heb. 11:27, NASB). Hebrews 11 also reviews the lives of several other Old Testament saints and concludes they endured all sorts of difficulties because they drew strength from God's presence and promises. Job endured physical misery and miserable friends until the Lord vindicated his faith (James 5:10). Abraham did not waver in his faith. He endured decades of frustration because he believed the promises of God (Rom. 4:20).

Jesus Christ gives us the greatest example of endurance. The writer of Hebrews said Jesus endured the cross, bore its shame, overcame Satan's opposition, and fulfilled the Father's will (Heb. 12:2–4). When we follow His example, we find strength and courage to persevere. Peter taught that we can find strength to endure suffering by reflecting on the crucifixion of Christ (1 Pet. 2:20–21). In fact, Peter said it is commendable in God's eyes when we willingly endure suffering for doing good. Patient endurance of life's struggles is one of the marks of a true believer.

God expects us to endure because He graciously provides the resources we need to do it. He expects us to live confidently because we have access to Him through Christ (Heb. 10:19–25). The Holy Spirit empowers our daily lives and gives us wisdom for hard decisions (1 Cor. 2:4–5, 12–13). Testing and trials are means God uses to develop perseverance in our character (James 1:2–4).

When life is over, our ability to endure will offer proof God has been conforming us to the image of His Son (Rom. 8:29). We endure because our hope is in the Lord Jesus Christ and all He has provided through His death and resurrection (1 Thess. 1:3). Patience—a near cousin of endurance—is one of the results of the indwelling Holy Spirit (Gal. 5:22).

Peter said we are to make every effort to allow qualities such as endurance to increase in our lives (2 Pet. 1:5–8). Those who trust the Lord can avail themselves of the complete armor God has provided in order to endure Satan's attacks (Eph. 6:13). Paul prayed that his readers would understand the power of God, which can bring us great endurance and patience (Col. 1:10–11). Paul himself modeled endurance for Timothy (and for us) as the apostle faced persecution and all kinds of adversity while serving the Lord (2 Tim. 3:10–11). Our endurance proves to a watching world that the grace of God is at work in our lives.   **—WGJ**

* * *

Be encouraged through the strength the Lord gives you to remain steadfast in the midst of difficult circumstances and temptations.

ETERNITY

The word *eternity* is a rare term in the Bible, but the concept is common. *Eternity* occurs only three times in the New International Version (Ps. 93:2; Prov. 8:23; Eccl. 3:11). However, the words *eternal, everlasting,* and *forever* occur regularly. God Himself has always existed and always will. He has no beginning and no ending. Moses wrote, "Before the mountains were born or you brought forth the earth and the world, from everlasting to everlasting you are God" (Ps. 90:2; see also Neh. 9:6; Is. 40:28; Hab. 1:12).

The Bible applies the term "eternal" to something that had a beginning in time but then has no end. Three biblical covenants are everlasting: the Abrahamic Covenant (Gen. 17:7, 13, 19; 1 Chr. 16:17; Ps. 105:10), the Davidic Covenant (2 Sam. 23:5), and the New Covenant (Ezek. 37:26; Heb. 13:20). The loving support of God's arms is everlasting (Deut. 33:27). God has graciously given us eternal life in Christ Jesus (John 3:15–16, 36; 5:24; 10:28; Rom. 6:23; 1 John 5:11). All that will be ours in Christ in glory can be called an "eternal inheritance" (Heb. 9:15).

The New Testament also applies the adjective "eternal" to damnation of the lost (Matt. 25:46; 2 Thess. 1:9). Some of the fallen angels are bound with everlasting chains (Jude 6). At the end of the Millennium, Satan will be "thrown into the lake of burning sulfur," where he "will be tormented day and night for ever and ever" (Rev. 20:10).

Because God is eternal, all of His characteristics are everlasting, including His love (Ps. 103:17; Jer. 31:3), righteousness (Ps. 119:40), kindness (Is. 54:8), power (Rom. 1:20), and purposes (Eph. 3:11). We look forward to an "eternal house in heaven" (2 Cor. 5:1), where we will enjoy "eternal glory" with Christ forever (2 Tim. 2:10). Meanwhile, in this life, God offers us His eternal joy (Is. 61:7) and His eternal encouragement (2 Thess. 2:17).   **—JFW**

***

Live each day with the realization that life in Christ does not end at death.

EVANGELISM

God started thinking about redeeming lost people before He created anything (1 Pet. 1:19–20). He will be thinking about redeeming lost people right up to the final judgment of those who reject His Son (Rev. 20:11–15). Getting the message of salvation to lost people is a high priority activity in God's eyes.

Evangelism is the term for spreading the Good News about salvation. The "good news" concerns the death and resurrection of Jesus, so evangelism is primarily a ministry of the church. Israelites were not commanded to evangelize other people. However, they were witnesses to the power and character of God (Is. 43:11–13).

During the time of Christ the message of salvation went out primarily to "the lost sheep of Israel" (Matt. 10:5–6). The message stressed the nearness of the kingdom (4:17; 10:7). A few Gentiles heard the gospel, but most evangelism targeted the Jews. After Christ rose from the dead, He commanded His apostles to go to all nations with the message of salvation (28:19–20; Luke 24:47). Jesus spent much of His time on earth preparing His disciples for this task.

We can't overstate the importance of evangelism. God loved the world and sent His Son to be the Savior. Those who do not believe in Christ are lost (John 3:16, 36). No one can be saved apart from the death and resurrection of the Lord Jesus (Acts 4:12). Someone has to tell unbelievers the gospel or they will not have the opportunity to receive Christ (Rom. 10:14–15). One reason the Lord has not returned is that He longs for many more to come to Him (2 Pet. 3:9).

Evangelism is the responsibility of everyone in the body of Christ. God expects everyone who has been reconciled to Him by the death of Christ to engage in "the ministry of reconciliation" (2 Cor. 5:18). We are ambassadors for Christ (5:20) and His witnesses (Acts 1:8). The gospel was so important to the apostle Paul that he felt compelled to proclaim it (1 Cor. 9:16). He considered himself a slave to everyone and he tried to win as many to Christ as possible (9:19–23).

The success of evangelism doesn't depend on the technique of the evangelist but on the power of the gospel (Rom. 1:16), the convicting ministry of the Holy Spirit (John 16:8), the authority and clarity of the Bible (2 Tim. 3:16; Heb. 4:12), and the prayers of God's people (Rom. 10:1). God does give the spiritual gift of evangelism to some (Eph. 4:11), but this gift is not neces-

sary for you to lead someone to Christ. Paul challenged Timothy to "do the work of an evangelist" (2 Tim. 4:5). All of us should accept that same challenge. Evangelism occurs through the way we live as well as by the words we say (1 Pet. 3:1–2, 4).

The necessary content for our evangelistic message is clear and uncomplicated. Paul described the essential gospel content to the Corinthians. It concerned Christ's death for sins and His subsequent burial and resurrection (1 Cor. 15:3–4). The death of Christ paid for the sins of the world. His burial emphasized His death, and His resurrection certified His conquest of sin and death. On the basis of their faith in Christ's sacrifice for sins, the Father delights to impart eternal life to sinners (Titus 3:5–7).

Paul declared that whoever trusts in Christ becomes a new creation (2 Cor. 5:17). Salvation is a gift from God apart from any human effort or work. It is received by faith (Acts 16:31; Rom. 10:9–10; Eph. 2:8–9). Anyone can learn to say the words of the gospel message, but the Holy Sprit must enlighten our hearts before we can grasp the full extent of our need and Christ's provision for it (John 16:8–11; Rom. 8:9; 1 Cor. 2:14). Effective evangelism always involves more than a clear and accurate summary of the facts of the gospel. The power of God rather than the eloquence or persuasiveness of the evangelist saves lost men and women (2:4).

The Book of Acts reports the early evangelistic activity of the apostles and the church. The details of the conversion experiences in Acts vary, but a pattern emerges. The convicting work of the Holy Spirit always preceded salvation. God used different means to convict people, but no one came to Christ who was not drawn by the Spirit. Faith in Christ was always the means of true conversion. Faith included repentance, though it was not considered a separate step or condition of salvation (Acts 20:21). Baptism followed faith in Christ, but was not necessary for salvation (1 Cor. 1:17; Eph. 2:8). Paul treated his own conversion experience as an example others could follow in coming to Christ (1 Tim. 1:15–16).

Of course, not everyone who hears the gospel responds by trusting Christ. This is illustrated by the first three soils in Jesus' parable of the sower (Matt. 13:3–7, 18–22) and by the fact that many people who heard Paul preach the gospel opposed him and his message.

Once we receive Christ as our Savior, God expects us to grow in our spiritual life. He expects us to join other believers for fellowship and the study of the apostles' teaching (Acts 2:42). The Epistles were written to assist our growth as we walk with the Lord (Titus 3:14; 2 Pet. 1:5–9). One of the evidences of our salvation is our desire to tell others about Christ (1 Pet. 1:4–10). Because of this, evangelism has always been a high priority in the church.

—**WGJ**

***

Ask the Lord to give you a burden for souls who are lost, and plan to witness for Christ when opportunities arise.

Ff

FAITH

Millions of people experience fellowship daily with a God they've never seen. Faith makes possible such encounters with the divine. Popular culture thinks of faith as the spiritual capacity inside people that helps them decide what their God is like. Christian faith is based on objective information about God in the Bible. We don't create God in our image. It was the other way around. He made us in His image and reveals Himself to us in His inerrant Word.

People have displayed heroic faith in God ever since creation (Heb. 11). The faith of Abel, Enoch, and Noah shows that salvation in Old Testament times came through faith in God and that without faith it was impossible to please Him (11:4–7). Abraham stands out as the supreme model of faith in the Old Testament. He left his homeland and his extended family to follow the leading of God that unfolded one step at a time. Genesis 15:6 states that he "believed in the LORD." God declared Abraham righteous when he believed. New Testament writers treated his faith in the Lord as an example for us when they explained the need to believe in Christ for salvation and justification (Rom. 4:18–25; Gal. 3:6; James 2:23).

Theologians differ about what Old Testament saints believed in. The Reformed view is that the object of faith was always Jesus Christ and His sacrificial death. The dispensational view is that God Himself was the object of faith. Old Testament believers trusted in God who had created them and revealed Himself to them in various ways. Before the Law was written, God often revealed Himself directly to people (Gen. 3:9; 4:6; 6:13). To Abraham He made Himself known in a vision (15:1; 17:3) and to Jacob in a dream (28:12–15). In every situation those who trusted the Lord knew who He was, and they respected and revered Him.

The Mosaic Law was the rule of life for Israel, but salvation never came from keeping it. Salvation came then as now by faith. Israel gained two things through the Law: first, a greater realization of God's righteous character and, second, a deeper understanding of their own unrighteousness. The Law demanded complete obedience to every detail, but no one could do that. Cen-

turies later when the apostle Paul explained Israel's failure, he said lack of faith was what caused the nation to fall out of God's favor (Rom. 9:30–32).

God made the covenant of the Law with Israel to drive the nation to depend on Him. He appeared to them on Mount Sinai with thunder, lightning, smoke, and an earthquake to underscore how helpless they were to approach Him in their own resources (Ex. 19:3–9; Deut. 1:30–32). But Israel plunged into idolatry and unbelief and wandered in the wilderness for forty years (Heb. 3:12—4:2). Before the people entered the land, Moses reminded them that they had to love the Lord and obey Him. He warned them that this could happen only if their hearts were right and they held fast to the Lord in faith (Deut. 30:16–17, 20).

When we read the Book of Psalms, we sense right away the importance of faith in the personal life of a worshiping Israelite. David said he trusted in the unfailing love of the Lord (Pss. 13:5; 52:8). He lamented over those who put their trust in idols rather than in the Lord (31:6). Trust in the Lord gave meaning to David's life and brought him the desires of his heart (37:3–5). The Psalms also express faith through the expression "to seek refuge in." David used this expression in Psalm 5:11; 7:2; 25:20 and elsewhere to describe his trust in the Lord. Belief in God brought salvation to people who lived in Old Testament times. Those who trusted the Lord obeyed Him and witnessed to His greatness (Is. 43:10).

In the New Testament we learn that Jesus Christ is now the object of our faith. He came in the flesh to reveal the Father more fully than all previous partial revelations had (John 1:14–18; Heb. 1:1–3). Those who believe in Him become children of God (John 1:12). Whoever trusts in Christ receives eternal life (3:16, 36). Jesus stated that to believe in Him also means believing in His words (6:63, 68–69). Belief in Christ extends to belief in what He accomplished on the Cross and in His Resurrection (3:15–16; 11:25–26). The miracles He performed were for the specific purpose of bringing people to faith in Him (20:30–31).

Jesus taught that faith is the means by which we gain all God has for His children (Mark 9:23). It's important to separate the *means* of gaining salvation (faith) from the *basis* of salvation (Christ's death on the cross). Jesus said we don't need huge amounts of faith to be saved (11:22–24). We don't need more faith to deal with big problems than with little ones, because it isn't our faith that solves life's problems. The grace of God gets us through tough circumstances (Luke 17:1–6). The effectiveness of our faith is totally dependent on the credibility of the object we rely on. God's grace is fully reliable.

The Book of Acts documents the importance of faith in the spread of the gospel. Peter declared that the crippled man by the temple gate was healed because of his faith (Acts 3:16). This incident gave Peter courage to proclaim the message of salvation to the Jewish leaders in Jerusalem (4:5–12). Because of his preaching about the Resurrection of Christ, many believed and received salvation (4:4).

Multitudes put their faith in Christ because of the miracles performed by the apostles (5:12–14). A large number of Samaritans were converted through faith in Christ (8:12). Saul the persecutor met the risen Christ on the road to Damascus and believed in Him (Acts 9; Phil. 3:9). The Gentile centurion Cornelius and his household believed in Christ and received the Holy Spirit. Peter gladly testified to their faith (Acts 11:14, 17). The proconsul of Cyprus, Sergius Paulus, was saved by believing Paul's message about the Lord (13:12).

Faith in Christ became the theme of Paul's preaching (13:38–39). The Philippian jailer believed in the Lord Jesus Christ and was saved (16:30–31). Paul told the Ephesian elders that he had been faithful in preaching the message of faith in Christ to both Jews and Greeks (20:21).

The New Testament Epistles repeatedly affirm that salvation and justification come by grace through faith in Christ (Rom. 1:16; 3:28; 10:9–10; 1 Cor. 1:21–23; Eph. 2:8–9; Gal. 2:16). The Christian life is a life of faith from beginning to end (Rom. 1:17; Gal. 2:20; 3:11; Heb. 10:38). Our faith in Christ provides the foundation for our Christian growth (2 Pet. 1:5–8). Trust in the Lord sustains us through the trials of life (1 Pet. 1:5–7). These trials in turn develop spiritual maturity (James 1:2–4). Faith gives victory to overcome the world (1 John 5:4–5), and it helps guard against the attacks of Satan (Eph. 6:16; 1 Thess. 5:8). James echoed the teaching of Christ by stressing the importance of praying with faith (James 5:15; compare Matt. 21:21–22).

The Holy Spirit gives the spiritual gift of faith to some members of the church, so they can stimulate the whole body to greater reliance on the Lord (1 Cor. 12:9). All believers are to walk by faith, but the spiritual gift of faith is a God-given capacity to attempt great things for God.

Several times in the New Testament the term *faith* is used to sum up the whole system of biblical truth we believe (1 Tim. 1:2; 3:13; 2 Tim. 4:7; Titus 1:13; Jude 3, 20). We often use *faith* in this way today, as in "the Christian faith." **—WGJ**

***

Trust in the unlimited power of God as you face every obstacle and challenge in life.

FAITHFULNESS

"Faithfulness" is a noun that can apply to both God and people. On the one hand, God is completely dependable and trustworthy. On the other hand, we all value dependability and trustworthiness in people we have to live and work with. God expects us to be faithful to Him and to the commandments of His Word. Faithfulness is one of the fruits of the Spirit (Gal. 5:22) because we aren't naturally faithful—either to other people or to God.

Christian faithfulness grows out of our faith in God. Human faithfulness is a learned character trait that reflects a person's moral strength. God's faithfulness is part of His infinite perfection. God is faithful to His promises and to us (1 Cor. 1:9; 10:13; 1 Thess. 5:24). Humans work at being faithful to others and to God (Matt. 24:45; 25:21, 23).

God shows His faithfulness in sustaining His creation, in providing redemption through Jesus Christ, and in keeping the various covenants He has made with humankind. God faithfully keeps all His promises to us as we trust in Him. Fulfilled prophecy demonstrates God's faithfulness to His Word. Moses called God the "faithful God" (Deut. 7:9; 32:4). The psalmist wrote that "the LORD is faithful to all his promises" (Ps. 145:13) and that He "remains faithful forever" (146:6), "through all generations" (100:5; 119:90). God's faithfulness to His own is like a protective shield (91:4). His faithfulness, Jeremiah wrote, is "great" (Lam. 3:23).

In the New Testament, Paul also stated that God "is faithful" (1 Cor. 1:9; 10:13; 2 Cor. 1:18) and will always "remain faithful" (2 Tim. 2:13). He is

F

faithful in protecting believers from Satan (2 Thess. 3:3) and in forgiving believers who confess their sins (1 John 1:9). Christ is the believers' faithful High Priest (Heb. 2:17; 3:6), and when He returns to earth He will bear the title "Faithful and True" (Rev. 19:11).

Human faithfulness refers to our reliability, truthfulness, and consistency. Can others count on us to do what we say we'll do? Can they count on us to tell the truth? Can they count on us to act and speak faithfully time after time? Apart from the work of the Holy Spirit in our lives, we tend to be self-centered. As He bears His fruit in our lives we become more faithful to others and the Lord (2 Chr. 19:9; Matt. 25:21, 23; 3 John 5). God expects us to be faithful as stewards of the resources He entrusts to us (1 Cor. 4:2). He prompts us to be faithful in prayer (Rom. 12:12).

One of the important New Testament Greek words is *pistis* ("faith"). The most basic meaning of that term is "faithfulness." It is related to the verb *pisteuō*, "to believe or trust in." This reminds us again that faith in God is basic to our own faithfulness. Our Christian life rests on the faithfulness of God and expresses itself as faithfulness to God and others.   **—JFW**

***

Be encouraged by the truth that God is totally dependable, and trust Him to help you meet every challenge in life triumphantly.

FALL, THE

The Fall of mankind refers to the moral and spiritual consequences of Adam and Eve's disobedience of God's command as reported in Genesis 3. Our first parents lost their innocence and perfection, and the entire human race came under the burden of their sin (Rom. 5:12).

Adam and Eve were created in innocence. They had no experience with sin, and they had no tendency to sin. Left to themselves, they would obey God gladly and continually. God gave them one simple command. They were not to eat of the tree of the knowledge of good and evil in the middle of the Garden of Eden.

A serpent indwelt by Satan tempted Eve to disobey God's command. Eve made the command stricter than it was by saying she must not touch the tree (Gen. 3:2–3). The serpent immediately replied, "You will not surely die" (3:4). Temptation likes to make God seem mean by implying He's stricter than He is, and then by questioning the goodness of such a mean God. Satan did this when he told Eve, "For God knows that when you eat of it your eyes will be opened, and you will be like God, knowing good and evil" (3:5).

What Satan said was partially true. Adam and Eve would increase their knowledge of good and evil, but they would not have the power to resist evil. In both of his statements Satan twisted the truth and misrepresented the situation.

Eve yielded to this temptation and ate some of the fruit. Adam, who apparently understood that it was wrong, also ate of it. First Timothy 2:14 indicates that Adam did this willfully. He was not deceived.

Catastrophe struck in Eden. Adam and Eve died spiritually. From then on they struggled with a sin nature. God judged all of creation on account of human sin. He "cursed" the ground (Gen. 3:17–19). He also cursed Satan and destined him for ultimate destruction. He condemned the serpent to crawl on the ground (3:14). Finally, God said there would be enmity between Satan and the woman and between his offspring and her offspring (3:15). "You will strike his heel," God said of Satan's centuries-later attempt to destroy Christ. "He [Christ] will crush your head," God added of Satan's doom insured by Christ's death on the Cross (3:15).

God predicted women would experience pain in childbearing and a power struggle with their husbands (3:16). Adam and all his offspring were condemned to a life of labor in an uncooperative world in order to have enough food to live (3:17–19).

God knew the Fall would occur, so He had planned the redemption of sinners, even before the foundation of the world. All of us who are Adam's descendants have inherited his act as the head of the race. Fortunately, Christ died as the Head of a new creation made up of those who trust Him as their redeemer from the effects of the Fall (Rom. 5:12–19; 1 Cor. 15:21–22, 45–49). Every person—except Christ—sins, because he or she is born in sin with a sin nature and is spiritually dead (Eph. 2:1).   —**JFW**

F

***

Acknowledge the effects of sin in the world but don't be defeated by sin, for Christ died to bring freedom from sin's bondage.

FAMILY

A family is the basic social unit made up of a husband and wife and any children they may have. "Family" may also mean an extended clan of related families led by a patriarch. The concept of family rises out of the creation account in the first chapters of Genesis.

After God created Adam, He found "no suitable helper" (2:20) for him anywhere in the rest of creation. As a result, God created Eve from one of Adam's ribs and brought her to Adam as his companion and helper (2:21–22). After Adam received and acknowledged her, God said, "For this reason a man will leave his father and mother and be united to his wife, and they will become one flesh" (2:24). After creating Adam and Eve, "God blessed them and said to them, 'Be fruitful and increase in number'" (Gen. 1:28).

Adam and Eve, as husband and wife, formed the nucleus of the first family. Children later became part of their family, starting with Cain (4:1). God intends for married partners to reproduce (1:28), but this is subject to His timing.

The basis of the family as created by God is a monogamous, loving relationship between a man and a woman. Lamech, the last of the line of Cain before the Flood, introduced polygamy into human behavior (4:19). Polygamy became widespread in the cultures of the ancient Near East, but God endorsed monogamy in the act of creation. The Bible clearly portrays the difficulties inherent in the structure of polygamous families.

God designed the monogamous marriage relationship to last through the lifetime of its partners. Only death separates a person from his physical flesh. Only death should separate a man and a woman from their marriage relationship, for they are "one flesh" (2:24). In the Law God made allowance for polygamy (Deut. 21:15–17) and divorce (24:1–4), but these conditions are not the ideal in marriage. The Lord Jesus endorsed lifelong monogamous marriage (Matt. 19:4–6) and explained that "Moses permitted you to divorce your wives because your hearts were hard. But it was not this way from the beginning" (19:8; see also 5:31–32).

It is important to note that God created Eve and brought her to Adam as a helper and companion (Gen. 2:18, 20–23), not as a possession or property. Eve, as well as Adam, was created "in the image of God" (1:27). Order is necessary in the family. The husband is the head of the home (1 Cor. 11:3) and the wife is submissive to him (Eph. 5:22–24; Col. 3:18; 1 Pet. 3:1–6). Conversely the husband is to "be considerate" of his wife, to "treat [her] with respect" (3:7), and to love her as his own body (Eph. 5:28, 33; Col. 3:18), even "as Christ loved the church and gave himself up for her" (Eph. 5:25). Harmony in the family prevails when such order is maintained.

The human family illustrates the relationship of God to His people throughout the Bible. In the Old Testament God is occasionally addressed as the Father of Israel (Ps. 89:26; Is. 63:16; 64:8; Jer. 3:4, 19; Mal. 2:10). God directed Hosea to bring his unfaithful wife Gomer back into his home (Hos. 1:2–3; 3:1–3) as a way of portraying His future restoration of unfaithful Israel. In the New Testament the title "Father" is frequently applied to God (Matt. 6:1, 4, 6, 8–9, 14–15, 18; John 20:17; Rom. 1:7; 2 Cor. 1:2–3; Eph. 5:20; James 3:9; 1 Pet. 1:2, 17; 1 John 3:1), The church is called "the family of believers" (Gal. 6:10) and "the family of God" (1 Pet. 4:17). Paul wrote, "I kneel before the Father, from whom his whole family in heaven and on earth derives its name" (Eph. 3:14–15). A harmonious Christian family can bear powerful witness to the love, joy, and peace that flows from knowing God the Father through faith in Jesus Christ our Savior.

—JAW

***

As you rejoice in the joy of knowing God as your Father, remember that you are only one child in an ever-growing family of God.

FASTING

Fasting was a common practice throughout biblical history that has become much less common today. The prophet Joel called the northern kingdom of Israel to repentance, exhorting them to return to the Lord with fasting (Joel 2:12) and to declare a holy fast (2:15). A tradition of fasting on certain days in the fourth, fifth, seventh, and tenth months developed during the Babylonian captivity (Zech. 8:19), although this was not commanded by the Lord. Certainly fasting was a frequent practice throughout Old Testament times, as numerous Scripture references indicate.

In the New Testament, Jesus fasted when He faced temptations from the devil in the wilderness (Matt. 4:1–2; Luke 4:1–2). Jesus didn't forbid fasting. In fact, He suggested there would be times in the future when it would be appropriate for the disciples to fast (Matt. 9:14–15; Luke 5:33–34). Saul (later Paul) fasted after his conversion experience on the road to Damascus (Acts 9:9). The church at Antioch fasted and prayed before they sent out Saul and Barnabas (Acts 13:2–3); and Paul and Barnabas fasted when they appointed elders for the churches in Lystra, Iconium, and Antioch (14:23). Fasting doesn't seem to have been a regular part of the early church life, because the New Testament Epistles teach nothing about it.

Fasting is abstinence from food and/ or drink for a period of time. Some contemporary fasting has only medicinal or dietary purposes. Fasting in the Bible can be a means of focusing one's attention on a spiritual task—prayer, decision-making, resisting temptation, etc. Pagan religions practiced fasting. In some biblical cases fasting was for evil purposes (1 Kin. 21:9–10). Some Jewish opponents of the early church vowed not to eat or drink until they had murdered Paul (Acts 23:12–15). Most fasting in the Bible is a response to a set of circumstances in which a person or group wants help from God. That's why fasting can be a companion discipline to prayer. Because the Bible simply reports fasting rather than teaching about it, it's difficult to develop a theology of fasting. All we can do is make observations about biblical examples.

The descriptions of fasting in the Bible are varied. People fasted on various occasions, such as in worship (Acts 13:2), times of calamities and approaching danger (2 Chr. 20:3; Ezra 8:21; Jon.

F

3:5–6), times of war (1 Sam. 7:6; 28:20), or when tragedy struck (31:13; 20:34; 2 Sam. 1:12). David fasted during the illness of his son (12:16), Moses fasted when he was devastated by the idolatrous actions of the people of Israel (Deut. 9:18, 25), and David fasted when wicked men spoke out against him (Ps. 109:24–25). The people of Israel fasted when they were seeking guidance in light of a difficult situation (Judg. 20:26), and Zechariah spoke of a future occasion when fasting would be associated with joy (Zech. 8:19).

People in the Bible fasted for various lengths of time. In Old Testament times it normally was from sunrise to sunset (Judg. 20:26; 1 Sam. 14:24). It could even be for a shorter period of time (Dan. 6:18). Other fasts lasted three days (Esth. 4:16; Acts 9:9), seven days (1 Sam. 1:13; 2 Sam. 12:16–18), and on one occasion three weeks (Dan. 10:1–2). Moses and Jesus each fasted for forty days (Ex. 34:28; Matt. 4:2). Duration didn't determine the genuineness of fasting.

Isaiah said that one's spiritual relationship to God forms the basis for fasting. Fasting does not necessarily bring a person closer to the Lord, nor does the act itself bring about a response from God (58:3–4). Fasting doesn't make a person humble, but it reveals how much humility exists in a person's heart. According to Isaiah, a fast from pure motives and a pure heart will lead to righteous actions. A proper fast results in consideration of others (58:3), peace instead of discord (58:4), efforts to help those in need (58:6), the sharing of abundance with others (58:7), and a tongue that is under control when it might otherwise be destructive (58:9).

Prayer and fasting are often mentioned together (Acts 13:3; 14:23). Fasting doesn't add to the impact of our prayers. God isn't impressed by fasting. Fasting focuses our attention on the issue we are concerned about. It's for our benefit as the pray-er. Fasting does not guarantee that our prayers will be answered (Ps. 35:13; Jer. 14:11–12). It might seem from Mark 9:29 in some Bible versions (for example, NKJV) that prayer *and* fasting are necessary to experience God's power in difficult situations. The New International Version and most other modern versions omit the word *fasting* in that verse because it isn't supported by the best Greek manuscript evidence. Even if the word was included in the original manuscript of the Gospel of Mark, Jesus' point would be that the apostles had stopped focusing on God as the source of any power or ability they possessed.

When done with a sincere heart, fasting has benefits. Meal times become times for meditation and reflection on the Lord and His Word. Personal discipline is strengthened through self-control. Fasting frees us from concentrating on ourselves and our needs. It can make us more aware that we do not live by bread alone. David seemed to indicate that fasting for his enemies who were ill helped him have a better understanding of them (Ps. 35:11–14). If this was true concerning enemies, then it certainly should give us more empathy for those around the world who have been deprived of food through no fault of their own.

Fasting can be easily abused. Fasting can lead to pride and presumption. Jesus told a parable to highlight this danger (Luke 18:9–12). Some people fast to try to manipulate God. At various times in church history, fasting was viewed as a means of achieving merit before God. An overemphasis on fasting inevitably leads to a devaluation of prayer, Bible study, and dependence on the Spirit. Paul wrote to Timothy that everything created by God was good, including food, and it should not be rejected if it is received with thanksgiving (1 Tim. 4:3–4). Fasting is an optional spiritual discipline that can help us focus on the Lord at times of special need.   **—WGJ**

***

Be willing to sacrifice time, money, and material privileges such as food to spend time in prayer and fellowship with the Lord.

FATHERHOOD

In the Old Testament, fathers had absolute authority over their children, as illustrated by Abraham's willingness to offer Isaac as a sacrifice. Later, however, the Mosaic Law prohibited human sacrifices. The Law also forbade fathers to force their daughters into prostitution (Lev. 19:29) or to sell their daughters as slaves to foreigners. Fathers chose whom their daughters married, but often the daughters expressed their opinion about the choice. Fathers could have rebellious children stoned (Deut. 21:18–21).

Fathers were the primary teachers of their children (4:9; 6:7; 31:13; Prov. 2:1–5; 3:1; 4:1, 10, 20; 5:1; 22:6), and fathers were to exercise discipline over them (13:24). Fathers influenced the lives of their grown, married sons, as illustrated by Terah's role in Abram's affairs (Gen. 11:31).

The relationship between a father and his child illustrates God's relationship to us as believers. Just as children obey their fathers (Eph. 6:1–2; Col. 3:20), so we should obey God, our heavenly Father. The Bible frequently speaks of God the Father's love for His children (Ps. 103:13). As a faithful Father, He disciplines us (Deut. 8:5; Prov. 3:12; Heb. 12:5–11) to encourage us to restore our fellowship with Him.

In one sense God is the Father of all creation, but in a special sense He is the Father only of those who are born again as His children through their trust in His Son. Because Israel is God's chosen people, He has a special

F

relationship to Israel as her Father (Is. 63:16; 64:8).

A unique aspect of God's Fatherhood is the relationship of God the Father to His Son, Jesus Christ. God is the "Father of our Lord Jesus Christ" (Rom. 15:6; 2 Cor. 1:3; Eph. 1:3; Col 1:3; 1 Pet. 1:3). Christ frequently called God His "Father" (John 5:18; 10:30, 38; 20:17). This Father-Son relationship does not contradict monotheism. While God is distinguished in three divine persons—Father, Son, and Holy Spirit—there is only one God (Deut. 6:4–5; Mark 12:29; Rom. 3:30). God is Father to the Son by nature and kind; He is Father to believers by redemption, regeneration, and adoption.

God guarantees us our status as His children and heirs by adoption (Rom. 8:14–15; Gal. 4:6). Those of us who trust in Christ as our Savior become children of God (John 1:12; Rom. 8:16; Eph. 5:1; 1 John 3:2). He lets us call Him our "heavenly Father" (Matt. 6:14, 26, 32; 15:13) and "the Father of us all" (Rom. 4:16; see also Eph. 4:6).   **—JFW**

***

Count all the benefits you as a believer can enjoy because God is your heavenly Father.

FEAR OF GOD

The normal sense of the word *fear* contains the idea of "dread" or "terror." As soon as the Fall occurred in the Garden of Eden, Adam and Eve found that sin caused them to dread God. Formerly they had delighted in every contact they had with Him "in the garden in the cool of the day" (Gen. 3:8). After they disobeyed God, "they hid from the Lord God" and Adam confessed, when confronted by God, "I was afraid" (3:10). Later, after their firstborn son Cain killed his younger brother Abel, Cain expressed terror when he told God, "Whoever finds me will kill me" (4:14).

Various Old Testament characters found themselves in terror when God displayed His power or holiness. The nation of Israel feared God when He descended on Mount Sinai to give Moses the Law. Moses wrote, "On the morning of the third day there was thunder and lightning, with a thick cloud over the mountain, and a very loud trumpet blast. Everyone in the camp trembled" (Ex. 19:16; 20:18). Even godly Isaiah cried out, when he received a vision of the Lord in the temple, " 'Woe to me! . . . I am ruined! For I am a man of unclean lips, and I live among a people of unclean lips, and my eyes have seen the King, the Lord Almighty' " (Is. 6:5).

Most believers in the Bible did not encounter God visibly. For them—as for us—the "fear of God" meant "awe" or "reverence" rather than dread or terror. This is evident in the use of the phrase "the fear of the Lord" in Psalms 19:9; 34:11; 111:10 and Proverbs 1:7;

8:13; 19:23; 22:4. In the New Testament the Son of God entered human flesh and taught us about God as our loving heavenly Father (Matt. 6:8, 32–33; Luke 12:30–31).

Our heavenly Father is still to be feared when sin stains our lives. The Epistle to the Hebrews reminds us, "It is a dreadful thing to fall into the hands of the living God" (Heb. 10:31). Today the tendency is to lose all fear of God by thinking of Him as a doting grandfather and forgetting that He is the eternal, infinite Creator to whom all are accountable. When Paul wanted to express the depths of human depravity apart from Christ, he quoted this line from Isaiah 59: "There is no fear of God before their eyes" (Rom. 3:18).

The God who loves us is awesome in majesty, might, and holiness. We are to reverently fear Him in all our ways. We should "walk in the fear of our God" (Neh. 5:9), remembering that "the fear of the LORD is the beginning of wisdom" (Ps. 111:10; Prov. 1:7; 9:10; see also Job 28:28). Fearing God results in serving Him (Deut. 6:13; Josh. 24:14; 1 Sam. 12:14; Ps. 2:11), trusting Him (Ps. 115:11), obeying Him (Eccl. 12:13), and worshiping Him (Rev. 14:7), Every believer should "know what it is to fear the Lord" (2 Cor. 5:11). —**JAW**

***

Address your heavenly Father,
the eternal, infinite Creator of all
things, in reverential awe.

FELLOWSHIP

The story of the Bible is a record of fellowship. The plurality within the Godhead suggests fellowship among the Father, Son, and Holy Spirit. God created humankind in His own image, and that included plurality of genders that resulted in the most intimate fellowship, that enjoyed in marriage (Gen. 2:24). The earliest scenes in the Book of Genesis depict God having fellowship with Adam. God enjoyed His creation and found it good.

The Old Testament provides many glimpses of God's fellowship with those He created. Because Enoch "walked with God" (5:22, 24) he did not die. The Lord appeared to Abram and established a relationship so close that he was called a friend of God (James 2:23). A dynamic fellowship existed between Moses and God. The Lord promised to go with Moses and revealed His glory to him (Ex. 33:18–23). Perhaps the epitome of fellowship in the Old Testament occurred between God and David, for David was a man after God's own heart (1 Sam. 13:14; see also Acts 13:22). David's psalms describe his side of this relationship. On one occasion David said the Lord confides in those who trust in Him (Ps. 25:14).

Jeremiah exemplified the kind of fellowship the prophets had with God. The Book of Jeremiah is filled with personal illustrations of God and Jeremiah communing with each other. In the

Old Testament even the average believing Israelite had fellowship with God through the prescribed rituals of the Levitical system (Lev. 7:11–21).

In the New Testament fellowship with God becomes more personal, and fellowship between believers bears witness to the world about the truth of the gospel. The incarnation of Christ brought God and man into closer contact than ever before. God rubbed elbows with everyday people, and those who believed in Jesus tagged along with God-made-flesh along the pathways of Judea, Samaria, and Galilee.

The death, resurrection, and ascension of Christ brought an even closer relationship with God for Christ's followers. The night before He was crucified Jesus began preparing His disciples for this new relationship (John 13—16). He knew they wouldn't understand it fully at that time, but later they would (13:7–14). This new relationship would be possible because the Father would send His Spirit to dwell in them. The Spirit had been *with* them up to then, but after Pentecost He would be *in* them (14:17). Jesus and the Father would come and make their home with those who would obey His words (14:23). Using the figure of the vine and the branches, Jesus described this close relationship in terms familiar to the disciples (15:4–10).

The amazing fellowship we enjoy with God through the Holy Spirit should bear fruit in our lives. It should give us a desire to love others (13:34), strengthen our prayer lives (14:13), and give us a peace that will sustain us even in our most difficult days (14:27).

The Bible's teaching about fellowship reaches its zenith in the epistles of Paul and John. Both of them used the word *koinōnia* to describe Christian fellowship. *Koinōnia* carries the meaning of "partnership." Paul told the Corinthians that God had called them into fellowship with His Son, Jesus Christ (1 Cor. 1:9). God had entered a partnership with them by graciously giving them gifts and making them promises. They in turn were to live in harmony with each other. There were to be no divisions in the body of Christ (1:10). In his second letter to the Corinthians Paul urged them to realize that their close association with Christ left no room for partnership with unbelievers (2 Cor. 6:14–16). The Lord's Supper gives us a strongly sensory way to sense our fellowship with the Lord. Eating the bread and drinking of the cup makes us partners in the body and blood of Christ (1 Cor. 10:16–17).

This wonderful fellowship is also expressed in other ways. Paul said we should share our material resources with others (Rom. 15:26–27; 2 Cor. 8:4; 9:13; Phil. 1:5; 4:15). We should share in each other's sufferings (2 Cor. 1:7; Phil. 1:7) and be like-minded, having the same attitude as Christ (2:1–2). This close fellowship is indispensable in living for Christ in a hostile world.

Paul himself wanted to know Christ in the most intimate and meaningful way. He set about understanding Christ's resurrection and experiencing the power related to it (3:10). The Resurrection became the source of Paul's daily strength and his hope for the future.

In the same verse Paul wrote that knowing Christ also meant partnering with Him in His sufferings. Paul willingly shared in Christ's humility and tried to copy Christ's obedience to the will of the Father. When we fellowship with Christ in humility and obedience to the Father, we too will find Christ's strength working through our weakness. Fellowship with Christ starts with the helplessness of suffering and ends with resurrection power.

The apostle John looked at "fellowship" as a summation of the believer's entire relationship with a holy God (1 John 1:3–7). If we want to get the most out of this relationship, we have to live in a way that reflects His holiness. We can't do this by ourselves. Christ removed the barrier of sin and speaks to the Father on our behalf. Thus, even when we do sin, our fellowship with God can be restored through confession and forgiveness (1:9). Like Paul, John stressed that walking in fellowship with God results in true partnership with others in the body of Christ. **—WGJ**

***

Enjoy the unique relationship that believers have in Christ, and encourage others to enjoy this privilege.

FIRSTFRUITS

"Firstfruits" is a biblical term referring to the first and best grain or fruit of a crop to ripen and be harvested. The Mosaic Law required Israelites to bring "the best of the firstfruits of [their] soil" to the tabernacle (Ex. 23:19). The firstfruits supported the priests who served at the tabernacle, and later at the temple. By bringing the firstfruits as an offering to the Lord, Israel acknowledged that the land and its produce were God's gift to them as His people. God also claimed the firstborn son of men and animals (13:2) in addition to the firstfruits of the land (22:29–30).

The offerings of the firstfruits included grain, fruit, honey, and wool, described as that which is "first ripe." Firstfruits also applied to the initial products of human labor, such as flour, oil, wine, dough, and bread (34:18, 22; Lev. 23:16–20). The manner in which the firstfruits were to be brought to the tabernacle or temple is described in Deuteronomy 26, but the Law did not stipulate how much to offer. As a result, the priests had plenty during times of revival and reform (for example, in Hezekiah's reign, 2 Chr. 31:5) and lived in poverty during times of spiritual indifference.

After the Captivity the exiles who returned to Jerusalem covenanted to be faithful in bringing the firstfruits to the temple (Neh. 10:37). However, while Nehemiah was away for a lengthy time, the people stopped the practice. When he returned he rebuked them sternly for neglecting to support the priests and Levites (13:10–12). The Book of Proverbs promised prosperity to those who honored the Lord with their firstfruits (Prov. 3:9).

Israel celebrated the Feast of Firstfruits (Lev. 23:9–14) at the beginning of the barley harvest in the spring. The first sheaf of the new crop was waved before the Lord. This act acknowledged two things: first, the harvest had come because of God's blessing and, second, it all belonged to Him. The "wave sheaf" also anticipated the abundant harvest to follow. On the fiftieth day after the Feast of Firstfruits, the Feast of Pentecost ("Pentecost" means "fiftieth") in early summer celebrated the completion of the wheat harvest. At this time the firstfruits of the wheat were presented to the Lord (Ex. 34:22; see also 23:16; Lev. 23:15–21).

The Scripture also uses the term *firstfruits* in metaphorical or figurative ways. Jeremiah called the nation of Israel "the firstfruits of [God's] harvest" (Jer. 2:3), that is, a nation holy to the Lord. The New Testament attaches the term "firstfruits" to the resurrected Christ. "But Christ has indeed been raised from the dead, the firstfruits of those who have fallen asleep" (1 Cor. 15:20). When Christ appeared in heaven in His glorified human body, He represented the vast harvest of all of us who will follow Him in our resurrection bodies (Phil. 3:20–21). As the "firstfruits," Christ's resurrection constitutes both a pledge of more to come and a sample of the rest of the "harvest."

We who believe in Jesus are described as "a kind of firstfruits" (James 1:18), that is, we are a guarantee of many more who will come to Christ for salvation. Also we possess "the firstfruits of the Spirit" (Rom. 8:23), which means we have a foretaste of what awaits us in heaven. In addition, the New Testament called the first converts in a given locality spiritual firstfruits (Rom. 16:5; 1 Cor. 16:15).

The term *firstfruits* describes the saved remnant in Israel in the present age (Rom. 11:16), as well as the 144,000 in the future Tribulation period (Rev. 14:4). The latter are seen as the firstfruits of the coming kingdom. In that millennial age, according to Ezekiel's vision and prophecy, the priests once again will receive the literal firstfruits of agricultural crops (Ezek. 44:30).

—DKC

***

Rejoice that God has guaranteed the resurrection of all saints because Christ is the "firstfruits of those who have fallen asleep" (1 Cor. 15:20).

FLESH

In its most basic sense, *flesh* refers to the meat (not in the sense of food) on the bones of an animal or a person. The word quickly takes on a variety of figurative meanings of natural and theological importance. In the Old Testament "the flesh" often refers to the human race (for example, Gen. 6:12, "people"). Other times it stands for the entire physical body of an animal or a person. Still other times it refers to the mortal nature of the human race, as when God said, "My Spirit will not contend with man forever, for he is mortal [literally, 'flesh']" (Gen. 6:3). "Flesh" also often points to the frailty of humanity (for example, 2 Chr. 32:8). It's important to note that "flesh" in the Old Testament does not convey the idea of a sin nature, as it so often does in the New Testament.

The New Testament word for "flesh" is *sarx*, which refers to the human race (John 17:2, "people"), the physical body (Acts 2:31; Gal. 2:20, "body"; 2 Cor. 12:7, "flesh"), or the sin nature (Col. 2:11, "sinful nature"; 1 Pet. 4:2, "evil human desires"). Sometimes *sarx* refers to individuals (Rom. 3:20, "no flesh will be justified," NKJV; Gal. 1:16, "man") or to the mortal aspect of human beings (2 Cor. 4:11). The New International Version uses a number of words and phrases to translate *sarx* in different contexts. Obviously the translation "sinful nature" is an interpretation, an attempt to get at the meaning of *sarx*

when it refers to our inner inclination to sin. Jesus of Nazareth was the only human being born into this world without an innate tendency to sin.

The New Testament regards the flesh as weak and unable to achieve holiness without God's help. The Holy Spirit indwells us at our new birth and begins the process of sanctification. The Spirit enables us, while still in our mortal flesh, to achieve a measure of holiness. Paul wrote, "Live by the Spirit, and you will not gratify the desires of the sinful nature ['flesh']" (Gal. 5:16). The sin nature is contrary to what the Holy Spirit desires in our lives (5:17). What the flesh wants is listed in 5:19–21. By contrast, the fruit the Spirit wants to bear in us consists of "love, joy, peace, patience, kindness, goodness, faithfulness, gentleness and self-control" (5:22–23). **—JFW**

* * *

Avoid the desires of the human nature that would hinder the work of the Holy Spirit in your life.

FOREKNOWLEDGE

The Scriptures uniformly assert that God knew from eternity past everything that would happen in creation (Job 28:23–24; 37:16; Pss. 44:21; 139:1–4; Is. 46:9–10; 48:2–3, 5; Jer. 1:5; 1 Cor. 2:10–11; 1 John 3:20). Nothing is hidden from Him. Foreknowledge is part of God's omniscience or total knowledge of everything, past, present, and future.

Foreknowledge also relates to God's omnipotence. Foreknowledge isn't passive awareness of what will happen. God's foreknowledge causes things to happen. He has the power to make happen what He wishes. In His omniscience God knows not only the course of events that will occur but all the combinations of events that won't occur.

Time is a dimension of the created universe. God is not limited by time. He stands outside it. His decree, His choices, and His foreknowledge not only occur outside of time, but they shape everything that happens inside of time. The difficulties and controversies relating to the interaction of divine foreknowledge and human free will result from our inability to imagine God's relationship to time.

Calvinists and Arminians disagree about what happens when a person is saved. Calvinists view God's foreknowledge and election as the starting point of salvation. Arminians view human choice to believe as the starting point. The Epistles teach that God's causative foreknowledge comes first. The scope of God's foreknowledge encompasses human will so people choose freely but always serve His ends. Consequently people always stand responsible for their sinful choices.

God must act first in salvation because every human being (except Jesus of Nazareth) is born spiritually dead and unable to comprehend the truth of God. God must perform a supernatural work before unbelievers can understand and receive the gospel. The Spirit of God must convict them of their guilt, of God's righteous standards, and of His judgment on sin (John 16:7–11).

It's hard to analyze what happens when a person believes in Christ because the divine and human initiatives are both involved. On the one hand, individuals by themselves cannot understand or come to God in faith. As Christ expressed it, "No one can come to me unless the Father who sent me draws him" (John 6:44). On the other hand, no one is saved contrary to his or her own will. In other words, God enables people to exercise faith in Him (John 6:37, 44–45, 65; Rom. 8:5–9; Phil. 1:29; 2 Pet. 1:1).

Ephesians 2:8–9 reads, "For it is by grace you have been saved, through faith—and this not from yourselves, it is the gift of God—not by works, so that no one can boast." Some readers assume that the word "this" refers to "faith." They assume "faith" is God's gift. However, the Greek term for "faith" is a feminine noun and the relative pronoun "this" is neuter. "This" refers to the whole work of salvation. It's all a gift of God.

Theologians debate how human choice and divine influence interact at the time a person believes in Christ. Foreknowledge says God actively knows what each person will do in advance as human and divine influences interact. Because of His foreknowledge, God is absolutely certain about the salvation of a person who believes in Christ. But God doesn't take credit for anyone's salvation. He points to the free choice of each believer. Though God enables and influences a person to believe, belief in Christ is an act of the human will.

God's foreknowledge of who will believe must not be viewed as coercion of faith. Certainty is not the same as coercion. Some things God accomplishes through natural laws and other things through human choices. All these events are absolutely certain because God knows completely what will flow out of every human choice.

God's foreknowledge makes all things absolutely certain from eternity past. However, this does not make God responsible for the sin of humankind. God created a world in which people are responsible moral agents. We make real choices and live with their consequences for good or ill. The entire fabric woven of human choices and consequences achieves every aspect of God's total plan without diminishing human freedom and responsibility.

First Peter 1:2 indicates that foreknowledge preceded election, that is, that God knew who would be saved and so He chose them. The Greek noun rendered "foreknowledge" means more than advance awareness of unfolding events, though it includes it.

It means "to have regard for, to have loving concern for, to choose." Thus those whom God chose in love, He elected (1 Pet. 1:2) and predestined (Rom. 8:29). **—JFW**

***

Realize that God's knowledge and planning do not absolve personal responsibility.

F

FORGIVENESS

The joyous drama of Adam and Eve in the early chapters of Genesis ended tragically when the first couple listened to the serpent and disobeyed God. The arrival of sin brought with it a desperate need for forgiveness. Forgiveness is God's act of grace whereby He pardons sinners, so they no longer face eternal condemnation for sin.

The Mosaic Law required specific rituals for asking God's forgiveness. Both individuals and the entire Israelite community had to bring the correct sacrifice for sin (Lev. 4:20, 26, 31, 35). The Hebrew verb used in these verses means "to forgive" or "to pardon," and was used only in relation to God's forgiveness. Solomon used this term in his prayer to God when the temple was dedicated (2 Chr. 6:21, 25, 27, 30, 39).

King David knew very well the need and the cost of forgiveness. He wrote Psalm 32 after his sin with Bathsheba. In its first two verses David used three different Hebrew words to explain what

God had done with his sin. The first means "to lift or carry away." The second means "to cover." The last one is used negatively in the sense that God will not "count or impute" David's sin to him. In a later psalm David rejoiced that God removed his sins as far as the east is from the west (103:12).

The prophets always followed their warnings about judgment with promises of God's forgiveness if the nation Israel would repent. Forgiveness formed the silver lining of the dark cloud of judgment (Is. 1:18). Jeremiah looked forward to a time when God would make the New Covenant with His people. He promised that when the Messiah came to reign, the Lord would pardon Israel's sins and restore their land (Jer. 33:6–8). Micah closed his book with a series of promises that one day God would pardon sin, forgive transgression, tread sins underfoot, and hurl iniquities into the depths of the sea (Mic. 7:18–20).

Forgiveness of sins in the Old Testament was real and effective for those who lived by faith, but it was temporary. Ultimately only the finished work of Christ at Calvary could forgive sins permanently. Paul proclaimed this in Romans 3:24–26. The writer of Hebrews concurred, declaring that Christ is the supreme Sacrifice for sins and the only Sacrifice bringing eternal redemption (Heb. 9:11–14; 10:3–11).

The New Testament uses two Greek words to express forgiveness: *aphiēmi,* "to send away" or "to let go," and *charizomai,* "to show favor" or "to pardon or forgive." *Aphiēmi* occurs more often. It's the general word for releasing from obligation or penalty. *Charizomai* is the more theological term because it contains the notion that grace (*charis*) is involved in forgiveness. Paul used it in 2 Corinthians 2:7, 10; Ephesians 4:32; Colossians 2:13; and 3:13.

John the Baptist introduced Jesus to his followers as the sacrificial Lamb who would take away the sin of the world (John 1:29). The Gospels say nothing more about the death of Jesus and forgiveness until the night before the Crucifixion. In the Upper Room Jesus instituted the Lord's Supper. When He explained the significance of the cup, He said His blood would be poured out for the forgiveness of sins (Matt. 26:28). Peter emphasized in his preaching that the death of Jesus provides forgiveness (Acts 10:43; 13:38). Paul's epistles stress this theme too (Rom. 3:25; Eph. 1:7; Col. 1:14).

In the Gospels Jesus gladly forgave the sins of all who believed in Him, regardless of their station in life. He healed a helpless paralytic (Matt. 9:5–8; Mark 2:10–12). A woman who had lived in sin received forgiveness because of her faith (Luke 7:48–50). Jesus told the heartwarming parable of the Prodigal Son to demonstrate the Father's love for and eagerness to forgive the lost (15:11–32).

The New Testament teaches that we have a responsibility to forgive one another because Christ forgave us. Two of Jesus' seven last sayings related to forgiveness (Luke 23:34, 43). He expects us to forgive our enemies as well as our brothers and sisters in Christ.

Jesus taught the importance of forgiveness from the beginning of His ministry. This is a major emphasis in the Sermon on the Mount (Matt. 6:14). The debt God has forgiven us is much greater than what anyone could owe us (18:15–17). Forgiveness should be the hallmark of the Christian. It should have no limit and should be genuine, not superficial (18:21–35).

The Epistles reinforce the teachings of Jesus on forgiveness. Spirit-controlled believers should reflect the kindness and compassion of the Lord and forgive each other just as God has forgiven them (Eph. 4:32). We are to clothe ourselves with the graciousness of Christ and forgive whatever grievance we may have against someone else (Col. 3:13).

The apostle John wrote that the Savior paid for all the sins of the world by His death on the Cross (1 John 2:1–2). God's children should walk in fellowship with the One who is absolutely holy and with others in the family of God (1:7). Daily sins disrupt our fellowship, but forgiveness is promised when we confess them, that is, when we view our sins the same way God looks at them (1:9). This regular cleansing lets us walk in the light and be in harmony with other believers. **—WGJ**

***

Each believer should have the same attitude of forgiving others that Christ has manifested.

FREEDOM

Freedom is liberty to live without restriction or coercion. Freedom often implies release from some form of oppression. In the Bible, oppression often took the form of slavery or captivity. Oppression is a somber theme weaving through the pages of the Bible.

The fear of death has held people captive since the fall of Adam and Eve (Heb. 2:14–15). Our adversary, the devil, has a viselike grip on unbelievers, a hold that makes them slaves to do his will (2 Tim. 2:26). Sin holds people captive. Even Christians struggle to get free from sin's power (Rom. 6:14; Gal. 4:4–7). The Law of Moses put people under bondage because they were powerless to fulfill its demands (Rom. 7:6). Creation, too, longs for the day when it will be free from its slavery to corruption (8:21). False teachers offer unsuspecting people a fraudulent freedom that drags them deeper into bondage (2 Pet. 2:17–19). The Maker of heaven and earth, who experiences freedom as an integral part of His nature (Ps. 146:5–9), offers lasting liberty to our downtrodden and desperate world.

The high point of redemption history

in the Old Testament was the exodus of Israel from Egypt. God delivered the Israelite slaves from bondage to their ruthless Egyptian masters (Ex. 6:6–8). The Exodus provided the greatest demonstrations of God's power between the creation of the universe and the resurrection of Christ. Subsequently Israel was often subject to bondage to surrounding nations as judgment for their sins. In reviewing the history of Israel, the psalmist reminded the people of the many times God had freed them when they were held captive (Ps. 106:43).

Because they had been enslaved in Egypt, Israel cherished individual freedom. The Law liberated slaves after six years of service and sent them away with gracious provisions (Lev. 25:39–42; Deut. 15:12–15). Every fifty years was to be a jubilee, when slaves were freed and debts forgiven throughout the land (Lev. 25:10). Isaiah promised Israel that the Messiah would bring them freedom (Is. 42:7; 61:1). God promised freedom for the captives on the day of salvation (49:8–9). Jerusalem, Isaiah said, will one day throw off the chains that enslave her (52:2). Because of God's desire to give the Israelites freedom, He expected them to pursue justice and free those bound in the chains of oppression (58:6–7).

The Gospels indicate that God sent His Son to earth at a time when the Jewish people longed for freedom from what they viewed as Roman tyranny (Luke 1:68–71). In one of His first public messages Jesus said He had come to preach the Good News to the poor and to proclaim freedom for the oppressed (Luke 4:16–19; Is. 61:1–2). Later He claimed that true spiritual freedom could come only from Him (John 8:31–36). All who believe in Jesus are delivered from death and given eternal life (5:24).

Much of the New Testament teaching about freedom comes from the writings of the apostle Paul. In Galatians, his very first letter, Paul repeatedly stressed freedom from the Mosaic Law (Gal. 5:1). Paul valued the eternal moral principles on which the Law was established. They had been valid even before the Law was given. Freedom from the Law meant freedom from law-keeping as the path to righteousness and justification (2:16; 3:2–3). He taught that our freedom in Christ makes us free to serve others (5:13). Peter echoed this idea when he instructed believers to use their freedom to live as servants of the Lord (1 Pet. 2:16).

Paul's Epistle to the Romans also highlights freedom. Paul taught that Christ died so we don't have to be slaves of sin (Rom. 6:6–7). We have been freed from sin so we can serve righteousness and God (6:18, 22). Through Christ we have complete freedom from the control of sin and death (8:1).

Paul taught the Corinthians that freedom in Christ does not mean the absence of all restraint. When we are free in Christ, we are controlled by concern for others (1 Cor. 10:23–24). In Paul's case, he wanted to reach Jews and Gentiles for Christ so badly that he made himself a slave to everyone (9:19). Freedom in Christ produces in us humility, love, patience, and a desire to magnify Christ above everything else.   **—WGJ**

***

Enjoy the freedom you have in Christ, and never allow your freedom to be a stumbling block to your friends.

FRUIT

In the Old Testament "fruit" has three primary meanings. First, it can describe the product or yield of the ground. Examples of this usage are in Genesis 4:3; Leviticus 25:19; Psalm 72:16; and Jeremiah 7:20. Second, "fruit" can refer to children or other descendants, as in Genesis 30:2; 49:22; Deuteronomy 7:13; 2 Kings 19:30; Psalm 21:10, 132:11; and Micah 6:7. Third, "fruit" can denote the final outcome of one's actions or character. Proverbs 1:31 uses "fruit" in this figurative way: "They will eat the fruit of their ways and be filled with the fruit of their schemes." See also Isaiah 3:10; Jeremiah 17:10; and Micah 7:13 (NKJV).

One of the best examples of the figurative use of the concept of fruitbearing occurs in the song of the vineyard (Is. 5:1–7). The vineyard in this passage represents Israel (see also Ps. 80:9–16 and Jer. 12:10). God gave Israel every possible advantage in a fertile land and He expected to harvest the good fruit of justice and righteousness. Instead He ended up with the bad fruit of bloodshed and cries of distress. Consequently, God tore down His protective hedge, and invaders devastated Israel.

The New Testament employs the Greek word for "fruit" in much the same three ways as the Old Testament uses the Hebrew word. "Fruit" can mean agricultural produce (Matt. 21:19; 26:29; Luke 22:18), children or other descendants (Luke 1:42; Acts 2:30), or the way a person's character expresses itself in actions. John the Baptist gave us an example of this third usage when He told the Pharisees and Sadducees to "produce fruit in keeping with repentance" (Matt. 3:8; Luke 3:8).

The apostles John and Paul bring a different perspective to the concept of fruitfulness. They look at fruitfulness, not as the outworking of one's character, but as the result of God indwelling believers. In John 15 Jesus identified Himself as the "true vine" and His disciples as branches intimately connected to Him. They would bear fruit to the extent that they let His life flow through them. Jesus concluded, "If a man remains in me and

F

I in him, he will bear much fruit" (John 15:5).

Jesus' use of the vine image is important. In the Old Testament, Israel had been the vine God planted (Ps. 80:8; Jer. 2:21). As noted above in the discussion of Isaiah 5:1–7, God tended His vineyard and nurtured it, but it produced rotten fruit. Jesus presented Himself as a new avenue to spiritual life and fruitfulness.

We find the apostle Paul's key passage about fruit-bearing in Galatians 5:16–26. Paul starkly contrasted the "bad fruit" (the fruit of our sinful human nature) with the "good fruit" (the fruit the Holy Spirit produces in and through us). The "bad fruit" of our sinful nature consists of "sexual immorality, impurity and debauchery; idolatry and witchcraft; hatred, discord, jealousy, fits of rage, selfish ambition, dissension, factions and envy; drunkenness, orgies, and the like" (Gal. 5:19–21). Anyone who lives continually on such a level of moral corruption demonstrates that he or she is not a child of God.

We should not produce such evil fruit. The Holy Spirit lives in us to bear His fruit through us. The "fruit of the Spirit" consists of "love, joy, peace, patience, kindness, goodness, faithfulness, gentleness and self-control" (5:22–23). The word *fruit* here is singular. These qualities are a package deal. A believer under the control of the Spirit should bear them all to some extent. Ultimately the fruit pf the Spirit is simply the life of Christ lived out in a Christian. John 15 and Galatians 5 speak of Christian fruitfulness from two different angles.

The Old and New Testaments speak with a united voice in the sense that that God expects His children to be fruitful. In this dispensation we enjoy the blessing of the permanent indwelling of the Holy Spirit, who enables us to produce qualities that are pleasing to God. **—DKC**

***

Pray that you may learn how to depend on the Holy Spirit so that He may produce good fruit in your life.

Gg

GENTILES

The general sense of the word *Gentiles* is that of "nations" as groups of ethnically related people. This word translates the Hebrew *gôyîm* and the Greek *ethnoi*.

The whole world could be called "Gentile" until the events of Genesis 12. All ethnic groups stood on an equal footing in the eyes of God. Then God selected Abraham and his descendants to stand in a unique covenant relationship with Him. God's chosen people, descending from Abraham, contrasted with all other nations, the Gentiles.

God promised Abraham, "I will make you into a great nation" (12:2). By this God distinguished Abraham's descendants from all other nationalities. In time the nation Israel organized into twelve divisions stemming from the twelve sons of Abraham's grandson Jacob.

Abraham had many other descendants besides the people of Israel. God had promised that Abraham would be "the father of many nations" (17:4). For example, his son Ishmael and his grandson Esau both sired great nations. Ethnically these people were Semites, but because they were not in the covenant line they were regarded as Gentiles.

Old Testament promises and prophecies about Israel must be distinguished from prophecies relating to other "peoples on earth" (12:3). God dealt with Israel according to the terms of the Abrahamic, Palestinian, Mosaic, and Davidic Covenants. He dealt with the Gentiles according to His common grace, His righteousness, and His justice.

In the Old Testament a few Gentiles stand as examples of outstanding faith in the God of Israel. They include Rahab (Josh. 2:1, 11), Ruth (Ruth 1:16; 2:12), the widow of Zarephath (1 Kin. 17:24), Naaman (2 Kin. 5:15), and Neb-

uchadnezzar (Dan. 4:37). But most Gentiles in the Bible worshiped idols.

In the Gospels, Jesus had significant but limited ministry contacts with Gentiles, such as a Syro-Phoenician woman (Mark 7:25–30), a Roman centurion (Luke 7:1–10) and some Greeks (John 12:20–22). However, He mainly focused His teaching and healing on the Jewish people. He commanded His disciples to go only to the people of Israel (Matt. 10:6). This changed after Jesus' resurrection when He commissioned the disciples to go to the world (Mark 16:15).

Soon after the Day of Pentecost the Ethiopian official and Cornelius, both Gentiles (Acts 8:26–40; 10:1–48), were saved. With some reluctance Jewish believers realized that "God has granted even the Gentiles repentance unto life" (11:18). Paul emerged as the apostle to the Gentiles. The churches he established usually started with a Jewish nucleus and expanded into the general Gentile population. It was in a predominantly Gentile church at Syrian Antioch that "the disciples were first called Christians" (12:26).　　　**—JFW**

***

Rejoice that God's grace is available to the Gentiles as well as to Israel.

GLORY

The glory of God is the visible display of His majesty and splendor. God's glory often expressed itself in the Bible as brilliant light (Ezek. 1:4, 27–28; Matt. 17:2; 1 Tim. 6:16; Rev. 1:12–16; 4:2–6). *Kābôd,* the Hebrew word for "glory," is related to a verb that means "to be heavy or weighty." This noun is sometimes used of someone's "weighty" reputation or honored status.

God's majesty and splendor appear in the created world ("the heavens declare the glory of God," Ps. 19:1) and in humankind who bear His image (God "crowned him [mankind] with glory and honor," 8:5). Because God resides in heaven, "glory" is sometimes used as a synonym for heaven's splendor (for example, Heb. 2:10).

Moses wanted to see God's glory, but God said he could not see His face and live (Ex. 33:18, 20). The Exodus brought glory to God (14:4), by revealing His power and sovereign control of the exalted Egyptian empire. So Moses referred to God as "awesome in glory" (15:11). The glory of the Lord in the form of a cloud filled the tabernacle (40:34) and the temple (2 Chr. 5:14; 7:1) when each was dedicated. Moses could not enter the tabernacle (Ex. 40:35), nor could the priests enter the temple (2 Chr. 7:2) because of these manifestations of God's glory.

David spoke of seeing God's power and glory (Ps. 63:2), and he wrote that kings should sing to the Lord because "the glory of the Lord is great" (138:5). An anonymous psalmist stated, "The Lord is exalted over all the nations,

his glory above the heavens" (113:4). In Isaiah's vision of the Lord angelic beings known as seraphs exclaimed, "Holy, holy, holy is the Lord Almighty. The whole earth is full of his glory" (Is. 6:3). God's presence, Jude wrote in the New Testament, is indeed "glorious" (Jude 24).

The supreme revelation of God is Jesus Christ, "the radiance of God's glory" (Heb. 1:3). John wrote of "the glory of the One and Only" (John 1:14), and James called Him "our glorious Lord Jesus Christ" (James 2:1). When Jesus became a man, His glory was veiled. But at His Transfiguration this limitation was temporarily lifted, and Peter, James, and John saw Christ in His glory as His face shone and His clothes were brilliantly white (Matt. 17:2). Peter spoke of the three disciples being "eyewitnesses of his majesty" (2 Pet. 1:16).

All of Christ's works on earth reflected God's glory, for Jesus prayed to God the Father, "I have brought you glory on earth by completing the work you gave me to do. And now, Father, glorify me in your presence with the glory I had with you before the world began" (John 17:4–5). The divine Son of God had enjoyed glory from eternity past. At His Resurrection He received a "glorious body" (Phil. 3:21), and at His Ascension He was "taken up in glory" (1 Tim. 3:16).

The gospel of salvation through Christ is glorious (1 Tim. 1:11), for it reveals God's attributes of grace, mercy, and love.

When Christ comes to the clouds to take us to Himself in the Rapture of the church, His coming will be so splendorous that Paul called it a "glorious appearing" (Titus 2:13). We "will appear with him in glory" (Col. 3:4). In heaven we will share in His glory—that is, we will experience the splendor of His presence (Rom. 8:17; 1 Pet. 5:1). We are called "to his eternal glory" (5:10). When He comes, we will be "overjoyed" (4:13); therefore we "rejoice [now] in the hope" of the coming manifestation of God's glory (Rom. 5:2).

When Christ returns to earth to establish His millennial reign, He will come "with power and great glory" (Matt. 24:30). He will reign "on his throne in heavenly glory" (25:31; see also 19:28). In the Millennium everyone will know of "the glory of the LORD" (Hab. 2:14).

The Westminster Catechism affims "man's chief end is to glorify God." To glorify Him means to live in such a way that we exhibit His qualities in our lives. In the apostle Paul's words, we are to live for "the praise of his glory" (Eph. 1:12, 14). Everything we do should reflect the Lord's splendor. "Whatever you do, do it all to the glory of God" (1 Cor. 10:31; see also Phil. 1:11). To glorify God (Rom. 15:6) or to give Him glory (Jer. 13:16) means to develop His virtues (1 Pet. 2:9). Our worship is to give Him glory (Rev. 4:11; 5:12). Answers to our prayers in Jesus' name glorify the Father (John 14:13). When we get to heaven, God will reveal His greatest display of glory in redeemed men and women (Rom. 8:18). Paul wrote that God is the One "to whom be glory for ever and ever" (Gal. 1:5).   **—JFW**

***

Display in your daily life the qualities of the Holy Spirit that will allow others to see Christ in you and to glorify God.

GOD

The simple word *God* refers to any deity, whether the true God of the Bible or the gods of polytheism and other pagan religions. In every use, however, it represents a supernatural being with great power. Not all gods of the world's religions, however, display righteous characters. Still fewer show love and mercy to humans.

In the Bible God is portrayed as the infinite, eternal, all-powerful Creator who is righteous in all His acts and ways.

The Old Testament directly and indirectly reveals a great deal about God's person, works, and attributes. The Hebrew word *Yahweh*, which is God's name, is used first in Genesis 2:4 and appears several thousand times in the Old Testament. Exodus 3:13–15 is one of the most important texts about God in the Bible. There God explained to

Moses the meaning of His name in preparation for the Exodus. "Moses said to God, 'Suppose I go to the Israelites and say to them, "The God of your fathers has sent me to you," and they ask me, "What is his name?" Then what shall I tell them?' God said to Moses, 'I AM WHO I AM. This is what you are to say to the Israelites: "I AM has sent me to you."' God also said to Moses, 'Say to the Israelites, "The LORD, the God of your fathers—the God of Abraham, the God of Isaac and the God of Jacob—has sent me to you." This is my name forever, the name by which I am to be remembered from generation to generation.'"

The name *Yahweh* refers to God as the self-existing One who has always existed in the past and will always exist in the future. He is the supreme God of the universe. A number of Bible versions represent the Hebrew *Yahweh* as LORD. ("Lord," without the small capital letters, translates the Hebrew word *ădōnāy*, which is discussed below.) *Jehovah* is an older English form of *Yahweh*.

The Hebrew words *ĕlōhîm, ĕl,* or *ĕlŏah* are more general terms for God in the Old Testament. They all can refer to false gods as well as of the living God. *Ĕlōhîm* is the most common of the three, and it has a plural ending. Some suggest that this implies the Trinity. Others say this is a "plural of majesty," such as when a king makes an official pronouncement and regally re-fers to himself as "we." The Bible certainly teaches Trinitarianism, so it is possible that *ĕlōhîm* hints at the full revelation of the Trinity in the New Testament.

Another Hebrew word used frequently in the Old Testament to refer to God is *ădōnāy*. It means "my Lord" or "my Master." It emphasizes the fact that God is Master and Ruler of our lives. Both *Yahweh* and *ădōnāy* are often combined with other titles to create compound names for God. *Yahweh* is often linked with *ĕlōhîm,* as in Exodus 34:6. Also *Yahweh* is linked to *Jireh,* meaning "the Lord will provide." *Yahweh-Rapha* (15:26) refers to God as the One who heals. *Yahweh-Nissi* (17:8–15) means "the Lord is my banner," under whose authority the believer is victorious. *Yahweh-Sabaoth* (1 Sam. 1:11) refers to the fact that God is over His hosts (angels). *Yahweh-Shalom* (Ex. 34:6) means "the Lord is our peace." *Yahweh-Shammah* (34:6; Ezek. 48:35) means "the Lord is there," and *Yahweh-Tsidkenu* (Ex. 34; Jer. 23:6) means "the Lord is our righteousness."

The New Testament employs a simple vocabulary to speak about God. The common noun *theos* ("God") appears a thousand times, and *kyrios* ("Lord") occurs about five hundred times. *Kyrios* is the interesting term of the two. By the first century, Jews refused to pronounce *Yahweh.* They feared accidentally profaning the holy name of God. As they read the Scriptures, prayed, or spoke of God, they substituted ʾădōnāy for Yahweh. Consequently in the New Testament kyrios is loaded with meaning. When applied to God, kyrios is the equivalent of Yahweh. In everyday usage, kyrios might mean no more than "sir" or "master," but in theological passages it was the most worshipful title one could apply.

The Old Testament hinted at the Trinity, but the New Testament clearly indicates that God exists in three persons: God the Father, God the Son, and God the Holy Spirit. Yet there is only one God, as affirmed in Deuteronomy 6:4, "Hear, O Israel: The LORD our God, the LORD is one." Literally, this verse reads "Yahweh, our ʾelôhîm Yahweh is one." The Hebrew word for "one" suggests that the persons of the Godhead are a unit. The same word is used in Genesis 2:24 of the unity of a husband and a wife. The New Testament also affirms the unity of the Godhead. For instance, Paul wrote that "God is one" (Gal. 3:20).

At Jesus' baptism God the Father spoke from heaven, God the Son stood in the waters of the Jordan River, and God the Holy Spirit passed between them in the form of a dove (Matt. 3:16–17). Jesus instructed that His disciples should be baptized "in the name of the Father and of the Son and of the Holy Spirit" (28:19). Each person of the Trinity has the same attributes as the other two. Each one possesses full deity and all the attributes of personality: intel-

lect, sensibility, and will. The Father is regarded as the first person, the Son as the second person, and the Holy Spirit as the third person. Paul's benediction in 2 Corinthians 13:14 mentions the grace of the Son, the love of God, and the fellowship of the Holy Spirit.

God is eternal (John 1:1). He is unchanging (Heb. 1:12). He is omnipotent (all-powerful), omnipresent (Ps. 139:7; Acts 17:27), and omniscient (all-knowing). The Bible also ascribes holiness, goodness, grace, love, mercy, faithfulness, justice, and wisdom to God.

In summary, the Scriptures fully support the concept that God is infinite in all His attributes. As such He is the God who is able to save and keep those who put their trust in Him and will in eternity reward those who have been faithful.　　　**—JFW**

***

Make the worship of the Lord a priority, and be sure the purpose of your life is to accomplish His will.

GOSPEL

The English word *gospel* comes from the Anglo-Saxon *godspell*, meaning "Godstory" or "good story." It translates the Greek word *euangelion*, "good news." In the Septuagint, the Greek translation of the Old Testament, *euangelion* is found only once (2 Sam. 4:10). Yet the concept occurs in such passages as Isaiah 52:7, "How beautiful on the mountains are the feet of those who bring good news, who proclaim peace, who bring good tidings, who proclaim salvation," and 61:1, "The Spirit of the Sovereign LORD is on me, because the LORD has anointed me to preach good news to the poor." Jesus read the latter passage in the synagogue at Nazareth and declared that it described His mission (Luke 4:18–21).

Euangelion occurs more than seventy-five times in the New Testament. It often is part of a special phrase, such as "the good news of God" (Mark 1:14), "the gospel about Jesus Christ" (Mark 1:1), "the gospel of his Son" (Rom. 1:9), "the good news of the kingdom" (Matt. 4:23; 9:35; see 24:14), "the gospel of God's grace" (Acts 20:24), the "gospel of peace" (Eph. 6:15), and "the eternal gospel" (Rev. 14:6).

The apostle Paul summarized the gospel this way: "that Christ died for our sins according to the Scriptures, that he was buried, that he was raised the third day according to the Scriptures, and that he appeared to Peter, and then to the Twelve" (1 Cor. 15:3–5). This was the gospel Paul preached to the Corinthians and it was the message by which they received salvation.

The New Testament gives glimpses of gospel messages in early Christian hymns (Phil. 2:6–11), creedal statements (1 Tim. 3:16), and the apostolic sermons of Peter and Paul. Paul's sermonic pattern began with a historical declaration of the death, resurrection, and exaltation of Jesus, moved to an explanation of the person of Jesus as both Lord and Christ, and ended with a call to believe and receive forgiveness of sins.

Dispensational interpreters believe that when the New Testament speaks of "the gospel of the kingdom," it refers to the Good News that God will establish an earthly kingdom in fulfillment of the Davidic Covenant (2 Sam. 7:16). Jesus offered this kingdom and presented Himself as the prophesied King, the Son of David. John the Baptist proclaimed this kingdom first (Matt. 3:1). Then Jesus (4:17), and the disciples (10:7) preached it until the Jews officially rejected Jesus as Messiah (Luke 17:25).

According to Matthew 24:14 the Good News of the kingdom will be proclaimed again during the Great Tribulation in anticipation of the Second Advent of the King in glory. The message will be, "The King is coming!" Also at that time "the eternal gospel" will be announced by an angel to earth dwellers (Rev. 14:6). The angel will herald coming judgment, not offer salvation. Still this will be good news to believers on earth because wicked persecutors will be judged. Believers will know with certainty that God is in control and that righteousness will triumph.

In the Pauline Epistles the apostle used *euangelion* sixty times. It was one of his favorite terms, found in each of his epistles except Titus. Paul wrote that he was "set apart for the gospel" (Rom. 1:1) and that preaching the gospel to the Gentiles was his special task (Gal. 2:7). He felt a special compulsion to fulfill his mission, asserting, "Woe to me if I do not preach the gospel" (1 Cor. 9:16).

Paul's most fervent defense of the gospel occurs in Galatians. He rebuked the Galatian believers and warned them that they were "turning to a different gospel—which is really no gospel at all" (Gal. 1:6–7). Paul insisted that a gospel of legalism, which adds works to faith, is not the same kind of gospel he preached and by which they were saved. He pronounced God's anathema on those who proclaimed such a false gospel (1:8).

The gospel is good news because it is a gift of God and not something that can be achieved by human effort. It is the gospel of God's grace (Act 20:24) because it originates in His loving-kindness, and it is the gospel of salvation (Eph. 1:13) because "it is the power of God for the salvation of everyone who believes" (Rom. 1:16).   **—DKC**

***

Thank God for the Good News of the gospel, the message by which we received salvation.

GOVERNMENT

Political units, both small and large, set up institutions to make and enforce policies that guide the life of the community. These institutions, their principle documents, and the people in control make up government. A government possesses and exercises sovereign rule in its sphere of authority.

Secular thinking regards governmental power as final. Biblical thinking recognizes that ultimate authority, ultimate control, and ultimate justice rest in the hands of God, the sovereign Creator and Ruler of the universe (Ex. 15:18; 1 Chr. 29:11–12; 2 Chr. 20:6; Pss. 10:16; 22:28). All governments ultimately answer to Him. God did not create the physical universe to operate independently of Him by inherent laws while He served as an absentee landlord (Col. 1:17; Heb. 1:3). Neither did God create people to function autonomously of Him in their social structures. God continually works both directly and providentially to fulfill His eternal plan to His glory (Eph. 1:11; 3:11). He uses both spiritual and human agents, but He remains in ultimate authority and control.

Human government emerged after the Flood. God established the foundation for authority and government when He pronounced to Noah that human life must be protected because "in the image of God has God made man" (Gen. 9:6). God added, "And from each man, too, I will demand an accounting for the life of his fellow man" (9:5). Formal government emerged to carry out this objective. The patriarchal era that developed after Noah gave rise to autocratic forms of rule, such as monarchy. Regardless of the form, as Paul wrote, "There is no authority except that which God has established. The authorities that exist have been established by God" (Rom. 13:1).

The Old Testament records numerous examples of God controlling the affairs of rulers and nations. One of the most graphic examples concerns His dealings with King Nebuchadnezzar of Babylon. Daniel knew that God "sets up kings and deposes them" (Dan. 2:21). As a result he explained to Nebuchadnezzar when interpreting his dream of "a large statue" (2:31) that "the God of heaven has given you dominion and power and might and glory; in your hands he has placed mankind and the beasts of the field and the birds of the air. Wherever they live, he has made you ruler over them all" (2:37–38). When Daniel interpreted Nebuchadnezzar's second dream, he told the king he would suffer insanity for seven years "until you acknowledge that the Most High is sovereign over the kingdoms of men and gives them to anyone he wishes" (4:25). A year later, as Nebuchadnezzar boasted of his power and accomplishments (4:28–30), God struck him with insanity. He lived like an animal until he acknowledged that God's "dominion is an eternal dominion; his kingdom endures from generation to generation" and that "he does as he pleases" (4:34–35).

The government of Israel in the Old Testament stands out from that of the surrounding nations. God governed His chosen people directly as a theocracy. At first He used various appointed human leaders as His agents, including Moses (Ex. 3:10, 12–15; Num. 12:1–2, 6–8), Joshua (Deut. 31:7–8, 14, 23; Josh. 1:1–9), and the successive judges until Samuel (1 Sam. 3:19–21; 7:15). Eventually Israel stubbornly demanded "a king to lead us, as all the other nations have" (8:5). God directed Samuel to grant the people's request, explaining that "it is not you they have rejected, but they have rejected me as their King" (8:7). God did not oppose monarchy. He would have given Israel a king when the time was right. The right time depended on the right person. King Saul was the wrong kind of king. King David, the man after God's own heart (1 Sam. 13:14; Acts 13:22), was the right kind.

The future worldwide millennial kingdom of Jesus Christ (Is. 9:6–7; 11:1–9; Luke 1:30–33) demonstrates that monarchy is the best, most efficient form of government, when God's appointed King sits on the throne. Until then, however, some form of government through representatives elected by the people is preferable. No matter the form of government, Scripture directs us to submit to "the governing authorities" (Rom. 13:1; see also Titus 3:1; 1 Pet. 2:13–14), because they are ordained by God. The Bible urges us to pray "for kings and all those in authority" (1 Tim. 2:1–2). We must remember that Paul and Peter gave these directions to believers while Nero, one of the most despicable and dissolute despots of history, was ruler of the Roman Empire.

During His time on earth Jesus Christ, the eternal Son of God (John 1:14, 18), set the example of submission to human government. The Pharisees and Herodians tried to trap Jesus by asking, "Is it right to pay taxes to Caesar or not?" (Matt. 22:17; Mark 12:14; Luke 20:22). He asked them to show Him the denarius used to pay taxes (Matt. 22:19). When given one, He asked, "Whose portrait is this? And whose inscription?" (20:20). His tempters responded, "Caesar's," and Jesus said, "Give to Caesar what is Caesar's, and to God what is God's" (20:21). Jesus also recognized the divine source of human authority. When Pilate asked, "Don't you realize I have power either to free you or to crucify you?" (John 19:10), Jesus responded, "You would have no power over me if it were not given to you from above" (19:11).

Human government does not possess autonomous authority to decree anything it chooses. There are occasions when God's people must refuse to obey human authorities that oppose the ways of God. If we do so, we need to know we will suffer the consequences. Daniel's three friends, Shadrach, Meshach, and Abednego, refused to bow to Neb-uchadnezzar's golden image. They were thrown into a blazing furnace (Dan. 3:12–18). Later Daniel disobeyed Darius's decree to pray only to him during a thirty-days period (6:6–9). He continued to pray to the Lord, and Darius reluctantly ordered him thrown into the den of lions (6:10, 16). When the Sanhedrin ordered Peter and John "not to speak or teach at all in the name of Jesus" (Acts 4:18), they replied, "Judge for yourselves whether it is right in God's sight to obey you rather than God. For we cannot help speaking about what we have seen and heard" (4:19–20). Later, Peter and the other disciples responded to the high priest, "We must obey God rather than men" (5:29).

Because of the secular nature of most human governments, some Christians oppose participation in them beyond obeying laws and paying taxes. The Scriptures, however, provide several examples of godly persons whom God used greatly in the pagan governments under which they lived. Joseph rose to exercise power in Egypt second only to Pharaoh (Gen. 41:37–47). Joseph came to realize that God providentially used his jealous brother who sold him into slavery as the means to put him in power and save the lives of his family and countless others (45:4–8; 50:19–21). God elevated to governmental power Daniel, Shadrach, Meshach, and Abednego in Babylon (Dan. 1:19–20; 2:48–49; 3:30; 5:29; 6:28), and Esther

(Esth. 4:12–14), Mordecai (10:3), and Nehemiah (Neh. 1:11) in Persia. God could call the Babylonian Nebuchadnezzar "my servant" (Jer. 27:6), and the Persian Cyrus His "anointed" (Is. 45:1) and "my shepherd [who] will accomplish all that I please" (44:28). The apostle Paul did not participate in government affairs, but on several occasions he insisted on his rights as a Roman citizen (Acts 16:22–24, 35–40; 22:23–29; 25:8–12, 21, 25–27; 26:32).

Not all government in the Bible concerns cities, provinces, nations, and empires. The resurrected Lord gave the apostles authority to govern the soon-to-be-inaugurated church (Matt. 28:18–20; John 20:21–23; Acts 1:8). The numerical growth of the Jerusalem church soon convinced the apostles to share their authority and ministry. They directed the disciples to choose seven wise, Spirit-filled men to care for the physical needs of the widows in the congregation (6:2–4). The office of deacon emerged from that first act of power sharing. As the church expanded around the eastern end of the Mediterranean Sea, elders took the place of the apostles in providing spiritual leadership for local congregations (14:23; 20:17; 1 Tim. 5:17; Titus 1:5; James 5:14; 1 Pet. 5:1–3). God provided for official leaders in local churches so they would have orderly direction and spiritual development.

—JAW

***

Take part in our system of government by voting and by doing what you can to help bring about justice.

GRACE

The concept of grace unfolds gradually in Scripture. It has its roots in the Old Testament, where the Hebrew word *ḥēn* describes the compassion a superior might feel for an inferior. The issue of social rank inherent in this term implies that the kindness was undeserved. Thus Moses prayed, "Now therefore, I pray, if I have found grace in Your sight, show me now Your way, that I may know You and that I may find grace in Your sight" (Ex. 33:13, NKJV). Another Hebrew word related to "grace" is *ḥesed*. This word emphasizes God's loyal love toward Israel, His covenant people (Ex. 20:6; Deut. 7:12; 2 Sam. 7:15; Jer. 31:3).

In the New Testament the concept of grace is fully developed (the Greek word is *charis*). With the coming of Christ, grace took on its complete meaning (John 1:17). The apostle Paul in his epistles used the word *grace* to describe the vital difference between striving to win God's favor and accepting God's gift of salvation. Salvation is an expression of His grace.

In Ephesians 2:4–5 Paul pointed out the relationship of three important doctrinal words, *love, mercy,* and *grace:*

"But because of his great love for us, God, who is rich in mercy, made us alive with Christ even when we were dead in transgressions—it is by grace you have been saved." *Mercy* may be defined as God's compassion that moved Him to send a Savior for the lost world. If God's mercy alone could have provided salvation, Christ wouldn't have needed to die sacrificially for us. In final analysis, it was divine *love* that motivated all God did in providing salvation. Yet even God's infinite love could not save sinners apart from a total satisfaction for the debt of sin. The atoning death of Christ satisfied the righteous demands of God's wrath. This set free God's *grace* upon the lost. Grace can be defined therefore as God's unmerited favor that gave His Son, through whom salvation is offered to all.

God's grace proceeds from His mercy and love. God freely chooses to favor us because of Christ. Such a salvation must function apart from all human efforts to earn it (Eph. 2:8–9). The Mosaic Law cannot justify the unsaved. Sinners are "justified freely by his grace through the redemption that came by Christ Jesus" (Rom. 3:24). Paul said bluntly, "You are not under law, but under grace" (6:14).

Grace gives us acceptance with God (3:24), enables us to live for God (Col. 1:29; Titus 2:11–12), places us in a new position (1 Pet. 2:9), and provides us every spiritual blessing for this life and the life to come (Eph. 1:3–14).

Many of the Epistles open and close with the hope that their readers will experience God's grace. In fact, the New Testament closes with the benediction, "the grace of the Lord Jesus be with God's people. Amen" (Rev. 22:21).

—**DKC**

***

Rejoice today in God's grace, His unmerited favor toward us.

G

GUILT

Today we commonly think of "guilt" as a feeling, but in the Bible "guilt" refers to a moral or legal fact. Guilt results from violating God's moral standards. Furthermore, biblical guilt includes the elements of sin and punishment. Though in a given passage of Scripture emphasis may be placed on just one of these elements, they all blend together.

The Old Testament employed various Hebrew words to express guilt, especially ᵓāšām, the common word for "trespass offering." ᵓĀšām added several nuances to the Old Testament meaning of "guilt." It can be incurred, enlarged, cleansed, punished, pardoned, remembered, or eliminated. Guilt in the Old Testament could be either individual (2 Kin. 14:6) or collective (Dan. 9:5). Isaiah described the coming Messiah, God's Suffering Servant, as the prophesied guilt offering (ᵓāšām) for our sin (Is. 53:10).

The New Testament frequently viewed guilt as a legal condition of criminals or sinners. For example, the Greek word *hypodikos*, found only in Romans 3:19, is translated "guilty" (NKJV) and "held accountable" (NIV). The world, Paul stated, is accountable to God and is declared guilty in divine court.

Other Greek words viewing guilt as a judicial concept are *aitia* and *aitios*. Both terms mean a "charge" or "accusation." The Gospels use them to describe the accusations or charges brought against Jesus by His enemies (Matt. 27:37; Mark 15:26; Luke 23:4, 14, 22; John 18:38; 19:4, 6). In Acts they describe the charges brought against Paul in Jerusalem, Caesarea, and Rome (Acts 22:24–25; 23:35; 25:7, 18, 27; 28:18).

Enochos, "worthy of punishment," occurs in Matthew 5:22; Mark 3:29; 1 Corinthians 11:27; James 2:10; and elsewhere.

The Scriptures charge people with guilt for transgressing God's laws (Rom. 3:23). Guilty sinners stand in grave jeopardy of incurring His judgment (Heb. 9:27). But the good news is that the guilt caused by sin can be removed through faith in Christ. His death provides a complete and final payment for sin. To be "in Christ" is to be free from guilt (Rom. 8:1). For believers the verdict of "guilty" has been finally and fully reversed. —DKC

***

Thank God for His verdict of "not guilty" because you have accepted Christ's final payment for sin.

Hh

HARDENING

Because of their sin nature, many unbelievers rebel against God and refuse to accept His truth. When people habitually reject truth, their hearts become hardened. The classic biblical example of this occurred when Pharaoh refused to release Israel in response to the ten plagues. Pharaoh hardened his heart against God's message in each of the first five plagues (Ex. 7:13, 22; 8:15, 19, 32; 9:7). Through the last five plagues, God hardened Pharaoh's heart (9:12; 10:1, 20, 27; 11:10; 14:4, 8).

When God hardened Pharaoh, He simply confirmed the disobedience Pharaoh was committed to. What God did to Pharaoh glorified Himself (10:1; 11:9; Rom. 9:17), for it demonstrated His superiority to the ruler of the Egyptian empire.

The Bible reports that Israel experienced a special kind of hardening. Paul wrote in Romans 11:7–10 that Israel's persistent dullness to divine truth hardened them against further revelation. As a result, Gentiles receive a large portion of God's present attention in the church. Yet Israel's blindness or hardening is both temporary and partial. "I do not want you to be ignorant of this mystery, brothers, so that you may not be conceited: Israel has experienced a hardening in part until the full number of the Gentiles has come in. And so all Israel will be saved, as it is written, 'The deliverer will come from Zion; he will turn godlessness away from Jacob. And this is my covenant with them when I take away their sins'" (11:25–27).

At the Rapture Israel will be delivered from their hardness and many will come to Christ and believe the gospel. We should learn from this that in order to keep going deeper into God's truth in the future, we must accept and respond to everything He shows us in His Word now. Present obedience becomes a stepping-stone to understanding more truth. Thus walking in the light is the opposite of becoming hardened to God's revealing, life-changing truth.   **—JFW**

***

Respond always to the convicting work of the Spirit, never allowing your heart to become insensitive to the truth of God.

HEADSHIP

The Bible doesn't use the word *headship,* but it assumes the concept at every turn. "Headship" refers to leadership and authority. It's a figurative term derived from the function of the head in relation to the human body. In a few biblical figures of speech, the head, as the controlling part of a person, represents the whole person (2 Chr. 6:23; Ezek. 33:4–5; Acts 18:6).

In the Bible God exercises the most significant headship. As the sovereign Creator of all things, God is Head of all creation (1 Cor. 11:3; 3:23; 15:28). God the Father appointed His Son, the Lord Jesus Christ, as "the head over every power and authority" (Col. 2:10; see also 1 Cor. 15:25–37; Eph. 1:21). God permits Satan—who "has been sinning from the beginning" (1 John 3:8) and who led some angels into rebellion against God—to rule as head or "prince of demons" (Matt. 12:24).

Of special importance to us is the fact that God appointed the Lord Jesus "to be head over everything for the church, which is his body" (Eph. 1:22–23). Christ is described as "the head of the church, his body, of which he is the Savior" (5:23) and "the head of the body, the church" (Col. 1:18). As Head, Christ is the one "from whom the whole body, supported and held together by its ligaments and sinews, grows as God causes it to grow" (2:19; see also Eph. 4:16). We must "grow up into him who is the Head, that is, Christ" (4:15), for we "are members of his body" (5:30).

At the human level the Bible says

much about headship within the family. Paul explained that "man did not come from woman, but woman from man; neither was man created for woman, but woman for man" (1 Cor. 11:8–9; see also Gen. 2:21–24). As a result "the head of the woman is man," just as "the head of every man is Christ" (1 Cor. 11:3). In another place Paul wrote that "the husband is the head of the wife as Christ is the head of the church, his body" (Eph. 5:23). Therefore, "as the church submits to Christ, so also wives should submit to their husbands in everything" (5:24; see 1 Pet. 3:1).

The other side of the coin is that "in the Lord, however, woman is not independent of man, nor is man independent of woman. For as woman came from man, so also man is born of woman" (1 Cor. 11:11–12). Men must keep in mind the tremendous sacrificial responsibility that comes with headship. Husbands are to love their wives "just as Christ loved the church and gave himself up for her" (Eph. 5:25; see also 5:28, 33). Peter also instructed husbands to "be considerate as you live with your wives, and treat them with respect as the weaker partner and as heirs with you of the gracious gift of life" (1 Pet. 3:7). In the final analysis, headship involves cultivating within the marital relationship mutual consideration, love, respect, and submission "to one another out of reverence for Christ" (Eph. 5:21).   **—JAW**

* * *

Obey the Lord Jesus, the Head of the church, so that you can participate with Him in accomplishing His work.

HEALING

People with physical and mental dseases want to be healed. Ill people long to be well. Whether infected with a communicable disease, injured in an accident, or mired in depression, they hope for an end to their misery. They pray for healing. Somewhere in our hearts we recognize that disease, injury, and infirmity are unnatural. And they are, because along with death they all result from the fall of Adam and Eve (Gen. 2:17). Their sin brought spiritual death, the immediate separation from God, and it also started the process of physical decline toward death. This does not mean that God makes us sick to judge us for sinning, though this was a common view during the time of Christ (John 9:2). Most sickness and injury are the unavoidable consequences of living in a sin-cursed world. Sometimes God permits specific instances of sickness and suffering, as was true of Job (Job 2:4–7). All illness and suffering can advance the sanctifying purposes of God in our lives, even though those purposes are usually unclear to us while we suffer (2:8–10; John 9:3).

The Old Testament relates many

instances of healing from diseases. For example, Abraham prayed for the physical healing of Abimelech and his household and God restored them to health (Gen. 20:17). In response to Hezekiah's prayer, God healed him and extended his life for fifteen years (2 Kin. 20:5–6). "Healing" also has figurative uses in the Old Testament. Jeremiah used the same word for healing (*rāpāʾ*) to describe God's restoration of Judah from captivity (Jer. 33:8). The prophets also used this image of healing to picture the forgiveness of sins and spiritual restoration (Is. 57:19; Hos. 14:4).

The New Testament uses "healing" to describe both physical and spiritual healing, but physical healing predominates. In the Gospels Jesus regularly healed the sick (Matt. 4:24; 9:35). Many of those he healed were demon oppressed (8:16; Mark 1:32–34; Luke 4:40–41). The healing ministry of Jesus gave evidence that He was the Messiah (Matt. 11:2–5). John structured his Gospel around several miraculous work of Jesus that he called "signs." Three of these "signs" involved healing (John 4:54; 5:8; 9:1–7). Jesus also gave His disciples the authority to heal every kind of disease and sickness (Matt. 10:1). However, physical healing was not the focus of Christ's ministry. Nor was it the focus of those He sent out to preach the Good News of the kingdom (Luke 10:19–20). His Great Commission makes no reference to healing or miracles of any kind (Matt. 28:19–20).

Healing continued in the early church, as recorded in the Book of Acts. God used Peter, John, and other apostles to heal the sick (Acts 3:1–10; 5:12–16). These healings authenticated the apostolic ministry. Paul's ministry included healing, but Luke records only a few incidents (14:8; 16:18; 28:8). Paul defended his apostleship to the Corinthians by referring to the miraculous signs he had performed in their midst (2 Cor. 12:12).

The Epistles say little about healing. Paul lists healings as one of the gifts of the Spirit to the church (1 Cor. 12:9, 30). He gave no instruction about healing. He didn't need to correct any abuses of the gift. The Prison Epistles and Pastoral Epistles give glimpses into the final years of Paul's ministry. Illness surrounded him, but he didn't seem to use his healing gift. During Paul's imprisonment Epaphroditus was ill and almost died (Phil. 2:25–30). Trophimus came to Miletus and got sick, but Paul didn't heal him (2 Tim. 4:20). He apparently never tried to heal Timothy of his frequent illnesses (1 Tim. 5:23).

Paul didn't regard healing as part of the gospel proclamation (1 Cor. 15:1–4). When Peter wrote his two letters, he made no mention of physical healing in either of them. In one of the earliest writings in the New Testament, James wrote about bodily healing (James 5:13–16). He addressed sickness resulting from sin (5:15) and advised the sick to

H

ask the elders of the church to intervene and pray for forgiveness and healing (5:14). James identified prayer offered in faith as the cause of healing. The anointing oil did not have special healing powers (5:15).

Today God in His grace and mercy often heals the sick in response to our prayers offered in faith. Yet it is evident that God does not heal every time we ask Him to (2 Cor. 12:7–10). It also seems that the gift of healing hasn't been exercised since the first century. However, God has let us learn about all kinds of sickness and disease. His grace has let the medical field make the strides it has in preventing and treating disease. Paul took advantage of the medical skills his beloved companion Luke possessed (Col. 4:14), and we should gratefully accept God's healing through medical treatment too.

Ultimately all who trust in Christ will find perfect healing when He makes all things new and wipes away every tear. Then there will be no more death, crying, or pain (Rev. 21:3–4).   **—WGJ**

* * *

Pray earnestly for those who are sick, knowing that God delights in healing people when it is His will.

HEART

The word *heart* appears more than eight hundred times in Scripture. It's definitely a major biblical term. A few times "heart" literally means the muscle that pumps blood through the body (for example, Ex. 28:29–30; 2 Sam. 18:14; 2 Kin. 9:24; Job 37:1). In the vast majority of cases, "heart" refers to the inner person. Our inner person can be thought of as our personality that controls our thoughts, emotions, and actions.

The unregenerate person has "heart" problems. He is spiritually "dead in . . . transgressions and sins" (Eph. 2:1) and controlled by Satan (2:2–3). "Every inclination of the thoughts of his heart [is] only evil all the time" (Gen. 6:5; see also 8:21). God stated that "the heart is deceitful above all things and beyond cure. Who can understand it?" (Jer. 17:9). As a result every individual needs to be born again (regenerated), for "if anyone is in Christ, he is a new creation; the old has gone, the new has come!" (2 Cor. 5:17). "What counts is a new creation" (Gal. 6:15). This new creation needs a transformed heart.

Sometimes the Bible uses the word *heart* as a synonym for the mind. It treats the heart as the seat of knowledge, thoughts, and wisdom (Prov. 2:2, 10; 3:1; 23:12, 15–16). It is capable of discerning good (1 Kin. 3:9, 12; 2 Chr. 6:7–8) or bad (Pss. 58:1–2; 64:6; Prov. 6:14, 18). The Lord Jesus warned, "For out of the heart come evil thoughts, murder, adultery, sexual immorality, theft, false testimony, slander" (Matt. 15:19).

In other places in the Bible the *heart* refers to the seat of human emotions, both positive and negative. The heart suffers hatred (Lev. 19:17), pride (Deut. 8:14), despair (28:65), fear and terror (28:67; 1 Sam. 28:5), grief and sorrow (2:33), sadness (Neh. 2:2), resentment (Job 36:13), anguish (Ps. 55:4), and stubbornness (Jer. 16:12; 18:12). It can also swell with gladness (Ex. 4:14), generosity (25:2; Deut. 15:10), joy (1 Sam. 2:1; 1 Kin. 8:66; 2 Chr. 7:10), devotion (17:6), and cheer (Prov. 15:15).

Jeremiah asked concerning the heart, "Who can understand it?" (Jer. 17:9). That's a rhetorical question that expects the answer "No one." Only God, the Creator of mankind, could reply, "I the LORD search the heart and examine the mind" (17:10; see also 1 Sam. 16:7; 1 Chr. 28:9; Prov. 17:3; Jer. 11:20; 20:12; Rom. 8:27; Rev. 2:23). God indeed knows the human heart fully (Acts 1:24; 15:8). David knew that and courageously prayed, "Search me, O God, and know my heart; test me and know my anxious thoughts" (Ps. 139:23). "Examine my heart and my mind" (26:2).

God does more than know the human heart. As the omnipotent Sovereign, He also controls it as He purposes. Before Moses ever confronted Pharaoah about releasing the children of Israel, God told him, "I will harden Pharaoh's heart" (4:21; 7:3; 14:4), and He did (Ex. 9:12; 10:20, 27; 11:10). Pha-

raoh certainly cooperated with God's purposes. He wasn't a mere puppet. He gladly hardened his own heart throughout the plagues (8:32; 7:13–14, 22; 8:15, 19; 9:7, 35). To prepare Saul to minister as king of Israel "God changed [his] heart" (1 Sam. 10:9). Centuries later "the LORD moved the heart of Cyrus king of Persia" (2 Chr. 36:22; see Ezra 1:1, 5) to allow Jews to return to their homeland. God put Solomon's astounding wisdom in his heart (1 Kin. 10:24; 2 Chr. 9:23), and Nehemiah wrote that "God had put in my heart" the plans for Jerusalem (Neh. 2:12; 7:5).

In a figurative sense the Bible says God has a heart with which He feels emotions and thinks thoughts. Since God is Spirit, this is a figure of speech, known as an anthropomorphism, that describes God in human terms. The point of the figure of speech is that God does think and feel. When God saw the wickedness of the human race before the Flood, He "was grieved . . . and his heart was filled with pain" (Gen. 6:6). God told Eli that He would raise up "a faithful priest, who will do according to what is in my heart and mind" (1 Sam. 2:35), and He described David as "a man after his own heart" (13:14; see also Acts 13:22). After Solomon built the temple, God told him, "My eyes and my heart will always be there" (1 Kin. 9:3; 2 Chr. 7:16). Israel is a nation "close to his heart" (Ps. 148:14).

The best thing we can do with our hearts is devote them to God. God's fundamental command to Israel was, "Love the LORD your God with all your heart and with all your soul and with all your strength" (Deut. 6:5). He restated that command a number of times (10:12; 11:13; 13:3; 30:2, 6, 10; Josh. 22:5). He wanted His people to serve Him wholeheartedly (1 Sam. 12:20, 24). He wants us to serve Him with all our hearts, that is, completely and enthusiastically (Eph. 6:7; Col. 3:23). The Bible commands, "Trust in the LORD with all your heart" (Prov. 3:5). **—JAW**

***

Be sure your heart is right with God through faith in Jesus Christ, so that you will have concern for others, both saved and unsaved.

HEAVEN

Jewish tradition held that the heavens are divided into seven different strata. The Bible doesn't support such a view. Paul however, spoke of being "caught up to the third heaven" (2 Cor. 12:2). Many Bible scholars, therefore, speak of three heavens. In this scheme the first heaven consists of the earth's atmosphere. Scripture speaks of this as the region of the clouds (Ps. 147:8), winds (Zech. 2:6, 6:5), rain (Deut. 11:11), thunder (1 Sam. 2:10), dew (Deut. 33:13), frost (Job 38:29), hail (Josh. 10:11), air (Gen. 1:26, 30; Matt. 6:26), and sky (Prov. 23:5).

The second heaven embraces outer space with our sun, moon, and planets and all the stars. God created these heavenly bodies as "lights in the expanse of the sky" (Gen. 1:14). Genesis 15:5 refers to the stars in the heavens and Job 9:9 and 38:31 name two constellations of stars, Pleiades and Orion. God forbade Israel to worship the heavenly bodies as the heathen did (Ex. 20:4; Deut. 4:19).

The dwelling place of the triune God—the Father, Son, and Holy Spirit—is called the "highest heaven" or the "heaven of heavens" (Deut. 10:14; 1 Kin. 8:27; Pss. 68:33; 148:4). This is what Paul called "the third heaven." In Solomon's prayer at the dedication of the temple he declared, "The heavens, even the highest heaven, cannot contain you. How much less this temple I have built!" (1 Kin. 8:27). Although omnipresent, God in a particular way makes heaven His habitation (Is. 57:15; 63:15).

Jesus taught that heaven is the dwelling place of God (Matt. 6:9). He repeatedly claimed to have come from heaven (John 3:13; 6:33–51), where He had lived eternally (17:5). Just before His trial and crucifixion Jesus told His disciples that heaven was a specific place where He was going to prepare abodes for them (14:1–2). In His high priestly prayer Jesus recalled His eternal preexistent glory with the Father in heaven (17:5). After His resurrection He spoke of His ascension to heaven (20:17), a dramatic event described twice by Luke (Luke 24:51; Acts 1:9). Two angels reminded the disciples that Jesus would return from heaven someday (Acts 1:10–11). Jesus had promised this Himself (John 14:3). Paul later gave the fullest description of His return from heaven for the church (1 Thess. 4:13–18). In the present age Christ is in heaven "at the right hand of God interceding for us" (Rom. 8:34).

The Father and the Son aren't the only residents of heaven. The souls of redeemed Old and New Testament saints dwell there. Paul taught that believers "prefer to be away from the body and at home with the Lord" (2 Cor. 5:8). To the dying thief Christ said, "Today you will be with me in paradise" (Luke 23:43). Two Old Testament saints, Enoch and Elijah, were translated into heaven (2 Kin. 2:1, 11; Heb. 11:5). Long before any human souls arrived in heaven, the angels served and praised God there as their natural element (Ps. 148:2; Heb. 12:22). Angels can come to earth from heaven. From heaven they go forth to minister to people, especially those who are heirs of salvation (Heb. 1:14).

Many conclude that we can't know anything about heaven because no one has gone there and returned to tell about it. Occasionally sensationalist preachers make fraudulent claims of visions of heaven or actual trips there, but the only believable information comes from Scripture. Jesus was the first such authentic eyewitness of heaven, His home from eternity past. The apostle Paul, who was "caught up to the third heaven" (2 Cor. 12:2) had eyewitness information. He probably saw the third heaven as he lay at death's door, after he was stoned at Lystra (Acts 14:19–22). God never allowed Paul to tell what he saw and heard. Instead He gave Paul a "thorn in the flesh" to humble him and remind him not to tell (2 Cor. 12:7). The biblical eyewitness who told us the most about heaven was the apostle John, who saw and heard remarkable things in a vision while exiled on the island of Patmos. He wrote, "After this I looked and there before me was a door standing open in heaven. And the voice I had first heard speaking to me like a trumpet said, 'Come up here, and I will show you what must take place after this'" (Rev. 4:1). In the Book of Revelation, John faithfully described the stunning revelations he received of God on His throne and of future judgments and glories.

God gave John the great privilege and responsibility of describing the present abode of God, many future events, and the future home of believers in Christ. The word *heaven* occurs fifty-two times in the Book of Revelation. Of particular interest is John's description of the New Jerusalem, the heavenly city (21:1—22:5). John wrote that he saw "the Holy City, the new Jerusalem, coming down out of heaven from God" (21:2). This city, which Jesus went to prepare for His saints (John 14:1–3), will descend from the third heaven to the earth. This will occur after the Great White Throne judgment. Thus at the beginning of the eternal state, heaven will come to earth! It will be the eternal abode of the redeemed of all ages.

The Bible mentions several things that won't be in heaven. For example, there will be no marrying or giving in marriage (Luke 20:35). There will be no tears, sorrow, pain, death, or night. Nor will there be any need of light because the Son of God will be heaven's light (Rev. 21:23, 22:5). John's description of the New Jerusalem contains lavish and magnificent descriptions of the city foundations, gates, and walls. Above all, it is a city in which the glory of God will be fully revealed (21:11). The cities of earth may reflect the glory of man, but the celestial city will reflect only the glory of God.

We will rejoice and rest in heaven, but we won't be inactive. The final chapter of the Bible portrays heaven as a place where we will serve God, see His face (that is, we will have immediate access to His presence), and reign with Christ forever (22:3–5).

—**DKC**

***

Look forward with eager anticipation to heaven, your real home, where every believer will worship and serve the Lord forever.

HELL

The English word *hell* represents the destiny of the souls of unbelievers. The concept is much less developed in the Old Testament than in the New. In the Old Testament the King James Version of the Bible translated the Hebrew noun *sheol* as "hell." The New International Version and most other modern translations render *sheol* as "the grave."

Sheol occurs more than sixty times in the Hebrew Old Testament. Sometimes it means the grave where a dead body is buried, but in other instances it refers to the present state of the unsaved dead. In the mid-nineteenth century Charles Hodge, a Presbyterian theologian at Princeton Seminary, taught that *sheol* was the abode of all the dead. He said it had two compartments, one for the saved and the other for the lost. Whenever *sheol* means the intermediate state, he said it refers to this two-compartment situation. However, W. G. T. Shedd, a contemporary of Hodge's, held that the two-compartment theory belonged to Greek mythology and not to the Old Testament. He held that the term *sheol* should always be translated "grave." Modern translations, such as the New International Version follow Shedd and generally translate *sheol* as "the grave." Among the exceptions are Deuteronomy 32:22 where *sheol* is translated "realm of death below," Job 17:16 where it is rendered "gates of death," and Job 26:6 which reads "death."

In the Gospels the Greek term *hades* functions as the equivalent of the Hebrew *sheol*. In Jesus' account of the rich man and Lazarus, the rich man was in *hades*. From there he could carry on a conversation with Lazarus, even though there was a great gulf between them (Luke 16:19–31). Hodge used this story to support his view of *sheol*. Some view this story as a parable and say we shouldn't draw theological conclusions from it. However, Jesus never named characters in His parables, and He identified the beggar Lazarus by name in this story.

The New Testament employs a number of Greek words for hell. Some refer to the temporary state of the wicked before the general resurrection of the dead and final judgment. Others refer to the eternal state of the lost after their resurrection and judgment. Like *sheol, hades* can refer to either the grave (of the unsaved) or their present conscious condition after death. Hades will hold unsaved people until the end of the millennial kingdom when the bodies of the dead will be resurrected and the Great White Throne judgment held. After the Great White Throne judgment they will be cast into their permanent place of punishment, "the lake of fire" (Rev. 20:15).

Jesus used the word *gehenna* several times to indicate the final destiny of the lost. It is apparently the equivalent of the lake of fire, because it isn't temporary. The nature of hell as eternal fire and torment is most explicit in Jesus' teachings (see, for example, Matt. 18:9; 25:46; Mark 9:44, 48)

Tartarus (2 Pet. 2:4), another word for hell, occurs only once in the New Testament. Peter identified *tartarus* as the place of punishment for some of the fallen angels. We don't have enough information to conclude whether *tartarus* is another name for *gehenna* or a special place of confinement for these fallen angels until they are cast into the lake of fire.

Our minds may be troubled by the notion that hell is a place of eternal punishment for the lost, even though it is the clear teaching of Scripture. We have to consider the righteous character of God and the infinite offense human sin gives Him. God must judge and punish all sin that is not forgiven through the death of Christ.

Some would like to believe that punishment for sin is temporary or that the wicked are annihilated. The Bible teaches that punishment goes on for eternity. Perhaps the clearest description of eternal punishment is found in Revelation 20:10, which states that the devil will be thrown into the lake of fire, to join the beast and the false prophet, who will have been cast there a thousand years earlier. All three "will be tormented day and night for ever and ever."

Jesus said the lake of fire was "prepared for the devil and his angels" (Matt. 25:41). God did not devise this punishment with humans in mind. The only people who end up there are those who side with the devil by rejecting Christ. They end up sharing the destiny of the devil and the fallen angels.

When Christians die, their souls go immediately to heaven rather than to *sheol* or *hades* (2 Cor. 5:8). In heaven they live consciously in the presence of the Savior, and await the resurrection of their bodies at the time of the Rapture (1 Cor. 15:52).   **—JFW**

***

Pray daily for those who are blind to the gospel so they will escape God's judgment on unbelievers.

HERESY

The English word *heresy* is almost a sound-for-sound reproduction of the Greek word it translates, *hairesis*. *Hairesis* originally meant "the act of choosing." By extension, it came to mean "what is chosen" or "an opinion." In classical Greek the word came to be used of a political party or a school of thought, such as the Stoics or the Epicureans. In this sense Scripture speaks neutrally of "the party [*hairesis*] of the Sadducees" (Acts 5:17) and "the party [*hairesis*] of the Pharisees" (15:5; see also 26:5). The lawyer Tertullus used this term negatively when he called Paul "a ringleader of the Nazarene sect [*hairesis*]" (24:5; see also 28:22).

Paul used this word to speak of "differences" of opinion (1 Cor. 11:19; "factions," NASB). These different opinions resulted in "divisions" in the church at Corinth (11:18). This situation deeply troubled Paul. "Factions," as he wrote in Galatians 5:20, are one of the "acts of the sinful nature." Peter took *hairesis* to the level that we generally think of when we hear the word heresy. He identified the views of false prophets and false teachers as "destructive heresies," for they denied the sovereign Lord who bought them (2 Pet. 2:1).

Primarily as a result of Peter's use of the word *hairesis,* a heresy became identified as a departure from an essential truth of the Christian faith. From the time of the apostles, Christians have had to identify and deal with false teachings. For example, Paul had to respond to those who said, "There is no resurrection of the dead" (1 Cor. 15:12–19). John warned against "the man who denies that Jesus is the Christ" (1 John 2:22). Jude urged his readers "to contend for the faith that was once for all entrusted to the saints" because of the "godless men, who change the grace of our God into a license for immorality and deny Jesus Christ our only Sovereign and Lord" (Jude 3–4). Identifying and combating heresies has made the church strong through the centuries. The early church in particular, established the essential doctrines of the Christian faith through its conflicts with heretics.   **—JAW**

***

Draw a line between accepting a doctrinal difference of opinion and tolerating a heresy concerning a key biblical truth.

HOLINESS

Holiness belongs uniquely to God. Israel called Him "majestic in holiness" (Ex. 15:11). He has "sworn by [His] holiness" (Ps. 89:35; Amos 4:2), and He reveals "the holiness of [His] great name" (Ezek. 36:23; see also 38:23). When God redeems and restores Israel in the future, the Gentiles "will acknowledge the holiness of the Holy One of Jacob" (Is. 29:23). Israel's worship leaders directed the people to worship Him for "the splendor of his holiness" (1 Chr. 16:29; 2 Chr. 20:21; Pss. 29:2; 96:9).

The Old Testament calls God "the Holy One" (Job 6:10; Ps. 22:3; Prov. 9:10; 30:3; Is. 40:25), More specifically it calls Him the "Holy One of Israel" (2 Kin. 19:22; Pss. 71:22; 78:41; 89:18; Jer. 50:29; 51:5; Ezek. 39:7). Isaiah used that name for God more than two dozen times in his prophecies. Often the expression God's "holy name," or simply "the Name," stood for God Himself (Lev. 20:3; 24:16; 1 Chr. 13:6; 29:16; Pss. 97:12; 106:47; 145:21; Ezek. 36:20–23; Amos 2:7; see also Is. 57:15).

The Old Testament expresses "holy" and "holiness" by the adjective *qōdeš* and various nouns based on it. The New Testament does the same thing with the adjective *hagios* and related nouns. These words describe people or things set apart for God. God Himself is holy because He is unique, perfect in every way, pure, and separate from evil. Habakkuk wrote concerning God, "Your eyes are too pure to look on evil; you cannot tolerate wrong" (Hab. 1:13).

God alone is inherently holy. People and things consecrated to God should take on His character as a result of intimate association with Him. In the Old Testament the Law revealed God's standards of holiness. In the New Testament His Holy Spirit indwells God's people to sanctify them and empower holy lives.

God made Israel holy by choosing them to be His special nation. He separated them from other peoples and consecrated them to Him (Ex. 31:13). Israel is described as "a people holy to the LORD your God" (Deut. 7:6; 14:2, 21; 26:19), God's "holy nation" (Ex. 19:6), and God's "holy people" (22:31; Deut. 28:9). God's covenant with Israel gave them this "positional" holiness. God expected the Israelites to manifest "personal" holiness in their conduct. God told Israel to "be holy, because I, the LORD your God, am holy" (Lev. 19:2; see also 11:44–45). "I am the LORD," God said, "who makes you holy" (20:7).

The Old Testament also reports that God made many objects holy by setting them apart for sacred use in the worship rituals of the tabernacle (Ex. 29:37; 40:9–10; Lev. 2:3, 10; 6:25–27; Num. 4:15–16; 16:37). Obviously no moral purity attached to these things, but they were dedicated to the service of God and therefore were holy. In the same way, certain events (Gen. 2:3; Ex. 16:23; 20:8, 11) and places (3:5; 26:33–34; 1 Chr. 29:3; Pss. 11:4; 20:6) were called holy.

The New Testament ascribes holiness to the Lord Jesus Christ and to the Spirit of God more often than to God the Father. Since the Old Testament only hinted at the Trinity, the New Testament emphasizes the character and work of the Son and the Holy Spirit. Looking back we can see that the Old Testament had Christ in mind when it referred to God's "Anointed One" and His "Son" (Ps. 2:2, 7). We now know who the Old Testament meant by its allusions to the "Spirit of God" and "Spirit of the Lord" (for example, Gen. 1:2; Judg. 3:10). The Old Testament only called Him the "Holy Spirit" three times (Ps. 51:11; Is. 63:10–11), but the New Testament adopted this as His primary title. The New Testament writers used the language of holiness to demonstrate the perfection and deity of the Son and the Spirit.

The angel Gabriel called Jesus "the Holy One" in his announcement to Mary (Luke 1:35). A demon did the same as Jesus drove it out (Mark 1:24; Luke 4:34). Simon Peter called Jesus "the Holy One of God" to express worshipful allegiance (John 6:69). Peter and Paul both called Jesus the "Holy One" in sermons recorded in Acts (2:27; 13:35). Peter also preached about "the Holy and Righteous One" (3:14). Peter and John led the early church in a prayer that called Jesus God's "Anointed One" (4:26) and His "holy servant Jesus" (4:27, 30). The glorified Christ identified Himself to the church in Philadelphia as "him who is holy and true" (Rev. 3:7). In two New Testament passages it's hard to tell whether "the Holy One" is the Father or the Son, so closely are the two associated in the New Testament (1 John 2:20; Rev. 16:5).

The New Testament sometimes calls Christians "holy" in the basic sense of being set apart to God (2 Tim.

2:21; 1 Pet. 2:9). Most often, however, the New Testament calls us "holy" to emphasize that we should be morally pure. Christ's sacrificial death justified us and made us holy in the sight of God the Father (Heb. 2:11; 10:10, 14; 13:12). As a result the Epistles typically refer to Christians as saints, that is, "holy ones" (for example, Rom. 1:7; 1 Cor. 6:1–2; 2 Cor. 13:13). Occasionally we are explicitly labeled holy (Eph. 5:3; Col. 1:2; 2 Thess. 1:10).

Because God looks at us as holy and blameless, He exhorts us to become increasingly morally pure in our daily lives by means of help from the indwelling Holy Spirit. Holiness involves more than doing the right things. It includes maintaining pure thoughts and attitudes (Heb. 4:12; Ps. 139:23). Peter concluded, "But just as he who called you is holy, so be holy in all you do; for it is written; 'Be holy, because I am holy'" (1 Pet. 1:15–16). Paul urged us "to live a holy life" (1 Thess. 4:7; see also 2 Tim. 1:9) because "it is God's will that you should be sanctified" (4:3).   **—JAW**

***

Strive to translate your holiness in your position in Christ into holiness in daily living.

HOLY SPIRIT

The Holy Spirit is a person, not an impersonal principle or force. He possesses all the qualities of personality.

He acts like a person. For instance, the Holy Spirit communicates. He testifies of Christ (John 15:26). He speaks (16:13) and reveals (16:15). The Spirit interacts with other personal beings. He fellowships with us (2 Cor. 13:14). He intercedes for us (Rom. 8:27). He leads and guides us (Gal. 5:18). He gives us spiritual gifts (1 Cor. 12:4, 11). He appoints us to acts of service (Acts 13:2). In turn, people respond to Him as a person. Ananias and Sapphira lied to Him (Acts 5:3). Various ones have grieved Him (Is. 63:10; Eph. 4:30) and insulted Him (Heb. 10:29).

The Scriptures clearly teach the deity of the Holy Spirit. He is a member of the Godhead, coequal with the Father and the Son. The Bible calls Him God (Acts 5:3–4). He is associated with God the Father and God the Son as their equal (Matt. 28:19; 2 Cor. 13:14; 1 Pet. 1:2). He does things only God can do. For instance, He led people to write Scripture (2 Pet. 1:21). He helped create the world (Gen. 1:2). He searches and knows the mind of God (1 Cor. 2:10–11). He raised Jesus from the dead (Rom. 8:11). He convicts the world of sin (John 16:7–11). He regenerates believers (Titus 3:5), and He sanctifies them (1 Pet. 1:2).

The Old Testament says a good deal about the Holy Spirit's involvement with creation. In Genesis 1:2, the Spirit acts as the Organizer of the order of creation. He turned chaos into order. All three members of the Trinity played a role in creation. The Holy Spirit's role related to creation's beauty and order (Job 26:13; 33:4; Pss. 33:6; 104:29–30; Is. 40:13). Job 26:13 speaks of the Holy Spirit causing the sky to become fair (the NKJV of this verse says the Holy Spirit "adorned the heavens"). The Holy Spirit acts continuously to sustain the physical world (Ps. 104:29–30).

The Old Testament also presents the Holy Spirit as one who revealed God to various individuals (2 Sam. 23:2–3; Is. 59:21; Acts 28:25).

In the New Testament the Holy Spirit assumes a more prominent role in God's work with His people. His new work began on the Day of Pentecost. The Spirit descended dramatically on the followers of Jesus to form the church, the body of Christ. In the work of regeneration, the Spirit gives life to spiritually dead people when they place their faith in Christ. All three persons of the Trinity play roles in giving a person spiritual life. Spiritual life is God's gift (James 1:17–18). The Son's death provides life (John 5:21; 1 John 5:12). The Holy Spirit is the agent of regeneration (John 3:5–6, 8).

On the Day of Pentecost the Holy Spirit also began His ministries of indwelling and sealing believers in Christ. In the Old Testament the Holy Spirit temporarily filled some believers for special acts of service. Since the Day of Pentecost the Spirit has indwelt every believer from the moment of salvation, and their bodies have become temples of God. Jesus promised His disciples that the Spirit "lives with you and will be in you" (John 14:17). The New Testament refers frequently to the Spirit's indwelling ministry (John 7:37–39; Rom. 5:5; 8:9, 11; 1 Cor. 2:12; 6:19–20; 2 Cor. 5:5; Gal. 3:2; 4:6; 1 John 3:24; 4:13). Anyone not indwelt by the Holy Spirit, is not saved (Rom. 8:9; Jude 19). By indwelling the believer, the Holy Spirit serves as God's seal or evidence of possession and protection (Eph. 4:30).

The baptism of the Spirit is yet another church age work of the Holy Spirit. Jesus predicted Spirit baptism in Matthew 3:11 and Acts 1:5, 8. Since the Day of Pentecost, the Holy Spirit has baptized every believer in Christ into the church (1 Cor. 12:13). The church is Christ's body, of which He is the Head (Eph. 4:15–16; Col. 2:19). Spirit baptism marks the church as a distinct body of believers, not known in the Old Testament. Spirit baptism occurs for every believer at salvation. It is not an experience to be sought subsequent to the new birth.

On the other hand, the filling of the Holy Spirit is an experience to be cultivated. The filling of the Spirit may occur at the same time as the baptism of the Spirit, but it may not. They aren't the same thing. Spirit baptism is once for all, but Spirit filling can happen many times. On the Day of

Pentecost the Spirit filled all the apostles (Acts 2:4). The Book of Acts goes on to report subsequent experiences of filling by various ones of these apostles for specific works of service (4:8, 31; 6:3; 7:55; 11:24; 13:9, 52).

Filling is the Holy Spirit's ministry with the most day-to-day practical application to our lives. Before the church age began, the Spirit temporarily filled some individuals (Ex.31:3; 35:31; Luke 1:15, 41, 67; 4:1). He enabled them to carry out special forms of service for God. Since Pentecost, however, each of us can be filled with the Spirit if we meet the scriptural conditions. Being filled with the Spirit does not get us more of the Spirit. Instead, it refers to the Spirit getting more of us. He takes control of our lives and empowers us. The Spirit can fill immature Christians and mature Christians. Mature Christians have more wisdom, experience, and spiritual depth to put at the Spirit's disposal.

The New Testament gives three necessary conditions before the Spirit fills a believer. First, we must not "quench" the Spirit (1 Thess. 5:19, NKJV). The New International Version says we should not "put out the Spirit's fire." This means we have to yield to the Spirit and not resist His guidance and empowerment. Ephesians 4:30 states the second condition for Spirit filling: "Do not grieve the Holy Spirit of God." We must regularly confess our sins in order to maintain close fellowship with Christ (1 John 1:9). The third command is to "live by the Spirit" (Gal. 5:16). More literally this reads to "walk by the Spirit." The idea is that we should constantly depend on God for victory over sin.

If we let the Spirit fill us, we will enjoy the "fruit" of the Spirit (Gal. 5:22–23). He will produce holiness in our lives. Other benefits we receive from the filling of the Spirit include guidance by the Spirit, assurance of salvation, love for God, answered prayer, and experience of the power of God. **—JFW**

***

Be sensitive to the many ways
the Spirit of God can enrich
your life.

HOMOSEXUALITY

God calls all of His children to live holy lives (1 Thess. 4:3). God does not call anyone to an impure life. To deviate from His will is to neglect or reject Him (4:7–8). When we know something displeases the Lord, we should not participate in it. The Bible says homosexual practices deeply offend God. We shouldn't cave in to societal pressure to okay what God abhors. There aren't a lot of Bible passages on the subject, but they are clear. God is not pleased when men and women violate His purposes for human sexuality.

The Bible's stance on homosexuality springs from the creation account in the Book of Genesis. God made male and female in His image (Gen. 1:27), and He called what He created "very good" (1:31). God did not intend for Adam to live alone because he would have been incomplete. God created woman for the man, and the two became one (2:18, 21–24).

The Lord did not create another male for Adam. Instead He made someone who was different from him but complementary to him. When God finished creating humanity, what He had made in His image was man and woman in relationship. This two-gender relationship completed Adam and Eve and reflects God's multi-person image. It also provided the means by which God intended to populate the earth. Homosexual relationships, of course, have no reproductive function.

The relationship between man and woman was ideal until sin entered the world. Sin immediately injected selfishness, defensiveness, distraction, and competition into male-female relationships (Gen. 3:12, 16–19). Genesis 4 and 5 trace the decline of mankind into violence and immorality. Some sort of sexual sin between "the sons of God" and "the daughters of men" triggered God's judgment on the whole earth by the Flood (Gen. 6:1–7).

The first biblical account that concerns homosexuality involved the men of Sodom and Gomorrah. God destroyed these two cities and all their inhabitants except Lot and his family (19:24–25). The Bible provides a brief glimpse of the conduct of the people whose actions grieved God (18:20). All the men from every part of the city of Sodom came to Lot and demanded to have sex with the men who were visiting his home (19:5). To "have sex with" (NIV) translates the verb yādâ, "to know," which is used in the Old Testament at least eleven other times to refer to sexual relations. Because this word is also translated "to become acquainted with" in other places in the Old Testament (Gen. 29:5; Ruth 2:11), some pro-homosexual advocates claim that this is its meaning in Genesis 19:5. However, this word is used in the same context to explain that Lot's daughters were virgins and had not "known" man (Gen. 19:8) or had "not had relations with man" (NASB). The New Testament confirms the traditional interpretation of Genesis 18—19. Jude described the sin of Sodom and Gomorrah as sexual immorality and perversion (Jude 7). Second Peter 2:6–10 refers to "the filthy lives of lawless men" (2:7) that triggered judgment on Sodom and Gomorrah.

The Mosaic Law includes specific teaching about homosexuality. The Lord told Moses to identify for Israel the practices that He would not allow in the land of Israel. A man was not to lie with another man in the same manner that a man would lie with a woman (Lev. 18:22). This kind of conduct, God said, was detestable and would defile them as well as the land (18:24–25). Because of His holy nature God would not tolerate this kind of lifestyle.

Leviticus 20:13 condemned homosexuals to death. This put homosexuality on the same level as adultery, witchcraft, and rebellion by children. It is true that the Mosaic Law as a system has ended (Rom. 12:4; 2 Cor. 3:7–11). We do not live in a theocracy where moral sins necessarily bear civil penalties. However, the moral principles on which the Law was established never change because they are evidence of God's holy character. The Old Testament prohibition of homosexual behavior also is supported by New Testament teaching against it.

Jesus did not discuss homosexuality, but His teaching on marriage was based on the Genesis account. He reiterated that marriage is a relationship between a man and a woman (Matt. 19:4–6).

Paul wrote that the wrath of God in his day was directed at the Greco-Roman world in part because of the prevalence of homosexual practice (Rom. 1:18–32). The apostle called homosexual activity "unnatural" (1:26–27). He described its practices as indecent acts and perversion (1:27). He said they didn't care that their sin warranted death (1:32). God judges homosexuality by abandoning its practitioners to the consequences of their lust (1:26, 28). Homosexual practices today are the homosexual practices of the ancient world condemned by Old and New Testaments.

In two other passages Paul included homosexuality in lists of actions that displease God. He wrote that people characterized by homosexual activity will not inherit the kingdom of God (1 Cor. 6:9–10). Some of the Corinthian believers had practiced homosexuality, but by God's grace they had been redeemed and sanctified from those practices (6:11). In 1 Timothy 1:10 Paul also warned about homosexual activity ("homosexuals," NASB; "perverts," NIV). He called homosexual behavior contrary to sound doctrine and displeasing to the Lord.

In light of the biblical teaching about homosexuality, Christians with an inclination toward this lifestyle need to heed Paul's admonition in Colossians 3:5–6. The sin of homosexual activity is forgiven like every other sin. Christ died for all the sins of the world. Those attracted to this kind of sexual activity need to realize that this sin need not master them (Rom. 6:13–14). Homosexuals who love Christ can find power and encouragement when they seek the Lord's help, as is true of any believer struggling to overcome sin. Don't minimize or justify sinful actions. Rather turn to the mercy of the Lord and seek forgiveness and deliverance from sin's dominance.

The Bible contains no explicit teaching about the causes of homosexual inclinations and orientations or about how to extinguish a homosexual orientation.   **—WGJ**

***

Ask God for a patient and sensitive heart in dealing with those who struggle with sexual temptations.

HOPE

In casual conversation the word *hope* has a wishy-washy flavor to it. What we hope for is doubtful. It probably won't happen. Luke 23:8 states that Herod "hoped" to see Jesus perform a miracle, and according to Acts 24:26 Felix "was hoping" Paul would give him a bribe. The Bible rarely uses "hope" in this way, however. In the Bible "hope" carries the sense of a confident or certain expectation.

In the Old Testament various Hebrew words for hope express the ideas of trust or expectation. Job, for example, raised the plaintive cry, "If the only home I hope for is the grave . . . , where then is my hope? Who can see any hope for me?" (Job 17:13, 15). In the end Job found the same answer as the psalmist who said, "LORD, what do I look for? My hope is in you" (Ps. 39:7).

The psalms echo with expressions of hopeful trust in God. He is seen as a deliverer, who will certainly act on behalf of believers someday. Meanwhile the godly are invited to wait and hope. "But the eyes of the LORD are on those who fear him, on those whose hope is in his unfailing love, to deliver them from death and keep them alive in famine" (33:18–19). Other verses that express the same hope are Psalms 31:23–24; 62:5–7; 71:5, 14; 119:49–50; 130:7; and 146:5–7.

The Old Testament prophets stressed the importance of hope, even in the face of the catastrophic Babylonian exile. Jeremiah addressed God as the "Hope of Israel" (Jer. 14:8), and he reassured the Jews, "[You] will return from the land of the enemy. So there is hope for your future" (31:16–17).

Both Testaments tell of people with hopes for success in some ordinary venture. They hope to bear children (Ruth 1:12), find water (Job 6:19), repay a loan (Luke 6:34), be delivered from a storm (Acts 27:20), share in a harvest (1 Cor. 9:10), or visit someone (Rom. 15:24; 1 Cor. 16:7; 1 Tim. 3:14).

In the New Testament the word *hope* occurs frequently in the Epistles. It was a favorite term of the apostle Paul (Rom. 12:12; 15:13; Eph. 1:18; Titus 1:2). Christ Himself is the believer's hope (Rom. 5:2; Col. 1:27; 1 Tim. 1:1). That hope springs from the death, burial, and resurrection of Christ (1 Pet. 1:3). Thus God gives believers hope through the gospel (Col. 1:23; Heb. 6:18–19).

Our hope looks toward the return of Jesus. Jesus was resurrected bodily, so we too will be resurrected (Acts 23:6; Rom. 8:18–25). In fact everyone, both the righteous and the wicked, will be resurrected (Acts 24:15). Because of this hope (or what J. B. Phillips called a "happy certainty") that we will be raised with Christ, we are not "to grieve like the rest of men, who have no hope" (1 Thess. 4:13) and are "without hope" (Eph. 2:12). Closely associated with our future resurrection is "the blessed hope" of the return of Christ for His own (Titus 2:13). At that time we will receive resurrection bodies (1 John 3:2).

Our hope isn't just some future thing. Christian hope also has present benefits. John declared that the hope of Christ's return has a sanctifying effect on us. "Everyone who has this hope in him purifies himself, just as he [Jesus] is pure" (1 John 3:3). Further, Paul said our troubles develop perseverance, and that perseverance produces strong character. That in turn strengthens our hope (Rom. 5:3–4). Paul commended the Thessalonian believers for their endurance, which was "inspired by hope in our Lord Jesus Christ" (1 Thess. 1:3).

Remember God's words to Jeremiah: "For I know the plans I have for you, declares the LORD, plans to prosper you and not to harm you, plans to give you hope and a future" (Jer. 29:11).

—**DKC**

***

Contemplate what life would be like without our hope in Christ.

HUMILITY

The philosophy of the world says look out for "number one" and do what it takes to get ahead. Humility says consider others ahead of yourself and realize that it's often better to take a position lower than what you deserve. The world thinks that's strange, but Jesus and the Bible commend humility as a primary Christian virtue (Eph. 4:2; Col. 3:12).

Even in the Old Testament, the prophet Isaiah expressed the Lord's attitude toward humility in these words: "This is the one I esteem: he who is humble and contrite in spirit, and trembles at my word" (Is. 66:2). Micah stated that God requires believers to walk humbly with Him (Mic. 6:8). In the New Testament, Jesus declared that humility is necessary for entrance into the kingdom of God (Matt. 18:3–4). Both James and Peter quoted Proverbs 3:34, which emphasizes that God gives grace to humble men and women (James 4:6; 1 Pet. 5:5).

Solomon dedicated the temple with a prayer that was both eloquent and humble. He said that whenever we turn from our sins in an attitude of true humility we can expect God to hear our prayers (2 Chr. 7:12–16). The remaining chapters of 2 Chronicles provide a running commentary on God's response to humility. Shishak, king of Egypt, threatened to overrun Jerusalem. King Rehoboam and the leaders of Israel humbled themselves before the Lord, and God spared them from judgment (12:6–7, 12). King Asa would not humble himself before God. His tragic death left an ugly blot on an otherwise sterling record (16:7–12). King Amaziah's pride caused his defeat at the hands of Jehoash, king of Israel (25:19–21). During Hezekiah's reign the Lord honored the humility of the people of Israel and allowed them to celebrate the Passover in Jerusalem (30:11–12). The humility of Hezekiah and his people averted judgment from God (32:24–26). Even when Manasseh, whose wickedness had devastated the nation, humbled himself, God responded (33:12–13). Jerusalem finally fell into the hands of the Babylonians because of the refusal of Amon and Zedekiah to humble themselves before the Lord (33:23; 36:11).

Humility marked the life and teachings of Christ. When He began His public ministry in Galilee, He emphasized the importance of humility with the words, "Blessed are the poor in spirit" (Matt. 5:3). How strange this must have sounded to the ears of the scribes and Pharisees. Jesus often confronted the Pharisees by telling parables that revealed their proud hearts (23:1–12; Luke 14:7–11).

Jesus used a child as an object lesson of the meaning of humility (Matt. 18:1–5). People must abandon their pride and become like little children to receive what God has for them. In this way Jesus illustrated that humility means placing ourselves in a position below what may be rightfully ours. An adult cannot become like a child without making a conscious choice to do so. Jesus issued His strongest admonition concerning humility when He called for those who were weary and burdened to come to Him. Relief can only come from the One who is "gentle and humble in heart" (11:28–30).

The heart of the New Testament teaching about humility is our Lord's own example of humility shown by His death on the cross. Paul's description of Christ's voluntary humility, found in Philippians 2:5–11, is the most beautiful expression of this truth in all of Scripture. While retaining His deity as the Son of God, Jesus voluntarily took on Himself the form of a servant (2:7). He consciously and willingly took a position lower than what He had. He did this to please the Father and to accomplish His will (Eph. 1:9). In so doing He demonstrated His great love for humanity (John 3:16).

In response to His humility, God exalted Jesus to the highest place and gave Him a name above all other names

(Phil. 2:9). Jesus' humility and subsequent exaltation will ultimately glorify God the Father when everyone will bow down before the Lord Jesus Christ (2:10–11). Paul exhorted us to follow the example of Christ by displaying the same attitude He had (2:5).

The night before He was crucified Jesus graphically illustrated humility. He wrapped Himself in a towel as a servant would, and washed the disciples' feet. Peter felt Jesus had demeaned Himself, until Jesus explained why He did it. Years later Peter wrote to Christians scattered throughout Asia Minor and urged them to act like Christ and clothe themselves with humility toward each other (1 Pet. 5:5). When we humble ourselves before God, Peter said, then He will lift us up (5:6).

Jesus called Himself humble (Matt. 11:29). And Paul said he "served the Lord with great humility" (Acts 20:19). It is possible to be aware of our humility without being proud of it. There is no formula for becoming humble. It is an attitude of the heart and mind. Humility begins with bowing before God. Then humility motivates us to meet the needs of people around us. How we think about and treat others may be the best gauge of our humility or lack of it. God knows our hearts. Others only see our actions and hear our words. We should make every effort to follow Christ's example of humility. **—WGJ**

***

Walk each day in the steps of Christ, exhibiting the same meekness that characterized His life, and don't be self-centered.

Ii

IDOLATRY

Idolatry means the worship of images, whether objects in nature or man-made idols. People have always wanted to see some representation of their gods. Animists worship spirits associated with natural objects, such as trees, rivers, and stones. Some idolators believe their gods live in creatures, such as bulls, serpents, and birds. Others have reverenced celestial bodies, such as the sun, moon, and stars, or the forces of nature (fire, water, and storms). Some idolatry focuses on abstract gods that may or may not be represented by images. Many people worship deceased ancestors or long-dead emperors and kings. Some revere the fertility principle. A few worship abstract ideas such as wisdom and justice.

The Old Testament warns sternly against the idolatry that infiltrated Israel from her heathen neighbors, especially the Egyptians, the Canaanites, and the Mesopotamian nations of

Assyria and Babylon. The Egyptians had a staggering array of deities numbering in the thousands. The Pyramid texts name two hundred gods, and the Book of the Dead lists another twelve hundred. Most Egyptian deities appeared as animals, though the chief gods assumed human form. Egypt also worshiped cosmic deities, such as Re, the sun god. The pharaohs even viewed themselves as incarnate deities. Egyptian religion with its multiplicity of gods and grotesque idols probably repulsed the Hebrews while they were enslaved there. Still Egyptian idolatry left its mark on Israel, as seen in the golden calf incident at Mount Sinai (Ex. 32).

Babylonian idolatry exerted the greatest influence on Israelite religion. Terah, Abraham's father, was an idolater (Josh. 24:2), and Abraham himself probably worshiped the Babylonian gods before God called him to leave his home in Ur. Some scholars estimate the Babylonian pantheon contained more than fifteen hundred gods, including Shamash, Marduk, Sin, and Ishtar, the goddess of lust and procreation. The Assyrians worshiped gods similar to the Babylonian ones. They brought greater cruelty and sadism to all their cultural practices than other ancient Near Eastern nations.

Canaanite idolatry featured fertility cults that engaged in orgiastic worship of nature and reproduction. Worship often consisted of nothing but ritualized debauchery. The chief Canaanite deities, El, Baal, and Astarte, were morally degenerate gods whose antics theoretically prompted crops and herds to multiply. Sacred prostitution and ritual sex supposedly spurred the gods to get busy and make everything grow. Obviously Canaanite religion appealed to the illicit sexual desires of the Israelites. Through Moses God sternly warned the Israelites to stay away from this debased form of paganism (Deut. 7:4; 20:18).

The history of Israel in the Old Testament is unfortunately the story of its flirtation with various forms of idolatry. For centuries, Israel disregarded God's Word about idolatry. Starting with the Ten Commandments, the Law forbade representing God in any form (Ex. 20:4–5; Deut. 5:8–9). The prophets often ridiculed those who made an idol with their hands and then worshiped it (Is. 40:19–20; 44:9–20; Jer. 10:20; Hos. 8:5; Hab. 2:18).

Idolatry was ingrained in Israel's origins and ancestry. Rachel, wife of Jacob, took the household gods when her family fled from her uncle Laban (Gen. 31:34). During the Egyptian sojourn the Israelites worshiped idols (Josh. 24:14; Ezek. 20:8–18; 23:3–8). They persisted in idolatry at Sinai while Moses received the Law from God (Ex. 32). At the end of the wilderness wanderings Israel angered God on the plains of Moab by worshiping Baal (Num. 25:1–3).

Just before Israel entered Canaan, Moses warned them against idolatry and intermarriage with the native populace (Deut. 4:15–19; 7:1–5). The nation disobeyed both prohibitions. The Book of Judges tells how the surrounding nations repeatedly led Israel into apostasy and idolatry (Judg. 2:11–13; 6:25–32; 17:1–13). At the end of the era of the judges, Samuel explained to the people that the Philistines had defeated them because of their idolatry. He promised Israel deliverance if they would put away their false gods (1 Sam. 7:3–4).

During the period of Israel's united kingdom Solomon opened a door for idolatry by taking many foreign wives. Each continued worshiping her native gods, including Chemosh and Molech who received children as sacrifices. By the time he was an old man, Solomon worshiped his wives' gods too (1 Kin. 11:1–8). As a consequence God brought civil war and divided Solomon's kingdom (11:9–13). Jeroboam, the first king of the northern tribes of Israel, thought it wise to prevent his subjects from going to Jerusalem several times a year. He set up golden calves at Dan in the north and Bethel in the south, and told the people that these idols represented the Lord. They could do all their worshiping without going to Jerusalem. Ever after the king was labeled "Jeroboam, who sinned and who made Israel sin" (14:16, NKJV).

Jeroboam represented the Lord as a golden calf. Canaanite cults sometimes represented Baal as a bull. It didn't take long to get the two confused. When King Ahab promoted Baal worship, Israel responded readily (1 Kin. 16:32–33). After that, calf worship and Baalism dominated the religious scene in the northern kingdom until the Assyrians conquered it in 722 B.C.

The southern kingdom of Judah struggled with idolatry too. The godly kings Asa, Jehoshaphat, Jehoash, Azariah, Hezekiah, and Josiah led spiritual revivals. However, their influence was more than negated by the royal apostates Rehoboam, Ahaz, and Manasseh. They all promoted false worship. God imposed the Babylonian exile on Judah as judgment for idolatry (Jer. 19:3–9; 20:4). The Jews recognized they were captives in a foreign land because of their idolatry. Babylonian life was saturated with idolatry, and the Jews reacted against it to form an abhorrence to idols that has characterized Judaism ever since.

The story of the New Testament plays out against the backdrop of first-century Gentile idolatry. The Roman Empire tolerated and promoted the religious traditions of each province. Early Christianity developed and flourished in competition with polytheistic idolatry. Paul wrote quite a bit about idolatry, and warned believers to avoid cultural events involving idol worship (1 Cor. 10:14). Paul insisted that an idol sitting in its temple was unreal and impotent. However, he recognized that demons involve themselves in idolatry, so idol feasts should be avoided (10:18–21).

Paul described the pervasive idolatry of the pagan world in a classic passage in the Book of Romans. Idolatry not only involves rejection of the true God but it has serious moral implications (Rom. 1:18–32). He did not view idolatry as a primitive form of religion that could lead on to higher forms. Rather, he saw idolatry as retrogressive. Idolators started with the true God and perverted their knowledge of Him into something that could only get worse.

In Athens Paul observed a god for every possible aspect of life. Idols had proliferated to the point that someone had set up an altar to an unknown god in case one had been overlooked (Acts 17:23). In Ephesus Paul's ministry succeeded to the point that the makers of images of the goddess Diana noticed a serious drop in sales (19:23–27). In Jerusalem the council of apostles and elders exhorted Gentile believers to "abstain from food sacrificed to idols" (15:29). The apostle John wrote that in the Tribulation, people will "not stop worshiping demons, and idols of gold, silver, bronze, stone and wood—idols that cannot see or hear or walk" (Rev. 9:20). John also recorded a dire warning against any who worship an image of the beast or antichrist (13:14–15; 14:9–11; see also Matt. 24:15–16).

The New Testament used the term idolatry a few times in a figurative sense. Paul equated greed (Eph. 5:5; Col. 3:5) and gluttony (Phil. 3:19) with idolatry. In effect, the apostle warned us not to make a god out of our passions and appetites.

At the end of his first epistle John wrote, "Dear children, keep yourselves from idols" (1 John 5:21). Since we know "the true God" (5:20) why would we turn to the false and embrace the moral laxness that accompanies idolatry? This message remains relevant today because idolatry includes anything that takes the place in our hearts that belongs to God alone.   **—DKC**

***

Beware of making a god out of your appetites, your passions, or your possessions.

IMAGE OF GOD

God made man the apex of His creative activity. "God said, 'Let us make man in our image, in our likeness.' . . . So God created man in his own image, in the image of God he created him; male and female he created them" (Gen. 1:26–27). At the beginning of the record of Adam's descendants, Genesis repeats the fact that humanity bears the image of God ("When God created man, he made him in the likeness of God," 5:1). After the Flood

God told Noah that murder is dreadful because humans bear the image of God (9:6). The New Testament states twice that people bear the image of God (1 Cor. 11:7; James 3:9). The passages in Genesis 1 and 5 refer to Adam before the Fall. The other passages describe people after the Fall. The Fall distorted the image of God in us, but it did not erase it.

How do people bear the image of God? What is it? It obviously is not our physical makeup and appearance. We don't "look like" God. It isn't that we walk upright unlike the animals. (Some have suggested that!) Our physical nature is of this earth. "The LORD God formed man from the dust of the ground" (Gen. 2:7). In contrast, as Jesus stated, "God is spirit" (John 4:24). Granted, Moses and the prophets encountered God in visions that included vague anthropomorphic shapes (Ex. 33:18–23; Is. 6:1; Dan. 7:9; Rev. 4:2–3), but these visions communicated God's splendor and glory in visible ways. They don't mean God has a body.

The image of God relates to our immaterial nature and results from God breathing "into [Adam's] nostrils the breath of life" so that he "became a living being" (Gen. 2:7). God's image includes the elements of personhood—self-consciousness and self-determination—and the capacities of intellect, sensibility, and will. God possesses all these personal traits to an infinite degree, whereas He has given them to us only in finite measures. God wanted us to represent Him as we "rule over the fish of the sea and the birds of the air, over the livestock, over all the earth, and over all the creatures that move along the ground" (1:26; see also 1:28). This finite responsibility mirrors God's infinite sovereignty and is also a part of the image of God in us.

Another aspect of the image of God in Adam and Eve was their innocent holiness as they came from the creative hand of God. When God had crowned His creation with a man and a woman who were pure in every way, He looked at "all that he had made, and it was very good" (1:31). Later Solomon wrote, "God made mankind upright" (Eccles. 7:29), meaning righteous, but, he continued, "men have gone in search of many schemes." Solomon alluded to our loss of innocence and holiness as the result of Adam and Eve's sin. The Fall had a horrible impact on the image of God.

To what extent did the Fall damage the image of God in humanity? Obviously we lost our original righteousness (or innocence), but how was the rest of the image of God affected? Some theologians believe the Fall totally destroyed the image of God in people. As noted earlier, however, the Bible refers to the image of God in humankind after the Fall. We still possess self-consciousness, self-determination, intellect, sensibility, and will, but these qualities have been so distorted in us that we cannot find God apart from His gracious revelation of Himself.

While we *bear* the image of God, the Lord Jesus Christ *is* "the image of God" (2 Cor. 4:4; Col. 1:15). John declared, "No one has ever seen God, but God the One and Only Son, who is at the Father's side, has made him known" (John 1:18). When Philip said, "Lord, show us the Father" (14:8), Jesus responded, "Anyone who has seen me has seen the Father" (14:9; see also 12:45; Heb. 1:3). As the eternal Word (John 1:1–2), Jesus Christ is the image of God the Father. Throughout His earthly life and ministry the incarnate Son of God, the Lord Jesus Christ, perfectly and sinlessly displayed the image of God.

As said before, the fall of Adam and Eve did not destroy the image of God in humankind, but it did distort and pervert it. When we receive the Lord Jesus Christ as our Savior by faith, we are born again and indwelt by the Holy Spirit. The Lord immediately begins the process of helping us become "conformed to the likeness of his Son" (Rom. 8:29; see also 1 Cor. 15:49; Eph. 4:24; Phil. 3:21; Col. 3:10; 1 John 3:2–3). God is refurbishing His image in us in this lifetime. He will complete the job when Jesus returns for us. "We know that when he appears, we shall be like him, for we shall see him as he is" (3:2). —**JAW**

***

Though you, as a human being, display the image of God marred by sin, as a Christian seek to reflect the image of Christ.

IMMORTALITY

Only God possesses immortality inherently because He can never be touched by death and decay as humans can. Romans 1:23 refers to "the immortal God," and 1 Timothy 1:17 refers to God as "the King, eternal, immortal." In 1 Timothy 6:16 Paul stated that God "alone is immortal." He exists as the infinite God from eternity past to eternity future without change. He is eternally the living God (Pss. 18:46; 90:2; 115:3–8; Jer. 10:11). God's immortality is an aspect of His infinitude that separates Him radically from finite humans, whose bodies die.

After the Fall, mortality was imposed on humanity as a judgment for sin. Because Adam sinned, he died (Gen. 2:17; 3:19). Because the entire human race sinned in Adam, we all die (Rom. 5:12). Every one of us lives in a mortal body. Yet though we die physically, we will exist forever after death in either heaven or hell. God is *inherently* immortal; humans *receive* immortality. Those who believe in Christ receive eternal life. After death we await the resurrection of our bodies to an eternity of life with God. We will enjoy immortality (2 Tim. 1:10).

Those who reject Christ face an eternal existence separated from God. After death they await the resurrection of their bodies, judgment, and eternal punishment that perhaps should not be called immortality. The Bible calls the eternal condition of the unsaved "the second death" (Rev. 21:8).

Christians alive at the time of the Rapture will not face death. At the moment of the Rapture, all church-age believers who have died will be resurrected. Both groups, those alive when Jesus returns and those resurrected then, will receive immortal, transformed bodies. Christ "will transform our lowly bodies so that they will be like his glorious body" (Phil. 3:21). "We shall be like him" (1 John 3:2). "So will it be with the resurrection of the dead. The body that is sown is perishable, it is raised imperishable; it is sown in dishonor, it is raised in glory; it is sown in weakness, it is raised in power; it is sown a natural body, it is raised a spiritual body" (1 Cor. 15:42–44). For church-age saints, the great enemy death will cease to exist (15:54–55).

At the end of the Millennium all the wicked dead will rise from their graves. God will judge them at the Great White Throne. They will be thrown into the lake of fire (Rev. 20:11–15), where they will suffer eternal torment (Matt. 25:46) as punishment for their sin (2 Thess. 1:9).   **—JFW**

***

Live every day in the light of the eternal life you possess in Christ.

IMPUTATION

The Bible frequently uses the verb "to impute" but not the noun "imputation." *Imputation* is a theological term that summarizes a concept important to the doctrine of salvation.

In both the Old and New Testaments "to impute" means "to set to one's account" or "to charge/credit something to someone." The Hebrew verb *ḥāšab* appears over one hundred times in the Old Testament. The parallel Greek verb *logizomai* is used forty-one times in the New Testament. You can see the idea of imputation in an everyday setting when Paul wrote to his friend Philemon about the runaway slave Onesimus: "If he has done you any wrong or owes you anything, *charge it to me*" (Philem. 18).

The theological concept of imputation appears in three different ways in the Bible's teaching about salvation. They are all acts of God. In each case He's acting as a judge issuing procedural rulings about a case in progress. The "case" involves prosecuting humanity for sinning against our Creator. First, God imputed Adam's original sin to the entire human race. Second, God imputed the sin and guilt of the human race to Christ on the Cross. Third, God imputes divine righteousness to all who believe in Christ as Savior.

The doctrine of the imputation of Adam's sin to his posterity is based on Genesis 3:1–19; Romans 5:12–19; and 1 Corinthians 15:21–22. The Genesis narrative contains God's curse on the serpent and the ground and His descriptions of how sin would damage human relationships. Further biblical revelation and history show that sin has devastated the human race. In Romans 5, Paul taught that Adam's sin was every man's sin. "Sin entered the world through one man, and death through sin, and in this way death came to all men, because all sinned" (5:12). That doesn't mean everyone eventually sins and dies because of it. Paul meant that we all sinned when Adam sinned and because of that sin in the Garden we all inherit the penalty of physical death. Consider these biblical expressions: "the many died by the trespass of the one man" (5:15); "the result of one trespass was condemnation for all men" (5:18); and "through the disobedience of the one man the many were made sinners" (5:19). Paul summed it up this way: "In Adam all die"(1 Cor. 15:22). Adam's sin has been charged to the entire human family.

Theologians differ about how the human race participated in Adam's sin. Some hold that when Adam sinned, he acted as the head and representative of the human race (the "federal headship" view). Others believe the whole human race was genetically present in Adam so that they sinned right along with him (the "seminal" view). The latter theory parallels the line of reasoning in the Book of Hebrews that Levi was in Abraham's loins when his great-grandfather paid tithes to king Melchizedek (Heb. 7:9–10).

There isn't a New Testament passage that uses the verb "to impute" to describe how the sins of humanity were laid on Christ when He died. But the idea appears in various Scriptures. Even in the Old Testament the sacrificial system pictured the imputation of sin to Christ. Worshipers laid their hands on sacrificial animals to symbolically transfer their sins to them. On the Day of Atonement the high priest transferred the sins of the whole nation Israel onto the scapegoat and banished it into the wilderness (Lev. 16). The prophet Isaiah affirmed that mankind's guilt was reckoned to the Servant of Yahweh. "Surely he took up our infirmities and carried our sorrows . . . the LORD has laid on him the iniquity of us all . . . he bore the sin of many" (Is. 53:4, 6, 12). The apostle Paul similarly wrote that "God made him [Christ] who had no sin to be sin for us" (2 Cor. 5:21) and that "Christ redeemed us from the curse of the law by becoming a curse for us" (Gal. 3:13). The apostle Peter declared, "He himself bore our sins in his body on the tree" (1 Pet. 2:24). Picture the sinless Son of God on the cross with the guilt of all mankind charged to His account and you more easily understand His impassioned cry, "My God, my God, why have you forsaken me?" (Matt. 27:46).

The final act of imputation occurs when God judicially credits the righteousness of Christ to those who exercise faith. The Bible looks back to an event in the life of Abraham as the basis on which God imputes righteousness to those who have faith in God. God had promised Abram in his old age that he would be the father of numerous offspring. "Abram believed the LORD, and he credited it to him as righteousness" (Gen. 15:6).

No person, the Bible asserts, possesses the righteousness God demands (Rom. 3:10). Yet God graciously provides the righteousness He requires, a righteousness that fully satisfies the demands of His holy character. Specifically, God imputes Christ's righteousness to believers (2 Cor. 5:21). This is a judicial act by which God *declares* the believer righteous. God grants the believer, at the moment of salvation, a righteous standing before Him, the holy God. Imputation does not *make* a believer experientially righteous. Some erroneously teach that when God justifies believers, they become righteous and live holy lives from then on. God credits Christ's righteousness to our account in response to our faith. He transforms our character through the experiential process of sanctification, not through the judicial imputation of Christ's righteousness.

The imputation of divine righteousness to the believer is one of the most important doctrines of the New Testament and is a major theme in Romans (Rom. 3:21—5:21). This divine act reverses the disastrous effect of the imputation of Adam's sin to the human race for all of us who believe. It is the sole basis on which God accepts us.   **—DKC**

***

Praise God that He provides for the believer the righteousness He requires for us to be in His presence.

INCARNATION

The word *Incarnation* does not occur in Scripture. However, evidence for the doctrine is scattered throughout the Bible. We find its main concentration in the New Testament. The eternal Second Person of the Trinity joined Himself with a complete human nature and was born as Jesus of Nazareth. The apostle John described Jesus, the God-Man, this way: "The Word became flesh and made his dwelling among us" (John 1:14).

The angel Gabriel told Mary she would "be with child and give birth to a son" (Luke 1:31). Mary asked, "How will this be . . . since I am a virgin?" (1:34). Gabriel's reply to her gives the Bible's most detailed explanation of how the Incarnation came about. He said, "The Holy Spirit will come upon you, and the power of the Most High will overshadow you. So the holy one to be born will be called the Son of God" (1:35). Mary and Joseph weren't married at that time, so an angel (probably Gabriel) told him not to "be afraid to take Mary home as your wife, because what is conceived in her is from the Holy Spirit" (Matt. 1:20).

The doctrine of the Incarnation affirms that the Holy Spirit united the eternal Second Person of the Godhead with a human nature at conception in the womb of a virgin so that Jesus of Nazareth was born fully God and fully human. Jesus' birth as the God-Man answers several false teachings concerning the Lord Jesus Christ that occurred in the early church. They called the earliest one Docetism. Docetism taught that Jesus was fully God, but He only seemed to have a human body (1 John 4:2–3; 2 John 7). John was attacking this kind of error when he said the apostles could claim "we have heard . . . have seen with our eyes . . . have touched . . . the Word of life" (1 John 1:1). John's great affirmation that the "Word became flesh" (John 1:14; see also 6:51–58) struck a fatal blow to Docetism. Docetism

didn't fit the facts of the Atonement either. If Jesus only seemed to have a human body, He didn't really die on Calvary and provide a redemptive sacrifice for sin.

A second early error about the Incarnation was called adoptionism. Adoptionists believed God was too exalted to have anything to do with human birth or death. They said Jesus was conceived and born a mere mortal. When John the Baptist baptized Jesus, the Second Person of the Trinity came on Him, adopted His body, and ministered through Him. The Son of God left Jesus before He was executed on Calvary. Jesus died simply as a human being. If this were true, Jesus' death had no redemptive value and He was conceived as an illegitimate child.

Another misunderstanding about the Incarnation grows out of Paul's statement that Jesus Christ "emptied himself" (Phil. 2:7, NASB). Some scholars conclude that Jesus laid aside His divine attributes of omnipotence, omnipresence, and omniscience at His Incarnation. But Jesus did not give up His deity, partially or totally. In fact, Jesus manifested those very attributes (Mark 4:39; Luke 8:24–25; John 1:47–48). Rather than discarding His deity, the incarnate Son of God veiled His divine glory (except to Peter, James, and John on the Mount of Transfiguration; Matt. 17:1–2), and He did not use His divine attributes for His own gratification.

Jesus possessed both a divine nature as the eternal Son of God and a human nature as the son of Mary. Yet He was one person, the God-Man, not two persons struggling with one another like a split personality. The two natures meshed harmoniously into the actions, emotions, and thoughts of the one person Jesus Christ.

God decreed the Incarnation as part of His eternal plan and program before the world began. John called Jesus Christ "the Word" (John 1:1–2, 14) because He was to enter human history and reveal God to humanity (14:7–11). The Old Testament prophesied the Incarnation as essential to God's eternal plan. As part of the curse on the serpent after the Fall, God said mysteriously that the offspring of the woman "will crush his head" (Gen. 3:15). God promised Abraham that "through your offspring all nations on earth will be blessed" (22:18; see Gal. 3:16). The promises He made to David took on royal overtones (2 Sam. 7:11–16; see also Pss. 89:3–4, 20, 26–37; 132:10–12, 17–18; Luke 1:32–33). When the prophets started anticipating the Messiah, He took on divine characteristics too (Is. 7:14 [see Matt. 1:23], Is. 9:6–7 [see Luke 1:32], and Mic. 5:2–4 [see Matt. 2:1–12]).

New Testament teaching about the Incarnation gets more specific. Paul wrote, "But when the time had fully come, God sent his Son, born of a woman, born under the law, to redeem those under law, that we might receive the full rights of sons" (Gal. 4:4–5; see also Eph. 1:10; 1 Tim. 2:6; Titus 1:3). John looked at the Incarnation as the way God fully revealed Himself to us. Paul liked to point out that the Incarnation was the starting point for Christ's redemptive work.

The Incarnation didn't end at the Resurrection or the Ascension. The Son of God rose from the dead with a glorified human body. He ascended into heaven with that glorified body, and He sits in that body at the right hand of God the Father (Rom. 8:34; Eph. 1:20; Col. 3:1; Heb. 1:3; 8:1; 10:12; 12:2). The incarnate glorified Christ will return to earth (Rev. 19:11–16) to establish His kingdom of righteousness and peace for a thousand years (20:4–6). After the Great White Throne judgment of the unbelieving dead (20:11–15) and the beginning of the eternal state (1 Cor. 15:24–28), the incarnate Lord Jesus Christ will reign forever with God the Father and God the Holy Spirit (Rev. 21:1–2, 22–27; 22:1–5). **—JAW**

***

Through the power of the indwelling Holy Spirit and the written Word of God, seek to "live out" the ascended Christ in your life.

INHERITANCE

The Bible describes both material and spiritual inheritances. A material inheritance consists of an estate that will pass from one generation to the next one. The spiritual inheritance the Bible talks about is the right believers received through Christ to enter the presence of God in heaven.

In the Old Testament the people of God looked forward to a material inheritance. When God called Abram to leave Haran and go to Canaan, He promised, "To your offspring I will give this land" (Gen. 12:7; see also 13:14–17; 15:18–21; 17:7–8; Acts 7:4; Rom. 4:13; Gal. 3:18; Heb. 11:8–10). God repeated this promise of Canaan as the inheritance to Isaac (Gen. 26:2–3) and Jacob (28:13).

After the exodus from Egypt, while Israel camped at Mount Sinai, God identified them as "a people holy to the LORD your God," a people for his own possession (Deut. 7:6; see 4:20; 14:2; 26:18–19; Ex. 19:5). He then directed Moses to lead His chosen people to possess the Promised Land as their inheritance (Ex. 33:1; Num. 26:52–56; 33:50–55; 34:1–12; Deut. 1:8). In turn God always looked at the people of Israel as His inheritance (Deut. 4:20; 9:29; 32:9; see also 9:26; Ex. 34:9; Ps. 33:12).

At Kadesh-Barnea the Israelites listened to the cowardly spies instead of Caleb and Joshua. They refused to enter the Promised Land, so God denied the inheritance to every Israelite twenty years of age and older, except Caleb and Joshua. Israel wandered in the wilderness until that generation died (Num. 14:22–23, 29–35; 26:64–65; 32:10–13; Deut. 1:34–36; 4:21–22, 26). God promised Canaan as the inheritance for the next generation (Num. 33:53–54; 34:13, 16–18, 29). The tribes of Gad and Reuben and half of the tribe of Manasseh inherited the east side of the Jordan River in return for helping the other tribes conquer Canaan (Num. 32:5, 16–22, 29–33; Deut. 1:12–20; Josh. 1:12–16; 22:1–4).

God directed Joshua to use lots to divide the Promised Land of Canaan among the tribes and families of Israel (Num. 26:52–56; 33:53–54; 34:1–2, 13–15; Josh. 14:1–5). God gave Israel detailed laws of inheritance so families could pass the ownership of their allotted land from generation to generation (Num. 27:1–11; 36:1–9). They could never sell their inheritance permanently (Lev. 25:23), though they could lease it (25:14–17). A seller could redeem his inheritance at any time he was able (25:26–27). A near kinsman could redeem an inheritance when the rightful owner could not (25:25; see Ruth 4:1–11). All land ownership reverted to its heirs in the Year of Jubilee, which occurred at fifty-year intervals (Lev. 25:8–10, 13, 28, 31, 33). The Lord justified these regulations by saying, "The land is mine and you are but aliens and my tenants" (25:23).

The people of Israel were dispersed from the land of their inheritance for centuries and scattered throughout the world. Israel exists as a political state among the nations of the world as a result of actions by the League of Nation, the United Nations, and various European powers. At some future time, God will restore Israel to her land on the basis of her original divine inheritance (Deut. 30:1–5; Jer. 29:14; 30:3; Zech. 8:2–3, 7–8, 15; 10:9–10). This restoration will have spiritual as well as physical significance, because it will result from Israel's return to God and her spiritual regeneration (Deut. 30:2, 6, 8; Jer. 31:31–34).

In the New Testament God promises us a spiritual inheritance, resulting from our trust in the Lord Jesus Christ as our Savior. Our inheritance includes salvation (Heb. 1:14) and the sure hope of eternal blessedness in God's presence (Col. 1:12; Titus 3:7; Heb. 9:15; James 2:5; 1 Pet. 1:3–5). The Holy Spirit dwells within us as the guarantee of our inheritance (Eph. 1:13–14). The Holy Spirit witnesses to us "that we are God's children" and "heirs—heirs of God and co-heirs with Christ" (Rom. 8:16–17). We will share in the inheritance of Christ, and He has been "appointed heir of all things" (Heb. 1:2; see Ps. 2:8). In another sense of the term, Christ's inheritance includes all believers (Eph. 1:18).   **—JAW**

* * *

In view of the rich spiritual inheritance reserved in heaven for you, don't live as a spiritual pauper in this life.

INSPIRATION

The doctrine of the inspiration of Scriptures affirms that men directed by God produced the Bible. In inspiration God directed the human authors of Scripture so that they accurately recorded His complete revelation. He superintended their writing without interfering with their individuality, personality, literary style, or their language of composition. In a few instances God dictated Scripture but usually He permitted the human authors to express freely their thoughts and emotions, even their doubts and fears. Yet the ultimate record says exactly what God wanted said and expresses His revelation without error.

Through the years conservative theologians have defended skeptical attacks on the doctrine of inspiration. Some questioned whether all of the Bible is inspired. Others suggested some parts are less inspired than others. When evangelicals speak of *plenary* inspiration, they mean that all of the Bible is equally inspired.

Then some writers contend that

inspiration applies to the ideas, but not the words, of the Bible. So evangelicals added the word *verbal* to their statements about inspiration. Then others suggested that the Bible speaks spiritual truth but contains "unimportant" factual errors, so evangelicals added the word *infallible.* Infallibility became a battleground between conservatives and liberals, so the word *inerrant* became necessary. Inerrancy teaches that the Bible never states as fact something that is in error. Of course the Bible may record the opinions of men or even Satan without necessarily approving them. But everything affirmed in the Scriptures is truth without error. The Bible's inspiration then is plenary, verbal, infallible, and inerrant.

The Scriptures themselves testify of their infallibility. The Bible records the sweep of God's activity from creation to the end of time. The Scriptures contain approximately one thousand passages that were prophetic when written. Five hundred have already been literally fulfilled. Fulfilled prophecy thus provides strong support for the accuracy of all Scripture. It also argues against suggestions that human ingenuity cooked up these prophecies.

Christ Himself affirmed the accuracy of the Scriptures. He declared, "The Scripture cannot be broken" (John 10:35). The Gospels also record many fulfilled prophecies (for example, Matt. 1:22–23; 4:14; 8:17; 12:17; 15:7–8; 21:4–5, 42; 22:29; 26:31, 56; 27:9–10, 35). The Gospels frequently refer to prophecies from Old Testament books that critics like to dispute, such as Deuteronomy, Daniel, and Jonah. When Jesus called Daniel a prophet (Matt. 24:15), He affirmed the inspiration and accuracy of the Book of Daniel.

New Testament writings look at themselves on a par with the Old Testament. In 1 Timothy 5:18 Paul treated both Deuteronomy 25:4 and Luke 10:7 as inspired. Peter called Paul's epistles "Scriptures" (2 Pet. 3:15–16). The central passage on inspiration is 2 Timothy 3:16: "All Scripture is God-breathed and useful for teaching, rebuking, correcting and training in righteousness." "God-breathed" translates the Greek *theopneustos,* which literally means "breathed out by God" or "proceeding from God." Thus under the influence of inspiration the human authors expressed in their unique styles the life-giving Word of God.

Peter described the process by which human authors could write without error in another classic New Testament text about inspiration: "For prophecy never had its origin in the will of man, but men spoke from God as they were carried along by the Holy Spirit" (2 Pet. 1:21). The wind of God's Spirit caught in the sails of human hearts and wills and carried the authors' pens across oceans of parchment to reach the destination—inspired Scripture free from error. Approximately two thousand times Old Testament passages begin, "Thus said the LORD." In each case what follows flows from God.

Plenary, verbal, infallible, inerrant inspiration applies only to the original manuscripts of biblical books as they issued from the pens of their writers. None of those manuscripts exists today. Our Bibles are translations based on copies that, in the case of the Old Testament, may be far removed in time from the originals. All historical and cultural evidence suggests that manuscript copying was done reverently and painstakingly so we can trust the accuracy of existing documents. The Dead Sea Scrolls, found during the decade after World War II, contain manuscripts of various Old Testament books about a thousand years older than those our Bibles are based on. They are essentially identical.

Each book of the Bible witnesses to its inspired and inerrant quality. Apocryphal books, included in some Bible versions, lack the same authoritative, life-changing quality found in the Bible's sixty-six books. The strongest statement of Jesus about divine inspiration of Scripture occurs in the Sermon on the Mount: "I tell you the truth, until heaven and earth disappear, not the smallest letter, not the least stroke of a pen, will by any means

disappear from the Law until everything is accomplished" (Matt. 5:18). "The smallest letter" in the Hebrew alphabet was the *yôd*, a character not much bigger than an apostrophe. "The least stroke" referred to the line or flourish that distinguished one letter of the alphabet from a similar one, something like the difference in English between a *b* and an *h*.

Even radical critics agree that Jesus accepted without question the authority of the Old Testament. His arguments in Matthew 22:43–45 and John 10:34–35 rest on the accuracy of a single word of the Bible. People who deny the inspiration of the Bible must deny the integrity (and deity) of Christ Himself. Add to the witness of Jesus the testimony of Paul and Peter, along with the other writers of Scripture, and you have a formidable array of witnesses to the divine inspiration of the Bible. As a result of inspiration by the Holy Spirit, the Bible is just as reliable in its spiritual and factual statements as if God Himself had taken a pen and written the words.   **—JFW**

***

Study the Scriptures with confidence, knowing they are trustworthy because they are from God.

INTERMEDIATE STATE

The term *intermediate state* doesn't appear in the Bible. It's a theological term created to describe the status of human souls between death and the resurrection of their bodies.

After death, disembodied souls remain conscious of what goes on around them (2 Cor. 5:6–9). Believers in Christ, after death, are "at home with the Lord" (5:8), but their bodies remain dead until the time of resurrection. In heaven their souls are alive and experience various things. Among these is the judgment seat of Christ (5:10) where the Lord will judge and reward believers according to the quality of their lives. Unbelievers will be in hell, or *hades,* where they will suffer until the resurrection of their bodies after the Millennium and before the Great White Throne judgment.

Some theologians speculate that believers have some sort of corporal form during the intermediate state. People saved during the Tribulation will receive white robes (Rev. 6:11). This may suggest they will have temporary bodies. Paul spoke of dead believers being "clothed with our heavenly dwelling" (2 Cor. 5:2, 4). If this refers to the intermediate state, it suggests a temporary body. If this text refers to the future resurrection, it has no bearing on the intermediate state.

In the Old Testament the word *sheol* often refers to the grave, but sometimes it refers to the intermediate state. In the New Testament the word *hades* serves as the Greek equivalent of *sheol.* In both the Old Testament and the Gospels the righteous and the unrighteous exist in an intermediate state, as illustrated by the rich man and Lazarus (Luke 16:19–31). The intermediate state ends when God resurrects the bodies of the dead. The saved will be resurrected at the Rapture of the church (1 Thess. 4:15–16) and after the Tribulation (Rev. 20:6). The lost will be resurrected after the Millennium, judged at the Great White Throne, and cast into the lake of fire (20:11–15). No one occupies the lake of fire presently. God prepared it for the devil and his angels. The unsaved will spend eternity there because they allied themselves with the devil intentionally or by default.

Christ called the intermediate state of the saved "paradise" (Luke 23:43). This refers to the portion of *hades* in which the righteous existed before His Resurrection. Since the Resurrection of Christ, the Scriptures regard paradise as the very presence of God (2 Cor. 12:3–4; Rev. 2:7). At the present time, therefore, only the unsaved occupy *hades.*

The important thing to remember about the intermediate state is that both saved and lost exist consciously between the death and the resurrection of their bodies. **—JFW**

* * *

Be comforted by the promise that after death God has prepared a place for us to live with Him.

INTERPRETATION

Many people are confused about how to interpret the Bible. Usually this happens because they haven't learned or applied several standard rules of interpretation. The starting point for interpreting the Bible is simple: God isn't trying to confuse us. He has said what He means directly and clearly.

Fairly early in church history, the Alexandrian school of theology in Egypt interpreted the Bible as a series of obscure allegories. The allegorical method of interpreting the Bible fell out of favor after a few centuries, but its legacy remains. Some churches still interpret large sections of prophecy in fanciful ways, and too many Christians think the Bible is full of hidden meanings that preachers discover as if by magic. The fact of the matter is that the Bible is understood at two levels. Intellectually, we discover the meaning of biblical statements much as we would understand any other literature. Spiritually we depend on the Holy Spirit to give us discernment of the life-changing power of the Scriptures that goes beyond their intellectual meaning.

The first rule of biblical interpretation is to interpret a passage of the Bible according to the normal sense of its words, unless there is good reason to believe a figure of speech has been used. Keep in mind these ques-tions: What did the author mean here? What did he intend for us to understand? If the author intended us to understand a statement in a figurative way, he probably indicated that in the context. A passage means what the author intended when he penned the words.

A related rule of interpretation is to interpret verses in the light of their immediate context. Context will reveal when a statement contains non-literal figures of speech. Consider the ten horns of the beast in Daniel 7:7. Verse 24 indicates the horns represent ten kings. Similes, metaphors, personifications, hyperboles, symbols, and other figures of speech are normal literary forms that depict objective, discernible truths in a picturesque way.

A third basic rule of biblical interpretation is to interpret obscure passages, for which the meaning is not clear, by passages that are clear. In most important doctrinal matters, the Bible states plainly and clearly in normal terms what God means.

When people misinterpret the Bible, they usually haven't let the Bible speak for itself. They've been careless or hurried. They often haven't examined the details of the passage under consideration. Too often they've ignored the context of the passage. Most often misinterpretation occurs when Bible students force the Bible to say what they want it to rather than what it does say.

Always keep in mind that God intended the Bible to communicate its deepest level of truth to those who have spiritual discernment. The intellectual sense of the Bible is objective and literary. The Holy Spirit illumines the spiritual sense. When we discover the Bible's normal meaning and receive the Sprit's illumination, the Scriptures have communicated all that God wants us to know in this life about Himself and His plans. **—JFW**

***

Ask the Holy Spirit to help you understand the truths in God's Word, and then apply them to your life.

ISRAEL

The Lord changed Jacob's name to *Israel* after Jacob wrestled with Him at Peniel (Gen. 32:28). "Jacob" means "supplanter" or "deceiver." "Israel" means "he wrestled with God" or "God rules." Israel became the name of the nation descended from Jacob. The name "Israel" identifies the nation about twenty-five hundred times in the Old and New Testaments. Each occurrence honors Jacob as the father of the twelve tribes of Israel. After the Babylonian captivity, Israelites are also called Jews, starting in Ezra 4:12. The term Jew derives from Judah, Israel's principal tribe.

Israel became a nation during its four centuries of slavery in Egypt. Because of famine Jacob had moved his entire family to Egypt because his son Joseph administered the famine relief program there. Jacob's descendants, the Israelites, grew from a clan numbering about seventy to a nation of perhaps two million. The Egyptians feared their number, enslaved them, and oppressed them greatly, as recorded in Exodus.

After four hundred years God raised up Moses and inflicted ten plagues on the land of Egypt. Under duress the pharoah allowed the Israelites to leave Egypt for the Promised Land. But because of their unbelief, God forced Israel to wander forty years in the desert of the Sinai Peninsula. After Moses died, Joshua led Israel across the Jordan River and they began to conquer and possess the land.

Before his death Moses gave Israel what is called Deuteronomy, "the second law," in which he summarized what God had revealed about His will for them. He told them that if they kept the Law they would be blessed and protected in the land, but if they broke the Law they would eventually be expelled. Israel neglected and disobeyed the Law century after century. When Israel exhausted the longsuffering of the Lord, the Assyrians conquered the ten northern tribes in 722 B.C. and the Babylonians conquered Judah and Benjamin in 586 B.C., destroying the city of Jerusalem and its beautiful temple.

Just before the Babylonian Captivity God raised up three major prophets. Jeremiah ministered to those in the land and almost lost his life because he said the nation should surrender to the Babylonians. The rulers in Jerusalem ignored Jeremiah, and the Babylonians slaughtered them and destroyed their city and temple. The second prophet, Daniel, grew up in Babylon and served in the government there. The Babylonians had deported him and the children of other noblemen in 605 B.C. when they were young teenagers to insure their fathers would not rebel. Daniel interpreted Nebuchadnezzar's dream (Dan. 2), and earned the post of chief executive to the Babylonian emperor during the remaining forty years of his reign. Daniel no doubt did much to alleviate Israel's sad condition. The third prophet, Ezekiel, went to Babylon in the second wave of deportees in 597 B.C. Ezekiel declared the word of the Lord to the captives in Babylon.

After the Jews' seventy years of captivity in Babylon, the Persian emperor Cyrus permitted some of them to return to their homeland, as God had predicted (Jer. 29:10). Nearly fifty thousand Jews returned to reestablish themselves in their land. Enemies prevented them from completing a small version of the temple until 516 B.C. It was 444 B.C. before Nehemiah led the Jews in rebuilding the fallen walls of Jerusalem. Over a long period of time the Jews restored Jerusalem and other Judean cities. As a result Christ was born in Bethlehem, not Babylon, just as Micah 5:2 had predicted.

Israel, however, continued to depart from God. They rejected Jesus as the Messiah and participated in His execution. Roman soldiers destroyed Jerusalem in A.D. 70, and most Jews were scattered to other nations. Only about fifteen thousand Jews remained in the land.

Israel has a future. The Old Testament predicts over and over that Israel will be regathered from the ends of the earth and restored as a glorious nation. Israel's restoration and prosperity highlight the end times.

The New Testament adds details about Israel's future. During the Tribulation, following the Rapture of the church, Israel will experience a terrible time of trouble (Jer. 30:5–11). At Christ's Second Coming God will rescue Israel and regather them from all over the world (Ezek. 39:25–29). Jews who don't come to Christ will be eliminated (20:33–38). Godly Israelites, those who receive Christ before His Second Coming, will be given the Promised Land. This will fulfill

God's promise that Israel will ultimately possess the land. God originally made this promise to Abraham (Gen. 15:18–21). During the Millennium the land will be partitioned into twelve sections, one for each of the twelve tribes (Ezek. 47:13—48:35). Jesus Christ, Israel's Messiah, will rule the millennial kingdom as the Son of David on the Davidic throne (Is. 9:7).

—JFW

***

God's faithfulness to the nation Israel is a reminder that He will never leave us or forsake us.

Jj

JERUSALEM

Jerusalem is the sacred city to three monotheistic world religions—Christianity, Judaism, and Islam. As a result Jerusalem has been called "the world's most significant city" and "the spiritual capital of the world."

Nobody knows for sure what the name Jerusalem means. At one time scholars assumed it meant "city of peace" (from the Hebrew *šālōm*). Many modern scholars believe Jerusalem breaks into two parts: *uru* meaning "city" and *salim,* the name of an Amorite god. Jerusalem then would mean "the city of (the god) Salim." The Bible variously refers to Jerusalem as Salem (Gen. 14:18), Jebus (Judg. 19:10–11), Ariel (Is. 29:1), the City of David (2 Sam. 5:7, 9), Zion (Ps. 87:1–3), the City of Righteousness (Is. 1:26), and the Holy City (Is. 48:2; 52:1; Rev. 21:2). Muslims call Jerusalem *al-Quds,* "the Holy [Town]."

Jerusalem perches on a ridge 2,550 feet above sea level some fourteen miles west of the northern tip of the Dead Sea and thirty-three miles east of the Mediterranean coast. Jerusalem, like Rome, is a city set on hills. Jerusalem's five hills are bordered on the east, south, and west by deep ravines. The psalmist wrote of Jerusalem, "It is beautiful in its loftiness, the joy of the whole earth" (Ps. 48:2).

The long, complex history of Jerusalem is littered with sieges, surrenders, restorations, and rebuildings. In about 3000 B.C. nomadic tribes first settled on the city's southeastern hill. Archeologists have found their kitchen pots and flint tools. About a thousand years later in patriarchal times, Abraham tithed battle spoils to Melchizedek, the priest-king of Jerusalem (Gen. 14:18–20). More than five hundred years later, Adoni-Zedek, king of Jerusalem, gathered a coalition and unsuccessfully opposed Joshua's conquest (Josh. 10:1–26). At that time the tribe of Judah temporarily held Jerusalem, But the Jebusites soon reoccupied it for roughly five hundred more years until Israel's monarchy.

David conquered Jerusalem about 1000 B.C. (2 Sam. 5:6–7) and made it the capital of his kingdom that ultimately stretched from Egypt to the Euphrates River. David planned to establish Jerusalem as a religious capital as well as a political capital. He therefore brought the ark of the covenant into the city and laid plans for building a temple for the Lord God of Israel. Solomon, David's son, built the temple in the seven years spanning 966–960 B.C. (1 Kin. 6:1). The presence of God filled the Jerusalem temple as the climax of its dedication ceremonies (8:10).

Solomon also made Jerusalem a cosmopolitan commercial center. Wealth poured into Jerusalem from caravans plying routes to Egypt and Babylon and shipping, using the Red Sea as a gateway to Arabia, Africa, and India. After Solomon's death civil war ended Israel's "golden age" and divided the nation into two minor kingdoms. Jerusalem, the capital of the southern kingdom of Judah, would never again be secure from strong enemies.

Within five years of Israel's division, Egypt invaded Judah, captured Jerusalem, and plundered the palace and temple treasuries of the wealth David and Solomon had amassed (14:25–26). During the reign of Jehoram (848–841 B.C.), both the Philistines and Arabs seized opportunities to plunder Jerusalem (2 Chr. 21:16–17). When Athaliah, Ahab and Jezebel's daughter, ruled as queen of Judah (841–835 B.C.), she made Jerusalem a center of Baal worship (2 Kin. 11; 2 Chr. 22:10—23:15). Early in the eighth century B.C., Jehoash, king of Israel, attacked and plundered Jerusalem (2 Kin. 14:8–14). King Uzziah repaired the damage caused by Jehoash and during a long reign revived the glory and influence of Jerusalem (2 Chr. 26:7–8).

Ominous international pressure threatened Jerusalem in 735–734 B.C. in the form of a joint siege by Syrian and Israelite armies. King Ahaz paid heavy tribute to the king of Assyria to get him to drive away the besiegers (2 Kin. 16:7–9). By 701 B.C. the Assyrians themselves had invaded Judah and besieged Jerusalem. In preparation King Hezekiah armed the people, repaired the walls, and safeguarded the water supply of Jerusalem. None of those measures could repel the Assyrians, but the angel of the Lord destroyed the Assyrian army as it slept one night (18:13—19:37).

The rise of Babylon as a world power and the military prowess of its ruler Nebuchadnezzar spelled the beginning of the end for Jerusalem. Babylonian forces invaded Judah in 605 and 597 B.C. to compel Judah's submission to Babylonian policy. Judah persisted in acting independently, so Babylon launched a crushing attack on Jerusalem. In 586 B.C. the city was decimated. The Babylonians systematically dismantled the Solomonic temple,

JERUSALEM170

the palace complex, and the city walls. Every survivor of any social significance was deported to Babylon. Only the poorest peasants and a handful of administrators were left behind. The prophet Jeremiah observed and lamented the tragic scene (Lam. 1:1–19).

In little more than fifty years the rise of Persia wiped Babylon from the stage of world domination. Cyrus, the first Persian emperor, decreed that all willing Jews could return to Judah and rebuild Jerusalem and the temple of the Lord (Ezra 1). It took twenty years for the first wave of repatriates to establish themselves and build the second temple under the urging of the prophets Haggai and Zechariah. That temple was dedicated in 516 B.C. (6:13–22). Jerusalem itself, however, was sparsely populated. Its walls were broken, and its gates burned down. Not until 444 B.C. did Nehemiah appear on the scene to serve as the leader and catalyst who would oversee the complete rebuilding of the walls and the repopulating of the city. Nehemiah left a secure post in the court of the Persian emperor Artaxerxes to provide vision and energy in Jerusalem. He spurred the people of Jerusalem to complete an impossible task—rebuilding the walls and gates in just fifty-two days!

A notable crisis took place in the second century B.C. in the intertesta-mental period. The Seleucids of Syria wrested control of Palestine from the Ptolemies of Egypt and tried to force Hellenistic culture on the Jews. The Syrian forces captured Jerusalem and desecrated the temple. The Syrian ruler abolished the worship of the Lord and installed a statue of the Olympian Zeus in the temple. Three years later, in 165 B.C., Jewish patriots led by the Maccabean family expelled the Syrians from Jerusalem. They cleansed the temple and rededicated it at the Feast of Lights. Jews continue to celebrate this feast (Hanukkah) to the present day.

Home rule lasted about a century. The Roman general Pompey took advantage of a period of civil strife between several Jewish sects and besieged Jerusalem. He entered the city in 63 B.C., dissolved the Maccabean government, and annexed Jerusalem and Judea to the Roman province of Syria.

During Roman rule, Jerusalem was the religious center of Judaism. Each year throngs of pilgrims gathered in the city on Passover and other religious feast days. While Jesus was born in Bethlehem and grew to manhood in Nazareth, He visited Jerusalem on numerous occasions. Mary and Joseph presented Jesus at the temple when He was eight days old (Luke 2:21–38). At age twelve, Jesus dialogued with the teachers in the temple (2:41–50). After Jesus' baptism, Satan took Him to Jerusalem and dared Him to leap from the high point of the temple (4:9–12). John recorded four visits of Jesus to Jerusalem (John 2:13—3:21; 5:1–47; 7—10; 12—20). The Synoptic Gospels detail Jesus' Passion Week in Jerusalem. Jesus' death, resurrection, and ascension all took place in and about Jerusalem.

The history of the early church also centered in Jerusalem. The first seven chapters of the Book of Acts occur in Jerusalem until persecution scatters disciples into Judea and beyond. As the gospel penetrates deeper into the Roman Empire, the apostle Paul returned to Jerusalem from successive preaching missions to confer with the leaders of the church there (Acts 15:1–35; 21:17–19).Following a four-year rebellion of the Jews, the Roman general Titus breached the walls of Jerusalem in A.D. 70 and burned the temple, just as Jesus had predicted (Mark 13:2).

In the postbiblical period the Jews rebelled again under Bar Kochba in A.D. 134. Once more the Romans razed Jerusalem. They quickly rebuilt it as a pagan city and named it Aelia Capitolina. Since then, Jerusalem has passed through nine periods of rule: Roman, to 330; Byzantine, to 638; Arab, to 1099; Crusader, to 1187 and from 1229 to 1244; Arab, to 1516; Turkish, to 1917; British, to 1948; Jordanian, to 1967; and Israeli, to the present.

When Christ returns to the earth at His Second Advent, Jerusalem once again will become the scene where biblical prophecies are fulfilled. Christ will descend to the Mount of Olives and rescue the believing Jewish remnant from a besieged Jerusalem (Zech. 14:1–4). The city will be the Messiah's millennial capital (14:20–21) and the home of a temple whose sacrifices will memorialize the sacrificial death of Jesus Christ.

The final biblical reference to Jerusalem is found in Revelation 21—22. John, in a glorious vision of the eternal state, saw "the Holy City, the new Jerusalem, coming down out of heaven from God" (Rev. 21:2). This city, anticipated by Abraham (Heb. 11:10, 16) and promised by Christ (John 14:2–3), is "the heavenly Jerusalem, the city of the living God" (Heb. 12:22), "Jerusalem that is above" (Gal. 4:26). The New Jerusalem will shine with the glory of God as the final and eternal home of redeemed humanity. In contrast to man-made cities that display only human achievements, this heavenly city will blaze with the light of the glory of God. At last Jerusalem will deservedly be called the Holy City.   **—DKC**

***

Rejoice in the fact that the believer's final home will be in the glorious Holy City, the New Jerusalem.

JUDGMENT

God, "the Judge of all the earth" (Gen. 18:25; see 1 Sam. 2:10) and the judge of "all men" (Heb. 12:23), judges with equity (Ps. 96:10), justice (Acts 17:31), impartiality (1 Pet. 1:17), righteousness (Ps. 9:8), and truth (Rom. 2:2). The Scriptures affirm that God judges all activities that occur on earth. He wields unlimited authority in heaven and earth. No one can question the accuracy of His judgments (Pss. 58:11; 99:4). God's justice is absolute, as the Scriptures often affirm (Gen. 18:25; Deut. 32:4; Pss. 33:5; 89:14; Jer. 11:20; 33:15; Ezek. 33:20; Rom. 3:5–6; 1 Pet. 2:23; Rev. 16:7; 19:2). He "loves justice" (Pss. 11:7; 99:4), and He has unlimited power to carry out His judgment.

Jesus' death on the Cross was an act of God's justice, just as much as it was an act of His grace and love. Jesus suffered the judicial punishment for the sins of the entire world "in his body on the tree" (1 Pet. 2:24). Isaiah wrote that "the LORD has laid on him the iniquity of us all" (Is. 53:6), and Paul wrote, "God made him who had no sin to be sin for us" (2 Cor. 5:21). Jesus Christ died on our behalf "to demonstrate his [God's] justice" against sin (Rom. 3:25–26). That is, God did not overlook sin. Someone had to pay its penalty, and Jesus Christ willingly did so.

The Old Testament records a number of historic instances in which God judged individuals and nations for their sins. His ultimate judgment on individuals occurs, however, after death. "Man is destined to die once, and after that to face judgment" (Heb. 9:27).

Because prophetic Scriptures are frequently ignored, many people assume there will be only one final judgment of the saved and unsaved sometime at the end of the age. The Scriptures, however, speak of a series of coming judgments. The judgment seat of Christ will take place after the rapture of the church. In that judgment in heaven believers will be evaluated on the basis of what they have done for Christ and will receive or not receive rewards (2 Cor. 5:10). The Tribulation occupies the seven-year between the Rapture and the Second Coming. As the name Tribulation implies, the period will be filled with judgments on the earth because of human wickedness (Rev. 6—18). Many wrongly tone down the severity of these judgments by saying they are not to be taken literally. Clearly they describe horrendous judgments.

Several other judgments will take place when Christ returns to the earth. The armies that gather to fight it out in the Holy Land will unite to fight the armies from heaven that accompany Christ. They will be immediately destroyed in an act of divine judgment (Rev. 16:13–16; 19:19). The Lord Jesus will capture the Antichrist, called "the beast," and his cohort, called "the false prophet," and cast them into the lake of fire (19:20). An angel will bind Satan and imprison him in the

Abyss for a thousand years (20:1–3). Jews who survive the Tribulation will be judged, and believing Jews will be given a place of blessing in the millennial kingdom.

Matthew 25:31–46 describes a judgment of Gentiles who survive the Tribulation. The sheep represent the saved, who will enter the millennial kingdom in their natural bodies, and the goats represent the lost, who will be judged by everlasting punishment in hell.

In the Millennium Christ will reign with an absolute rule and will judge any open rebellion against Him. At the end of the thousand years Satan will be loosed, judged, and cast into the lake of fire (Rev. 20:7–10), and the wicked will be judged at the Great White Throne judgment (20:11–15). Eternal punishment of the lost is dreadful to contemplate, but it is an act of divine justice. Sin cannot go unpunished. As Paul wrote, "God is just" (2 Thess. 1:6).

God isn't the only person in the Bible who exercises judgment. We are told not to judge fellow believers needlessly (Matt. 7:1–5). Yet we should call sin sin. We should exercise such discerning judgment in a spirit of gentleness, always recognizing that we too are sinners (Gal. 6:1). When we come to the Lord's Table, we should judge ourselves, to be sure we have no unconfessed sin in our lives (1 Cor. 11:27–32).

God the Father has committed all judgment to Jesus Christ, His Son (John 5:22, 27).   **—JFW**

***

Be gracious in dealing with others, knowing that God alone judges impartially and in righteousness.

JUSTICE

Justice involves what is right or correct, as conveyed by several Hebrew words in the Old Testament (primarily *mišpat*) and several Greek words in the New Testament (mainly *krisis* and *dikaiosynē*). Technically "justice" and "righteousness" mean the same thing. Both English words translate the same Hebrew and Greek words (*mišpat* and *dikaiosynē*). "Justice" and "righteousness" deal with treating other people (including God) correctly. Connotatively, "righteousness" involves integrity of personal character and "justice" relates to legal fairness.

Justice springs from the heart of God, who is infinitely just by nature and always fair in all His dealings with His creatures. Isaiah declared that "the LORD is a God of justice" (Is. 30:18). Elihu, one of Job's friends, said, "I will ascribe justice to my Maker" (Job 36:3; see also Ps. 9:16; Is. 5:16). In the New Testament Paul simply asserted, "God is just" (1 Thess. 1:6). Through Isaiah God said, "I, the LORD, love justice; I hate robbery and iniquity" (Is. 61:8).

God's justice is almost invariably emphasized in contexts that speak of His grace, love, and mercy. Justice involves much more than punishment. However, God will punish when He must, because He is "the Judge of all the earth" (Gen. 18:25; see also Pss. 58:11; 94:2), who "has entrusted all judgment to the Son" (John 5:22).

Because of God's just character and actions, God expects justice to prevail in people's dealings with each other. He has higher expectations of justice for those who are in authority over others. God frowns severely on those who misuse their position and power. Before the Israelites entered Canaan, Moses told them to "follow justice and justice alone." At Sinai he warned them not to "pervert justice by siding with the crowd" (Ex. 23:2; see also 23:6; Lev. 19:15; Deut. 1:17; 16:19). Through Zechariah God warned Israel, "Administer true justice" (Zech. 7:9). This involved showing "mercy and compassion to one another," not oppressing "the widow or the fatherless, the alien or the poor," and not thinking "evil of each other" (7:10).

Of necessity, the exercise of justice involves the establishment of laws and courts. As quoted above, God said, "I hate robbery and iniquity" (Is. 61:8). Laws can be interpreted and administered so rigidly, however, that judges fail to show mercy when it's called for. The Pharisees of the New Testament mechanically condemned Jesus' disciples for plucking and eating heads of grain to satisfy their hunger on the Sabbath (Matt. 12:1–2). They criticized Jesus for healing on the Sabbath (John 5:1–16; see also Matt. 12:9–14; Mark 3:1–6; Luke 6:6–11). The Pharisees committed injustices by emphasizing the letter of the Law while missing the Law's spirit. Justice requires that laws be executed with wisdom.

The exercise of justice also required the establishment of governmental authorities with power to enforce laws. God ordained existing governing powers, even ungodly ones (Rom. 13:1). The Bible directs us to submit to our governments (13:1–7; Titus 3:1; 1 Pet. 2:13–14). In the millennial kingdom the Lord Jesus Christ will implement the ultimate perfect justice throughout His realm and His reign (Is. 2:2–4; 42:1–4; 2 Thess. 1:6–7; Rev. 19:11).

—**JAW**

***

Be vigilant to exercise justice
and fairness in every area
of your life.

JUSTIFICATION

Justification is an act of God. God justifies sinners who believe in Christ by declaring them righteous on the basis of what Christ did for them on the Cross. Justification is a legal ruling by God the Judge. On the one hand God determined that Christ's sacrifice satisfied the demands of His wrath. On the other hand God imputes the righteousness of Christ to regenerated sinners.

The death of Christ could justify all humanity, but only those who trust in Christ as their Savior receive justification. Romans 3:28, Galatians 2:16, and 3:24 speak of being "justified by faith." Romans 3:24 and Titus 3:7 state that we are justified "by his grace." Abraham provides the classic Old Testament example of justification by faith: "Abraham believed the LORD, and he credited it to him as righteousness" (Gen. 15:6). In justification God credits Christ's righteousness to believers so that God sees them in right standing before Him (Rom. 4:5, 23–24).

Christ said very little about justification. On one occasion He said that a tax collector who prayed, " 'God, have mercy on me, a sinner' . . . went home justified before God" (Luke 18:13–14).

The apostle Paul developed most of the New Testament teaching about justification. He related justification to many other aspects of salvation, such as redemption, reconciliation, and righteousness. He explained that no one can be justified by works (Gal. 2:16; 3:11; Rom. 4:5) because no quantity of good deeds can change a person's past or his or her sin nature. Only the death of Christ on the Cross gave God a basis on which He can justify believing sinners. This is why Paul wrote that we are "justified by his blood" (5:9).

Justification includes more than forgiveness of sins. Forgiveness debits guilt from a believer's spiritual "bank account." Justification credits righteousness (Christ's righteousness) to a believer's account. Justification is an act of God's grace, because no one deserves it. However, it is also an act of righteousness, because Christ paid in full the penalty for human sins. The Christian doctrine of justification by faith stands in stark contrast to other world religions which base salvation on human efforts.   **—JFW**

***

Because of your right standing
as a believer before God, reflect
God's righteousness in your
dealings with others.

K

Kk

KING

A king is a life-long, hereditary, sovereign ruler of a city or state. The first biblical reference to kings as supreme political leaders occurs in Genesis 14. Several kings captured Lot while he lived in Sodom. Abram, Lot's uncle, defeated those kings, rescued Lot and other captives, and retrieved the plunder. Immediately following this rescue, Melchizedek, king of Salem (Jerusalem), blessed Abram. Melchizedek also served as "priest of God Most High" (14:18). In recognition of that position Abram gave him a tenth of his possessions (14:20).

Throughout biblical history, the supreme political rulers of nations were called kings. Often minor biblical kings ruled city-states.

The nation Israel was a theocracy. The covenant God made with Israel at Mount Sinai made Him her leader. By the end of the period of the judges, a strong popular movement demanded a king so Israel could be like other nations (1 Sam. 8:5, 20). Samuel, Israel's last judge and a prophet, warned Israel that a king could oppress in many ways (8:11–18). The people insisted, so God told Samuel to anoint Saul, son of Kish, as king. Saul rather quickly turned from God, and Samuel anointed David as king (16:12–13). David did not become king until Saul died. After David died, his son Solomon succeeded him. When Israel divided into two kingdoms in 931 B.C., ten tribes formed the northern kingdom known as Israel, while Judah and Benjamin formed the southern kingdom known as Judah. The nineteen kings of the south were David's descendants from the tribe of Judah. The books of Kings and Chronicles labeled eight of Judah's kings as godly rulers. The twenty kings of the north came from various tribes. A single dynasty never took hold. Assassinations and coups occurred frequently. The Bible judged all twenty northern kings as wicked rulers.

The Law and the Prophets identified the Lord God as Israel's King in the sense of being her Sovereign (Is. 33:22; 43:15; Zeph. 3:15). And of course He has always reigned over the universe (Pss. 9:8; 47:7–8; 99:1).

In His First Advent Jesus Christ presented Himself to Israel as her King, but the nation rejected Him (Luke 7:30; 17:25). At His trial and crucifixion Jesus was mockingly derided by Roman authorities as the "King of the Jews" (Matt. 27:29, 37). Pilate did that to irritate Jewish leaders who wanted nothing to do with Jesus as their king. So His reign on the earth awaits His Second Coming when He will reign on David's throne (Is. 9:7).

In an important prophecy in 2 Samuel 7 God told David that his descendants would rule over the house of Israel forever. Ultimately Jesus Christ, a direct descendant of David of the tribe of Judah, will fulfill this prophecy. Amillenarians say this Davidic kingdom is entirely a spiritual reign in which Christ rules over His church today from heaven. Premillenarians, however, interpret the millennial promises of the Old and New Testaments literally. We believe that Christ will rule on the earth for one thousand years. He will reign over Israel in a political kingdom and over the entire world as the King of kings and the

Lord of lords (1 Tim. 6:15; Rev. 19:16; see also 17:14). **—JFW**

***

Praise God for the realization that the day is coming when Christ will be recognized as the Ruler over all the earth.

KINGDOM

A kingdom refers to the realm ruled by a king, whether a city-state, a nation, or an empire. The Bible refers to many earthly kingdoms and to several spiritual kingdoms, including the kingdom of heaven, the kingdom of God, and the future millennial kingdom. The Bible also calls God's rule as the Creator and Sovereign of the whole earth a kingdom (2 Kin. 19:15; 1 Chr. 29:11; Pss. 47:2, 7–8; 103:19).

Amillennial theology stresses that there is one kingdom of God with various subdivisions. These include the rule of God as Creator, His rule of Israel in Old Testament times, and most preeminently His spiritual rule over all humanity and especially over those who believe in Him.

Premillennialism, on the other hand, emphasizes different forms of the kingdom of God, each with its own characteristics. God's rule over creation arises from His role as Creator of all things. It includes all humanity, whether believers or unbelievers, as well as the world of nature. In the Old Testament God was the ultimate sovereign over the nation of Israel. He expected Israel's government to reflect the principles of His kingdom. After the nation became a monarchy, God entered a covenant with the house of David that established His reign through that dynasty. After the death of David's son Solomon, political Israel divided. Ten northern tribes broke away but kept the name Israel. Benjamin and Judah remained true to the Davidic monarchy. The resultant southern kingdom was known as Judah. After the Babylonian captivity, a remnant returned from exile under Zerubbabel, Ezra, and Nehemiah to reestablish Judah. Except for the Maccabean era, Judah existed as a province of successive empires, the last one being Rome. Many Jews scattered to other parts of the Mediterranean world.

When Christ returns to the earth, He will restore the nation Israel to her land (Jer. 31:17; Ezek. 36:24; Amos 9:11–15) and reestablish the kingdom of David (2 Sam. 7:12–16; Is. 9:7; Luke 1:31–33). David will be raised from the dead and will reign with Christ in Jerusalem (Jer. 30:9; Ezek. 34:23–24; 37:24–25). In Christ's millennial rule of one thousand years (Rev. 20:6) He will reign in justice (Is. 2:2–5; 11:1–5; 32:1) on David's throne (9:7).

Just before His Ascension the disciples asked Jesus if He was going to restore the kingdom to Israel then (Acts 1:6). They hoped He would set up the millennial kingdom at that time. They

K

did not envision the church age separating the First and Second Advents of Christ.

After the Millennium, in which Christ will "reign until he has put all his enemies under his feet" (1 Cor. 15:25; see also Pss. 8:6; 110:1), He will hand over the kingdom to God the Father (1 Cor. 15:24). God will reign through eternity.

Premillenarians interpret these prophecies literally, whereas amillenarians take them in a nonliteral sense and apply them to God's present spiritual rule over believers.

The New Testament speaks of the *kingdom of heaven* and the *kingdom of God.* Most expositors regard these two kingdoms as one without noting the differences. Sometimes the expressions are used synonymously, but when they are contrasted the kingdom of heaven includes not only true believers but also those who profess Christ but are not actually saved. The kingdom of God, however, includes only those who are genuine believers.

The term *kingdom of heaven* is found only in Matthew. Bible teachers who equate the kingdom of heaven with the kingdom of God point out that Matthew is the most Jewish of the Gospels. Strict Jews reverenced the name *Yahweh* and regularly replaced it so they wouldn't accidentally profane it. These scholars theorize that Matthew replaced the common expression *kingdom of God (Yahweh)* with *kingdom of heaven* out of respect for the divine name. However, even in Matthew the term *kingdom of God* occurs four times (Matt. 12:28; 19:24; 21:31, 43). According to these passages those who are in the kingdom of God are saved. There are no false professions of salvation in this kingdom. However, in Jesus' parables of the kingdom of heaven in Matthew 13, false profession is an issue. There are weeds among the standing grain (13:24–30, 36–42) and bad fish in the net among the good ones (13:47–50). Such parables can illustrate the kingdom of heaven, but not the kingdom of God. Dispensational scholars take both sides of this interpretive debate. Dispensational interpretation of prophecy does not depend on this distinction.

In John 3:3, 5 Jesus said the kingdom of God belongs only to the born again, those who receive eternal life by trusting Jesus as their Savior. The kingdom of God is the spiritual rule of God in the hearts of believers. God has brought believers, Paul wrote, from the realm of darkness "into the kingdom of the Son" (Col. 1:13; see also 4:11).

The major contrast between the premillennial and amillennial points of view on the kingdom is that premillennialism holds that Christ will reign from Jerusalem in a future literal political kingdom on earth. Amillennialism denies that such a literal event will occur after the Second Coming. They believe Christ fulfills all millennial prophecies in His present rule over creation and the church.

—**JFW**

***

Count it a privilege that every believer is under the rule of God now and will participate in serving the Lord in the coming millennial kingdom.

— **LI** —

LAMB

A lamb is a young sheep, usually less than a year old. Lambs figure prominently in the Scripture as sacrificial animals and as symbols of gentleness and innocence. Abel offered the first animal sacrifice in the Bible (Gen. 4:4). The first reference to a lamb as a sacrifice occurs in conversation between Isaac and Abraham as they traveled to Mount Moriah where Abraham expected to sacrifice his son (22:7–8). One of the best-known references to a sacrificial lamb is the Passover lamb (Ex. 12:1–5). All three of the above passages contain the Hebrew term *śeh*, "one from the flock," which could refer to a lamb or a kid. Ancient Near Easterners often didn't distinguish very carefully between young goats and young sheep. We don't know which animal Abel offered. God provided Abraham a ram to replace Isaac. The Passover sacrifice could be an unblemished one-year-old male lamb or kid.

The Law employed a more species-specific term, *kebeś*, to describe the lambs for the daily sacrifices in the tabernacle (Ex. 29:38–41; Num. 28:1–8). Every day the priests offered two one-year-old male lambs, one in the morning and the other at twilight. These burnt offerings would be a "pleasing aroma" to the Lord. Besides the daily offerings, lambs were also used for Sabbath offerings (Num. 28:9–10) and monthly offerings (28:11–15). Lambs played important roles at Passover (28:16–25), the Feast of Weeks (28:26–31), the Feast of Trumpets (29:1–6), the Day of Atonement (29:7–11), and the Feast of Tabernacles (29:12–40). Lambs sacrificed as sin offerings were females without defects (Lev. 4:32). A lamb could be sacrificed for purification after childbirth (12:6), and three lambs were offered to cleanse someone ceremonially who had been healed of an infectious disease (14:10).

Lambs were common in Israelite daily life, so the term *lamb* picked up metaphorical meanings. In recounting the power of God in bringing Israel out of Egypt, a psalmist compared quaking mountains to skipping lambs

(Ps. 114:1–4). Isaiah used a lamb metaphor to express the tranquility of the Millennium (Is. 11:6; 65:25). He pictured the Messiah carrying the people of Israel in His arms as a shepherd would carry his lambs (40:11). The lamb portrays the meekness of Messiah (53:7), as well as the submission of the enemies of Israel when future judgment comes (Jer. 51:40).

The New Testament uses three words for "lamb"—*amnos, arēn,* and *arnion*—and applies the first and third to Jesus. John the Baptist introduced Jesus to his followers by identifying Him as "the Lamb of God" who takes away the sin of the world (John 1:29, 36). The Greek word *amnos* is used in those two passages to describe the lamb. This term appears four times in the New Testament, always in reference to Jesus as our sacrifice for sin. Peter wrote that believers have been redeemed "with the precious blood of Christ, a lamb without blemish or defect" (1 Pet. 1:19). *Amnos* also occurs in Acts 8:32, in Luke's record of the Old Testament passage the Ethiopian eunuch read (Is. 53:7). Paul referred to Jesus as "the Passover Lamb, who has been sacrificed" (1 Cor. 5:7), but the word *lamb* has been supplied by the New International Version translators. Though the writer of Hebrews did not use the word *lamb,* he did consider Jesus the Sacrifice offered to God for the sins of humankind (Heb. 9:14; 10:10, 14; 13:12).

Like the prophets, Jesus used the term "lamb" (*arēn*) in a figurative sense when describing the precarious circumstances His disciples would face in fulfilling their responsibilities (Luke 10:3). In His conversation with Peter after the Resurrection (John 21:15), Jesus again used the word *arnion* metaphorically as He exhorted Peter to feed His lambs.

The entire Book of Revelation centers around Christ, the Lamb of God. More than two dozen times John refers to the "Lamb," using the Greek word *arnion.* Historically *arnion* meant "little lamb," but by New Testament times the diminutive sense had dropped from the word.

The Book of Revelation described the Son of God as the Lamb who has been slain (5:6). The future of the world will revolve around Him. The Lamb is the only One worthy to break the seals and unleash the judgments that will come on the earth in the Tribulation (5:1–10). People from all walks of life will fall down before the Lamb as He alone has the authority to judge (6:15–17). Those saved during the Tribulation will be redeemed by the blood of the Lamb (7:12). The Lamb is also the Shepherd, who provides eternal life (7:17). As the Lamb, Christ will triumph over Satan, the great adversary of Israel (12:7–12). Israel's hope and salvation during the Tribulation will be the Lamb (14:1–5). The Lamb will also triumph over the kings and rulers of the earth (17:14). John had a vision of the wedding of the Lamb to His bride (19:6–9). The final two chapters of Revelation describe the new heavens and the new earth and the splendor of life in the presence of the Lamb (22:3–5). Throughout eternity believers will enjoy the salvation of the Lamb and will worship and serve Him forever (21:27; 22:3–5). —**WGJ**

***

Always be thankful that Jesus, the Lamb of God, gave Himself for the sins of the world.

LAST DAYS

The Bible uses the phrases "the last days" and "the last times" in several different ways to describe the end times. Since the coming of God's promised Messiah is identified with the last days, there is a sense in which they began with the incarnation of Jesus Christ: "In these last days he [God] has spoken [finally, once for all] to us by his Son" (Heb. 1:2), and "He was chosen before the creation of the world, but was revealed in these last times for your sake" (1 Pet. 1:20).

Broadly speaking, therefore, the last days include the earthly life and ministry of Jesus Christ, the entire history of the church, and all events prophesied in the Scriptures that are still unfulfilled. Even near the beginning of church history the apostle John pointed out that "many antichrists

have come" and are evidence that this "is the last hour" (1 John 2:18).

The last days will bring tribulation and judgment on all peoples of the world. Even before the Rapture, the church will experience the precursors of what will happen in the Great Tribulation. Paul warned Timothy that "there will be terrible times in the last days" (2 Tim. 3:1). Then he described the corrupt people at the end as those "having a form of godliness but denying its power" (3:5). Both Peter and Jude warned that in the last days "scoffers" will come (2 Pet. 3:3; Jude 18). Although such opponents of the Christian faith appeared in the early generations of church history, they apparently will multiply and become increasingly aggressive as the last days draw near.

When the Old Testament talks about the last days, it looks to the Millennium when God will regather and restore His chosen people Israel (Deut. 30:1–10). God will pour His Spirit on the people of Israel and save them (Jer. 23:3–8; Joel 2:28–32). The people of Israel will return to the Lord (Hos. 3:5), and God will restore them to the Promised Land and Jerusalem will become the capital of all nations (Is. 2:2–5; Mic. 4:1–8). Numerous other prophecies speak of these future blessings for Israel independently of the phrase "the last days."

Before that future time of blessedness will occur, a time of conflict and

L

judgment will come in which God will defeat both His human and His satanic enemies (Joel 2:30–31; 3:9–15). This time of tribulation is called "the day of the LORD" (Is. 13:6, 9–13; Zeph. 1:14–18; Mal. 4:1–3, 5). The Tribulation in turn will be followed by "the coming of salvation" (1 Pet. 1:5) and the fulfillment of Christ's promise of resurrection "at the last day" (John 6:39–40, 44, 54).   —JAW

***

Anticipate the Lord's coming for His own at any moment, since we are already in the last days.

LAW

The primary Old Testament and New Testament words for "law" are the Hebrew *tôrā* and the Greek *nomos.* Both share the basic meaning of guiding principle. From this root sense developed the idea of a rule to be obeyed under threat of punishment. Laws can be either positive, demanding certain actions, or negative, prohibiting certain actions.

Law begins with God, since He is the Creator and Sovereign of all things (Is. 45:5–7, 18). He fulfills His eternal plan to His glory and praise. God's will thus shapes the "guiding principle," the *tôrā* or *nomos,* for all systems of law. This is true even for the laws of godless nations, because "there is no authority except that which God has established. The authorities that exist

have been established by God" (Rom. 13:1). In fact, law began in the Garden of Eden when God commanded Adam not to "eat from the tree of the knowledge of good and evil." God spelled out the consequences of disobedience: "When you eat of it you will surely die" (Gen. 2:17).

After the Flood, God made the Noahic Covenant with humanity. This covenant introduced laws concerning murder. Humans deserve special protection because we bear the image of God. God said, "Whoever sheds the blood of man, by man shall his blood be shed; for in the image of God has God made man" (9:6). All laws of capital punishment for murder spring from this divine pronouncement.

"Law" takes on special religious significance when we consider the Mosaic Covenant God made with Israel. The Law consisted of a multitude of instructions God gave the Israelites to regulate their relationship with Him and with one another. These are crystallized in the Ten Commandments (Ex. 34:28; Deut. 4:13; 10:4), known by the Jews as "the Ten Words" because the Hebrew *dābā,* translated "commandments," literally means "word." *Commandment* is an unfortunate translation because it makes the "words" sound authoritarian and negative. The Hebrew expression *word* emphasizes the revelational and instructional character of this crucial message from God to His people.

God communicated the Ten Commandments and all the other civic, religious, and social regulations to Israel through Moses. Consequently the whole set of legislations that comprised God's covenant with His people was called "the Law of Moses" (for example, 1 Kin. 2:3; 2 Kin. 23:25; Dan. 9:11; Luke 2:22; 24:44; John 7:23; Acts 13:39; 1 Cor. 9:9). This inevitably was shortened to "the Law" (for example, Neh. 10:34, 36; Is. 2:3; Mic. 4:2; Matt. 5:17–18; Luke 2:27; John 1:45). To emphasize its divine origin it often was called "the law of the LORD" (for example, 2 Kin. 10:31; 1 Chr. 16:40; Pss. 1:2; 19:7; 119:1; Is. 5:24; Luke 2:23, 39).

The Law can signify more than the Ten Commandments or Israel's covenant with the Lord. The Law can mean the entire Pentateuch, as in the phrase this "Book of the Law" (Deut. 28:61; Josh. 1:8; 2 Kin. 22:8; Neh. 8:3, 18; 9:3). Some scholars would limit the "Book of the Law" to part of Exodus or to Deuteronomy, but this is inadequate. Many of the regulations of the Law appear in Leviticus, and Numbers records many rulings by God or Moses that carried the force of Law. The phrase "the Law and the Prophets," used to sum up the entire Old Testament, certainly intended "the Law" to refer to the entire Pentateuch (Matt. 7:12; Acts 13:15; Rom. 3:21; see also Luke 16:29, 31; 24:27; Acts 28:23).

God never viewed the Ten Commandments and all the laws He gave Israel through Moses as a way to earn salvation and eternal life. The Law provided avenues for demonstrating obedience to God and maintaining fellowship with Him. Israel was God's chosen people (Ex. 19:5–6; Deut. 7:6–8; 4:20; 14:2; 26:18) on the basis of a covenant established and confirmed with their forefathers. When Israel obeyed God's laws, they enjoyed His covenant blessings. When they disobeyed, they suffered His covenant judgments. The Ten Commandments gave Israel opportunity to express God's perfect standard. When Israel failed to live by God's Law, God expected them to turn to Him in faith for forgiveness and salvation. Israel could express faith in God by offering the prescribed sacrifices that anticipated the ultimate redemptive sacrifice of the Lord Jesus Christ.

Jesus told the rich young man, "If you want to enter life, obey the commandments" (Matt. 19:17). Did Jesus think the young man could achieve eternal life by law-keeping? No. He knew the rich young man had a superficial understanding of the Law of God. Upright as he was, the rich young man was violating the first and second commandments, because his wealth was his idol (19:21–22; Ex. 20:3–4). As Paul stated, no one will be justified by observing the Law (Rom. 3:20; Gal. 2:16).

Does the Law serve any purpose

for believers in Christ? It does. First, "through the law we become conscious of sin" (Rom. 3:20; 7:7). "Sin is not taken into account when there is no law" (5:13; see also 4:15). Second, "the law was put in charge to lead us to Christ that we might be justified by faith" (Gal. 3:24).

Paul added, "Now that faith has come, we are no longer under the supervision of the law" (3:25). Then he warned the Galatian Christians against "turning back to those weak and miserable principles" (4:9), because "when the time had fully come, God sent his Son, born of a woman, born under law, to redeem those under law" (4:4–5). He illustrated this principle by the marriage covenant, which is valid so long as both partners live but which is nullified when one spouse dies (Rom. 7:1–3). As believers we "died to the law through the body of Christ" to "belong to another, to him who was raised from the dead" (7:4).

Jesus said that "until heaven and earth disappear, not the smallest letter, not the least stroke of a pen, will by any means disappear from the Law until everything is accomplished" (Matt. 5:18; Luke 16:17). How does that harmonize with Paul's teaching that we are not under the Law? First, Paul agreed with Jesus and David that "the law of the LORD is perfect" (Ps. 19:7–10). He called the Law "holy . . . righteous and good" (Rom. 7:12, 16) and "spiritual" (7:14). Second, the apostle insisted that justification by faith does not "nullify the law," saying "Not at all! Rather, we uphold the law" (3:31). Third, Paul explained that "through Christ Jesus the law of the Spirit of life set me free from the law of sin and death. For what the law was powerless to do in that it was weakened by the sinful nature, God did by sending his own Son in the likeness of sinful man to be a sin offering. And so he condemned sin in sinful man, in order that the righteous requirements of the law might be fully met in us, who do not live according to the sinful nature but according to the Spirit" (8:2–4).

Nine of the Ten Commandments—all except the one "to observe the Sabbath day" (Deut. 5:15; Ex. 20:8–11)—are repeated in the New Testament Epistles. However, church-age believers are to live on a higher level than the Law. We are empowered by the indwelling Holy Spirit. Paul wrote the Galatian Christians: "Live by the Spirit, and you will not gratify the desires of the sinful nature" (5:16). The verb translated "live" signifies the habitual conduct of one's daily life. Paul explained that "if you are led by the Spirit, you are not under law" (5:18).

After listing the fruit of the Holy Spirit (5:22–23), Paul stated, "Against such things there is no law" (5:23). The nine virtues of the Spirit operate on a higher plane than the Mosaic

Law. If, however, we do not walk under the leadership of the Holy Spirit but choose to sin, the Law condemns us. We have descended to the level of the Law, God's perfect standard for human conduct. Since we live by the Spirit, let us "keep in step with the Spirit" (5:25). The verb translated "keep in step" is a military term meaning "to march in a row" as on parade. The verb tense emphasizes continuing action. We should regularly live each day in step with the Holy Spirit. This is God's desire for us. May it be our desire as well.   —JAW

***

Fulfill God's "law" by displaying the fruit of the Holy Spirit in your life.

LAYING ON OF HANDS

Laying on of hands was a biblical practice in which a person ceremonially transferred guilt, blessing, or authority to something or someone else. In the Old Testament, for example, Jacob laid his hands on the heads of his grandsons Ephraim and Manasseh and blessed them (Gen. 48:14–20). It was also a symbol of identification for purposes of consecration. Aaron and his sons as priests placed their hands on a bull and a ram that were killed as sin offerings in the ceremony that consecrated these men as Israel's first priests (Ex. 29:10–21; Lev. 8:14, 18).

On the Day of Atonement, after slaying a bull and a goat as sin offerings for the priests and the people, the high priest was "to lay both hands on the head of the live goat and confess over it all the wickedness and rebellion of the Israelites—all their sins—and put them on the goat's head" (16:21). The goat was then released into the desert as a scapegoat.

Individual Israelites similarly identified themselves with their fellowship offerings (3:1–2, 6–8, 12–13) and sin offerings (4:27–29, 32–33) by laying their hands on the heads of the sacrificial animals. The elders of Israel placed their hands on the sin offering for the community (4:13–15). The priests and other leaders of Israel did the same when making offerings for their own sin (4:3–4, 22–24).

Various Old Testament leaders were consecrated for ministry by the act of laying on of hands. The Israelite people laid hands on the Levites to acknowledge their authority (Num. 8:10, 12–14). Moses commissioned Joshua by laying his hands on him (27:18–20, 22–23; Deut. 34:9). The rite also was used at the execution of a blasphemer. All the Israelites who heard the blasphemy were "to lay their hands on his head" and then "the entire assembly [was] to stone him" (Lev. 24:13–14).

The Lord Jesus Christ used laying on of hands as a sign of His blessing. He laid hands on little children who were brought to Him for blessing and prayer (Matt. 19:13–15; Mark 10:13–16;

Luke 18:15–17). At His Ascension, although Jesus apparently did not lay His hands on the apostles' heads, He "lifted up his hands and blessed them" (24:50). Jesus also laid His hands on people when He healed them (Matt. 9:18–19, 25; Mark 5:22–24; 6:5; Luke 4:40).

The apostolic church continued the practice of laying on of hands to consecrate leaders for a ministry or an office. The Jerusalem church selected seven men to care for the daily distribution of food to needy widows (Acts 6:1–5) and presented them to the apostles, "who prayed and laid their hands on them." The church at Antioch obeyed the leading of the Holy Spirit by commissioning Barnabas and Saul to undertake a missionary venture. "After they had fasted and prayed, they placed their hands on them and sent them off" (13:3).

Paul ordained Timothy to the ministry "through the laying on of my hands" (2 Tim. 1:6; see also 1 Tim. 4:14) and warned him against being "hasty in the laying on of hands" (5:22) in ordaining others. In the apostolic church the laying on of hands indicated that those who received the Holy Spirit were united with other believers (Acts 8:12–13, 14–17; 19:1–7). Simon the Sorcerer wrongly sought the power to bestow the Holy Spirit through the laying on of hands (8:18–21). Paul used laying on of hands in performing miracles of healing (28:8). Undoubtedly so did others in the apostolic church (Mark 16:18). The elder of the church laid on hands, anointed with oil, and prayed that God would heal the sick (James 5:14–15).

Modern churches continue the practice of laying on of hands in their rituals of ordaining church leaders.

—JAW

***

Whether or not you receive the laying on of hands by others, seek the Lord's approval in your life.

LEADERSHIP

Leadership is the authority and ability to direct the affairs of an informal group of people or a formal institution. The Old Testament tends to focus on military or political leadership. The New Testament pays more attention to the spiritual dimensions of servant leadership.

All authority and leadership derives from God. Psalm 145 gives a breathtaking summary of God as the ultimate Ruler over His everlasting kingdom. "Your kingdom is an everlasting kingdom, and your dominion endures through all generations" (Ps. 145:13). The Lord delegated authority to men like Abraham, Isaac, Jacob, Moses, and Joshua to exercise leadership while Israel grew from a family to a nation. The role of these men lacked the formality of modern-day leadership, but there was never a question about their call and authority to lead. After the days of Joshua God raised up eleven men and one woman to provide leadership for Israel in the capacity of judges. Besides governing, they acted as military leaders to rescue their people from oppression.

Later, kings exercised the ultimate leadership role in Israel. Moses had given specific instructions from the Lord on the process of selecting a king (Deut. 17:14–20). The people were to look to the Lord for the man of His choosing, and this king would rule in accord with instructions in the Word of God. Of all the kings of Israel, one man, David, stood out from all others as the epitome of a godly and gifted leader (Ps. 78:72; Acts 13:22, 36).

Kings weren't Israel's only leaders during the monarchy. When the kings in the palace turned away from God and His laws for the nation, the Lord raised up prophets to provide alternative spiritual leadership. Elijah, Elisha, Isaiah, Jeremiah, Ezekiel, Daniel, and a host of other writing and speaking prophets led the people of God by confronting sin and cultivating righteousness. These men were not always acclaimed as leaders (Heb. 11:36–38), but what they accomplished for God has forever been recorded in the pages of Scripture.

The New Testament established a whole new order of leadership, following the example of our Lord Jesus Christ. The writer of Hebrews called Jesus our Apostle and High Priest (Heb. 3:1). Jesus had all the credentials of a successful leader. He was sent by the Father to accomplish His will (10:5–10), and all authority in heaven and on earth had been given to Him (Matt. 28:18). In spite of all this, Jesus led like a shepherd rather than like a king. He identified Himself as "the good shepherd" (John 10:11). Peter called Jesus "the Chief Shepherd" (1 Pet. 5:4), and he declared that all leaders in the church should follow His style of leadership (5:2–3).

An examination of the leadership style of the Lord Jesus reveals several things. First, leadership involves taking responsibility. Jesus willingly came to this earth to lay down His life (John 10:14–18). Paul identified eager willingness as a basic quality for church leaders (1 Tim. 3:1). Second, Jesus acted as guide. He led from in front and invited people to follow Him. His example helped His followers stay focused on the proper goals. He was not afraid to rebuke His disciples when they lost sight of His purposes (Matt. 16:22–27). Third, Jesus illustrated that leaders should be goal-oriented. His overall goal was to fulfill the Father's will.

After Jesus ascended to the Father, the apostles became the first leaders of the church. Jesus had appointed them and given them authority to carry out their mission (Mark 3:13–15). Along with Christ the leadership of the apostles laid

L

the foundation on which the church was built (Eph. 2:20). Besides the original Twelve, a few others, most notably Paul, were called apostles in recognition of distinct ministries they were commissioned to carry out (1 Cor. 15:6–9).

The pattern for church leadership emerged in response to the needs of groups of disciples in towns where the gospel was preached. The need for organization came as a result of growth. New converts coming to Christ needed to learn the apostles' doctrine and to be integrated into the life of local congregations. Problems also developed that required leadership and organization to solve (Acts 6:1). By the end of the first decade of church life, elders had been selected in the church at Jerusalem, but there is no indication when and how they were appointed (11:30). When Paul and Barnabas went on their first missionary journey, they appointed elders in all the churches (14:23). The common factor in early church leadership selection was to find leaders who were "full of the Spirit and wisdom" (6:3).

When Paul addressed the elders from the church at Ephesus on his final journey to Jerusalem, he summarized some of the responsibilities of elders. Elders were responsible for the spiritual growth of the congregation (20:28), the doctrinal purity of the people and the leadership team (20:29–31), and the teachings of the grace of God (20:32).

Elders existed to enrich the congregation spiritually (20:33–35).

Later in Paul's ministry he identified specific characteristics of elders (1 Tim. 3:2–7; Titus 1:6–9). Elders should desire to serve and should take responsibility willingly. Elders should have exemplary personal lives and strong marriages. They should be self-controlled and worthy of respect. Elders should be accessible, skilled in communication, gentle, focused on spiritual not monetary matters, able to manage their families, spiritually mature, alert to the devil's tricks, well-respected by unbelievers, and knowledgeable about the doctrines of the church so they can teach others and detect error.

The office of deacon emerged as churches experienced numerical growth and needed qualified assistants in the work of the Lord. The term *deacon* means "servant" or "minister." The Bible doesn't tell us how this office came into being. Some believe that the seven men chosen to assist the Twelve in Acts 6 were the first deacons. Acts 6 doesn't use the term "deacon" or any other title to describe the service those men performed for needy widows. What is evident from the passage is that organization developed out of need. Growth required additional leadership.

The initial occurrence of the term *deacon* in an official capacity appears in Paul's salutation to the leaders of the church in Philippi (Phil. 1:1). The

Philippian deacons evidently had a respected leadership role along with elders. By the time Paul wrote his letters to Timothy, the office of deacon was well established (1 Tim. 3:8–13). As he did for elders, Paul detailed the qualities a deacon should possess. Deacons should demonstrate consistent growth in spiritual matters and exhibit qualities that demand respect (3:8, 10). They must evidence a deep commitment to the truths of the Christian faith (3:9), must have a wholesome family life (3:12), and have wives who partner with them in ministry (3:11).

Some believe the Greek term *gynaikas* in 1 Timothy 3:11 should be translated "women" rather than "wives." This would identify the women as deaconesses. This occurrence of *gynaikas* does leave the door open to the possibility that women ministered in an official capacity. A growing number of people in the early church were women, and some would have had special needs. Paul identified some of these needs later in the letter (5:3–16). Paul seemed to anticipate that these needs could be handled informally by deacons' wives or officially by deaconesses.

The New Testament clearly teaches that church leadership originates with God, who gives people as gifts to the church (Eph. 4:11). Through the Holy Spirit, He also gives spiritual gifts to leaders so they can carry out their tasks effectively (Rom. 12:8; 1 Cor. 12:28).

Church members should respect, encourage, honor, and appreciate their leaders (1 Thess. 5:12–13; Heb. 13:7, 17).

—WGJ

***

Pray about how God wants to use you in cooperative relationship with leaders in the body of Christ to facilitate the work of God.

LIFE

Life is a mysterious and unexplainable quality of animate creatures. Scientists can observe and describe life but are hard pressed to define what it is. If a body were weighed both before and after death, the weight would be the same, yet something, life itself, has departed. Life then is what gives consciousness or sensibility to the body.

The Old Testament uses two main words for life. The first is *ḥayyîm,* meaning physical life, with special reference to its duration (1 Kin. 4:21). It also can denote a life that enjoys the favor of God, as shown by spiritual and material blessings (Deut. 30:15–20; Pss. 30:5; 42:8).

The second major Hebrew word for life is *nepeš,* which is translated as "soul," "life," or "breath" (its root meaning). In Genesis 2:7, 19 God is said to be the Source of life. In these verses both humans and animals are called "living beings," an expression that combines *ḥayyîm* and *nepeš.* The Bible distinguishes people from animals on the basis of the image and likeness of God they bear. Bible passages about capital punishment emphasize the importance of human life: "Show no pity: life for life" (Deut. 19:21; see also Gen. 9:5–6; Ex. 21:23). In the sacrificial system of the Mosaic Law God provided an atonement for sinners by the blood of an animal, "For the life of a creature is in the blood, and I have given it to you to make atonement for yourselves on the altar; it is the blood that makes atonement for one's life" (Lev. 17:11). God accepted life for life—an animal life in place of a human life.

The Law of Moses regulated the life of Israel. It set out the Lord's standards for a righteous life. God spoke to His people through Moses just before they invaded Canaan: "This day I call heaven and earth as witnesses against you that I have set before you life and death, blessings and curses. Now choose life, so that you and your children may live" (Deut. 30:19). Some Bible students think a few references to life in the Old Testament refer to eternal life (Pss. 16:10–11; 21:4–6; Prov. 12:28; Is. 26:19; Dan. 12:2).

The New Testament uses three words to describe various aspects of life: *bios*, *psychē*, and *zōē*. The first word, *bios*, refers to the physical aspects of a person's present earthly life (Luke 8:14; 1 Tim. 2:2; 2 Tim. 2:4, NKJV). It or its derivatives also describe one's conduct (Acts 26:4, 1 Pet. 4:2–3), and means of support (Mark 12:44; Luke 15:12, 30; 1 John 2:16; 3:17). This word is never used of eternal life.

The word *psychē*, used over one hundred times in the New Testament, is often translated "soul" (for example, Mark 8:36; 1 Pet. 2:11; 3 John 2) and occasionally it is rendered "life." *Psychē* corresponds to the Hebrew word *nepeš*. It is a multifaceted word that refers to the inner self or personality. In Matthew 20:28 Jesus said He came "to give his life as a ransom for many." Jesus challenged His followers with the words, "Do not worry about your life (*psychē*), what you will eat; or about your body, what you will wear. Life (*psychē*) is more than food, and the body more than clothes" (Luke 12:22–23).

Zōē is used in diverse ways. On occasion it is employed of natural or physical life (Acts 17:25; 1 Cor. 15:19). It also speaks of the life of God (John 5:26) and of the life of Christ residing in the believer (2 Cor. 4:10–11; Col. 3:4). This life is received by faith (John 3:16) and is a present possession (5:24). It extends through death to eternity (2 Cor. 5:4).

We cannot fully fathom the mystery of life, but we can acknowledge it as a gift of God. This is true of both physical life and eternal life. Though our natural life on earth is brief (James 4:14) and subject to physical death, our existence is nonetheless endless whether we are saved or unsaved. The unsaved will exist eternally apart from God, whereas the eternal destiny of the saved involves unending communion in heaven with the triune God: Father, Son, and Holy Spirit. Only then will we understand and appreciate the full meaning of the eternal life we received here on earth.   **—DKC**

***

Thank God for physical life and for eternal life through Jesus Christ our Lord.

LIGHT

Physics may define light as elecromagnetic radiation in the range of wavelengths that stimulate our eyes. What a sterile definition! Light is one of God's greatest gifts to the inhabitants of earth. The first recorded words of God are "Let there be light" (Gen. 1:3), and on the fourth creative day God set the light-bearing sun, moon, and stars in the sky (1:14–17). But what was the source of light before God made the light-bearing bodies? Some suggest it was a cosmic light that was not centered anywhere, like that of the aurora borealis. On the other hand it should be noted that in eternity's New Jerusalem, "The city does not need the sun or the moon to shine on it, for the glory of God gives it light" (Rev. 21:23).

The Old Testament tells of special lights that God provided for His people the Israelites. During one of the plagues in Egypt the Israelites had light in their homes while the Egyptians stumbled around in thick darkness (Ex. 10:22–23). When the Israelites left Egypt, God led them by means of a pillar of cloud by day and a pillar of fire that gave them light by night (13:21; 14:20; Ps. 78:14). God also favored His people with awesome light when the Shekinah glory appeared at the completion of both the tabernacle (Ex. 40:34–38) and the temple (1 Kin. 8:11; 2 Chr. 5:13–14).

The New Testament also makes frequent reference to light. Among the many kinds of light mentioned are the supernatural brightness of the Transfiguration scene (Matt. 17:2), the bright light at Paul's Damascus road conversion (Acts 9:3), the light of day (John 11:9), and ordinary lamps (Acts 20:8).

"Light" is used metaphorically in both the Old and New Testaments. God is declared to be light (1 John 1:5) and the "Father of the heavenly lights" (James 1:17). He is described as One who "wraps himself in light as with a garment" (Ps. 104:2), and the one "who lives in unapproachable light" (1 Tim. 6:16). Frequently light symbolizes God's blessings (Job 12:22; 29:3; Pss. 18:28; 27:1; 97:11; 118:27). The expression "the light of his countenance" appears frequently in Psalms and usually connotes God looking with favor on His people (4:6; 44:3; 89:15). Sometimes it means that nothing, not even secret sins, escapes God's close scrutiny (90:8). Light is associated with justice (Is. 51:4) and with good conduct

L

(Prov. 4:18; 6:23). It is a perversion to regard moral darkness as light and moral light as darkness (Is. 5:20). The Word of God is compared to a light (Ps. 119:105), and a righteous king, David, was identified with light. He was considered a source of illumination for his subjects (2 Sam. 21:17; 1 Kin. 11:36).

Of all the New Testament writers John delighted in symbols. He particularly fancied "light" as an image for things and people that revealed the truth. John used the Greek word for light, *phōs*, twenty-three times in the first twelve chapters of his Gospel. It almost always refers to Jesus or His teachings. Jesus is called the "light of men" (John 1:4), "the true light" (1:9), and "the light of the world" (8:12). The apostle John declared, "Light has come into the world, but men loved darkness instead of light because their deeds were evil" (3:19). Just before withdrawing from the crowd to be with His disciples in the Upper Room, Jesus said to the people, "You are going to have the light just a little while longer. Walk while you have the light, before darkness overtakes you. . . . Put your trust in the light while you have it, so that you may become sons of light" (12:35–36).

Paul developed similar themes in his epistles. He wrote that Satan blinds the minds of the lost lest they see "the light of the gospel." God, however, overcomes Satan's opposition and causes

the believer to receive "the light of the knowledge of the glory of God in the face of Christ" (2 Cor. 4:4–6). Such a transaction having taken place, believers are expected to live as "children of light," producing such fruit as "goodness, righteousness, and truth" (Eph. 5:8–9).

In his first epistle John emphasized what God requires of those who walk in the light. "God is light" (1 John 1:5), and as such He exposes and condemns people's sins. A Christian therefore cannot claim to have communion with God while living in darkness (sin). The only way to have fellowship with God is to live in the light where He is. Then there is openness to the light of divine truth and cleansing from every sin by the shed blood of Christ (1:6–7). Cleansing takes place when the believer acknowledges the failure revealed by the light of God (1:9). John then mentioned the specific sin of hating a fellow believer, behavior that is typical of the realm of darkness (2:9). The believer, on the other hand, who loves other Christians "lives in the light, and there is nothing in him to make him stumble" (2:10; see also Rom. 13:8–10).

Jesus issued the greatest challenge concerning light when He told His followers, "You are the light of the world" (Matt. 5:14; see 5:16). (Jesus also said He is the Light of the world; John 8:12.) Like John the Baptist, all of us who believe in Christ are to be witnesses to the light, that is, to our Savior (John 1:8). Because dangers loom in a dark world, Paul urged Christians to put on "the armor of light" (Rom. 13:12) and to keep themselves apart from false teachers. We must take seriously his rhetorical question, "What fellowship can light have with darkness?" (2 Cor. 6:14). **—DKC**

* * *

Walk in the light by allowing the piercing, cleansing brightness of Christ's holiness to destroy all hidden corners of fear, jealousy, greed, and selfishness in our hearts.

LOGOS

The English word *logos* is a letter-for-letter reproduction of the Greek noun normally translated "word." "Word" in this case doesn't mean a noun, verb, adjective, etc. It means "concept," "idea," or "thought" that results in communication (1 Cor. 14:9, 19). As a result, *logos* (John 6:60; 14:23) and its plural *logoi* (Matt. 7:24; 10:14; Mark 8:38; Luke 1:29; John 2:22) refer to an entire statement or even an entire teaching. In this sense *logos* refers to God's message to humankind (Mark 7:13; 1 Cor. 14:36; Phil. 1:14).

The apostle John's message concerning the Word (*logos*) in the opening verses of his Gospel (1:1–5) is of special significance. In it he identifies the Word with the Lord Jesus Christ (1:14,

18). Later John confirmed this identification when he called the Rider on the white horse at the Second Coming "Faithful and True" and "the Word of God" (Rev. 19:11, 13).

John makes stupendous affirmations concerning the Word in his prologue to his Gospel. He takes his readers back to the beginning of time by opening his Gospel with wording reminiscent of the opening words of Genesis: "In the beginning was the Word" (John 1:1). Whenever the world began, the Word already existed. In this way John affirmed the eternal existence of the Word. Then he restated the idea for emphasis in verse 2. "He was with God in the beginning." The preposition translated "with" followed by the accusative case signifies close face-to-face proximity in fellowship. The Word and the Father have fellowshipped harmoniously forever.

"The Word was God," the final affirmation in verse 1, states that the Word has the character or quality of God. The word "God" in the Greek text does not have the definite article with it, so Jehovah's Witnesses translate the clause, "the Word was a god." In the Greek sentence, however, the predicate comes first (*theos* without the article). That makes the idea of deity emphatic. It also makes it characteristic of the subject (*logos* with the definite article). The Word emphatically is God. A parallel Greek construction occurs in Jesus' statement to the

Samaritan woman at the well, "God is spirit" (John 4:24). No one translates that "God is a spirit." It means God is emphatically and characteristically spirit.

John explained that this eternal Word "became flesh" and lived as a man "for a while" (1:14). His Incarnation enabled people to behold "his glory, glory as of an only-born from a father full of grace and truth" (literal translation). We know that "God is spirit." Accordingly, "no one has ever yet seen God; the only-born God, the one being in the bosom of the Father, that one has led him forth" (1:18, literal translation). The eternal Word is equal with God the Father. The Word expressed God's infinite power and wisdom in the work of creation (1:3, 10). The incarnate Word manifested and revealed God's glory, grace, love, and mercy among people of His day (10:38; 12:45; 14:9–11). Creation and Incarnation are the great works of the Word. Through them the Word communicates God and His plan.

John is the only biblical author who used *logos* ("Word") to speak of the eternal, coequal Son who created the world and became incarnate as Jesus Christ. However, other New Testament writers expressed the same idea using other terms. Paul wrote of Christ's equality with God (Phil. 2:6; Col. 2:9), His eternal existence (1:17), and His work of creation (Rom. 8:3; Gal. 4:4; Phil. 2:7–8). The author of Hebrews also wrote of the deity and eternality of Christ, His involvement in creation (Heb. 1:2–3, 10–11), and His Incarnation (1:5–6).

Why did John use the term *logos* of the eternal, preincarnate Lord Jesus Christ? First, at the close of the apostolic century, when John wrote his Gospel, Greek philosophy had begun to influence Christian theology. A movement called Gnosticism taught that a Logos, a minor deity, acted as an intermediary between the supreme deity and the material world, including people. Some believed in a long pecking order of subordinate gods, sometimes called *logoi* (plural of *logos*), between people and the supreme deity. This system taught that the more special knowledge (*gnōsis*) a person could get, the further up the pecking order he moved toward contact with the supreme deity. John wrote of Jesus Christ as the *logos* to refute this false teaching.

Second, John was affirming a strand of Old Testament thought that was losing popularity. The Old Testament spoke of creation being accomplished "by the word [*dābār*] of the LORD" (Ps. 33:6, 9; compare Gen. 1:3, 6, 9, 14, 20, 24, 26, 29; Ps. 148:5; Heb. 11:3). The Old Testament identifies God's word with His person (Ps. 147:15, 18) and gives it an almost personal character (107:20; Is. 55:1; Hos. 6:5). The Book of Proverbs personifies wisdom (Prov. 1:20–21; 8:1–21, 32—9:6). Wisdom is described as eternal and involved with God in the work of creation (3:19–20; 8:22–31). Intertestamental Jewish wisdom literature coupled wisdom with the Word of God and elevated both. At the time of Jesus, however, Philo of Alexandria, a Jewish philosopher influenced by Greek thought, said that wisdom (which he identified as *logos*) was a secondary force or person. He wanted to protect strict Jewish monotheism. John's teaching concerning the *logos* advanced the Old Testament ideas of the Word and wisdom in opposition to Philo.

The Bible also uses the term "word" to mean God's message to a person, as in the phrase "the word of the LORD" (for example, Gen. 15:1, 4; Num. 3:16, 51; 1 Sam. 15:10; 1 Kin. 6:11; Zech. 1:1). Subsequently the phrase "the word of God" is used for all or any portion of the Scriptures (Luke 3:2; 8:11; Acts 6:2, 7; 2 Cor. 2:17; Eph. 6:17; Heb. 4:12) and for the proclaimed message of God (Acts 12:24; 13:46; 17:13). Sometimes that phrase is reduced simply to "the word" (6:4; 8:4; 14:25; 1 Cor. 15:2; 2 Tim. 4:2). Whether referring to the Lord Jesus or to the Scriptures, the Word (*logos*) is the revelation of the nature, message, and plan of God.

—**JAW**

***

Thank the Lord that He has revealed Himself to us through Jesus Christ and the Scriptures.

LORDSHIP

How many people actually heard Jesus speak in the course of His lifetime? No doubt the number reached into the thousands, but by modern standards He didn't touch very many. However, what Jesus communicated to His handful of devoted followers has impacted the entire world. Just before His Ascension Jesus told His disciples that all authority in heaven and on earth had been given to Him (Matt. 28:18). Think of what He claimed. He has "all authority in heaven"—over angels and the souls of believers who have died—and authority over everything "on earth." Nothing escapes His domain. By this dramatic statement Jesus Christ claimed He is Lord. No one but God could utter such words.

The theme of lordship is central to the message of the New Testament. Though writing from different perspectives, the Gospel writers left no doubt that the One they featured is the Lord. Each Gospel ends with an affirmation of the lordship of Christ (Matt. 28:16–20; Mark 13:26; Luke 24:44–48; John 20:28). Paul painted many word pictures of Jesus as Lord. Colossians 1:15–20 is the most stirring. The Book of Hebrews begins with an eloquent presentation of Jesus' superiority to angels and of His claim to our worship (Heb. 1:1–13). The Book of Revelation prophesies the return of the Lord to earth in triumph, with believers giving Him all praise, honor, and glory (Rev. 19:1–8; see also 4:8–11; 5:12–13). He truly is the sovereign Lord.

In one sense, the lordship of Jesus arises from His triumph on the Cross (Phil. 2:8–9) and His resurrection from the dead (Acts 2:36; Rom. 1:4). In another sense, He has always been Lord because He has always been the Son of God, co-eternal and co-equal with the Father and the Spirit in the Godhead (Ps. 110:1; Luke 20:42). The angel Gabriel announced the infant Jesus to the shepherds as "Christ the Lord" (Luke 2:11). In the Incarnation Christ did not lose or relinquish any of His attributes (Phil. 2:6), but in keeping with His humanity He didn't use His divine attributes for personal convenience. God has exalted the Son as Lord, and some day everyone will acknowledge His lordship (2:9–11).

We can see implications of Christ's lordship throughout the New Testament. We should worship Christ because He is the sovereign Lord. Jesus rebuked Satan and reminded him that only God is to be worshiped (Luke 4:4–8). When Peter realized that Jesus is Lord, he worshiped Him and felt unworthy in His presence (5:8). The disciples who witnessed His Ascension worshiped Him (24:52), and after the Day of Pentecost believers worshiped Him every day (Acts 2:36–42).

The Lord was the focal point of the preaching by the apostles (10:36; 2 Cor. 4:5). As Lord He is head over the church, the body of Christ, which is subject to Him (Eph. 1:22–23; Col. 1:18; 1 Pet. 3:22). All our prayers are to be directed to the Father through Christ the Lord (John 14:13–14; 16:23–24; Eph. 2:18; Heb. 7:25). He gives gifts and gifted people to the church (Eph. 4:7–11). As the wisdom of God the Lord Jesus provides the guidance we need to accomplish His purposes (1 Cor. 1:30–31; 2 Cor. 2:12). He gives us strength (12:8–10; Phil. 4:10–13). Because Jesus is Lord, we need not fear death (1 Cor. 15:25–26). We recognize that ministry for the cause of Christ will never be in vain (15:28). We have hope because of the Lord's promise to come back for all who believe in Him (1 Thess. 4:13–18). Since He is Lord, we are accountable to Him for the way we relate to others in the body of Christ (Rom. 14:4–12).

Every one of us should eagerly submit to the lordship of Christ. Our voluntary yielding to His lordship is not a requirement for salvation. Lordship results from the sanctifying work of the Holy Spirit in our lives (Rom. 6:8–14; 12:1–2; Eph. 4:1–5; 5:20–32; Phil. 3:10–16; Col. 3:1–10). Some of the practical outworkings of our submission to Christ are noted in 1 Peter 2:11—3:7.   **—WGJ**

***

Worship the Lord regularly and rejoice in the truth that Jesus is Lord over everything and that someday this will be recognized by everyone.

LORD'S SUPPER

The phrase "the Lord's Supper" appears only once in the New Testament (1 Cor. 11:20), but the three Synoptic Gospels all report in detail its establishment on the night before Jesus' crucifixion (Matt. 26:26–29; Mark 14:22–25; Luke 22:19–20). The apostolic church called it "the breaking of bread" (Acts. 2:42, 46; 20:7), and some groups still retain that title for the observance.

More liturgical groups call the Lord's Supper the Eucharist, because the Lord Jesus "gave thanks" (*eucharistēsas*) before breaking the bread (Matt. 26:26; Mark 14:22; Luke 22:19; see 1 Cor. 11:24). Most likely He also gave thanks before passing the cup of wine (Matt. 26:27; Mark 14:23). None of the writers say the Lord gave thanks before the cup, but Luke and Paul imply it by saying He handled the cup "in the same way" (Luke 22:20; 1 Cor. 11:25).

The phrase "the Lord's Supper" emphasizes the word "Lord." The Lord Jesus established this observance and commanded His followers to repeat it regularly. The Lord's Supper focuses exclusively on the Lord. We remember His finished redemptive sacrifice which provides salvation and eternal life. We also fellowship with the ascended Lord and anticipate His imminent return to gather us to Himself.

The apostolic "believers were together and had everything in common" (Acts. 2:44; see also 4:32; 6:1–4), so they ate their meals together (2:46). This raises the question whether "breaking of bread" refers to ordinary common meals or to the Lord's Supper. Apparently the Lord's Supper was part of every common meal. Paul's discussion of the Lord's Supper is found in the context of abuses at the Corinthian church's love feast, which was the common meal (1 Cor. 11:17–22, 27–34).

So it seems the earliest believers observed the Lord's Supper every day (Acts 2:46). We don't know how long this continued, but by the time Paul stopped at Troas (20:6) on his way to Jerusalem (20:16, 22) the Supper was observed weekly, "on the first day of the week" (20:7). Some groups presently still observe the Lord's Supper weekly, but most churches observe it once a month and on special occasions. The Lord did not specify the frequency; He simply said, "Do this, *whenever* you drink it, in remembrance of me" (1 Cor. 11:25). Paul added, "For *whenever* you eat this bread and drink this cup, you proclaim the Lord's death until he comes" (11:26).

The apostolic church apparently observed the Lord's Supper in the evening (Acts 20:7). Some church groups continue this practice, but most groups conduct the Lord's Supper as a part of the Sunday morning worship service. Jesus established the Lord's Supper in the evening because it arose out of part of the Jewish Passover meal that was an evening ceremony (Matt. 26:17–30; Mark 14:12–26; Luke 22:7–20).

The exact chronology of the Lord's Supper in relationship to the Passover has puzzled scholars through the centuries. Matthew, Mark, and Luke all say Jesus established the ceremony in the course of the Passover meal (Matt. 26:19–20; Mark 14:16–17; Luke 22:13–14); yet it hardly seems likely that the Jewish leaders would arrest Jesus and try Him on Passover night. Furthermore Christian tradition teaches that Jesus was crucified on Passover day as God's "Passover Lamb" (1 Cor. 5:7).

Some scholars solve the puzzle by saying that the evening meal Jesus ate with His apostles was not *the* Passover meal, but it was simply *a* meal during Passover season. Others note that two Passovers were observed at that time: the first by Galileans, the Qumran community, and other dissident groups and the second by the mainline Jerusalem establishment. In this scenario, Jesus and His apostles ate the earlier Passover on Thursday, and He was tried and crucified during the day of the second Passover that began Friday evening (John 18:28).

A third and preferable solution is that the preparations for the Passover meal took place on Nisan 14 (Thursday), and the Passover meal was eaten by Jesus and His disciples after sundown. By the Jewish calendar they ate the meal on Nisan 15.

That same day (according to Jewish reckoning) Jesus was arrested, condemned, and crucified on the Passover day (which corresponds with our Friday). He was indeed God's Passover Lamb, since His crucifixion occurred before Friday sundown, the start of Nisan 16. This Passover day on which Jesus was crucified also marked the preparation for the Feast of Unleavened Bread, which lasted seven days and was sometimes called Passover Week.

Jesus said, "This is my body" (1 Cor. 11:24) and "This cup is the new covenant in my blood" (11:25). Some groups believe that the bread and wine of the Lord's Supper are transformed into Christ's body and blood by the minister's words. Others believe that Christ becomes present *with* the elements. Still others hold that He is *spiritually present.* Undoubtedly believers are spiritually blessed and enriched by observing the Lord's Supper, for Jesus spoke of its observance as a memorial of Him, saying, "do this in remembrance of me" (Luke 22:19; see also 1 Cor. 11:24–25). Since Jesus held the unleavened bread and broke it with His hands and later held the cup of wine, they elements are only *symbols* of His body and blood.

As a memorial observance, the Lord's Supper gives us a threefold perspective on our Lord. First, it looks to the past, reminding us of the Lord's redemptive sacrifice on the Cross. Second, it looks to the present and our continuing fellowship with Christ as our Advocate and Great High Priest. Third, it looks to the future in anticipation of the imminent return of Christ for us.

John's Gospel doesn't mention the Lord's Supper, although it deals with the Passover and the evening meal (John 13:1–2). Instead John emphasized the extensive teaching ministry of Jesus through the course of the meal and the evening (John 13:1—18:1). Earlier in his Gospel, John did record Jesus' teaching following the feeding of the five thousand. He called Himself "the bread of life" (6:35, 48) whose body had to be eaten and His blood drunk to receive and enjoy eternal life (6:50–59). John also recorded Jesus' claims to be the source of "living water" (4:10, 7:37–38) received by faith.

The Lord's Supper is our supreme act of worship. We should participate in it only after serious self-examination (1 Cor. 11:28), because whoever partakes "in an unworthy manner will be guilty of sinning against the body and blood of the Lord" (11:27). That is what the Corinthian Christians were doing in their love feast that preceded the Lord's Supper (11:17–22, 29–34). They negated the purpose and value of their observance. In the Lord's Supper we commune with other believers as well as with the Lord Himself.

—JAW

***

When you partake of the Lord's Supper, examine your life and be sure you are in fellowship with Christ.

LOVE

Henry Drummond, Scottish naturalist and theologian, called love "the greatest thing in the world." In fact, he wrote a book by that title that sold exceptionally well late in the nineteenth century. Love has also been described as everything from "the grandest theme of Scripture" to an "exceedingly ambiguous term." We need to go to the Bible to get a clear picture of love, both as an attribute of God and as a Christian virtue.

In the Old Testament ʾāhēb is the most common Hebrew word for "love." It describes the warm relationship between a father and a son (Gen. 22:2) and a master and a slave (Ex. 21:5). It is also used of love for a neighbor (Lev. 19:18), love for a stranger (Deut. 10:19), love for God, and of God's love for humankind. In particular ʾāhēb explains God's choice of Israel and His commitment to her as a people (Deut. 4:37–38; 7:7–8). The prophets, too, associated God's love with major events of Israel's history (Hos. 11:1; Mal. 1:2–3). Consider God's amazing words to Israel: "I have loved you with an everlasting love; I have drawn you with loving-kindness" (Jer. 31:3). God will also bless Israel's future with His love (Is. 43:1–7; Hos. 14:4).

A second significant Hebrew word for love is *hesed,* rendered "loving-kindness" or "steadfast love." This unshakable, steadfast love stood in contrast to the impulsive, capricious moods and actions of heathen deities. God's love as *hesed* is closely linked with His covenants. Moses described the Sinai Covenant as a "covenant of love" (Deut. 7:9, 12). The Lord Himself said His covenant promises to David were based on love: "I will maintain my love to him forever, and my covenant with him will never fail" (Ps. 89:28). God's unchanging love promises the redeemed many things: deliverance from their enemies (6:4; 17:7), safekeeping (21:7; 32:10), forgiveness (25:7; 51:1; Mic. 7:20), answers to prayer (Ps. 66:20), redemption (130:7), and the future establishment of David's throne and kingdom (Is. 16:5; 55:3).

God expected Israel to respond to His loving provision with wholehearted love and obedience. He called Israel to "love the LORD your God with all your heart and with all your soul and with all your strength" (Deut. 6:5). Israel was to demonstrate her love by obedience: "These commandments that I give you today are to be upon your hearts" (6:6). In addition to loving God, the people of Israel were also to love their neighbors (Lev. 19:18).

When we move to the New Testament, we find a fuller exposition of love, both divine and human. Two of the three common Greek words for love occur frequently in its pages. The word not used, though it was common in Greek literature, is *erōs,* sexual love. The New Testament does employ *phileō* (verb form), which refers to spontaneous natural affection expressed between relatives and friends. The most frequent New Testament word for love is the noun *agapē. Agapē* occurred infrequently in secular Greek literature. The New Testament gave *agapē* new depths by using it to describes God's love for all people (Rom. 5:8) and of believers' love for one another (John 13:35).

Jesus had much to say about love. As He prepared to leave the world, He told His disciples, "A new command I give you: Love one another. As I have loved you, so you must love one another" (John 13:34). What could have been "new" about this command? It was new because this love among believers would be modeled after Jesus' sacrificial love. This mutual love helped the first disciples survive in the hostile world they soon faced. Earlier in His earthly ministry Jesus had emphasized that His followers were to love even their enemies (Matt. 5:44–48).

The apostle John affirmed that God's love is the foundation of all that happened to bring about salvation. "For God so loved the world that he gave his one and only Son, that whoever believes in him shall not perish but have eternal life" (John 3:16; see also 16:27; 17:23). In his first epistle John declared that "God is love" (1 John 4:16), and that because God loved us first we in turn should love Him and fellow believers (4:19–21).

In Romans 5:6–8 the apostle Paul wrote what has been called "the finest exposition of God's love found anywhere in the Bible." He explained that what people would scarcely do for the good, God has done for the vile and despicable! Christ, indeed, died for the *ungodly* who are God's enemies! Such a demonstration, wrote Paul, demands a response on the part of the believer: "Live a life of love, just as Christ loved us and gave himself up for us as a fragrant offering and sacrifice to God" (Eph. 5:2). The apostle also exhorted, "Serve one another in love. The entire law is summed up in a single command: 'Love your neighbor as yourself'" (Gal. 5:13–14). Paul was quoting Leviticus 19:18 at that point. He then argued that Christian love is the "fulfillment" or the "carrying out" of the Law. He fully developed this point in Romans 13:8–10.

How do we comprehend the dimensions of God's love for all people and the demands of that love on us? We have to saturate ourselves with the scriptural portrayal of the love of God expressed through our Lord Jesus. We have to grasp that the self-sacrificing love of God that sent Christ to die for sinners. We are called to demonstrate that same love to one another and to unbelievers. Such love is the "fruit of the Spirit" (Gal. 5:22). Our effort cannot work it up. The Holy Spirit does it through us as we maintain a vital union with Christ (John 15:1–8).

—**DKC**   M

***

Strive to love other believers as
Jesus commanded.

Mm

MARRIAGE

God established marriage when He formed Eve out of the rib taken from Adam to be a "suitable helper" for him and brought her to him (Gen. 2:20–22). "For this reason a man will leave his father and mother and be united to his wife, and they will become one flesh" (2:24). God created a monogamous union. The Law regulated polygamy to protect the weak (Deut. 21:15–17), but it did not endorse the practice. Monogamy has always been God's ideal. Similarly the Law regulated without approving the dissolution of a marriage by divorce (24:1–4). God envisioned marriage as a lifelong union dissolved only by the death of one of the partners.

Lamech, the fifth generation in the

line of Cain, was the first to marry more than one wife (Gen. 4:19). A polygamous marriage always created tension in the family, as illustrated by Jacob's experience with Leah and Rachel and Elkanah's experience with Hannah and Peninnah. David married several wives for political purposes and created chaotic discord in his family. Solomon's many wives led him away from the Lord to serve other gods (1 Kin. 11:4–6, 9–10). By contrast Noah, Isaac, and Joseph each had only one wife and more successful homes. When an Old Testament writer wanted to depict scenes of domestic harmony, he sketched a monogamous marriage (Ps. 128:1–4; Prov. 31:10–31).

The Old Testament compared God's exclusive relationship with Israel to the monogamous relationship of a husband and his wife (Is. 54:5–8; Jer. 3:14; Hos. 2:19–20). Both the northern kingdom (Israel) and the southern kingdom (Judah) were judged by God as adulterous because they abandoned Him for other gods (Is. 57:3; Jer. 3:6–10; 5:7; 13:24–27; 23:10, 13–14; Ezek. 6:9; 16:32–43). God would not accept a syncretistic relationship in which His people worshiped Him as well as other gods. God did not accept the spiritual equivalent of polygamy. Instead, He gave His people Israel a "certificate of divorce" (Is. 50:1) and "sent her away because of all her adulteries" (Jer. 3:8).

Although God judged His people Israel for her spiritual adulteries, He did not abandon her. The prophet Hosea provided in his family life an object lesson paralleling God's dealings with Israel. God directed Hosea to "take to yourself an adulterous wife" (Hos. 1:2) to illustrate that "the land is guilty of the vilest adultery in departing from the Lord." Hosea married Gomer (1:3), who bore him three children. Then Gomer deserted Hosea in favor of a series of adulterous relationships. After a time God directed the prophet to "go, show your love to your wife again, though she is loved by another and is an adulteress. Love her as the LORD loves the Israelites, though they turn to other gods" (3:1). Hosea bought Gomer back to be his wife and isolated her for a time before resuming relations with her (3:3). Similarly after separation and judgment God will restore Israel as His people (2:14–16, 19–20, 23).

The New Testament includes several passages about marriage. Jesus taught or answered questions about marriage on more than one occasion. He attended a wedding at Cana of Galilee and performed His first miracle there (changing water into wine to save the bridegroom from embarrassment; John 2:1–11). He obviously approved of marriage and its accompanying joyous festivities.

When questioned by the Pharisees about the validity of divorce (Matt. 19:3; Mark 10:2), Jesus endorsed monogamous, lifelong marriage. He quoted part of Genesis 1:27 and 2:24 and said, "So they are no longer two, but one. Therefore what God has joined together, let man not separate" (Matt. 19:6; see Mark 10:8). The Pharisees pressed Jesus by asking Him why Moses allowed for divorce (Matt. 19:7; Mark 10:3–4; Deut. 24:1–4). He replied that it was "because your hearts were hard. But it was not this way from the beginning" (Matt. 19:8; Mark 10:5). Jesus then identified "marital unfaithfulness" as the only valid basis for divorce (Matt. 19:9; 5:32).

The writer to the Hebrews summarized the basic New Testament attitude toward marriage when he said, "Marriage should be honored by all, and the marriage bed kept pure" (Heb. 13:4). Paul endorsed monogamous, lifelong marriage, and demanded it of elders (1 Tim. 3:2; Titus 1:6) and deacons (1 Tim. 3:12). Paul was unmarried and promoted celibacy (1 Cor. 7:7–8; 9:5) as a way to serve the Lord single-mindedly (7:32, 34), but he recognized marriage as the norm for most believers (7:2–6). Much of what Paul told the Corinthians in support of celibacy was in response to the "present crisis" (7:26) in the church and because "the time is short" (7:29).

Paul deplored divorce (7:10–11) but directed that "if an unbeliever leaves, let him do so. A believing man or woman is not bound in such circumstances" (7:15). He did not approve of a believer marrying an unbeliever (2 Cor. 6:14–15), but a believing partner should not divorce an unbeliever who is willing to remain in the union (1 Cor. 7:12–13). Such a marriage is sanctified in some sense by the believing partner (7:14), and the unbeliever might be saved (7:16; 1 Pet. 3:1). As the gospel of Christ penetrated pagan communities in the first century, many men and women came to faith in Christ whose marriage partners did not. Those were the believer-unbeliever marriages Paul had in mind.

Paul taught that the relationship of husband and wife portrays the relationship between the Lord Jesus Christ and His church (Eph. 5:22–33). He described the husband "as the head of the wife as Christ is the head of the church" (5:23; see also 1 Cor. 11:3; Eph. 1:22; 4:15; Col. 1:18; 2:19), and he called on wives to "submit to your husbands as to the Lord" (Eph. 5:22; see also 5:24, 33; Titus 2:5; 1 Pet. 3:1, 5–6). Conversely, he called on husbands to "love your wives, just as Christ loved the church" (Eph. 5:25) and sacrificed Himself for her. He also said husbands are to "love their wives as their own bodies" (5:28) and to "love his wife as he loves himself" (5:33; see 1 Pet. 3:7). Husbands who fulfill these admonitions even to a small degree will find that their wives will lovingly fulfill their own roles. As Paul said concerning the whole subject, "This is a profound mystery—but I am talking about Christ and the church" (Eph. 5:32).   **—JAW**

Whether married or not, every believer is responsible before God to promote the sanctity of marriage.

MEDIATOR

Job pleaded with God for a mediator by saying, "If only there were someone to arbitrate between us, to lay his hand upon us both" (Job 9:33). A mediator stands between two estranged individuals or groups to achieve a mutually agreed-on settlement that reconciles them.

In human affairs either party can propose a mediator. When both sides agree on a mediator, he can begin his work to achieve a compromise between competing interests. In our relation to God, however, only God Himself can provide a mediator. There is no compromise to work out, because only one party has done anything wrong. Only God knows how to repair the damage done by our sin. As Paul proclaimed, "For there is one God and one mediator between God and men, the man Christ Jesus, who gave himself as a ransom for all men" (1 Tim. 2:5–6).

Human sin created the need for a mediator between God and people. Adam and Eve disobeyed God and ate the fruit of the tree of the knowledge of good and evil (Gen. 2:17; 3:6–7). Before that time they enjoyed fellowship with God, but afterward "they hid from the LORD God" when they heard Him

"walking in the garden" (3:8). At first God simply spoke to His estranged creatures (3:9, 11, 13, 16–17; 4:5, 9–10, 15; 6:13–21; 7:1–4; 8:15–17; 9:1–16; 12:1–3; 13:14–17). Later He used visions (15:1), angels (19:1), and many chosen men (for example, Moses, Ex. 3:7–10) as mediators to communicate His will, execute His program, and reconcile people to Himself.

In the Old Testament mediators ministered between God and individuals in a number of ways. The first kind of mediator was one who communicated God's message to people. The Angel of the Lord often delivered messages from God (Gen. 16:7–14; Ex. 3:2–6; Num. 22:22–35; Judg. 6:11–24). He was a visible appearance of the preincarnate Jesus Christ. Later chosen men such as Moses (Ex. 19:3–9) and the prophets (1 Sam. 3:11–21; Ezek. 2:1–10) mediated God's messages to His people. When Jesus walked on earth, He served as a mediator in this sense. The people recognized Him as a prophet (Matt. 21:11; John 9:17), and He identified Himself as a prophet (Matt. 13:57; Luke 13:33).

The second kind of mediator represented God as a political ruler. God is the sovereign Creator and Ruler of the universe, but He exercised authority among men on earth, particularly among His chosen people Israel through mediators. Various leaders acted as mediators: for instance, Moses (Ex. 18:13–16), Joshua (Num. 27:15–

23; Deut. 34:9; Josh. 1), the judges (Judg. 2:16, 18), and Israel's kings (1 Sam. 9:16–17; 10:1; 16:12–13; 1 Kin. 11:29–39). In a sense all "governing authorities" continue to mediate the rule of God on earth (Rom. 13:1–7; Titus 3:1; 1 Pet. 2:13–17). Christ will be the ultimate political mediator between God and humanity. "The Lord God will give him the throne of his father David, and he will reign over the house of Jacob forever; his kingdom will never end" (Luke 1:32–33).

The third, and most important, kind of mediator stood between God and humankind to deal with sin. God created this category of mediators to minister before Him on behalf of people. In patriarchal times fathers performed the priestly ministry of offering sacrifices and prayers for their families (Gen. 8:20; Job 1:5). God also began to raise up specially gifted individuals to serve as priests in their communities (Gen. 14:18–20; Job 42:7–9; Heb. 7:1–3). When God established the Mosaic Covenant with Israel, He designated Moses' brother Aaron, his descendants, and the tribe of Levi as priests for Israel.

The New Testament recognizes our Lord Jesus as the supreme priestly Mediator "in the order of Melchizedek" (Ps. 110:4; Heb. 5:5–10; 6:19–20; 7: 15–17, 20–22, 24—8:2). Jesus offered Himself as the final redemptive sacrifice for sin (Eph. 5:2; Heb. 7:27; 9:14; 10:5–7, 10, 14). He now ministers at the right hand of God as our "Advocate" (1 John 2:1, NASB) and our High Priest, who "always lives to intercede" for us (Heb. 7:25; see also Rom. 8:34; Heb. 9:24; John 17).

Since we are identified with Christ by faith, we have been made "a holy priesthood" (1 Pet. 2:5) and "a royal priesthood" (2:9). Christ has made us "a kingdom and priests to serve his God and Father" (Rev. 1:6; see also 5:10; 20:6). We have the unique privilege to "approach the throne of grace with confidence, so that we may receive mercy and find grace to help us in our time of need" (Heb. 4:16). We should intercede for each other, because we have "the priestly duty of proclaiming the gospel of God" (Rom. 15:16).

—JAW

***

As a Christian, you have an opportunity to be a mediator for others with God and a mediator with others.

MEDITATION

While the children of Israel prepared to enter and possess the Promised Land, Joshua received a commission from God. The Lord told Joshua He would be with him. In return He asked for Joshua's complete obedience to the Law of Moses. The Lord also revealed to Joshua how he and the people of Israel could be successful. Joshua was to keep the "Book of the Law" at the center of his life. He was to *meditate*

M

on it day and night and do all it required of him (Josh. 1:7–8).

The word *meditate* means "to ponder or reflect." Several Hebrew words in the Old Testament convey this concept. The word used in Joshua 1:8 implies Joshua would ponder the Book of the Law in his heart and regularly rehearse it in his thoughts. Joshua was expected to do more than review the Law as a set of ideas. He was to contemplate God Himself and dwell on His power and greatness.

The Book of Psalms repeatedly stresses the importance of meditation for the Israelites. The very first psalm draws a sharp contrast between the righteous and the wicked. The righteous person meditates on God's Word day and night (Ps. 1:2). Often such meditation by the godly is motivated by the difficult situations they face. When David was in distress, he found relief as he pondered the goodness of God. He spoke of peace and gladness that flooded his soul in the night (4:4–8). On another occasion, when he was in the house of the Lord, David struggled because of opposition from his enemies. He found strength as he meditated on the beauty of the Lord (27:4, NASB). At that time David faced immediate danger, but he felt it necessary to take time to meet with the Lord in the place of worship and to reflect on the One who was his light and salvation. Even in isolated places like the Judean desert David found that meditating on God's love and greatness sustained him. When he suffered physically, David looked for spiritual relief through meditating on the Lord at night (63:6, NASB).

The psalmist Asaph said he meditated on the power of God by rehearsing in detail how God delivered the Israelites from Egypt. As he thought about all the Lord's mighty works, he found strength for his present situation (77:11–15).

Meditation on the Word of God was central to Israel's worship. Psalm 119 refers to the place of the Scriptures in the lives of God's people in almost every one of its 176 verses. Purity of life results from meditating on His precepts and considering His ways (119:15). The antidote to sorrow is to meditate on the wonders of God revealed in His precepts (119:27–28). Pondering God's truth provides hope when enemies taunt us (119:42–48). When the enemy speaks lies against us, we are sustained by reflecting on the truth of God (119:78). In the darkest night we find hope by meditating on God's promises (119:148).

The New Testament says little about meditation. Jesus and His followers presumably were trained as children and young adults to meditate on the Word of God, as were all young Jewish men. The New Testament teaches that our minds need to be renewed by God's Word and God's Spirit (Rom. 12:2; Eph. 4:23; Col. 3:10). Such renewal presupposes Spirit-led meditation on the Scriptures.   **—WGJ**

* * *

Take time each day to ponder the goodness and greatness of God as revealed in the Scriptures.

MERCY

God's mercy is His compassion expressed in response to dire human need. Even as Moses predicted Israel's future failures and punishments, he declared, "The LORD your God is a merciful God; he will not abandon or destroy you or forget the covenant with your forefathers" (Deut. 4:31). Micah described the Lord as a God of compassion who will "delight to show mercy" (Mic. 7:18–19).

Mercy is a complex, many-faceted concept. The Scripture employs a variety of Hebrew and Greek words to express and describe it. In the Old Testament God showed His mercy in rich and different ways as He interacted with His covenant people Israel. The Bible portrays God as a Father who has compassion on His children (Ps. 103:13), even though they are sometimes wayward and rebellious (Hos. 11; Jer. 31:20). Hosea described Israel as an unfaithful and adulterous wife to whom God shows compassion and mercy (Hos. 1—3; see also Is. 54:4–8). Isaiah depicted God as a mother who has compassion on the child at her breast (49:15).

Israel often petitioned the Lord for mercy and forgiveness in times of need (Pss. 6, 40, 51, 69, 79, 130, 143). The Lord responded to all such petitions by affirming, "I will have mercy on whom I will have mercy, and I will have compassion on whom I will have compassion" (Ex. 33:19). In Nehemiah's time the Levites led the restored remnant of Judah in a moving prayer of confession in which they reviewed the history of Israel from the call of Abraham to the Babylonian exile. The historical summary showed how God had responded to the frequent sins of the people with mercy and forgiveness (Neh. 9:5–31).

Jesus responded with mercy to a wide variety of human needs. Blind men pleaded for sight (Matt. 9:27; 20:30–31; Mark 10:46–48; Luke 18:35–39). A Canaanite woman begged Jesus to deliver her daughter from demons (Matt. 15:22). A father sought help for a demon-possessed son (17:15). Ten lepers asked for healing (Luke 17:12–13).

The Gospels show that Jesus expected His followers who had received God's mercy to extend mercy to those around them. In the Beatitudes, Jesus called the merciful "blessed" (Matt. 5:7). He exhorted His disciples, "Be merciful, just as your Father is merciful" (Luke 6:36). He charged that the religious leaders "neglected the more important matters of the law—justice, mercy and faithfulness" (Matt. 23:23). By contrast, the good Samaritan showed

M

mercy to a man who was beaten and robbed (Luke 10:36–37). In teaching the need for showing mercy to others, the Lord confirmed the commands of the Old Testament to be merciful, especially to the poor, the needy, widows, and orphans (Prov. 14:21, 31; 19:17, NKJV; Mic. 6:8).

The writers of the Epistles typically thought of mercy as a motivation of God's provision of salvation for helpless sinners. Thus God "who is rich in mercy, made us alive with Christ even when we were dead in transgressions" (Eph. 2:4–5). "In His great mercy he has given us new birth into a living hope" (1 Pet. 1:3). "He saved us, not because of righteous things we had done, but because of his mercy" (Titus 3:5). Paul affirmed that God's mercy is sovereignly bestowed (Rom. 9:15–16, 18, 23) and reaches out to the disobedient (11:32). God's mercy motivated Paul to engage in special ministries (2 Cor. 4:1; 1 Tim. 1:16). We should be greatly encouraged that we may "approach the throne of grace with confidence, so that we may receive mercy and find grace to help us in our time of need" (Heb. 4:16).

God's mercy has delivered us from eternal misery and blessed us with everlasting glory and joy. If we truly grasp the significance of God's mercy for our lives, we will gladly worship Him with every breath, every word, and every action of our daily lives. Paul said it like this: "I urge you, brothers, in view of God's mercy, to offer your bodies as living sacrifices, holy and pleasing to God—which is your spiritual act of worship" (Rom. 12:1).

—**DKC**

***

As you are conscious of God's mercy to you, delight in showing mercy to others.

MESSIAH

The word *messiah* comes from the Hebrew *māšîah*, which means "anointed one." The related verb *māšah* means "to anoint with oil." Each Old Testament priest was anointed with oil as the means of consecrating him to God (Ex. 29:7). He then could be called "the anointed priest" (Lev. 4:3, 5, 16). Israel's kings also were called the Lord's "anointed" (1 Sam. 2:10, 35; Pss. 20:6; 28:8), including Saul (1 Sam. 12:3, 5; 26:9, 11, 23; 2 Sam. 1:14, 16) and David (19:21; Pss. 2:2; 18:50). Isaiah even called Cyrus, king of Persia, the Lord's anointed because God had set him apart to restore Israel from captivity (Is. 45:1). Prophets were God's "anointed ones" (1 Chr. 16:22; Ps. 105:15). While the "Anointed One" in Psalm 2:2 originally referred to a king of Judah, it referred ultimately to Jesus Christ, as Peter and John noted in Acts 4:26.

Twice Daniel spoke of "the Anointed One," that is, the Messiah, Jesus Christ (Dan. 9:25–26). The English title "Christ" comes from *christos*, the Greek equivalent of *māšîah*. When Andrew told his brother Peter about Jesus, he said, "We have found the Messiah" (John 1:41). The Samaritan woman told Jesus that she knew that the Messiah would come (4:25). Obviously people in the first century anticipated the Messiah, whose coming the Old Testament had predicted.

In his sermon on the Day of Pentecost, Peter stated that God the Father had made Jesus "both Lord and Christ" (Acts 2:36), that is, both the Sovereign and the Messiah. Later Peter said again that God had sent Jesus as Israel's Messiah (3:20). Other apostles also proclaimed "the good news that Jesus is the Christ" (5:42). Soon after his conversion Saul presented arguments to the Jews to demonstrate that Jesus was the Messiah whom the people were anticipating. Saul even "baffled" the Jews by his reasoning "that Jesus is the Christ" (9:22). Also in Thessalonica and Corinth, Paul reasoned with Jews that Jesus is the Messiah (17:3; 18:5).

Though a number of Jews believed, many others could not accept the idea that the Messiah would die an ignominious death by crucifixion. Most of the Jews who heard Jesus teach had also rejected Him as their Messiah. He Himself said that He must "be rejected by this generation" (Luke 17:25), and the apostle John wrote that "his own did not receive him" (John 1:11). But at His Second Coming the nation Israel will turn to the Lord and will welcome Jesus as their Messiah. He will reign from Jerusalem over Israel as Messiah and over the world as the King of kings and Lord of lords.   —**JFW**

***

Be faithful in sharing with others the Good News that Jesus is God's Anointed One and the only way of eternal salvation.

MILLENNIUM

The word *Millennium* comes from a Latin word meaning "one thousand years." In Revelation 20:2–7 the apostle John refers six times to the future reign of Christ on earth as a period one thousand years in length.

John placed the Millennium after the Second Coming of Christ. An angel will bind and imprison Satan (20:1–3). Believers who will be martyred in the Tribulation will be resurrected (20:4–6) to reign with Christ for one thousand years. At the end of the Millennium Satan will be loosed, and he will organize a rebellion against Christ that will result in destruction of the rebels (20:9). Satan will then be cast into the lake of fire (20:10), the present earth will be destroyed, and new heavens and a new earth will be created (2 Pet. 3:10–13; Rev. 21—22).

A variety of opinions have arisen concerning the Millennium. Premillenarians believe that Christ will reign on the earth for a literal thousand years in fulfillment of prophecies in the Old Testament that Christ will reign on David's throne in Jerusalem. Amillenarians deny a future reign of Christ on this earth. They interpret the thousand years symbolically as a long, indefinite period of time. Most amillenarians say the prophecies concerning the Millennium are being fulfilled in the spiritual kingdom of Christ in the present age. Others say they refer to the present blessed condition of believers in heaven. Still others suggest that the thousand years speak of the future new heavens and the new earth extending indefinitely after their creation. The postmillennial position holds that Christianity will eventually spread over the whole world. Then Christian values will hold sway for a thousand years (or an indefinite long era), and then Christ will return. Very few theologians hold such an optimistic position today. Contemporary liberals do not take biblical prophecies seriously and are almost always amillennial.

A Bible student's view of the Millennium has particular application to interpreting Revelation 20, but it also affects major sections of the Old Testament that speak of a messianic kingdom on earth (Ps. 72) and of Israel's future possession of her land (Gen. 12:7; 15:18–21; Ezek. 39:25–29; 47:13–23). Those who treat the Millennium figuratively usually disregard these passages or treat them nonliterally.

In Christ's millennial reign He will rule over Israel, who will be restored to her land. For the first time Israel will possess all the land God promised in the Abrahamic Covenant (Gen. 15:18–21). Christ will fulfill all aspects, both physical and spiritual, of the New Covenant with Israel (Jer. 31:31–34; Ezek. 36:24–38) He also will fulfill the Davidic Covenant as He rules from David's throne in Jerusalem (2 Sam. 7:12–16; Ps. 89:3–4, 28–29). Christ will bring universal peace as He rules over the entire world. He will rule with supreme justice (Ps. 2:9; Is. 11:3–5; 32:1). Satan will be bound "to keep him from deceiving the nations" (Rev. 20:3). The land will be unusually productive (Is. 27:6; 35:1–7), and people will live long lives (65:20).

Believers look forward to that remarkable time, for they will reign with Christ as His coregents (2 Tim. 2:12; Rev. 3:21; 20:4) and judge the world (1 Cor. 6:2).   **—JFW**

* * *

Think about all God has planned for His children when we will reign with Christ for one thousand years.

MIND

Humans have the innate capacity to think, meditate, plan, and desire. We also can communicate the outcomes of these processes in various ways. All these inner activities occur in the center of conscious mental activity called "the mind."

There is no specific Hebrew word for "mind," but the Old Testament discusses all the functions that relate to the mind. At least sixty-six times the New International Version uses the word "mind" to describe these conscious mental functions. Many passages ascribe an activity of the mind to God. When we read these, we have to realize that the Bible does this to accommodate our limited human understanding. God isn't making up His mind as the events of history unfold. He works according to His sovereign plan, and no circumstance or human action can alter His purposes (1 Sam. 15:29; Ps. 110:4).

Jesus made limited references to the mind in His teaching. The Lord regarded the mind as a vital component of one's inner being. When asked about the greatest of the commandments, Jesus quoted Deuteronomy 6:5, which says, "Love the LORD your God with all your heart and with all your soul and with all your strength." But Jesus inserted "with all your mind" into the list of personality aspects with which we are to love God (Matt. 22:37; Mark 12:30; Luke 10:27). Jesus valued our minds, and He closely associated the activity of our minds with the actions of our hearts and souls.

On another occasion Jesus rebuked Peter for not understanding about His death and resurrection (Matt. 16:23). The thinking of those who did not believe in Christ was influencing Peter's mind. All of the disciples had major difficulties comprehending Jesus' teachings (16:8–11). After His resurrection, however, Jesus opened the minds of the disciples so they could understand the Scriptures more adequately (Luke 24:25). Our minds are not able to discern the things of God apart from supernatural enlightenment (1 Cor. 2:14).

We cannot overstate the importance of the New Testament concept that the mind of Christ must be the pattern for our attitudes, thoughts, values, and choices. His mind is in perfect harmony with and submissive to the will of the Father. The Incarnation and subsequent sacrificial death of Christ show us the major characteristics of the mind of Christ (Phil. 2:5). It is a mark of maturity to possess the mind and attitude of Christ (3:15; 1 Cor. 2:16).

The apostle Paul wrote extensively about the minds of unbelievers and believers alike. It's important to understand that he did not use language about the mind and thinking in the way a modern psychologist would. The mind may refer to the immaterial part of a person and include much more than mere thought processes.

The minds of unregenerate people, Paul noted, are hostile to God. Their minds are focused on sinful human desires and stand in stark contrast to the mind controlled by the Spirit of God (Rom. 8:5–7). This kind of mind leads to futile thinking, separation from God, lack of restraint, and insensitivity to what is pure and wholesome (Eph. 4:14–19). People who oppose the truth have depraved minds (Rom. 1:28; 2 Tim. 3:8). Those whose minds resist the grace of God are called enemies of the Cross of Christ and are headed for destruction (Phil. 3:18; Col. 1:21).

In contrast to the unregenerate mind, the mind of a believer is focused on the desires of the Spirit (Rom. 8:6). Because the Spirit controls our minds, we are able to discern all things and have the mind of Christ (1 Cor. 2:15–16). Our minds are a center from which spiritual activity originates. They are renewed as we give ourselves wholeheartedly to the Holy Spirit (Rom. 12:2; Eph. 4:22–23). As we put off the things related to our former way of life and live as children of light, we will comprehend the mind of the Lord and do the will of God (Eph. 5:8–17). Through prayer the peace of God guards our minds and hearts and prevents anxiety (Phil. 4:6–7). When our minds are under the control of the Holy Spirit and sensitive to the mind of Christ, we bring glory to God.

James encouraged us to be single-minded and to trust the Lord in the midst of difficult circumstances. He warned that a double-minded person is unstable and unworthy of God's assistance (James 1:5–8; 4:8). Writing to believers who were facing pressure to conform to evil desires, Peter said we should prepare our minds

for holy living (1 Pet. 1:13). Peter said Christ set the example as One who suffered in the flesh and resisted Satan's temptations. He exhorts us, "Arm yourselves also with the same attitude" (4:1). The word "attitude" is *ennoia,* one of several Greek words that can be rendered "mind." *Ennoia* literally identifies what is *in* the mind, in the sense of thought, idea, or attitude. Having Jesus' attitude toward suffering enables us to reject evil desires and to do God's will (4:2). The apostle John reminded us that Christ has given us insight (*dianoia*) to know the true God (1 John 5:20).   **—WGJ**

***

Guard your mind and heart from the ever-present influences of the world, and center your attention on the Lord and the promises of His Word.

MINISTRY

Serving God has always been the privilege and responsibility of human beings. Before sin came on the earth, Adam served God by working the ground (Gen. 2:15). In this verse the Hebrew word for "work" is ʿābad, the same word translated "worship" in Exodus 3:12. We use the word *ministry* to cover the same broad spectrum of activities from work to worship when they serve God's purposes. Ministry in the Old Testament was service performed in obedience to God. Ministry became primarily the responsibility of the priests and Levites after the tabernacle and temple came on the scene. The prophets spoke for God, and in that sense they served the Lord, though the term *ministry* was not normally used to explain their calling.

The New Testament presents a much broader concept of ministry. All Christians are priests who worship and serve the Lord (1 Pet. 2:5, 9; Rev. 1:6). When Christ died at Calvary, His death established a new priesthood. The Levitical priesthood instituted by Moses ended. Jesus established a new and permanent priesthood (Heb. 7:24). Through the finished work of Christ's sacrifice, we have obtained an eternal redemption, on the basis of which we must serve the Lord (10:11–14).

As priests under the lordship of Christ, we minister differently than the Levitical priests did. Jesus told His disciples that humble service is the way to greatness (Mark 10:45). On that same occasion Jesus said His own purpose in coming to the earth was to serve (*diakoneō*). Peter, who followed Jesus closely, described His ministry as "doing good" (Acts 10:38). Peter learned firsthand about the servant ministry of Jesus when Jesus washed the feet of His disciples. In what may have been Peter's last encounter with the resurrected Jesus, the Lord repeatedly challenged him to feed and care for His sheep (John 21:15–17).

Jesus demonstrated for us what the psalmist taught: effective ministry stems from a faithful, pure, and humble heart (Ps. 101:6).

Ministry is a recurring theme in the Epistles. Paul's formal service of the Lord in ministry began during the year he spent with Barnabas at Antioch (Acts 11:25–26). At the end of that year, Paul and Barnabas were deployed for an itinerant ministry (13:2–3). Paul cared deeply about the people of Israel, but God had commissioned him to minister primarily to the Gentiles (21:19; Rom. 11:13).

When Paul described his ministry to the Ephesian elders, he used the verb *douleuō*, "to serve as a bondservant" (Acts 20:19). His ministry was noted for humility and compassion. He said that teaching the Word of God played a major role in his ministry (20:21, 24, 27). Having been a shepherd to the Ephesians, he exhorted their elders to follow his example and to pastor (literally, shepherd) the congregation (20:28).

Paul emphasized the significance of the Holy Spirit in our ministry (2 Cor. 3:3–6). The ministry of reconciliation, he said, has been committed to all of us (5:18–19). Since ministry can be discredited, we should not be a stumbling block to others (6:3). For some of us, like Paul, ministry may involve many hardships (6:4–10).

Paul also emphasized the importance

of spiritual gifts in ministry (1 Cor. 12:4–11). In Ephesians 4:11–12 he taught that gifted people are given to the church "to prepare God's people for works of service." Christian ministry is not something we do in our own strength; we are dependent on the enablement of the Spirit of God.

Paul's letters to Timothy and Titus show that the apostle believed in organized leadership for ministry within the church (1 Tim. 3:1–13; Titus 1:5–9). Good ministers believe the truth, exemplify God's grace, and faithfully teach the truth to others (1 Tim. 4:6). In his last letter Paul exhorted Timothy to fulfill all the responsibilities of the ministry God had entrusted to him (2 Tim. 4:5).

Peter added an important concept concerning our ministry: All our service, besides benefiting others, ultimately brings praise and glory to God (1 Pet. 4:11).   **—WGJ**

***

Pursue opportunities to serve the Lord each day, and write down specific ways you can minister to people in the body of Christ.

MIRACLES

A miracle is an event in which God reveals His divine power for the purpose of drawing people to Himself. Miracles not only inspire awe and wonder; they also have revelatory significance. Philosopher David Hume asserted that a miracle is "a violation of the laws of nature," but the Bible does not teach that natural law is something independent or separate from God as if He created the universe and then left it to operate by itself. On the contrary, natural law is God's *ordinary way* of operating in the natural world (Ps. 19:1–3; 104; Heb. 1:3), and a miracle is, therefore, God's *extraordinary* manner of operating in the natural world. Sometimes people use the word *miracle* too loosely. Some occurrences may be unusual in their nature or their timing, but that does not mean they are miracles in the strict biblical sense.

Several Old Testament terms are translated "sign" and "wonder." Both indicate God's intervention in history to affirm His presence and His control over events. The New Testament uses eight Greek words in association with miracles. Four of these are the most prominent. *Dynamis* ("power") describes a miracle as an expression of divine power. *Sēmeion* ("sign") affirms that the miracle attests to God's presence. *Teras* ("wonder") portrays the effect of the miracle on the observer. These three terms occur together in Acts 2:22; Romans 15:19–20; 2 Thessalonians 2:9; and Hebrews 2:4. The fourth is *erga* ("works"). What men considered a "wonder," Christ regarded simply as a work of His hands.

Miracles are not scattered haphazardly throughout Scripture. They are concentrated in four specific periods of biblical history: the time of Moses and Joshua, of Elijah and Elisha, of Daniel, and of Christ and the early church.

In the Old Testament, miracles took place during critical periods of Israel's history. They served to accredit God's message and messenger. When Moses responded to God's call to return to Egypt to lead the Hebrews out of bondage, he needed miraculous signs to convince the people that he had been sent by God and to convince Pharaoh to release the enslaved Israelites. The ten miraculous plagues in Egypt demonstrated to Israel that God was exercising His power on their behalf (Ex. 6:6–7). In addition, each of the plagues was directed at a particular god of Egypt. God declared, "The Egyptians will know that I am the LORD when I stretch out my hand against Egypt" (7:5; see also 7:17; 8:6, 17; 9:15, 29; 12:12). This truth applied as well to the great miracle of the crossing of the Red Sea. After the Exodus, God performed numerous miracles on Israel's behalf when they were in the wilderness and as they invaded and conquered Canaan under Joshua's leadership.

In the period of the united monarchy (the reigns of Saul, David, and Solomon) miracles are conspicuously absent. God worked through these kings, even with their frailties, to accomplish His purposes. When the kingdom divided after Solomon's reign, apostasy took hold in the northern kingdom. King Jeroboam introduced calf worship. Later King Ahab and Queen Jezebel promoted Baal worship. Elijah and Elisha performed miracles that demonstrated the powerlessness of Baal (for example, the contest on Mount Carmel, 1 Kin. 18) and the omnipotence of the one true God.

During the Babylonian captivity Daniel and his friends stood out as godly leaders who reassured the exiles that their God was still alive. The miracles performed in Babylon demonstrated God's greater prowess over the false gods of Babylon and Persia, and showed that He could still protect His people even though they were away from their homeland (see Dan. 3, 5, 6).

The New Testament abounds in miracles because of the advent of Jesus Christ. In Old Testament times God injected His acts into the flow of human history, but through the incarnation of Christ, God entered and participated in human history. Christ performed miracles during His earthly ministry to prove His deity, to demonstrate His messiahship, to show compassion to those in need, and to prepare the disciples for their future ministry. The Gospel writers reported only thirty-five of the miracles Jesus performed.

M

They selected only those miracles that fit their purposes. They made numerous references, however, to the sheer volume of miracles Jesus performed (Matt. 4:23–24; 8:16; 9:35; 11:4–5, 20–24; 12:15; 14:14, 36; 15:30; 19:2; 21:14). Behind the miracles Jesus performed were the miracles of His mission: His Incarnation, Resurrection, and Ascension. These miracles, in a class by themselves, set the stage for God to provide salvation for lost people.

Miracles continued in the early church (Acts 3, 5, 8, 9, 12, 13, 14, 16, 19, 20, 28). On some occasions they were direct divine interventions, as with the opening of the prison doors for the apostles (Acts 5, 12), but more often the miracles were performed by the apostles themselves in the power of the Holy Spirit. Paul spoke of signs, wonders, and miracles as "the things that mark an apostle" (2 Cor. 12:12; see also Rom. 15:18–19). The author of the letter to the Hebrews said that with signs, wonders, and miracles God bore witness to salvation (Heb. 2:4). The miracles performed in the apostolic age were signs that authenticated the Christian message as well as the messenger. With the Christian faith established and the canon of Scripture completed, the need for authenticating signs no longer exists. As has been seen, not every generation experiences miraculous signs. They have appeared in critical periods in biblical history, fulfilled their purpose, and then passed off the scene.

On the other hand, it is unwise to say God never performs miracles today. It can be affirmed, however, that they are not typical of God's present working as they were during Jesus' ministry. Further, when God does heal someone miraculously, He does so sovereignly, rather than through a human agent. Believers should follow the example of Jesus in Gethsemane when He prayed, "Not my will but yours be done" (Luke 22:42).

As the end of history approaches and the return of Christ to establish His kingdom on earth draws near, deceiving miracles will burst out. Christ warned of this future day when "false Christs and false prophets will appear and perform great signs and miracles" (Matt. 24:24). Paul, too, spoke of "the lawless one," whose coming "will be in accordance with the work of Satan displayed in all kinds of counterfeit miracles, signs and wonders" (2 Thess. 2:9). In the Tribulation the Antichrist will perform miraculous works to convince people to worship him (Rev. 13:14; 19:20). At Christ's glorious appearance the beast will be defeated, and he will be "thrown alive into the fiery lake of burning sulfur" (19:20).

—**DKC**

***

Learn significant truths about Christ by studying the seven miracles of John's Gospel.

MYSTERY

This English word reproduces letter-for-letter the first syllables of the Greek word *mystērion*. "Mystery" pops up with some frequency in the New Testament, primarily in the writings of the apostle Paul. The Bible does not use the word in the contemporary sense of something hard to understand or something incomprehensible. (That meaning, however, may be involved when Paul wrote that when a person "speaks in a tongue . . . no one understands him; he utters mysteries with his spirit," 1 Cor. 14:2. That meaning may also be in view when Paul said that a person possessing the gift of prophecy was able to "fathom all mysteries and all knowledge," 13:2.)

In the pagan religions of Egypt, Persia, Greece, and Rome, mystery cults developed. In these groups teachers progressively initiated new members into closely guarded secret rites and teachings. These mystery religions developed before the Christian era, but coexisted for a long time with the church. Some mystery religions influenced heresies in the church. Paul's hometown of Tarsus was a center for a mystery religion. This may explain why Paul used the word *mystery*, but the meaning he gave it is uniquely biblical.

One of the clearest uses of "mystery" in the Bible is Paul's reference to "the mystery that has been kept hidden for ages and generations, but is now disclosed to the saints" (Col. 1:26). Elsewhere he wrote that his ministry was "to make plain to everyone the administration of this mystery, which for ages past was hidden in God" (Eph. 3:9). Just before this he explained that "the mystery [was] made known to me by revelation" (3:3) and that it "was not made known to men in other generations as it has now been revealed by the Spirit of God's holy apostles and prophets" (3:5; see also Rom. 16:26).

Biblically a mystery is divine truth that God did not disclose in Old Testament times. He reserved it until the New Testament era when the apostles and prophets proclaimed it freely to everyone who would listen. The free, open sharing of the truth is what distinguishes a biblical mystery from one in a mystery religion. Mystery religions only shared their mysteries with their initiates. They prohibited members, sometimes on pain of death, from leaking their mysteries to outsiders.

The New Testament phrases its "mystery" in various ways, but it seems to be just one mystery. It's called "the mystery of Christ" (Eph. 3:4; Col. 4:3) and "the mystery of God, namely, Christ" (2:2). It can be expanded as "this mystery, which is Christ in you, the hope of glory" (1:27), a truth never revealed in the Old Testament. In greater detail the mystery asserts "that through the gospel the Gentiles are heirs together with Israel, members together

M

of one body, and sharers together in the promise in Christ Jesus" (Eph. 3:6; see also Col. 1:26–27). This idea that Gentiles could have equal standing with Jews in the church, the body of Christ, is foreign to the Old Testament. However, it was Paul's gospel (Rom. 16:25–27). Paul asked the Colossian

Christians to pray that he "may proclaim the mystery of Christ . . . clearly" (Col. 4:3–4). **—JAW**

***

Remember that the gospel of Christ remains a mystery only when it is not proclaimed.

Nn

NATURAL MAN

Christians exhibit certain spiritual characteristics that distinguish them from the general populace. The critical distinguishing mark, according to the apostle Paul, is how a person responds to the things of God (1 Cor. 2:14–15). Individuals indwelt and controlled by the Holy Spirit will welcome the things of God (Rom. 8:9, 14). Those who have never received Christ by faith do not have the Spirit (8:8–9) and are unable to understand the thoughts of God (1 Cor. 2:11, 14).

The Greek words Paul used to describe someone without Christ are *psychikos anthrōpos* (2:14). The New American Standard Bible translates this phrase as "natural man," and the New International Version loosely renders it "the man without the Spirit." This exact Greek phrase appears nowhere else in the New Testament. The expression the "natural man" represents unregenerate people as a group. A "natural man" grapples success-

fully with all things human because his human spirit sympathizes with human strengths and weaknesses. But he is incapable of comprehending what God has revealed. Spiritual comprehension is possible only by the Spirit of God (2:13). Unsaved people may be brilliant, talented, prosperous, and even moral and good. However, their human wisdom is natural and unspiritual, not supernatural and from heaven (James 3:15).

The "natural man" is simply one who is born into the world, unrelated to God because of sin (Jude 19). He is "in Adam" (1 Cor. 15:22) in contrast to the saved, who are "in Christ." We who are "in Christ," are a new creation, possessing a unique relationship to God (2 Cor. 5:17). **—WGJ**

***

Be sensitive to the fact that a person without Christ is incapable of understanding spiritual truth, and pray for the enlightenment of the Spirit that brings salvation.

OBEDIENCE

Obedience to God and his Word is never an option for believers. It is mandatory. The term *obedience* and related words occur more than 250 times in the New International Version. The majority of these passages are in the Old Testament. The predominant Hebrew word is *šāmâ*, which means "to hear, to understand, and to respond appropriately." In the New Testament, the Greek verbs *akouō* and *hypakouō* mean essentially the same thing as the Hebrew *šāmâ*.

In the Old Testament the concept of obedience is built on the premise that God expects His people to listen to what He says and do as He commands. When God created Adam and Eve and placed them in the Garden of Eden, He gave them one command to obey: "You must not eat from the tree of the knowledge of good and evil" (Gen. 2:17). They failed to obey, they became separated from God, and their sin brought condemnation on the entire human race (Rom. 5:12). God expected Adam and Eve to hear His warning and to obey His instructions.

God selected Israel to be His people and rescued them from Egypt. He expected them to obey the covenant He established with them through Moses (Ex. 19:5). The people promised to obey everything the Lord said (19:8). Obedience to the Mosaic Law would bring about a variety of blessings. God would defeat their enemies (23:22–23). He would take away sickness from among them (23:25), and they could expect a full life span (23:26). The land would be fruitful, and they would dwell there in safety (Lev. 25:18–19; 26:6–8).

Moses restated the Law to Israel after the nation had wandered in the wilderness for forty years. Once again God highlighted His demands for obedience. He conditioned Israel's possession of the land on their obedience to His commands (Deut. 4:1–2). Their obedience would show the surrounding nations that Israel was wise (4:6). Ultimately, obedience to God and His commands would guarantee Israel life (30:15–20). Disobedience would result in death.

The capstone of Old Testament teaching about obedience is in Deuteronomy 6:4–5. Because God revealed His true character to Israel, the nation was expected to love Him totally. Obedience should flow from the heart. Obedience should be an integral part of the life of an Israelite who loved God. God's commands were to be the first thing he thought about in the morning and the last thing at night (6:7).

Consequently obedience was always a spiritual issue. It began in the heart (30:1–2) as an act of faith. The people were to obey God with all their heart (30:2). God said this was not too difficult for them to comprehend or to carry out. He had made His commands known and they had access to them

O

(30:11–14). Paul referred to whole-hearted obedience in Romans 10:1–11. Obedience has to be more than carrying out the letter of the Law. He lamented the superficiality of self-righteous legalism (10:3). The obedience God wanted of Old Testament saints was based on faith in Him and His Word.

Abraham exemplified the faith God desired of all His old covenant people. God had told him to go to a place that he would later receive as his inheritance. Abraham obeyed and went. He obeyed because he believed everything God told him. Without faith, it is impossible to please God (Heb. 11:6–10).

The prophets called Israel to obey the Law or face judgment. Tragically Israel never persevered in any of her revivals. She repeatedly rejected her God, and her *dis*obedience resulted in destruction, captivity, and deportation to either Assyria or Babylon. Jeremiah provided a ray of hope for the people as he prophesied about the New Covenant. God promised He would one day put His Law in their minds and write it on their hearts so that they would obey (Jer. 31:33).

The New Testament adds certain new dimensions to the biblical teaching about obedience. In the Sermon on the Mount Jesus made it clear that obeying the Mosaic Law didn't mean following the narrow interpretations given by the Pharisees (Matt. 5:20). Obedience required responding to the spirit of God's Law. Disciples listen carefully to the words of Christ in order to obey them (7:24).

At the close of His earthly ministry Jesus explained the significance of obedience to His disciples in the Upper Room. He explained that faith in Him is an absolute necessity (John 14:1). He added that if they loved Him, they would obey His commands (14:15; 15:23). He taught that abiding in Him requires obeying His Word (15:10).

Jesus modeled obedience for all believers (15:10). He became a servant and died on the Cross in obedience to the will of the Father (Phil. 2:6–9). Every aspect of the Incarnation illustrates the true nature of obedience. It is a responsive attitude that wants to please God.

John presented the Upper Room Discourse and its teaching about obedience in his Gospel. Not surprisingly he also wrote in his epistles about the necessity of obedience in our lives. Obedience demonstrates our salvation to others (1 John 2:3). The love of God is perfected in us through obedience (2:5). Obedience has a positive effect on our prayer life (3:22). And obedience demonstrates that we are abiding in fellowship with Christ (3:24). John didn't want to be misunderstood. He made it clear that obedience to rules doesn't save us. Salvation is rooted in our faith in Christ. Our obedience is the visible evidence of our faith (3:23–24; 5:1–4).

The writer to the Hebrews said that Christ is "the source of eternal salvation for all who obey him" (Heb. 5:9). This passage uses obedience as a synonym for believing in Christ. Other passages that do the same thing include Acts 5:32; Romans 16:26; and 2 Thessalonians 1:8. To believe in Him is to obey His command to turn to Christ in salvation.

We demonstrate to others that we belong to Christ when we believe in Him, obey His Word, and demonstrate our obedience by loving others and doing His will.

The Bible also tells us to obey in other areas. Children should obey their parents (Eph. 6:1), and citizens should obey their political leaders (Rom. 13:1, 5) so long as doing so does not involve disobeying God (Acts 5:29).　　**—WGJ**

***

Trust in the Lord and live in obedience to His Word, which is the pathway of happiness for every believer.

OIL

In biblical times oil was made from a variety of natural sources. Almonds and castor beans could be pressed for oil. But most oil in the ancient Near East came from olives. In fact, the English word "oil" is derived from the Latin *oleum*, which in turn translates the Greek *elaian*, "olive oil." In ancient times olive oil played a major role in food preparation, home illumination, medicine, cosmetics, hospitality rituals, religious rites, and the consecration of political and religious leaders. As a result olive oil was highly valued commercially.

Olive trees are now cultivated all over the Mediterranean Basin and in other climatically favorable areas. In biblical times, however, Palestine especially was known as "a land with . . . olive oil" (Deut. 8:8). Its production was basic to Israel's economy both for domestic consumption and export (2 Chr. 2:8–10, 15–16). Elisha multiplied the olive oil of a widow whose creditors threatened to take her two boys as slaves. He miraculously multiplied her "little oil" and directed her to "sell the oil and pay your debts. You and your sons can live on what is left" (2 Kin. 4:1–7).

Some olive oil came from green olives, but most was produced from ripe, black olives. The harvest season for olives ran from September through November. Growers allowed the olives to fall to the ground or they beat them from the trees with long rods. Then they gathered the ripe olives from the ground. As with other crops, the poor people of Israel could glean overlooked olives from the groves of landowners after the harvest was completed (Deut. 24:20).

Farmers produced the best grades

of oil by pressing the olives without crushing the kernels. Sometimes they did this by treading the olives underfoot like grapes (Mic. 6:15), or by crushing them with a pestle. This premium oil was called "clear oil" (Ex. 27:20). In later times farmers used mills to crush the kernels as well as the fruit into a pulp. They pressed the pulp to extract the oil. The pulp was squeezed progressively harder to extract oil in several grades of purity. The better grades were used in cosmetics and religious ceremonies, and the impure grades were used for cooking and lamp fuel.

People in Bible times used oil medicinally in a variety of ways. Frequently it was one of the ingredients in medicines taken internally. It was applied to open wounds as an ointment (Is. 1:6) or mixed with wine as an antiseptic (Luke 10:34). The elders of the church applied oil to sick people as they prayed for their healing by God (James 5:14). On the basis of these Scriptures, the Roman Catholic Church has developed the sacrament of extreme unction and the Greek Orthodox Church the rite called Euchelaion.

From ancient times into the last century, olive oil was used in the Mediterranean area as lamp fuel to light homes and businesses. In Bible times the typical lamp was a small shallow clay bowl. The rim of the bowl was pinched on one side to create a wick holder. Such lamps turn up in large numbers in almost any excavation. Tourist shops sell them as souvenirs throughout the Near East. The average home had these lamps in most rooms (2 Kin. 4:10). They didn't hold much oil, so anyone going out at night had to carry a supply of fuel. Five of the ten virgins in Jesus' parable neglected this everyday precaution to their chagrin and loss (Matt. 25:1–10).

The sun, wind, and heat of the eastern Mediterranean climate dried people's skin. In the desert areas in particular, men and women rubbed olive oil on their skin to moisten and protect it. Many applied olive oil as a hair treatment and face lotion. As a result, it became customary to anoint the heads of visitors in one's home with olive oil, sometimes perfumed, as a token of hospitality (Ps. 23:5; Amos 6:6, NASB).

When Jesus visited the home of Simon, the Pharisee, Simon withheld the common courtesy of anointing an honored guest's head with oil. Everyone present would have caught the snub. Then Simon silently criticized Jesus for allowing "a woman who had lived a sinful life in that town" to anoint Him with perfumed oil and wash and kiss His feet. Jesus rebuked Simon for omitting the normal courtesies of washing His feet, greeting Him with a kiss, and anointing His head with oil and commended the woman for doing those very things as acts of devotion and worship (Luke 7:36–50).

In a similar incident in Bethany of Judea, Mary, one of Lazarus's sisters, anointed Jesus with "a pint of pure nard, an expensive perfume." When Judas Iscariot and other disciples denounced her act of devotion and worship as a waste, Jesus rebuked them, saying that she had done it to prepare Him "for the day of [his] burial" (John 12:1–8; see also Matt. 26:6–13; Mark 14:3–9). Merchants made perfumes by combining olive oil with scented substances such as myrrh, anise, cedar, cinnamon, ginger, peppermint, rose, or sandalwood. Once the essences had scented the oil and the solid residue had settled, the perfumer poured off the oil, bottled it, and sold it as perfume (Ruth 3:3; 2 Sam. 12:20; Esth. 2:12).

The most important biblical use of olive oil, both ordinary and perfumed, was in worship. God appeared to Jacob the night he left Beersheba for Haran. The next morning Jacob "took the stone he had placed under his head and set it up as a pillar and poured oil on top of it. He called that place Bethel" (Gen. 28:18–19), which means "God's house" (28:22; 35:14–15). Likewise, Moses anointed the tabernacle and all its furnishings and instruments with a special oil (Ex. 30:26–29; 40:9–11; Lev. 8:10–11; Num. 7:1) made to a specific formula (Ex. 30:22–24), "a holy anointing oil" (30:25; 37:29).

Moses used the same holy anointing oil to consecrate Aaron as the high priest and his sons as priests to serve God (Ex. 29:7; 30:30; 40:12–16; Lev. 8:12; 21:10, 12; Ps. 133:2). The care of the anointing oil was given to Aaron's son Eleazar (Num. 4:16) and later committed to some of the priests (1 Chr. 9:29–30). Samuel anointed Saul to be Israel's first king (1 Sam. 10:1). He anointed David to replace Saul as king after Saul disobeyed the Lord's command (16:1, 12–13). After David designated Solomon to succeed him (1 Kin. 1:30, 32–35), Zadok the priest anointed Solomon as king over Israel (1:39). At Elisha's direction, one of his prophets anointed Jehu to kill "the whole house of Ahab" and serve as king of Israel (2 Kin. 9:1–3, 6–7, 12–13).

In the Bible olive oil can symbolize a number of things. A lack of oil signified famine (Joel 1:10; Hag. 1:11), while oil in abundance represented prosperity and God's blessing (Job 29:6; Joel 2:19, 24). Olive oil stood for joy (Ps. 45:7; Is. 61:3; Heb. 1:9). Wasting oil is a sign of profligacy (Prov. 21:17), while using it carefully is evidence of prudence and wisdom (21:20). Supremely, however, anointing with oil symbolizes the Holy Spirit's descent on an anointed individual (1 Sam. 10:1, 6–7, 9; 16:13).   **—JAW**

***

Since olive oil in the Bible is a symbol of gladness and joy, become a "merchant" who dispenses joy freely.

PARADISE

Paradise refers to the place where the souls of the righteous dead go to await the resurrection of their bodies. It is a place of happiness and delight. *Paradise* is believed to be a word of Persian origin. *Pardēs* appears three times in the Old Testament: Song of Solomon 4:13 ("orchard"), Nehemiah 2:8 ("forest"), and Ecclesiastes 2:5 ("parks"). In the Septuagint, the Greek translation of the Old Testament, *paradeisos* refers to the Garden of Eden in Genesis 2 and 3. In Genesis 13:10 and Joel 2:3, biblical writers looked back to Eden and called it *paradeisos*.

Jewish tradition in New Testament times taught that the region of the dead, hades, was located in the heart of the earth. Hades was divided into two compartments. In one the wicked dead suffered torment, and in the other the righteous dead enjoyed bliss. They were in paradise.

Christ used the word *paradeisos* only once. He told the thief on the cross, "I tell you the truth, today you will be with me in paradise" (Luke 23:43). "Paradise" can be equated with "Abraham's bosom" where Lazarus went after his death in Jesus' story of the rich man and Lazarus (16:22, NKJV). Some theologians hold the view that paradise is no longer a portion of hades. They maintain that following the Resurrection and Ascension of Christ, paradise was relocated in the third

heaven. Paul may have described the movement of saints from hades to heaven in Ephesians 4:8–10. Other theologians feel the Scriptures simply equate paradise and heaven with no allusion to hades. Paradise refers to where Christ is (Luke 23:43; Phil. 1:23; 2 Cor. 5:8). When Jesus promised the thief the bliss of paradise (heaven), He was affirming a prospect that belongs to all believing Christians.

A second New Testament mention of paradise occurs in 2 Corinthians 12:4. Paul was telling about his "visions and revelations from the Lord" (12:1). He countered his opponents' boasts regarding their spiritual experiences by telling one of his that had happened fourteen years earlier. What Paul told about may have happened when he was stoned at Lystra (Acts 14:19). He was "caught up" (*harpazō*, the same verb used in 1 Thess. 4:17 of saints at the Rapture) and transported to the third heaven (2 Cor. 12:2). In paradise he saw and heard wondrous things he wasn't allowed to repeat to anyone (12:4). The "third heaven" is the abode of God as distinguished from the first heaven of the clouds and atmosphere and from the second heaven of the stars and planets. The heavenly experience nonetheless did enable him to write knowledgeably, "I desire to depart and be with Christ, which is better by far" (Phil. 1:23).

The third New Testament reference

to paradise occurs in the Book of Revelation. Jesus promised the church in Ephesus, "To him who overcomes, I will give the right to eat from the tree of life, which is in the paradise of God" (Rev. 2:7). Though the tree of life was originally in the Garden of Eden (Gen. 3:22), the Old Testament prophets predicted a restoration of the Edenic paradise (Is. 51:3; Ezek. 36:35). The prophets were writing about conditions during the Millennium, but the tree of life itself won't reappear until the New Jerusalem arrives in the eternal state (Rev. 22:2). To eat its fruit is to partake of the fullness of eternal life.   **—DKC**

***

Thank God that because of Jesus' sacrifice on the Cross paradise is the believer's certain hope.

PASSOVER

Passover was one of Israel's three great annual festivals. All the men of Israel were commanded to appear before the Lord at the sanctuary for these celebrations (Ex. 23:14–17). The Passover marked the most significant divine intervention in Israel's history, the nation's deliverance from bondage in Egypt. It fell on the fourteenth day of the first month of Israel's lunar calendar (Ex. 12:2, 6). Since Jesus was killed at Passover time, Passover falls in the spring near the Easter season.

The Passover protected Israel from the tenth plague, which brought death to the firstborn sons of Egyptian families. The Israelites smeared the blood of a lamb on the lintels and doorposts of their homes. When the Lord visited the land, He "passed over" (*pāsaḥ*) the blood-marked homes of the Israelites (Ex. 12:13), but the firstborn sons of the Egyptians died. That night Hebrew families ate the roasted lamb with bitter herbs and unleavened bread to remind them of their bitter Egyptian bondage. They tucked their cloaks into their belts, put on their traveling sandals, and held their staffs in their hands before they ate to show their readiness for a hasty departure from Egypt.

Before Israel left Egypt, God gave detailed instructions about how the Passover should be observed every year. He instructed that when Israel entered Canaan, they should add a week of celebration to the Passover season during which nothing made with leaven could be eaten. This Feast of Unleavened Bread marked the beginning of the barley harvest (13:3–10).

God expected Israel to repeat the Passover celebration annually as a memorial of their deliverance from Egypt and as a means of instructing future generations about their heritage (12:24–27; Lev. 23:5–8; Num. 28:16–25; Deut. 16:1–8). But His people often neglected the Passover as well as many other divine instructions and laws. After its institution (Ex. 12:28), the Passover was observed a year later at Sinai (Num. 9:1–5) but not again until Israel entered Canaan (Josh. 5:10). Only three Passover observances are recorded between Israel's entrance into the Promised Land (1406 B.C.) and the Babylonian captivity (586 B.C.). The three Passovers occurred during the reigns of Solomon (2 Chr. 8:13), Hezekiah (30:15), and Josiah (2 Kin. 23:21; 2 Chr. 35:1–19). After the return of the Jews from captivity, the exiles celebrated a noteworthy Passover following the dedication of the second temple (Ezra 6:19–22).

The New Testament refers many times to the Passover. Hebrews 11 includes Moses among its Old Testament heroes of faith by saying, "By faith he kept the Passover and the sprinkling of blood, so that the destroyer of the firstborn would not touch the firstborn of Israel" (Heb. 11:28). Passover and the Feast of Unleavened Bread figure prominently in the life and ministry of Christ on earth. As a boy Jesus accompanied His parents as they went to Jerusalem each year for the Feast of the Passover (Luke 2:41). John's Gospel records at least three Passovers during Christ's ministry (John 2:13, 23; 6:4; 12:1; 18:28, 39; 19:14). Some believe the feast mentioned in John 5:1 was a fourth Passover. When Jesus met with His disciples in the Upper Room on the evening before His crucifixion, He ate the Passover meal with them (Matt. 26:17–19; Mark 14:12–18; Luke 22:14–20). Jesus pictured His death on the cross by breaking bread and passing a cup of wine. To this day we memorialize the death of Jesus with the Lord's Supper in anticipation of His imminent return (1 Cor. 11:24–26). It is probable that Christ actually hung on the cross when the Passover lambs were being killed (these animals were slain between 2:30 P.M. and 5:30 P.M. in the temple court). Thus Jesus graphically portrayed the "Lamb of God, who takes away the sin of the world" (John 1:29).

An estimated 120,000 to 180,000 Jews were present in Jerusalem to celebrate the Passover when Jesus died. Most of them had come from surrounding countries. Many of them stood in the crowd at the cross as Jesus, God's Lamb, died between two thieves. In A.D. 70 the Romans destroyed Jerusalem and its temple. Large-scale Passover celebrations ended because there was no longer an altar served by priests where animal sacrifices could be made. Since then the Jewish Passover has functioned as a family observance with no shedding of blood.

Today Samaritans make an annual pilgrimage from their homes in Nablus, Israel, up nearby Mount Gerizim. There they celebrate the Passover feast after seven lambs are slain and roasted. Thus two groups—Jews and Samaritans—continue to observe a feast that Jesus fulfilled two thousand years ago on Mount Calvary outside Jerusalem.

The Passover and the Feast of Unleavened Bread prefigured truths about Christ and the church. Paul declared that Christ is "our Passover lamb" (1 Cor. 5:7). We should therefore put away the "old leaven" of malice and wickedness and in its place embrace "the unleavened bread of sincerity and truth" (5:8, NKJV).   **—DKC**

***

Meditate on the significance to you of Christ, the Passover Lamb.

PEACE

In the Bible the word *peace* includes the ideas of wholeness, wellbeing, prosperity, and security, all based on God's presence with His people.

The Hebrew word *šālôm* is translated "peace" over two hundred times in the Old Testament. Sometimes it is simply a form of greeting (Gen. 29:6; 2 Kin. 4:26), but more often "peace" describes relationships—between individuals (Gen. 34:21, NKJV; Josh. 9:15), between nations (Deut. 2:26; Josh. 10:21, NKJV; 1 Kin. 4:24; 5:12), or between God and people (Ps. 85:8; Jer. 16:5, NKJV).

One of the Old Testament offerings was called the peace offering ("fellowship offering," NIV). Since the Hebrew concept of peace embraces health, prosperity, security, and peace with God, "peace offering" makes a better translation. (R. K. Harrison suggests the translation "sacrifice of well-being.") The unique feature of this offering was the communal meal. Worshipers, their families, and a Levite feasted on most of the sacrifice after it was offered. A worshiper brought a peace offering to express gratitude, to make a vow, or as a freewill offering. The peace offering was a fitting response to God for all His blessings that led to peace (Lev. 3; 7:11–36).

In the psalms, God's people cherish peace, both nationally and individually. God declared He would bless "his people with peace" (Ps. 29:11). David felt deep anxiety when he was pursued by Saul and betrayed by friends and family, yet he could declare with confidence, "I will lie down and sleep in peace, for you alone, O LORD, make me dwell in safety" (4:8). The psalms repeatedly contrast the wicked and the righteous (for example, 1:3–5; 37:35–37), calling the latter a "man of peace" (37:37). Further, the psalmist declared that those who love God's Law possess "great peace" (119:165).

The prophets emphasized the same themes. God grants peace to those who are rightly related to Him (Is. 26:3),

P

but there is no peace for the wicked (57:20–21). The prophets also expected that peace would come someday to the nations, a peace will only come with the Second Advent of the Messiah, the "Prince of Peace" (Is. 9:6–7). Redeemed Israel will enjoy this peace preeminently, but it will also extend throughout the whole earth. Zechariah predicted, "He will proclaim peace to the nations. His rule will extend from sea to sea and from the River to the ends of the earth" (Zech. 9:10). In that day God will dwell with His people and confirm to them His "covenant of peace" (Ezek. 34:22–25).

In the New Testament the Greek word *eirēnē*, "peace," occurs ninety times. In classical Greek this word described an era of rest from war when people lived orderly, tranquil lives. Later *eirēnē* expanded in meaning to include the concept of inner, personal peace. The New Testament added all the meanings of *šālôm* to *eirēnē*. Spiritual peace is personal wholeness, inner health, and tranquility based on a person's relationship with God (Rom. 5:1).

Angels announced the birth of Christ by saying, "Glory to God in the highest, and on earth peace to men on whom his favor rests" (Luke 2:14). The death of Christ removed the barrier between God and humankind. Paul declared that God reconciled all things to Himself, "by making peace through his blood, shed on the cross" (Col. 1:20; see also Eph. 2:14–18). After His resurrection Christ's greetings and benedictions to His disciples contained words of peace (John 20:19, 21, 26). The gospel itself is "the good news of peace through Jesus Christ" (Acts 10:36; see also Eph. 6:15). Christ left a legacy of peace to His followers (John 14:27; 16:33) and assured them it was their inalienable privilege and possession (Phil. 4:6–7). Paul's common greeting, "grace and peace," in each of his thirteen epistles (for example, Rom. 1:7; 1 Cor. 1:3) is not an empty wish. These words remind us that Christ grants grace and peace to every believer.

If we are at peace with God, we are responsible to pursue peace in all our relationships with others. Peacemaking is an important aspect of growth in sanctification (Heb. 12:14; Col. 3:15; 1 Pet. 3:11). The indwelling Holy Spirit makes this possible for us (Rom. 8:6; 15:13), because "the fruit of the Spirit is . . . peace" (Gal. 5:22).

The Bible urges us to pray for rulers and to work for peace in our communities so that we may enjoy peaceful and quiet lives and be unhindered in proclaiming the gospel of peace (1 Tim. 2:1–2). **—DKC**

***

Be thankful today that because of Christ we can be at peace with God.

PERFECTION

Every believer should set perfection as a personal goal (Matt. 5:48). However, no one can attain perfection if it means unvarying victory over temptation or the eradication of the capacity to sin. Perfection in the sense of sinlessness is true only of God. Teachings that promotes the possibility of becoming sinless in this life must either redefine the nature of sin or reject the clear teaching of Scripture in 1 John 1:8, 10.

No one has ever truthfully claimed to be sinless, except Jesus Christ (John 8:46; 1 Pet. 2:21–22). The Scriptures state that Jesus was *made* perfect through suffering (Heb. 2:10, 5:8). That doesn't mean He was imperfect before He suffered. He was, after all, the eternal Son of God. But suffering gave Jesus experiences He could not have prior to the Incarnation. Suffering fully prepared Jesus for His role as our High Priest. His earthly suffering enables Him to sympathize with our weaknesses, even though He never sinned (4:15). As believers we ultimately will be perfect like Christ (1 John 3:2; Heb. 11:40), but that will not take place until He comes back for us. This hope should have a purifying effect on us, but until He returns we must face the reality of sin in our lives.

The Hebrew word for "perfect" is *tām* or *tāmîm*. It can refer to a complete day (Josh. 10:13), something whole or healthy (Ezek. 15:5), or something ethically sound or upright (Ps. 19:13). Job was "perfect" in the sense that he was morally upright (Job 1:1, 8; 2:3). The Hebrew word is also used of unblemished animal sacrifices (Lev. 22:21–22).

The corresponding Greek word, *teleios*, "whole or complete," is used of believers who are mature (1 Cor. 14:20; Phil 3:15; Heb. 5:14; 6:1; James 1:4). Paul also used the word in connection with the perfect (that is, complete) will of God (Rom. 12:1–2).

When Jesus exhorted His disciples to be perfect (*teleios*) as God the Father is perfect (Matt. 5:48), He meant that they should measure themselves in every area of life against the standard of God's character. Every commendable quality and characteristic finds its highest expression in God. He is not deficient in anything; He is the epitome of completeness. We are exhorted to be perfect in the sense of striving, in the power of the Holy Spirit, to be like Him. We will never reach this ultimate goal in this life, but we are to pursue it.

In Matthew 19:16–24 Jesus told a rich young ruler, "If you want to be perfect, go, sell your possessions and give to the poor, and you will have treasure in heaven. Then come and follow me." What deficiency did this man have? Matthew said that because of his great wealth the man was not willing to follow Christ (19:22)., Money was more important to him than God. In a sense, money was his god, so he lacked genuine faith in the Lord. He preferred to cling to his riches rather than humble himself before the Lord and by faith receive eternal life. Nowhere does the Bible teach that eternal life can be attained by keeping the Ten Commandments.

Paul crystallized his teaching on spiritual maturity in Philippians 3:12–16. He affirmed in this text that his personal goal in life was to know Christ and be like Him. Even though Paul's credentials were impeccable, he admitted that he had not attained the goal. He had not "been made perfect." The ultimate goal was still before him. Yet from another standpoint Paul claimed he and others were perfect (*teleios*), that is, mature (3:15). There is no contradiction here. Perfection or absolute maturity was not something he could attain, but growth and development did mark his life as one who was devoted to the Savior. This passage points out the balance between absolute and relative perfection as it relates to maturity. Paul was committed to preaching and teaching because he wanted to see every believer perfect (mature) in Christ (Col. 1:28). Paul applied the same standard of perfection (maturity) to churches that he did to individual believers (Eph. 4:12–13).

The writer of Hebrews adds another ingredient to the concept of spiritual maturity. He equates maturity with growth in ability to process and apply doctrine, the solid food of the Word of God (Heb. 5:12–14). We can't repeat the conversion experience, so we should focus on growth (6:1–6). Advancing in scriptural knowledge and wisdom is a key component of spiritual maturity (2 Tim. 3:16–17).

When God lets us face various trials and testings in life, He intends to foster our maturity (*teleios*, James 1:4). James wrote that mature believers do more than listen to the perfect law (the Word of God). They habitually do what it says (1:25). James also declared that if we can control our tongues we are perfect, that is, mature (3:2).

To the apostle John, love was the critical ingredient of perfection. He wrote that God's love is perfected in anyone who obeys the Word of God (1 John 2:5). Our love for one another is evidence that God dwells within us and that His love is made perfect (complete) in us (4:12). In fact, perfect love casts out fear (4:18).

We should look forward to the time when Christ will come again and we shall be changed so we can stand complete in Him. Yet in another sense there is the positional truth that because Christ died, we are already complete (perfect) in Him (Heb. 10:12–14). His death has paid the penalty for all our sins.   **—WGJ**

***

Ask the Spirit of God to teach you how to grow in your Christian life so you can reach a consistent level of maturity in your walk with the Lord.

POSITION

"Position" is a theological term rather than a biblical one. It refers to our standing in the Lord Jesus Christ as believers. "Position" relates to the biblical truth of the security of the believer. When someone receives the Lord Jesus as Savior by faith and is born again, that person moves from a position outside of Christ to a new position "in Christ" (Eph. 1:3, 9, 13) and is identified with Him. The daily *condition* of someone's Christian life may fluctuate, but his *position* remains constant. Paul wrote that nothing "in all creation, will be able to separate us from the love of God that is in Christ Jesus our Lord" (Rom. 8:39).

To understand and appreciate our position in Christ, it is necessary to understand a lost person's position apart from Christ. The unbeliever is "dead in . . . transgressions and sins" (Eph. 2:1, 5; see Col. 2:13). He is dead spiritually, not physically. All unsaved people, because they are human be-ings, are identified with Adam, the first man (Gen. 2:7) and progenitor of the human race. When Adam disobeyed God's command (2:16–17; 3:6–7), he immediately died spiritually (3:8–12) and became subject to physical death (3:17–19; 5:5). God looks at the human race as having been in Adam (1 Cor. 15:45–49) and having participated in his sin (Rom. 5:12). Therefore all humans are subject to Adam's condemnation (5:15–19; 1 Cor. 15:21–22).

Unbelievers also live in a world of spiritual darkness (Acts 26:18; Eph. 5:8; 6:12; Col. 1:13). They are spiritually blind (2 Cor. 4:4; 3:14–16). They are unknowingly energized by "the prince of the power of the air" (Eph. 2:2, NKJV), also called "the prince of this world" (John 12:31; 14:30; 16:11), "the god of this age" (2 Cor. 4:4), "the evil one" (John 17:15; 1 John 2:13, 14; 5:18–19), "the devil" (Matt. 4:8–9; Luke 4:5–7; John 8:44; Acts 13:10; 1 Tim. 3:6; James 3:15; 1 John 3:8, 10), and "that ancient serpent . . . Satan" (Rev. 12:9; 20:2). Because they are empowered by Satan, all unbelievers are "alienated from God" (Col. 1:21; see also Eph. 2:12) and are "God's enemies" (Rom. 5:10) subject to His wrath (2:5; Eph. 2:3; 5:6; Col. 3:6).

When we received Jesus Christ as our Savior by faith, we were regenerated, that is, made alive spiritually. We became identified with Christ; we

P

are "in Christ" (Rom. 16:7, 10; 2 Cor. 5:17; 12:2; Gal. 1:22). Christ in turn took up residence in us (John 14:20; 17:23; Gal. 2:20; Eph. 3:17 Col. 1:27) by means of the indwelling Holy Spirit (John 14:17; Rom. 8:9, 11; 1 Cor. 3:16; 6:19; 2 Tim. 1:14). The Holy Spirit baptized us into Christ's spiritual body, the church (1 Cor. 12:12–14, 20; Eph. 1:22–23; 4:4, 11–16; 5:22–30, 32). In this way we were joined to Him.

By faith we were born into the family of God as children of God (John 1:12–13; Rom. 8:14–17; see also Gal. 3:26; 4:5–7). This is another aspect of our position as Christians. As Paul wrote, "Now if [literally, 'since'] we are children, then we are heirs—heirs of God and co-heirs with Christ" (Rom. 8:17; see also Gal. 3:29; 4:7; 1 Pet. 3:7). God the Father has appointed the Lord Jesus, "his Son . . . heir of all things" (Heb. 1:2), and we share in that future inheritance (1 Pet. 1:3–5), "the hope of eternal life" (Titus 3:7). The entire creation "waits in eager expectation for the sons of God to be revealed" (Rom. 8:19). Then the creation will "be liberated from its bondage to decay and brought into the glorious freedom of the children of God" (8:21). Our inheritance includes our "adoption as sons, the redemption of our bodies" (8:23). We have a sure hope of spending eternity "blameless and holy in the presence of our God and Father" (1 Thess. 3:13), "con-formed to the likeness of his Son" (Rom. 8:29).

The Bible describes our position in several other ways as well. Before receiving Jesus Christ as Savior, we were "excluded from citizenship in Israel and foreigners to the covenants of promise, without hope and without God in the world" (Eph. 2:12). However, as a result of trusting Christ, we "are no longer foreigners and aliens, but fellow citizens with God's people and members of God's household" (2:19). As a result "our citizenship is in heaven. And we eagerly await a Savior from there, the Lord Jesus Christ" (Phil. 3:20).

We who believe in Christ are also described as "living stones" that are being "built into a spiritual house" (1 Pet. 2:5). Each of us is "a temple of the Holy Spirit" (1 Cor. 6:19), who indwells him (Rom. 8:9, 11; 2 Tim. 1:14), and collectively we are "a holy temple in the Lord" (Eph. 2:21) built on "the foundation of the apostles and prophets, with Christ Jesus himself as the chief cornerstone" (2:20; see also 1 Cor. 3:10–17; 2 Cor. 6:16).

The Holy Spirit baptizes each of us into Jesus Christ as a member of His body and gives us spiritual gifts to function appropriately (1 Cor. 12:4–11). The various parts of the physical body with their individual functions illustrate this (12:14–26). Paul concluded: "Now you are the body of Christ, and each one of you is a part of it" (12:27). Christ directs His church as the head directs the body (Eph. 1:22–23; 4:15; 5:23, 29–30; Col. 1:18; 2:19).

Although each of us sins, confession brings forgiveness and purification (1 John 1:8–10). When we sin, we have "one who speaks to the Father in our defense—Jesus Christ, the Righteous One" (2:1–2). That provision is not a license to sin (Rom. 6:1–14) but a guarantee of the security of the believer's position in Christ.   **—JAW**

***

Constantly bear in mind that, although your fellowship with Christ is affected by sin, your position in Christ remains secure.

POVERTY

The Bible identifies two kinds of poverty: economic poverty (Prov. 10:15) and spiritual poverty (Matt. 5:3; "poor in spirit" means to be humble). God has special concern for those suffering economic poverty (Deut. 15:7–11; 24:14–15; 1 Sam. 2:8; Ps. 12:5), especially orphans and widows (Ex. 22:22; Deut. 10:17–19; Ps. 146:9; Is. 1:17; Jer. 22:3; Zech. 7:10; James 1:27). God's Law contained statutes protecting the poor among His people Israel. For instance, the poor could glean the residue of crops from the harvest fields each year (Lev. 19:9–10; 23:22; Deut. 24:19–21; Ruth 2:2–9, 17).

Ultimately "the LORD sends poverty and wealth; he humbles and he exalts" (1 Sam. 2:7). He permitted Satan to take away Job's enormous wealth and leave him destitute (Job 1:12–21). He threatened Israel with poverty as a consequence for persistent failure to serve Him (Deut. 28:47–48). On the other hand, the Book of Proverbs looks at the immediate causes of poverty. It describes poverty as the natural long-term consequence of laziness (Prov. 6:9–11; 24:30–34), of engaging in mere talk (14:23), of entertaining fantasies (28:19), of acting with haste (21:5), of ignoring discipline (13:18), and of being stingy (11:24; 28:22).

The Bible commends those in poverty who maintain a generous spirit. Matthew, Mark, and Luke report how Jesus praised the sacrificial giving of the "poor widow" who dropped into the temple treasury "two very small copper coins, worth only a fraction of a penny" (Mark 12:42; see Luke 21:2). Paul applauded the Macedonian churches because "out of the most severe trial, their overflowing joy and their extreme poverty welled up in rich generosity. For I testify that they gave as much as they were able, and even beyond their ability. . . . They urgently pleaded with us for the privilege of sharing in this service to the saints" (2 Cor. 8:2–4). Their secret—and that of all Christian generosity—was

P

that "they gave themselves first to the Lord and then to us in keeping with God's will" (8:5).

Jesus Christ voluntarily embraced poverty to provide salvation for the human race. He "did not consider equality with God something to be grasped, but made himself nothing, taking the very nature of a servant [literally, 'slave'], being made in human likeness. And being found in appearance as a man, he humbled himself and became obedient to death—even death on a cross" (Phil. 2:6–8; see also 2 Cor. 8:9). He was born to Mary, who was engaged to Joseph, a poor carpenter (Matt. 1:18–25; Luke 1:26–38). As an adult He lived as a poor, itinerant preacher, who lacked the funds to pay the temple tax (Matt. 17:24–27). Jesus had to borrow a denarius, the poll tax coin, to point out Caesar's picture on it (Matt. 22:18–21; Mark 12:15–17; Luke 20:24–25). And He was buried in a borrowed tomb (Matt. 27:57–60).

The spiritual condition of lost humanity can only be described as extreme poverty. People must recognize that their "righteous acts are like filthy rags" (Is. 64:6). David recognized this about himself and wrote, "I am poor and needy; may the Lord think of me" (Ps. 40:17; see also 70:5; 86:1; 109:22). Once we come by faith to Jesus Christ, we become spiritually wealthy (2 Cor. 8:9).   **—JAW**

***

Give to help meet the needs of the poor, remembering that it stores up riches in heaven.

PRAISE

Praise can be defined as strong verbal commendation of another person or as verbal adoration of God. Synonyms include "laud," "acclamation," "affirmation," and "eulogy."

Scripture does report instances of praise directed toward men and women (Prov. 31:28–31; 1 Pet. 2:14, NKJV), but the predominant biblical emphasis is on praising God. The Old Testament abounds with references to praise of God. The angels continually praise God in heaven (Pss. 103:20; 148:2; Rev. 7:11–12). Psalm 148 says the angels, the elements of nature, and both animate and inanimate creation praise God together. Heaven and earth praise God (Pss. 89:5; 96:11; 98:4). The song of Moses (Ex. 15), which praised God for His redemptive acts in the Exodus, is an early example of Israelite homage. God's chosen people covenanted to praise Him. Their praise was meant to lead Gentile nations to know and praise the Lord (67:2–3).

The Book of Psalms contains the highest expression of Israelite worship. In the Hebrew Bible the psalms carry the title "Book of Praises." Almost all the psalms contain some note of praise. According to this treasured book, God's people should praise Him for His goodness and mercy to Israel and all peoples, for His vindication of the righteous in times of persecution, for His rulership over all mankind, and for His might as the Creator and Sovereign of the universe. Various psalms also praise things intimately connected to God: the Scriptures, Zion as God's earthly dwelling place, and the Davidic dynasty destined to occupy the throne of Israel.

The Old Testament designated Sabbaths, new moons, and various festivals as special times of praise. Psalms 113—118, called collectively the *Hallēl* ("Praise"), were sung at Israel's great festivals —Passover, Pentecost, and Tabernacles—and on other holy days. At the Passover Feast, Psalms 113 and 114 were sung before the meal and Psalms 115—118 afterward. In addition, the psalms make clear that people of God should continually praise Him: "Seven times a day I praise you for your righteous laws" (119:164); "From the rising of the sun to the place where it sets, the name of the LORD is to be praised" (113:3); "I will praise the LORD all my life; I will sing praise to my God as long as I live" (146:2).

The advent of the Savior, Jesus Christ, brought a fresh outburst of praise from angels and from the shepherds (Luke 2:10–13, 20). In a remarkable doxology that opens the Epistle to the Ephesians, the apostle Paul praised God the Father for choosing us for salvation (Eph. 1:6). He praised God the Son for redeeming us through His sacrificial death (1:12). He concluded by praising God the Holy Spirit for sealing us as God's own children (1:14). In Romans Paul used a series of Old Testament quotations to call believing Gentiles to praise God for welcoming them into His family (Rom. 15:7–12).

Peter declared, "But you are a chosen people, a royal priesthood, a holy nation, a people belonging to God, that you may declare the praises of him who called you out of darkness into his wonderful light" (1 Pet. 2:9). Likewise, the author of Hebrews exhorted us, "Let us continually offer to God a sacrifice of praise—the fruit of lips that confess his name" (Heb. 13:15).

In the Book of Revelation the apostle John recorded a triumphant song of praise, a mighty hymn of thanksgiving in heaven that "sounded like the roar of a great multitude" (Rev. 19:1). Four times the great chorus sang "Hallelujah!" "Hallelujah" only occurs here in the New Testament. It transliterates the Hebrew expression "Praise Yah." "Yah" is a shortened version of the divine name *Yahweh*. The heavenly throng praise God for judging the unrighteous at the end of the Great Tribulation (19:2–3). Then they praise God that Christ is coming to reign on earth (19:6). Revelation 19:1–8 contains the true "Hallelujah Chorus." It sets the stage for eternity when God's redeemed people will fulfill the admonition of the psalmist, "Let everything that has breath praise the LORD" (Ps. 150:6).

> Praise God, from whom all
>   blessings flow;
> Praise Him all creatures here
>   below;
> Praise Him above, ye heavenly
>   host;
> Praise Father, Son, and Holy
>   Ghost.   **—DKC**

***

*Strive to praise God consistently
for His blessings.*

PRAYER

Nineteenth-century hymn writer James Montgomery penned "Prayer Is the Soul's Sincere Desire." His hymn echoes the disciples' request, "Lord, teach us to pray" (Luke 11:1). "Prayer," Montgomery's hymn says, "is the soul's sincere desire, uttered or unexpressed, the motion of a hidden fire that trembles in the breast." In its simplest form prayer is talking to God. Often it takes the form of a request. Other times it is an expression of praise and gratitude. We can pray for ourselves or for others. We can talk to God in private or with others. The Old Testament, particularly the Book of Psalms, is filled with examples of prayers. The New Testament also records many prayers and gives instruction on how and why to pray.

A survey of the variety of words used in the Old Testament concerning prayer gives us an idea of prayer's scope. Intercession (Num. 21:7), entreaty (Ex. 32:11), confession (Ezra 10:1), supplication (1 Kin. 8:30), call for help (Gen. 32:9–11), request (30:22), thanksgiving (Deut. 26:10–11), praise (Ps. 103), protection and deliverance (2 Chr. 32:20), judgment (1 Kin. 17:1–2), healing (Is. 38:1–5), cleansing (2 Chr. 30:18–20)—all these are included in Old Testament prayers.

People who prayed in the Old Testament believed in God and considered Him approachable. They sensed that He cared for them and would respond to their petitions. Prayers were not limited to places of public worship or to special occasions. Many Old Testament saints called on the name of the Lord as naturally as they talked to people around them. Some prayers were spontaneous, and others give evidence of careful thought and expression.

We can glean principles about praying from the many prayers recorded in the Old Testament. Abraham interceded for the people of Sodom and Gomorrah on the basis of the righteousness of God (Gen. 18:22–33). Abraham's servant sought God's guidance in selecting a bride for Isaac (24:12–14, 26–27). He demonstrated our need to pray according to the will of God. Jacob's encounter with God at Peniel illustrates the struggle that often occurs in prayer (32:24–32). When Moses sensed the anger of the Lord against the Israelites, he based his plea on their behalf on the Lord's many promises to His people (Ex. 32:9–14). Through Moses' prayers on behalf of the Israelites we learn that nothing is impossible with God (Num. 11:1–2, 10–23).

God's rebuff of Joshua's prayer after the defeat by Ai shows how sin can interfere with the answer to our prayers (Josh. 7:8–12). David's prayer in 2 Samuel 7:18–29 teaches that God works on behalf of His great name. Solomon's prayer after his kingdom was established highlights the importance of humility in talking to God (2 Chr. 1:7–12). Evil King Manasseh prayed in repentance and God responded to his humility (33:12–13). Disobedience to the Word of God can also affect the outcome of our prayers (Ezra 9:1–15). God told Jeremiah not to pray for Israel, because He would not answer while they were disobedient (Jer. 7:16, 23–26). Jonah's prayer from inside the fish illustrates how God responds to those whose hearts have become open before Him (Jon. 2:1–9).

The New Testament also employs a rich vocabulary with regard to prayer. One of the most common terms used, primarily in the Gospels and Acts, is *aiteō*, "to ask something of someone." Interestingly Christ never used this word when He prayed to the Father. The word Jesus used most of the time was *erōtaō*, "to request or ask a question" (for example, Matt. 16:13; John 14:16; 17:20). Another basic word is *deomai*, "to request, beseech, or beg," based on a need. The most common term for prayer is *proseuchomai*, used of voicing a request to a deity.

When the apostles wrote about prayer in the New Testament Epistles, they were elaborating on the teaching of Jesus. The Lord said much about prayer. The Gospels refer often to Jesus in prayer. Strangely they report little about the disciples at prayer. Even when they accompanied Jesus as He prayed, they seem to have observed rather than participated (Matt. 26:36–45; Luke 22:39–46). Perhaps Christ's presence made prayer on their part seem unnecessary or redundant. At any rate, after Jesus' ascension the disciples prayed frequently and intensely (Acts 1:14).

The example of Jesus at prayer must have taught the disciples much about the importance of prayer. It still teaches us today. Luke's Gospel gives the most comprehensive picture

P

of Christ's commitment to prayer. Luke stated that Jesus prayed while He was baptized (Luke 3:21). Prayer was an essential part of His daily life (5:16). He prayed all night before choosing His disciples (6:12). Before He multiplied the loaves and fish to feed the five thousand, He looked up to the Father in prayer (9:16). He was praying when the Transfiguration occurred (9:29). Praise to the Father broke from His lips when He heard the report of the seventy-two after their appointed mission (10:21). At the disciples' request, He provided a model for prayer (11:1–4). He spoke parables that exhorted them to pray (18:1). He prayed regularly for His disciples that they might resist the devil (22:31–32). The night before He was crucified He spent a lengthy time in prayer to the Father (22:39–44). Those who stood by the cross and watched Him die heard his last words. They were directed to God (23:46). After the Resurrection He prayed before eating with two of His friends (24:30).

We learn the Lord's teaching on prayer from two main Gospel passages: the Sermon on the Mount (Matt. 5—7) and the Upper Room Discourse (John 13—17). When we study these texts, certain concepts about prayer emerge. Our attitude in prayer is crucial (Matt. 6:5–6, 14–15). Quality is more important than length (6:7). God's will should always be paramount (6:10).

Nothing is too mundane to pray about (6:11). We must be sensitive to sin and confess it (6:12). We must be aware of our adversary the devil (6:13). God answers prayer (7:7–8). God gives us the best in answer to prayer (7:9–12). We should pray in the name of Christ, that is, in accord with His character (John 14:13–14). Prayer must be for the glory of the Father (14:13). Our prayers should spring from an intimate relationship with the Lord (15:1–7). The content and aims of our prayers should be consistent with His Word (15:7).

Other Gospel passages teach about prayer. Some teachings are new. Some repeat lessons of the two primary texts. We should pray in faith (Matt. 21:22; Mark 11:24). Our prayers should be genuine (9:29). God welcomes and responds to persistent praying (Luke 11:5–10). God will not hold back what is best for His own (11:9–13). We should not give up voicing our requests to God (18:1–5). We should pray in accord with the will of God (22:42).

The Book of Acts reveals the role of prayer in the early church. From the very beginning of the church at Pentecost, believers prayed as part of their daily routine (Acts 2:42; 4:24, 31; 6:4). Prayer played a critical role in spreading the gospel to Samaria (8:15). Peter's carried on his ministry through prayer (9:40; 10:9, 31). The corporate prayer of the church helped Peter escape from prison (12:5, 12). The church at Antioch sent out Barnabas and Saul as missionaries after a time of prayer and fasting (13:3). Barnabas and Saul selected leaders for the churches of their first missionary journey after praying and fasting (14:23). Some churches, like the one at Philippi, grew out of prayer groups (16:13). Prayer sustained Paul and Silas during their imprisonment (16:25). The closing chapters of Acts show how prayer marked the life and ministry of Paul as he struggled to preach the gospel in the midst of great opposition.

Paul's letters to the churches show how these congregations were to conduct prayer. The spread of the gospel depended on the prayers of God's people (Rom. 15:30–31; Eph. 6:19–20; Col. 4:4; 2 Thess. 3:1). Group prayer allowed many to be involved in ministry (2 Cor. 1:11). Paul cared about the decorum of men and women in their practice of prayer (1 Cor. 11:3–16; 1 Tim. 2:8). His prayers for the Ephesian, Philippian, and Colossian believers, filled with strong theological content, give insight into Paul's pattern of praying (Eph. 1:15–23; 3:14–21; Phil. 1:9–11; Col. 1:10–12). We must pray in order to stand against Satan (Eph. 6:18). We should pray continually (1 Thess. 5:17). Paul exhorted Christians to pray for those in places of authority (1 Tim. 2:1–2). His letters show Paul's prayer burden for the nation Israel (Rom.

10:1). He said that not all his prayers received affirmative answers, and that God had reasons for saying "No" (2 Cor. 12:7–10).

Other New Testament writers taught about prayer. James and Peter discussed hindrances to prayer and the significance of a godly life (James 4:1–3, 5:13–18; 1 Pet. 3:7, 4:7). John emphasized praying according to God's will (1 John 5:13–15) and in obedience to His commands (3:22). Jude reminded believers to pray in the Holy Spirit (Jude 20). The writer of Hebrews described the ministry of the risen Christ as our Great High Priest, who intercedes for us (Heb. 4:14, 7:24–25). Probably no teaching in Scripture is more pertinent to the Christian life and the progress of Christianity than that on prayer.   **—WGJ**

***

Take every opportunity to talk with the Lord, and keep an updated list of requests that you can pray about daily.

PREDESTINATION

Predestination means that events and situations in the plan of God are made certain in advance. It is part of God's work in eternity past when He adopted a complete plan for the universe that included all that would come to pass.

The verb *predestine* appears in four

verses in the New International Version, translating the Greek *proorizō* (Rom. 8:29–30; Eph. 1:5, 11). *Proorizō* also occurs in Acts 4:28, which reads "to determine beforehand," and in 1 Corinthians 2:7, where the word "destined" is used. Romans 8:29–30 spells out what predestination involves. These verses link predestination with God's plan to transform believers into the image of Christ. "For those God foreknew he also predestined to be conformed to the likeness of his Son, that he might be the firstborn among many brothers" (8:29). Paul then detailed the process for getting from predestination to conformity to Christ: "And those he predestined, he also called; those he called, he also justified; those he justified, he also glorified" (8:30). Paul then pointed out that no one can bring any charge against those who have been justified in God's sight (8:30–34) because God is the one who orchestrated their salvation. Paul concluded that nothing can separate a believer from the love of Christ (8:35–39).

Like the doctrine of election, the doctrine of predestination differs from fatalism, even though all events have been rendered certain by the intelligent act of God. In eternity past God chose (elected) some individuals and predestined them to receive salvation and to be conformed to His Son. He also determined the method by which they would be brought to the knowledge of the gospel, come to believe in Christ, and be saved. God's election, however, does not force anyone to believe. It does insure that they will certainly believe. Certainty differs from coercion. The relationship between God's will and individual human wills is ultimately beyond human understanding, but election and predestination are expressly biblical doctrines. We can rejoice in the fact that God included us in His plan from eternity past. **—JFW**

***

If you are a believer, enjoy the certainty of salvation in Christ.

PRIESTHOOD

A priest is a spiritual leader who represents people to God. The Scriptures regard the priesthood as an institution of critical importance. In Old Testament times the work of the priesthood allowed God's people to approach Him and fellowship with Him. The New Testament uses the ministry of the priesthood as a picture of the redemptive work of Jesus Christ.

In patriarchal times heads of families served as priests for their clans. After the Flood, Noah built an altar and sacrificed burnt offerings (Gen. 8:20–21). Abraham built altars at Bethel, Mamre, and Moriah (12:7; 13:4; 22:1–13). Job offered sacrifices on behalf of his children (Job 1:5). The Bible refers also to non-Israelite priests, such as Melchizedek (Gen. 14:18), the priests of the Egyptians (41:50; 46:20; 47:22), and the priests of the Midianites (Ex. 2:16; 3:1; 18:1). Moses apparently appointed priests for Israel prior to the Levitical priesthood (19:22, 24; 24:5). Even after the institution of the Hebrew priesthood, some who were not priests occasionally performed priestly duties, such as Gideon (Judg. 6:24–26), the men of Bethshemesh (1 Sam. 6:14–15), Samuel (7:9), David (2 Sam. 6:13–17), Solomon (1 Kin. 8:22–24), and Elijah (1 Kin. 18:23). God accepted these priestly acts, but they must be viewed as exceptional cases.

At God's instruction, Moses appointed Aaron and his sons as priests (Ex. 28:1) to serve as mediators between God and Israel and to care for the operation of the tabernacle. Moses consecrated Aaron and his sons in a seven-day ceremony that was elaborate, solemn, and meaningful (Ex. 29; Lev. 8). All the priests wore special priestly garments, but Aaron's high priestly robe was especially elaborate (Ex. 28:2–39). The main task of the high priest was to officiate at the ceremonies of the Day of Atonement (Lev. 16). The ordinary priests officiated at all the sacrifices and offerings (Lev. 1—6) and administered the elaborate rituals for cleansing worshipers who had become ceremonially unclean (Lev. 13—

14). The Levites functioned as servants to the priests. They maintained the tabernacle and moved it from place to place in the wilderness (1:47–53; 3:1–38; Deut. 11:8–9). The Chronicles record that the Levites also served as musicians and treasurers as Israel's worship became more sophisticated (1 Chr. 6:31–32; 9:19; 16:4–5, 7; 25:1–7; 26:1, 20; 2 Chr. 8:14).

The priests and Levites did not receive a tribal portion of the Promised Land as an inheritance to farm for income. The people of Israel supported them with their tithes, firstfruits, and various sacrifices (Num. 18). The Levites, however, did receive forty-eight cities and surrounding pasturelands to live in. Aaron's descendants, the priests, received thirteen of those cities (Num. 35; Josh. 21). In this way God dispersed the priests and Levites among His people.

The Old Testament records numerous failures by Israel to keep the priesthood functioning as God intended it. In the period of the judges, an Ephraimite named Micah set up an idolatrous shrine and paid a displaced Levite to be his priest (Judg. 17). A prophet predicted that the family of Eli the high priest would lose the priestly office because of the gross sins of his sons (1 Sam. 2:27–36). This prophecy was fulfilled in the days of Solomon when the priestly line passed to the family of Zadok, descendants of Aaron through his son Eleazar (1 Kin. 2:27; 1 Chr. 6:4–8; 24:3). At the time of the division of the united kingdom, Jeroboam I appointed priests from tribes other than Levi (1 Kin. 12:31) and served as a priest himself (12:32–33). Ahaz offered sacrifices on an altar modeled after a pagan one he had seen in Damascus (2 Kin. 16:10–16). God struck Uzziah with leprosy because he usurped the priest's office (2 Chr. 26:16–20).

The Law prescribed that the high priest should serve for life, but by New Testament times the Roman provincial government prevented that. The Romans did not want power concentrated in one person so they changed high priests frequently. Annas, for example, was appointed high priest by Quirinius, governor of Syria in A.D. 6 but was deposed in A.D. 15. He was succeeded by five of his sons and his son-in-law Caiaphas (Luke 3:2; John 18:12–13).

Jesus interacted regularly with the Levitical priesthood. When He healed lepers, He sent them to the priests at the temple in keeping with the Mosaic regulation (Mark 1:44; Luke 5:14; 17:14). If these priests acknowledged Jesus' miracles, they would find themselves giving testimony to Jesus' mighty works. The priesthood connived with Roman secular authorities to execute Jesus (Matt. 26:3, 14, 57–65; 27:1). Priests were also major antagonists of the leaders of the early church (Acts 4:1–6; 9:1–2). Yet Luke recorded that during these days "a large number of priests became obedient to the faith" (6:7).

When the Romans destroyed the temple and Jewish state in A.D. 70, the Old Testament Jewish priesthood disappeared from history. For a time the Jews made sporadic attempts to reinstitute the priestly order and the sacrificial system, but all such efforts failed. Eventually they abandoned the institution entirely.

The letter to the Hebrews declares that Jesus Christ fulfilled the spiritual significance of the Old Testament priesthood. Aaron and Melchizedek connect the Old and New Testaments in that both foreshadowed Christ's priesthood. Christ's priestly *duties* are patterned after Aaron's priesthood in that He offered Himself as a sacrifice for sin (Heb. 7:27), He entered heaven, the Most Holy Place, by virtue of His blood (9:7, 12, 24), thereby securing our eternal redemption (9:12) and giving us free access to the throne of grace (4:16).

As to the priestly *order*, Jesus' priesthood is patterned after that of Melchizedek. The New Scofield Reference Bible notes several ways in which the Aaronic high priesthood proved inferior to the Melchizedekian. Aaron paid tithes to Melchizedek in Abraham (7:4–10). The Aaronic priesthood could make nothing perfect (7:11–22). The Aaronic priests died whereas Christ lives eternally (7:23–28). The Aaronic priests served as shadows of Christ, who is the reality (8:1–5). Christ mediates a superior covenant (8:6—10:18). We can conclude that Jesus Christ, as both High Priest and atoning Sacrifice, fulfilled everything the Old Testament priesthood pictured.

The term *priest* is never used in the New Testament of a minister in the church. However, believers are described as a "holy priesthood who offer spiritual sacrifices acceptable to God through Jesus Christ" (1 Pet. 2:5). We are "a kingdom and priests to serve his God and Father" (Rev. 1:6; see also 5:10). In Christ's millennial kingdom we "will be priests of God and of Christ and will reign with him for a thousand years" (20:6). From the time of Martin Luther, Protestants have viewed these verses as the basis for affirming the universal priesthood of all believers. They reject the idea of a priestly caste that mediates between God and individual believers.

The priesthood of Christians involves, above all else, sacrificial obedience to God. Paul wrote, "I urge you, brothers, in view of God's mercy, to offer your bodies as living sacrifices, holy and pleasing to God—which is your spiritual act of worship" (Rom. 12:1). The author of Hebrews exhorted, "Through Jesus, therefore, let us continually offer to God a sacrifice of praise—the fruit of lips that confess his name. And do not forget to do good and to share with others, for with such sacrifices God is pleased" (Heb. 13:15–16).   **—DKC**

***

List several spiritual sacrifices that believers as New Testament priests are exhorted to offer to God.

PROPHECY

The term "prophet" describes one who received supernatural messages from God along with a commission to pass those messages on to God's people. A true prophet served as a channel for God's truth. What God revealed through His prophets covered a wide gamut of truth, some of it moral and some of it predictive. In all cases the prophets' messages carried God's authority.

Not all prophets wrote Scripture, but many did. The others were speaking prophets. About one-fourth of Scripture was predictive when it was first revealed. Many books of the Old and New Testaments are largely prophetic, including Daniel, Ezekiel, Jeremiah, significant portions of the Gospels and the Epistles, and the Book of Revelation. Major topics of prophecy include Israel, the nations, and the church.

Prophecy often features symbols and figurative language, but the Bible itself usually explains the meaning of

P

the symbols and metaphors. In the end the prophecy makes an understandable factual statement. The popular idea that prophecy can mean anything the interpreter wants it to is not supported by Scripture. About half of the Bible's prophecies have already been fulfilled literally. God expects us to understand prophecy according to the normal usage of language. Literal statements convey literal meanings. Figurative statements also convey specific meanings.

Prophets delivered their messages from God both orally and in written form. Written prophecy often reports what the prophet earlier proclaimed orally. Prophets received revelations of truth in various ways. Sometimes God spoke directly to the prophet, and sometimes He spoke in dreams and visions. In every case God communicated truth about the present and the future through His prophets.

In the four hundred years before Christ no prophet ministered. Then just before Jesus began to teach and perform miracles, Anna, a prophetess (Luke 2:36), and John the Baptist (Matt. 21:26) appeared. Christ Himself was the greatest of all prophets (Deut. 18:15; Matt. 21:11; Acts 3:22; 7:37). Then in the first century God spoke through both men and women prophets. Once the Scriptures were completed, however, the gift of prophecy ceased (1 Cor. 13:8).

The Scriptures are God's completed revelation. Prophets no longer reveal further truth. Instead, the Holy Spirit illuminates the Scriptures to give us further insight into this finished revelation. As prophecies have been fulfilled, we should gain a renewed appreciation of everything else the Bible predicts.

The Bible told how to distinguish false prophets from true ones. The prophecies of true prophets always came to pass (Deut. 18:21–22). Often the messages of God's prophets were verified by accompanying miraculous signs.

In recent centuries higher critics have regularly attacked the inspiration of the Bible and undermined the confidence of many in the Scriptures as the inspired, inerrant Word of God. Obviously any low view of Scripture results in a low view of prophecy. Prophecy assumes the reality of supernatural revelation from God. To deny the possibility that God can predict what lies ahead inevitably denies that the Bible is supernaturally inspired and that the prophets who spoke had genuine messages from God.

To interpret prophecy properly, we need to keep certain things in mind. First, the Scriptures are inerrant and reliable. Second, we understand prophecy according to the normal meanings of literal and figurative expressions.

Third, interpret the details as well as the main thrust of a prophecy to get the full picture. Fourth, in some cases prophecies have multiple fulfillments. A prophecy may be partially fulfilled at one point in history and completely fulfilled at a later time.

The fundamental purpose of prophecy is to give us the necessary information to plan wisely for spiritually crucial future events. However, God didn't give us prophecy to fill our heads with knowledge. He gave us prophecy to challenge us to both holy living and hopeful living. (See, for example, 1 Cor. 15:58; 1 Thess. 3:13; 4:18; Titus 2:11–13; James 5:7–9; 2 Pet. 3:11, 13; 1 John 3:2.)   **—JFW**

***

Write down the specific promises God has for the future, knowing that these will certainly be fulfilled as written.

PROPITIATION

"To propitiate" means to satisfy the anger of God. Unrighteousness provokes God's wrath. His holy and righteous character cannot abide sin, so His wrath must be satisfied if we are to experience salvation and the forgiveness of sins. The Bible recognizes only one way to propitiate God's just wrath: the supreme sacrifice of the Lord Jesus Christ in the place of sinners on the Cross.

The light of God's impeccable holiness never shines brighter than when it is contrasted to the sinfulness of humankind. Similarly the doctrine of propitiation lays a jeweler's black velvet cloth under the diamond of God's grace. God's grace gleams against the backdrop of His wrath. God's gracious love moved Him to sacrifice His Son to avert His wrath and satisfy His holiness. Grace prompted the Father to accept the Son's sacrifice on the Cross as the total payment for the sins of the world (1 John 2:2).

A small family of Greek words expresses the concept of propitiation in the New Testament. A verb and two nouns each occur twice in widely separated writings by Luke, Paul, the writer of Hebrews, and John. The verb *hilaskomai* means "to propitiate" (Luke 18:13; Heb. 2:17). The nouns *hilasmos* (1 John 2:2; 4:10), and *hilastērion* (Rom. 3:25; Heb. 9:5) both mean "propitiation." The Greek Old Testament used *hilastērion* to translate the Hebrew for "mercy seat," the lid to the ark of the covenant. That's its usage in Hebrews 9:5.

The New International Version translates these words in slightly different ways because *propitiation* has become an uncommon word even in church circles. In Luke 18:13 the tax collector recognized his unrighteousness in the sight of God and asked the Lord "to have mercy on" him, and in Hebrews

2:17 the word is rendered to "make atonement." In Romans 3:25 the word is translated by the phrase "a sacrifice of atonement." The two occurrences of *hilasmos* in 1 John are both translated "atoning sacrifice." The New American Standard Bible and the New King James Bible still translate these passages (except Luke 18:13) with "propitiation" or "propitiate."

Some modern theologians object to the idea that people could ever be the objects of God's wrath. They downplay the history of the Greek terms in reference to angry gods and assert that the words refer to asking the gods to be gracious. These theologians favor a more neutral term, such as *expiation*, in place of *propitiation*. However, the *hilaskomai* word family assumes the anger of God. The Bible assumes that our sin angers God. "Propitiation" is the appropriate theological terminology.

In using these terms Paul emphasized the substitutionary death of Christ (Rom. 3:25). The writer of Hebrews described Jesus as the faithful High Priest atoning for sin (Heb. 2:17). The apostle John declared that Christ is the Righteous One, worthy to be the Sacrifice for the sins of the whole world (1 John 2:2). Romans 3:25 and 1 John 4:10 clearly show that God Himself is the Provider of the all-sufficient sacrifice, thus establishing the depth of God's love in the process of propitiation.   **—WGJ**

***

Rejoice in the fact that God is satisfied with Christ's death as the payment for your sins and that you will never be condemned for these sins.

PROVIDENCE

While the word *providence* does not occur in Scripture, it does represent a true biblical doctrine. The Westminster Confession of Faith states, "God, the great Creator of all things, doth uphold, direct, dispose, and govern all creatures, actions and things, from the greatest even to the least, by His most wise and holy providence" (5.1). *Providence* comes from a Latin word meaning "to watch over." It refers to divine oversight of all that occurs. Scripture declares that the world in which we live continues because "the Son is the radiance of God's glory and the exact representation of his being, sustaining all things by his powerful word" (Heb. 1:3). Further, "He [Christ] is before all things, and in him all things hold together" (Col. 1:17).

Providence contradicts deism, the philosophy that likens God to a watchmaker who wound up a watch and left it running. So God supposedly created the world with its natural laws and left it to run on its own. A biblical view of providence also eliminates such concepts as dualism, chance, and fatalism. Dualism theorizes that the universe operates under the influence of two equal powers, one good and the other evil. Chance is the belief that everything that happens is an accident devoid of meaning. Fatalism believes all events are predetermined and unalterable, but the plan serves no purpose. Psalm 33:12–15 and Acts 17:24–28 counter these false views and clearly describe how God personally sustains and governs both the world and humankind.

Israel experienced God's providential love and care in Old Testament times (Amos 3:1; Mal. 1:2). After the present period of Gentile visitation, God will reveal His unbroken love for Israel in her future restoration (Acts 15:14–16; Rom. 11:1–27). In the present dispensation God directs His providential love at the church, the body of Christ (Eph. 3:14–19).

Providence may be defined as "God's timely provision for the needs of humans." The Bible contains numerous examples of such divine actions. For instance, when God instructed Abraham to sacrifice his son Isaac, the boy asked his father where the offering was. Abraham affirmed, "God himself will provide the lamb for the burnt offering" (Gen. 22:8). When God provided a ram to replace Isaac, Abraham named the mountain where they were "The LORD Will Provide" (22:14). Joseph experienced God's providence in Egypt as the tragedies of his youth changed into the triumphs of his adulthood. When Joseph's brothers cowered before him in anticipation of retaliation, Joseph said, "Don't be afraid. Am I in the place of God? You intended to harm me, but God intended it for good to accomplish what is now being done, the saving of many lives" (50:19–20).

The Lord providentially guided Jonah's life by means of a great fish and a small worm. The entire Book of Esther portrays the amazing workings of God's providence that preserved the Jewish people in the heart of the hostile Persian Empire. The small Book of Philemon tells the interesting story of how God providentially directed the slave Onesimus from Colosse to the apostle Paul hundreds of miles away in Rome.

We are constantly the object of God's providential watchcare. The psalmist declared, "You hem me in—behind and before; you have laid your hand upon me" (Ps. 139:5), and, "For he will command his angels concerning you to guard you in all your ways" (91:11). In the New Testament both Jesus (Matt. 6:26) and Paul (Rom. 8:28–39) affirmed divine providence.

The eye of faith always recognizes

P

God's timely interventions in our lives. Let us thank God for taking such personal and loving interest that He showers us with wonderful providential care.   **—DKC**

***

In a journal or diary write daily examples of God's providence. Look back at the end of the year and you will be greatly encouraged!

Rr

RAPTURE

The Old Testament revealed the First and Second Comings of Christ, but it nowhere prophesied a rapture of the church. Israel misunderstood the Old Testament prophecies and expected the Messiah to establish His millennial reign on earth at His First Coming. They overlooked or ignored Old Testament predictions about His sufferings and death. This is why the disciples who followed Christ expected to have a part in His glorious kingdom. Toward the end of His public ministry Jesus told them He would suffer and die and then be raised the third day. They had difficulty believing this because it did not fit into their understanding of prophecy.

The Rapture refers to the whole generation of believers alive at the Second Coming of Christ being caught up into heaven without dying. Jesus hinted at this truth in the Upper Room when He talked about going to His Father's house, a reference to heaven. He promised, "And if I go and prepare a place for you, I will come back and take you

to be with me that you also may be with me where I am" (John 14:3).

Jesus did not go onto detail about His return at that time because the disciples were confused about His First and Second Comings. They would not have comprehended fuller teaching about an additional coming when He will take His own out of the earth. Later the apostle Paul explained the doctrine of the Rapture more fully (1 Thess. 4:13–18). When opposition to the gospel forced Paul to leave Thessalonica, He sent Timothy back to inquire about the believers' condition (3:2–5). Timothy found them standing true to the faith (3:6–8), but they were puzzled about what would happen to some of their loved ones who had died in the interval since Paul left. In answer to their questions Paul detailed what will happen at the Rapture.

Paul asserted that the Rapture is as certain as the death and resurrection of Christ (4:14). When Jesus returns, living believers will be caught up to be with the Lord. Their dead loved ones will be resurrected immediately before them. Both the believers who have died and those who are still living will at that moment receive bodies suited for heaven. "For the Lord Himself will come down from heaven with a loud command, with the voice of the archangel, and with the trumpet call of God, and the dead in Christ shall rise first. After that we who are still alive and are left will be caught up together with them in the clouds to meet the Lord in the air. And so we will be with the Lord forever" (4:16–17). The expression "will be caught up together" could be translated "will be raptured together." It means to be snatched from the earth and taken to heaven. When Christ comes in the clouds to take us to Himself, our rapture will occur "in a flash, in the twinkling of an eye" (1 Cor. 15:52). In this way the Rapture gives hope to Christians whose believing loved ones have died. It assures us that we will see our loved ones again.

The Bible frequently describes dead church-age believers as "asleep." In one sense that's because dead bodies look like people who are sleeping. In another sense the sleep image acknowledges that death for believers is temporary, like a good night's sleep (1 Cor. 15:6, 18, 20, 51; 1 Thess. 4:13–15; see also Mark 5:39; John 11:11, 13). But at the Rapture their bodies will come out of the graves, be changed in conformity to Jesus' glorified body, and

join with their souls. Living saints will also receive resurrection bodies the moment they are caught up. "When he appears, we shall be like him, for we shall see him as he is" (1 John 3:2). Paul described the transformation of the dead and the living at the Rapture when he said that the corruptible (dead bodies) will become incorruptible, and the mortal (living saints whose bodies are decaying) will become immortal (1 Cor. 15:42, 52–54). The apostle called this "the redemption of our bodies" (Rom. 8:23).

In 1 Thessalonians 5:1–11 Paul indicated the Rapture will occur just before the Tribulation. He wrote that after the Rapture, the Day of the Lord will begin—a time of judgment that will embrace the whole world. Some people teach that the Rapture will occur after the seven-year Tribulation. But passages that discuss the Rapture give no hint of anything that must occur (such as the Tribulation) before the Lord comes for His church. By contrast, passages about Christ's Second Coming to set up His kingdom on earth indicate the events of Revelation 6—18 must occur first. Many systematic arguments support pretribulationalism, the view that the Rapture will occur before the Tribulation, and several Bible passages give it support.

For instance, Matthew 25:31–46 depicts an event that will occur soon after the Second Coming. Christ will

R

assemble the Gentile believers who are living then. The text calls all people alive at the time sheep and goats. The sheep represent the saved and the goats represent the lost. If the Rapture occurred at the time of the Second Coming, there would be no sheep. They would have been taken out in the Rapture, leaving only the goats. No further separation would be necessary.

In Revelation 3:10 Jesus Christ promised that believers will be kept out of, not kept through, "the hour of trial that is going to come upon the whole world." They will be kept from the Tribulation by being raptured before it begins. Along the same lines, the Tribulation will be a time of God's wrath (6:16), and Jesus has rescued us "from the coming wrath" (1 Thess. 1:10; see also 5:9). The Rapture provides the rescue.

Posttribulationalists—those who say that the church will go through the Tribulation and that the Rapture will occur at the end of the Tribulation—support their view with Jesus' words in John 16:33, "In the world you will have tribulation" (NKJV). However, this statement refers to troubles or difficulties believers face in this life. Posttribulationalists also suggest that the Scriptures make no clear statement about the Rapture preceding the Tribulation. They maintain that the Bible doesn't divide Jesus' Second Coming into two events (the Rapture and His later return to the earth) separated by years of time. The fact is, however, that posttribulationists cannot point to any Scripture that says the Rapture will occur at Jesus' Second Coming. On the whole the biblical evidence suggests that the Rapture of the church will precede the Tribulation.

The Rapture gives us hope (it is called "the blessed hope," Titus 2:13). It encourages us to lead pure lives (1 Thess. 3:13; James 5:8–9; 1 John 3:3). And it comforts those whose believing loved ones have died (1 Thess. 4:18). The Rapture could happen at any time, so we should "eagerly wait for our Lord Jesus" to come (2 Cor. 1:7). "We eagerly await a Savior from [heaven], the Lord Jesus Christ" (Phil. 3:20; see also 1 Thess. 1:10).   **—JFW**

***

Conduct your life in a manner that reflects the hope of Christ's soon coming for His church.

RECONCILIATION

Reconciliation is the process of bringing two or more parties into agreement by removing the cause of their disharmony. In the Bible, reconciliation focuses on bringing harmony between God and sinful humanity. Sin alienates us from God. Christ's death on the cross provides the basis for reconciliation.

Paul develops the concept of reconciliation in some detail in Romans 5:6–11. In that passage the apostle said unsaved people are "powerless," "ungodly," "sinners," and "God's enemies." Sin creates a barrier between God and humanity that leaves us in a position of hostility toward our Creator. The death of Jesus Christ removes the enmity between people and God and achieves reconciliation. "When we were God's enemies, we were reconciled to him through the death of his Son" (5:10). "He has reconciled you by Christ's physical body through death to present you holy in his sight, without blemish and free from accusation" (Col. 1:22).

Paul declared in 2 Corinthians 5:19 that God reconciled "the world to himself." Through the death of Christ for lost humanity, the whole world moved into a different relationship to God. Christ's death rendered people savable. Now each person needs to respond by faith to the finished work of Christ on the Cross. Every time someone does, that person becomes reconciled to God. This sober realization moved the apostle Paul to write, "We implore you on Christ's behalf: Be reconciled to God" (5:20).

The Scriptures speak only of humans being reconciled to God. God is not reconciled to us. Our relationship changes because we change. Our sin offended God and created disharmony. Christ paid the penalty for our sins, and we responded to His sacrifice in faith. God graciously imputed the righteousness of Christ to us, and our relationship with God was reconciled.

The Bible also speaks of reconciliation between estranged people. In Ephesians 2:11–12, Paul wrote about an inveterate hostility that divided Jews and Gentiles. He compared the hatred and contempt that divided Jews and Gentiles to a wall. Jews called Gentiles "dogs," that is, unclean beasts, and avoided then whenever possible. Gentiles despised Jews as religious oddballs and inferior people. Christ Jesus, the Peacemaker, broke down this barrier of hostility so that believing Jews and believing Gentiles can live together in unity and harmony (2:14). Paul based social reconciliation between Jewish and Gentile believers on spiritual reconciliation of both groups to God "through the cross" (2:16). The message of this passage is timely and relevant for our world that is divided by ongoing hatred and hostilities. Only when angry sinners have been brought into harmony with God at the Cross, can they be truly reconciled to each other.

To this end Paul declared that God "has committed to us the message of reconciliation" (2 Cor. 5:19). What is the message of reconciliation? "God made him who had no sin to be sin for us, so that in him we might become

R

the righteousness of God" (5:21). The apostle himself exemplifies for us what it means to be Christ's ambassador. He faithfully proclaimed "the message of reconciliation" all over the Mediterranean world.　　**—DKC**

***

Pray that God will lead you to someone with whom you can share "the message of reconciliation."

REDEMPTION

When someone pays a ransom to free another from bondage, the process is called redemption. The Bible uses the word *redemption* to make two things clear about salvation: the Savior paid a price and the saved have been set free from bondage.

In the Old Testament, Israelites could redeem both property and life by a prescribed payment. Israelite parents redeemed their firstborn sons with money in remembrance that God spared Israelite firstborns during the final plague that fell on Egypt (Ex. 13:13–15). If an Israelite lost his estate or sold himself into slavery, a kinsman could pay a ransom and redeem the person and/or the property (Lev. 25:25–27, 47–54; Ruth 4:1–12).

God was Israel's Redeemer (Ps. 78:35). God told Israel in Egypt, "I will redeem you with an outstretched arm" (Ex. 6:6). Centuries later when Bab-

ylon took the people of Judah into captivity, God promised to be their Redeemer (Jer. 31:11; 50:33–34). Usually when the Old Testament calls God Israel's Redeemer, the redemption under consideration was physical rather than spiritual. However, Israel's deliverance from Babylon only happened after the sin that had caused the calamity had been confessed and forgiven. The Old Testament did not ignore redemption from sin. Psalm 130:7–8 urged: "O Israel, put your hope in the LORD, for with the LORD is unfailing love and with him is full redemption. He himself will redeem Israel from all their sins."

The New Testament looks at redemption strictly as a work of God accomplished by and through Jesus Christ. Jesus declared that His mission was to be the Redeemer: "For even the Son of Man did not come to be served, but to serve, and to give his life a ransom for many" (Mark 10:45). Jesus never doubted that His earthly life would end with a self-sacrifice that would ransom sinners from their bondage to sin.

In the early church the idea arose that Christ redeemed lost sinners by paying a ransom to the devil. Anselm (1033–1109), archbishop of Canterbury, refuted this theory in his *Cur Deus Homo* (Why God Became Man). The Scriptures are silent as to whom the ransom was paid. The Cross crushed

Satan; it did not enrich him. Conceivably Christ's ransom was paid to God to free sinners from the debt of their offenses. In any case, the emphasis of Christ's redemption is on the sufficiency of the payment He made, not on who received it.

The most extensive development of the doctrine of redemption appears in the writings of Paul. He declared that Christ "gave himself for us to redeem us from all wickedness" (Titus 2:14). Christ "redeemed us from the curse of the law by becoming a curse for us" (Gal. 3:13). "He redeemed us in order that the blessing given to Abraham might come to the Gentiles through Christ Jesus, so that by faith we might receive the promise of the Spirit" (3:14). The apostle sometimes coupled redemption with justification and propitiation (Rom. 3:24; 1 Cor. 1:30). He stressed the *present* benefits of redemption: "In him we have redemption through his blood, the forgiveness of sins" (Eph. 1:7; see also Col. 1:14). He also anticipated the *future* blessing of redemption: "We wait eagerly for our adoption as sons, the redemption of our bodies" (Rom. 8:23; see also Eph. 4:30).

Other New Testament writers also taught about redemption. Peter emphasized the great price required to purchase redemption, namely, "the precious blood of Christ, a lamb without blemish or defect" (1 Pet. 1:19).

The author of Hebrews stressed the perfection of the redemptive work of Christ (Heb. 9:25–27).

In the vocabulary of the Christian no word can be considered more precious or treasured than "Redeemer." It reminds us that our salvation, while free to us, was paid for by the One who gave Himself for our sins. Fanny J. Crosby expressed this truth beautifully in one of her many hymns.

*Redeemed—How I love to
proclaim it!
Redeemed by the blood of the
Lamb;
Redeemed by His infinite mercy,
His child, and forever, I am.*
—DKC

***

*Praise God for the past, present,
and future benefits of
redemption.*

REGENERATION

It is impossible to overemphasize the importance of the doctrine of regeneration. Regeneration, or the new birth, forms the dividing line between heaven and hell. From God's perspective every individual is either spiritually dead or spiritually alive. The spiritually dead await eternal perdition, while those regenerated by God await eternal glory.

The word *regeneration* occurs in

English translations only at Matthew 19:28 and Titus 3:5 (NKJV). In the former passage the word refers to the millennial reign of Christ when the earth will be renewed and the nation of Israel reborn. In Titus the word applies to individual spiritual rebirth.

In the early church numerous theologians taught that the Holy Spirit regenerated people by means of water baptism. Among the better-known church fathers who held this view were Justin Martyr, Irenaeus, Clement of Alexandria, Tertullian, Cyprian, and Athanasius. They also failed to distinguish regeneration from justification. Theologians of the Reformation period clarified the biblical truth that regeneration is solely a work of God accomplished by the Holy Spirit. Modern-day liberal theology regards regeneration as an ethical issue. It says people are regenerated on the basis of personal conduct and not a divine work. Evangelicals assert that God regenerates believers apart from ecclesiastical rites. Regeneration is an instantaneous change from spiritual death to spiritual life as a result of God's gift of eternal life.

Much of Jesus' conversation with Nicodemus involved his need for regeneration. Three times Jesus told Nicodemus he needed to be born again (John 3:3, 5, 7). Four reasons underlie Christ's strong declaration to Nicodemus: we are totally depraved, we are spiritually dead, heaven cannot receive sinners, and a holy God cannot associate with sinners. First, in our natural condition all of us are totally (that is, in every part) depraved. That means sin has touched every aspect of our personality. We are corrupted by sin and have no merit in God's sight (Job 15:14–16; Rom. 3:9–18). The only remedy for such a condition is a re-creation by God (Gal. 6:15).

Second, apart from salvation we are all spiritually dead (Eph. 2:1–3; 4:17–19). We are alienated from God and insensitive to the realities of the spiritual world. A corpse will never have much of a social life apart from a miraculous resurrection. Neither can a spiritually dead person get to know God apart from the miracle of regeneration.

Third, the nature of heaven cries out for regeneration. Heaven is the abode of God. There isn't going to be any sin or defilement there (Rev. 21:27; 22:15). Sinners wouldn't want to go there. Only spiritually alive people can appreciate and respond to the beauties and joys of the heavenly kingdom. When God regenerates believers, they become "partakers of the divine nature" (2 Pet. 1:4, NASB).

That leads to the fourth issue. God's holiness is absolutely incompatible with human depravity. A holy God cannot look on sin (Ezra 9:15; Is. 59:1–2). God views regenerated people through the blood of Christ. He imputes to them the righteousness of Christ and declares them qualified "to share in the inheritance of the saints in the kingdom of light" (Col. 1:12).

Who regenerates sinful men and women? The Bible makes clear statements about regeneration, but many people arrive at wrong answers to this question. If we look closely at the biblical teaching on the subject, we discover several facts. (1) Regeneration isn't the product of human choice (John 1:13; 6:44; Rom. 9:16). (2) Regeneration is the product of the will of God (Ezek. 36:23–38; John 3:5; 1 Cor. 3:6–7; James 1:18; 1 Pet. 1:3). (3) The Holy Spirit is the Agent of regeneration (John 3:5–8; Titus 3:5). The work of regeneration begins and ends with God. It is His work.

God accomplishes regeneration *by means of* the Scriptures. "He chose to give us birth through the word of truth" (James 1:18). "For you have been born again . . . through the living and enduring word of God" (1 Pet. 1:23). Other passages that describe the Word of God as the instrument in regeneration are John 5:24–25; Romans 1:16; 10:17; Philippians 2:16; and 1:23. Not everyone who reads the Scriptures is regenerated. The Holy Spirit must illumine the Bible and work through its truth to effect regeneration.

The Bible pictures the divine work of regeneration as a new birth, a spiritual resurrection, a new creation, and a spiritual transformation. We are most familiar with the phrase "new birth" because Jesus used it. In John 3:3–7 He compared the birth of body to the birth of soul. At physical birth we received life, the same kind of life our parents had. At spiritual birth we receive the same kind of life God has. We receive eternal life. We entered the human family by physical birth, and we enter God's family by spiritual birth.

The second biblical metaphor for regeneration is spiritual resurrection. Resurrection is a more common metaphor in the New Testament than new birth (John 5:21, 24–25; Rom. 6:13; Eph. 2:1, 5; Col. 2:12; 3:1–2). Since we have been resurrected spiritually (that is, have new life in Christ), we are exhorted to live as resurrected people.

Third, the change accomplished by regeneration can be described as a new creation (2 Cor. 5:17; see also Eph. 2:10; 4:24). Referring to the future regeneration of Israel, God said, "I will give you a new heart and put a new spirit in you" (Ezek. 36:26). And similarly in this church age God imparts a new heart or a new nature to every believer, whether Jew or Gentile. Our new nature gives us new capacities to glorify God. Our new nature struggles against our "old," or sinful, nature that remains (Rom. 7:14–25).

Fourth, regeneration can be called a spiritual transformation. Paul wrote,

R

"He has delivered us from the power of darkness and conveyed us into the kingdom of the Son of His love" (Col. 1:13, NKJV). God has rescued us from the rebel kingdom of the tyrant Satan and made us citizens in the kingdom of Christ, God's beloved Son. This kingdom will be visibly manifested on earth in the age to come. Today it is a spiritual kingdom populated by those who have received Christ by faith and who possess "righteousness, peace and joy in the Holy Spirit" (Rom. 14:17).

All of our Christian experience springs from our regeneration by God. He gave us eternal life and a new nature. Because we have been regenerated, we have new desires and new capabilities. We perceive new spiritual realities. We experience new spiritual delights based on a new love for God, for prayer, for the Bible, for God's people, for godliness, and for lost humanity. **—DKC**

***

Recall the persons and circumstances in your life that led to your new birth.

REMNANT

A remnant is what's left after the majority of something is used up or removed. We speak of the remnant of a bolt of cloth or of carpet remnants. The Bible often speaks of a remnant in this general sense. Joseph told his brothers in Egypt, "God sent me ahead of you to preserve for you a remnant on earth" (Gen. 45:7). Similarly, after Israel defeated Og's kingdom of Bashan, Moses wrote, "Only Og king of Bashan was left of the remnant of the Rephaites" (Deut. 3:11). Also God promised concerning Judah's idolatry, "I will cut off from this place every remnant of Baal" (Zeph. 1:4).

The Bible often applies remnant terminology to the survivors of a conquered kingdom. This was true of Gibeon (2 Sam. 21:2), Babylon (Is. 14:22), Philistia (14:30), and Moab (16:14). More important to biblical history, a remnant of the northern kingdom of Israel survived conquest by Assyria (2 Chr. 34:9, 21), and a remnant of the southern kingdom of Judah survived conquest by Babylon (36:20). Later Ezra labeled the group that returned with him to Judah from Babylon as a remnant (Ezra 9:8, 13–15).

The prophets also applied the idea of a remnant to the Jewish people in a spiritual sense. When Israel faced God's judgment at the hands of the Assyrians (Is. 10:5, 12), Isaiah looked to the future and wrote, "In that day the remnant of Israel . . . will truly rely on the LORD" (10:20), and "A remnant will return . . . to the Mighty God" (10:21). No remnant in Israel's history has fulfilled this prophecy so far. The remnant that returned from

Babylon in Ezra's time did not "truly rely on the LORD." No, Isaiah wrote of a coming day when "the Lord will reach out his hand a second time to reclaim the remnant that is left of his people . . . from the four quarters of the earth" (Is. 11:11–12). Jeremiah also wrote that God promised, "I myself will gather the remnant of my flock out of all the countries where I have driven them" (Jer. 23:3–8; 31:7–8).

And God did drive His people far and wide. After the Romans destroyed Jerusalem in A.D. 70, the Jewish people scattered throughout the empire. Micah prophesied that the "remnant of Jacob will be in the midst of many peoples like dew from the LORD" (Mic. 5:7) and "like a lion among the beasts of the forest" (5:8). Political Israel has existed now since 1948, and millions of Jews have relocated there. They have come for a variety of personal, cultural, and political reasons. The gathering of the remnant that God prophesied will occur for spiritual reasons at the end of the age. God has promised Israel's remnant that "when you and your children return to the LORD your God," He will "gather you again from all the nations where he scattered you" (Deut. 30:2–3). At that time, the Lord told the remnant He would "circumcise your hearts and the hearts of your descendants, so that you may love him with all your heart and with all your soul, and live" (30:6; see also Jer. 31:33–34).

The apostle Paul used remnant language to describe Israel's relationship to the church. Paul asserted that God had "chosen by grace" (Rom. 11:5) a remnant of Israel, including himself, to be saved as part of the church. The church, however, is not the remnant of Israel spoken of in the Old Testament. God has not abandoned His prophetic plan for His people Israel (Jer. 31:35–37). In God's plans, however, only a remnant of Israel (Is. 10:21–22; Rom. 9:27) as well as of all humanity (Acts 15:16–18) will be saved.

—JAW

***

Seek to win all you can for Christ, but recognize that all believers will be only a remnant of humankind.

REPENTANCE

John the Baptist captured the attention of the people of Israel when he appeared in the wilderness of Judea and commanded them to repent (Matt. 3:1–2; Luke 3:3; see also Acts 13:24). John startled his listeners by saying they needed to repent because the kingdom of heaven was close at hand. John had a reputation as a prophet, so his message attracted Israelites who were praying for a spiritual awakening (Luke 1:8–17; 2:25–26, 36–38). Jesus

R

repeated John the Baptist's call to repentance when He began His ministry in Jerusalem (Matt. 4:17).

The primary New Testament word for repentance is *metanoia,* "a change of one's mind." The context of a given usage determines what kind of change of mind is in view. One other word, *metamelomai,* "to regret, to be sorry" (2 Cor. 7:8–10), adds little to a discussion of the biblical doctrine of repentance. As moderns, we tend to think of repentance as sorrow for our sins, but sorrow and regret play a minor role in New Testament repentance. Both John the Baptist and Jesus challenged the Jews of their day to change their thinking about the approaching kingdom (Matt. 3:2) and about the forgiveness of their sins (Luke 3:3). First-century Judaism had well-developed teachings about "forgiveness" and "the kingdom," but with the coming of Christ the people needed to change their thinking about these issues in keeping with His gospel.

The King James Version translated two Hebrew words with the English word "repentance." *Nāham,* "to regret, to be sorry, to be comforted," reflects the emotions involved in change. Normally the Scriptures used this Hebrew word to describe a change in God's response to human sin (Ex. 32:14; Num. 23:19; 1 Sam. 15:11). In each of these verses the New International Version translators used a different English word to express a change of heart. The primary Hebrew word that describes human change is *šûb. Šûb* occurs more than a thousand times in the Old Testament. Its basic meaning is "to turn" or "to return." It certain contexts, the turning refers to repentance from sin. The Septuagint, the Greek translation of the Hebrew Old Testament, usually translated *šûb* by the Greek word *epistrephō,* "to turn about."

When the Gospel writers chose *metanoia* to express repentance, they had something different in mind than *šûb* and *epistrephō.* Our English word *repentance* derives from Latin and has more of the idea of sorrow and regret in it than *metanoia* does. *Metanoia* in the Gospels refers to a radical change in thinking—a major paradigm shift in understanding. Christ had entered the world, and people needed to understand who He was and why He had come. This demanded a change in their thinking. So the word *metanoia* accurately expresses how Israel needed to respond to Christ and His message.

Jesus called for repentance in relation to several subjects: the kingdom (Matt. 4:17; Mark 1:15); judgment (Matt. 11:20–21; 12:41; Luke 10:13; 11:32; 13:3, 5); faith (Mark 1:15); forgiveness of unbelievers' sins (Luke 5:32; 24:47); and forgiveness of believers' sins (17:3–4). The context of each of these verses shows why people needed to change. In some cases the context mentions the consequences for those who did not repent (Matt. 11:20–24; Luke 13:3, 5; 15:7, 10).

Repentance and faith are closely related concepts, as seen in Acts 20:21. When Jesus called on people in the Gospels to repent of their sins to receive salvation, He used repentance as a virtual synonym for faith, rather than an action distinct from faith.

The apostles often mentioned repentance when they preached the gospel (Acts 2:38; 3:19; 5:31; 8:22; 17:30; 20:21; 26:20). Peter related human repentance to God's forgiveness of sins (2:38; 3:19; 5:31; 8:22). In Paul's defense before King Agrippa he declared that the message God gave him to preach included "repentance" and "turning to God" (implying faith in God). He also stated that the way believers lived should give evidence of their repentance (26:20).

Interestingly, Luke does not refer to repentance in the various conversion experiences in Acts—the Ethiopian eunuch (8:26–39); Saul of Tarsus (9:1–18; 22:6–16; 26:12–18); Cornelius (10:1–43); Sergius Paulus (13:6–12); Lydia (16:13–15); and the Philippian jailer (16:25–34). While the details of each account differ, we can observe an unvarying sequence in the stories. Each conversion record includes (1) the convicting work of the Holy Spirit, (2) faith in Christ who died and rose again to provide salvation, and (3) the baptism of the new believer. These conversion stories support the proposition that faith and repentance are not separate steps in the salvation process. Whereas the Gospels used *repentance* to represent the conversion experience, the Book of Acts used the term *faith* to serve that same function. In Acts 20:21 the Greek construction linking *repentance* and *faith* presents them as two sides of the same coin.

Romans 2:4 and 2 Corinthians 7:10 indicate the apostle Paul believed only God can bring people to repentance. He grieved that some Corinthian believers had sinned and never repented of their impurity (12:21). He urged Christian leaders to exercise patience in dealing with unbelievers in the hope that they might repent and come to salvation (2 Tim. 2:25). Hebrews 6:6 teaches that "repentance" (or salvation) cannot be repeated because Christ cannot be crucified a second time. And Peter declared that God wants everyone to come to repentance (2 Pet. 3:9).

The apostle John did not use the word *repentance* in his Gospel or in his Epistles, but he used it eleven times in the Book of Revelation. Revelation 2—3 reports the messages of the risen Christ to seven local churches. The Lord rebuked the churches and called for changed behavior that comes from repentance (2:5 [twice], 16, 21–22; 3:3, 19). The four other uses of repentance (9:20–21; 16:9, 11) pertain to unbelievers during the Tribulation. They refuse to repent, and so they will suffer judgment at the hand of God. —**WGJ**

* * *

Follow the admonition of the risen Christ and cling to your first love; be quick to change your mind and your affections if your love wanes.

REST

God Himself set the pattern for resting when "on the seventh day . . . he rested from all the work of creating that he had done" (Gen. 2:2–3). God is omnipotent (17:1; 35:11), so He didn't rest because He was tired. He rested because He was satisfied with the work He had completed. The Bible, however, does present God's rest as the justification for our need of physical rest every seventh day (Ex. 16:23–26; 20:8–11; Lev. 23:3; Deut. 5:12–15). One other aspect of creation figures into a discussion of *rest*. God created the cycle of light and darkness to provide daily rest for people and animals (Gen. 1:14–19).

Jesus Christ needed physical rest. He rested by the well at Sychar in Samaria while His disciples went to buy food (John 4:4–6). He fell asleep in a boat crossing the Sea of Galilee (Mark 4:38; Luke 8:22–23). When the crowds pressured Jesus and His disciples, He said, "Come with me by yourselves to a quiet place and get some rest" (Mark 6:31). Adequate physical rest is a divinely ordained human need.

The Bible also uses the word *rest* in several figurative ways. *Rest* may refer to physical death. Jacob instructed Joseph not to bury him in Egypt: "When I rest with my fathers, carry me out of Egypt and bury me where they are buried" (Gen. 47:30). God told Moses on the east side of the Jordan River, "You are going to rest with your fathers" (Deut. 31:16). David's death was similarly described (2 Sam. 7:12; 1 Kin. 1:21), and Job spoke of death as a rest (Job 3:13, 17).

The Scriptures use *rest* to speak of peace, in the sense of freedom from turmoil and warfare. Moses told the Israelites that when they crossed the Jordan River and settled in Canaan, God "will give you rest from all your enemies" (Deut. 12:10; see 25:19; Josh. 1:13). When Joshua "took the entire land" and "gave it as an inheritance to Israel according to their tribal divisions . . . the land had rest from war" (11:23–24; see 23:1). David was the warrior king, but God gave him "rest from all his enemies around him" (2 Sam. 7:1). He gave Solomon rest as well (1 Kin. 5:4; 8:56). He did the same for Asa (2 Chr. 14:6–7; 15:15), Jehoshaphat (20:30), and Nehemiah (Neh. 9:28).

Rest may speak of peace in the personal sense—emotional, mental, and physical. When Job was perplexed by his difficult experiences, he wrote, "I have no peace, no quietness; I have no rest, but only turmoil" (Job 3:26). When Ruth reported that Boaz was interested in her, Naomi said he would "not rest until the matter is settled today" (Ruth 3:18). David wrote, "My soul finds rest in God alone" (Ps. 62:1; see 62:5). And other psalms read, "He who dwells in the shelter of the Most High will rest in the shadow of the Almighty" (91:1), and "Be at rest once more, O my soul, for the LORD has been good to you" (116:7). Such statements express both spiritual and psychological peace.

Such spiritual peace results from faith in Jesus Christ and God the Father. The Lord Jesus had this in mind when He said, "Come unto me, all you who are weary and burdened, and I will give you rest. Take my yoke upon you and learn from me . . . and you will find rest for your souls" (Matt. 11:28–29). God said that rest and faith are essentially the same thing: "In repentance and rest is your salvation, in quietness and trust is your strength" (Is. 30:15; see also Jer. 6:16; 31:25).

If Israel had faithfully worshiped and served the Lord, then they would have experienced His peace and security in a physical sense. However, from the beginning they did not. Because of their persistent unbelief, God did not allow the adult generation that came out of Egypt to enter Canaan. He said, "I declared on oath in my anger, 'They shall never enter my rest'" (Ps. 95:11).

The physical rest Israel longed to experience in Canaan, however, became a biblical metaphor for spiritual salvation. The author of the Epistle to the Hebrews alluded to Psalm 95:7–11 repeatedly in Hebrews 3:7–11, 15; 4:3, 5, 7. He wanted to stiffen the resolve of wavering Jewish Christians so they would experience all Christ had for them. We live in the age of grace. God lovingly offers spiritual rest and salvation to every Jew and Gentile who will receive Jesus Christ as his or her Savior. Following the rapture of the church, however, Jesus Christ will return to minister once again to His chosen nation, Israel. He will give Israel physical and spiritual rest during the Millennium. He promised through Jeremiah, "I will come to give rest to Israel" (Jer. 31:2).

—JAW

***

As you labor for Christ and the glory of God, learn to rest in Christ and the grace of God.

R

RESURRECTION

The writer to the Hebrews claimed that Old Testament saints hoped for life beyond the grave (Heb. 11:10). Several Old Testament incidents support this conclusion. God commanded Abraham to offer his son Isaac as a sacrifice (Gen. 22:2). But Abraham believed that somehow Isaac would return with him from Mount Moriah, and he told this to his servants (22:5). The writer of Hebrews stated that Abraham believed God could raise the dead, and that "figuratively speaking, he did receive Isaac back from death" (Heb. 11:19).

David expressed his hope of resurrection in Psalm 16:8–11. Peter used David's words to explain Christ's resurrection (Acts 2:24–28). Isaiah brought hope to believing Israelites when he declared that the dead will live and their bodies rise (Is. 26:19). The prophet Daniel spoke of resurrection, some to everlasting life and some to everlasting contempt (Dan. 12:1–3). Many who lived in New Testament times believed in the Resurrection on the basis of the Old Testament (Acts 23:8).

All New Testament teaching about a literal bodily resurrection of the dead is based on the resurrection of Christ. Jesus spoke of His resurrection from the beginning of His ministry, but no one understand what He meant until after the event occurred (John 2:20–

22). At least three times Jesus made major predictions of His death and resurrection (Matt. 16:21; 17:22–23; 20:18–19). Jesus also occasionally demonstrated His power by raising individuals from the dead (9:24–25; Luke 7:14–15; John 11:43–44). These resuscitations differed from resurrection in that these people died again later. Their bodies had not been glorified and made immortal.

On a few occasions Jesus spoke about resurrection. In John 5:28–29 He said everyone will be resurrected: those who had done good (exhibiting their faith in Christ) and those who had done evil (revealing their unbelief). After Lazarus died, Jesus told Martha that He Himself was the Resurrection and the Life and that those who believe in Him will never die (11:25–26).

Jesus' resurrection was a major theme in the preaching of the apostles in the Book of Acts. Because Christ had risen, the Holy Spirit was poured out on believers (Acts 2:32–33). The power of the risen Christ healed an invalid by the temple gate (4:10). Because of the Resurrection, Peter and others faced severe opposition with amazing courage (5:29–32). Saul came to faith because he saw the risen Christ (9:4–5; 22:6–10; 26:15–19). The resurrection of Jesus was a central element of the gospel message that went to the Gentiles (10:39–43; 13:30–38).

Whenever Paul preached in Jewish synagogues, he stressed Jesus' resurrection (17:2–4). The resurrection of Christ, Paul affirmed, proves God will judge the world (17:31). Paul implied that the Jews in Jerusalem rejected him because of his belief in the Resurrection (23:6; 24:15, 21; 26:8). Peter affirmed that we experience new birth because Jesus Christ rose from the dead (1 Pet. 1:3).

One of Paul's most significant statements about the Resurrection appears in 1 Corinthians 15. He began by stating that Jesus' resurrection is one of the two essential tenets of the gospel (1 Cor. 15:4). He ended by affirming that the resurrection of Christ assures all who believe in Him that they will be raised from the dead (15:52).

Paul also presented a basic order of events for the future resurrection. First, Christ rose from the dead (15:23). Then believers who die during the church age will be raised at the Rapture (15:51–56; 1 Thess. 4:16). Other Scripture completes the resurrection time sequence. Old Testament saints (Dan. 12:2) and those martyred during the Tribulation (Rev. 20:4) will be raised at the Second Coming. At the end of the Millennium all the dead who have not put their faith in God will be raised to stand before the Great White Throne judgment (20:11–15). The Scriptures are silent as to how the Lord will handle the resurrection of saints who die during the Millennium.

Paul's other contribution from 1 Corinthians 15 to what we know about the resurrection concerns the nature of the resurrection body. Our natural bodies will be changed into bodies like Christ's. They will share continuity with our physical bodies to the extent that we will be recognizable. They will be imperishable in power and glory (1 Cor. 15:43, 50, 53–54). Resurrection bodies are spiritual bodies (15:44); that is, they will be like the body Christ possesses now in heaven (15:45–49). Resurrection bodies will be recognizable, permanent, glorious, and fully adapted to the eternal life we will enjoy with the Lord.

The Bible doesn't tell us things for mere information's sake. The truth of the Resurrection has practical implications for our daily lives. The apostle Paul stated that we can appropriate for our daily lives the power God exercised to raise Jesus from the dead (2 Cor. 13:4). This power means strength for overcoming obstacles. Paul longed to experience more fully the power of the risen Christ every day (Phil. 3:10). In his second letter, Paul exhorted Timothy to remember the resurrection of Jesus Christ (2 Tim. 2:8). We can draw strength for life and ministry by meditating on Christ's resurrection.   **—WGJ**

R

***

*The Resurrection allows each
believer to enjoy the presence
of Christ every day and
assures us of our hope
for the future.*

REVELATION

Revelation is the process by which God communicates to humans. Apart from God's revelation, human intelligence would be limited to what we can experience with our senses and what we can infer from our experience.

Revelation provides us with "God's secret wisdom, a wisdom that has been hidden and that God destined for our glory before time began" (1 Cor. 2:7). The Bible calls revealed truths "the deep things of God" and "the thoughts of God" (2:10–11). "No eye has seen, no ear has heard, no mind has conceived" this body of truth, "but God has revealed it to us by his Spirit" (2:9–10). God reveals His truth "in words taught by the Spirit, expressing spiritual truth in spiritual words" (2:13).

Revelation can come in many forms, including natural revelation through the physical world. Natural revelation demonstrates the knowledge, power, and love of God (Ps. 19:1–4; Acts 14:17; Rom. 1:20). In Bible times God sometimes revealed truths through dreams and visions. Other times His revelation was direct, as when He communicated with Adam or Moses. On many occasions angels were God's agents of communication. In one sense the entire Bible is a revelation of God because every word in Scripture has been inspired by God (2 Tim. 3:16) to teach us spiritual truth (John 17:17). The human authors of the Bible wrote under the inspiration of the Holy Spirit and expressed exactly what God wanted recorded. The Bible is truth from God Himself. The Holy Spirit indwells believers in Christ. He is "the Spirit of truth," who teaches us and helps us understand the things of God (John 14:26; 16:13).   —**JFW**

***

*Each day carefully read the
Bible, God's primary means
of revelation today.*

REWARDS

The Scriptures reveal that God has promised many rewards to Christians who serve Him faithfully. Rewards differ from wages. Wages compensate for services. Wages correspond in monetary value to the significance of the service to the employer. Rewards are tokens of appreciation for unusual effort and dedication. They are given at the discretion of the rewarder, and their value is not necessarily related to the service rendered.

God is not obligated to reward His children with lives of ease. Millions of

Christians in the past and at present experience persecution and even martyrdom. Our present rewards for serving God are primarily spiritual. We receive the fruit of the Spirit, composed of "love, joy, peace, patience, kindness, goodness, faithfulness, gentleness, and self-control" (Gal. 5:22–23). We will never enjoy life or find meaning apart from yielding ourselves to God and depending on the Spirit (Rom. 12:1–2; Gal. 5:16).

God will reward His children following the Rapture. At that moment we will receive new, immortal bodies that are not affected by sin. After the rapture of the church, we will be judged at the judgment seat of Christ. "For we must all appear before the judgment seat of Christ, that each one may receive what is due him for the things done while in the body, whether good or bad" (2 Cor. 5:10; see also Rom. 14:10). Our Lord will not judge us for our sins; He will reward us for our faithful service to Him. We have been justified by faith (5:1) and stand before God without condemnation (8:1, 33–34). Several times Jesus told His disciples that rewards would be given in heaven (see Matt. 5:12; 6:1, 4, 6, 18). In the last chapter of the Bible, Jesus said, "Behold, I am coming soon! My reward is with me" (Rev. 22:12).

The apostle Paul compared the judgment of our works to a building on fire. Everything flimsy and impermanent burns up. Only what is precious and enduring survives (1 Cor. 3:10–15). Some believers will receive rewards, whereas others who have not been faithful will experience loss of rewards. Paul also compared heavenly rewards to the laurel wreath received by the winner of a race (9:24–27). He wrote that he desired to serve God faithfully so that he would receive "a crown that will last forever" (9:25). At this judgment each believer will have to "give an account of himself to God" (Rom. 14:12), that is, to report how he or she lived. Those who long for Jesus' return will receive "the crown of righteousness" (2 Tim. 4:8). Some of our rewards may consist of positions of privileged service throughout eternity.

—JFW

***

*To receive reward from
God, live with heavenly
values in mind.*

RIGHTEOUSNESS

The Hebrew and Greek words for "righteousness" refer generally to a life that conforms to an accepted and approved standard. In biblical usage, righteousness refers to a life that conforms to God's standard. God's Law expresses God's character. By nature God is infinitely holy (Is. 6:3; Rev. 4:8), so righteousness is one of His attributes (Ezra 9:15; Pss. 116:5; 119:137;

129:4; 145:17; Jer. 12:1; Lam. 1:18; Dan. 9:7, 14). All His actions are righteous. God loves righteousness (Pss. 11:7; 33:5) and has established a standard of righteousness for His creatures (Deut. 6:24–25).

We are unable to live up to God's standard of righteousness. We have to realize that, in comparison to His righteousness, "all our righteous acts are like filthy rags" (Is. 64:6). Righteousness involves inward thoughts as well as outward actions. Jesus explained that "anyone who is angry with his brother will be subject to judgment" (Matt. 5:22), and "anyone who looks at a woman lustfully has already committed adultery with her in his heart" (5:28).

On one occasion when Jesus listed the social commandments (19:18–19), a rich young man replied, "All these I have kept" (19:20). Jesus then told him to sell all his possessions, give it to the poor, and become His disciple (19:21). The young man went away sad because wealth was his god (19:22). Paul said he could have "confidence in the flesh," because "as for legalistic righteousness, [he was] faultless" (Phil. 3:4–6). But then he wrote, "But whatever was to my profit I now consider loss . . . I consider them rubbish, that I may gain Christ and be found in him, not having a righteousness of my own that comes from the law, but that which is through faith in Christ—the righteousness that comes from God and is by faith" (3:7–9).

The rich young ruler (Luke 18:18–23) and Paul before his conversion (Phil. 3:4–6) both fell woefully short of God's standard of righteous. Yet they, and even the Pharisees (Matt. 5:20; 23:28), demonstrated a human righteousness. They conformed outwardly to the Ten Commandments. Many unregenerate men and women carry out commendable deeds, but apart from Christ God will judge them as unrighteousness. In God's sight the so-called righteous acts of the unsaved "are like filthy rags." They can never form the basis for salvation (Is. 64:6). However, degrees of punishment in hell may be based on unsaved individuals' deeds (Luke 12:47–48; Rom. 2:6; Rev. 20:11–13). Similarly the righteous actions of Christians will be rewarded variously according to their motives and their conformity to the will of God (1 Cor. 3:10, 12–15). When Jesus returns, He "will reward each person according to what he has done" (Matt. 16:27; see also Rev. 22:12).

God cannot accept human beings into His presence on the basis of human righteousness. He has, however, carried out a plan that enables Him by grace to grant the righteousness of Christ to each person who by faith accepts the salvation provided through the His death (Rom. 3:21–26). The Ten Commandments state God's righteous standard and demonstrate to us our inability to achieve that standard. In this way the Law leads us to faith in Christ (Gal. 3:21–24).

The eternal Son of God incarnate in human form, the Lord Jesus Christ, is the only human being who lived a totally righteous life. He was "the Holy and Righteous One" (Acts 3:14; see also 7:52; 22:14; 1 John 2:1). Only Jesus could say, "The prince of this world is coming. He has no hold on me" (John 14:30) and "Can any of you prove me guilty of sin?" (8:46). God accepted Jesus' sacrifice of Himself as the perfect "Lamb of God" (John 1:29, 36; see also 1 Pet. 1:19). He bore the Father's judgment on the sin of the world. This enabled God to apply Christ's righteousness to each of us who receives Him as Savior.

By *position* each of us who have identified with Christ enjoys perfect righteousness, but none of us enjoys righteousness as our *possession*. We will not possess righteousness until we enter the presence of God at death or by the rapture of the church (Eph. 2:4–7; Col. 3:1–4). Meanwhile in this life we live among those believers in Christ "who hunger and thirst for righteousness" (Matt. 5:6). We can pray with David, "Lead me, O LORD, in your righteousness" (Ps. 5:8).   **—JAW**

***

As a Christian, transform your righteous standing before God into righteous living for God through the Word of God and the power of the Holy Spirit.

Ss

SABBATH

The Jews called their day of rest and worship the Sabbath (from the Hebrew verb *šābbat,* meaning "to cease" or "to desist from work"). The Sabbath originated when God rested on the seventh day after creating the universe in the first six (Gen. 2:2–3). By declaring the seventh day holy, God set a pattern for the human race to follow. The Old Testament doesn't mention the Sabbath again until God told the Israelites not to gather manna on

it (Ex. 16:23–30). Shortly after that God included a command to keep the Sabbath among the Ten Commandments (20:8–11; Deut. 5:12–15). The Exodus passage bases the Sabbath command on God's rest after creation. Deuteronomy adds that the Sabbath rest should remind Israel of her release from Egyptian slavery.

The Mosaic Law decreed that Israel should keep the Sabbath by refraining from all work that day. This included such minor things as gathering wood

(Num. 15:32–36) and starting a fire for cooking (Ex. 35:3). They could not carry heavy loads (Jer. 17:21), travel (Ex. 16:29), or engage in commerce (Amos 8:5, Neh. 10:31; 13:15, 19). Instead Israel was to observe the Sabbath with a sacred assembly (Lev. 23:3) at which they doubled the number of daily sacrificial lambs along with their voluntary drink and grain offerings (Num. 28:9). Every Sabbath the priests put fresh bread on the table of pure gold in the holy place (Lev. 24:8).

The Sabbath symbolized Israel's covenant relationship with God. "The Israelites are to observe the Sabbath, celebrating it for the generations to come as a lasting covenant" (Ex. 31:16). Thus Sabbath-keeping became the sign of the Mosaic Covenant, much as circumcision represented the Abrahamic Covenant (Gen. 17:11).

In addition to the weekly Sabbath, Israel observed three annual feast days with a Sabbath rest. All of them fell in the seventh month (September/October): the Feast of Trumpets on the first day, the Day of Atonement on the fifteenth day, and the Feast of Tabernacles on the twenty-third day (Lev. 23:24, 32, 39). Every seventh year was a sabbatical year (25:2–7). The Hebrews grouped years by sevens (heptads) rather than by tens (decades). After seven "sabbatical years" the Law called on Israel to observe the fiftieth year as a Year of Jubilee. In that year all land

reverted to its original owner (25:8–31) and enslaved Israelites were set free (25:32–54; see Deut. 15:12). The prophets emphasized to Israel the importance of keeping the Sabbath (Is. 58:13–14). But the nation failed to do so and was removed from the land so that it might have its Sabbath rest (Lev. 26:32–35; 2 Chr. 36:20–21; Ezek. 20:10–24).

During the intertestamental period Jewish scribes created a complicated code of regulations governing Sabbath observance. These regulations led to the formulation of thirty-nine articles, which forbade all kinds of ordinary activities on the Sabbath. These petty, legalistic Sabbath regulations brought Jesus into conflict with the rabbis' additions to the Law of Moses. The Gospels report six occasions on which Jesus collided with Jewish Sabbath traditions. The scribes cared more about strict observance of the day than about the needs of people. Jesus insisted, "The Sabbath was made for man, not man for the Sabbath" (Mark 2:27). He also startled the authorities by asserting He was Lord of the Sabbath (2:28).

The early Christians worshiped on the first day of the week (Acts 20:7), although for a time Christian Jews apparently also attended synagogue services and observed the Sabbath. The Council of Jerusalem (A.D. 49 or 50), however, made no mention of Sabbath-keeping for Gentile Christians. Paul considered the Mosaic Law a yoke of bondage from which Christians are freed (Gal. 5:1). He made no distinction between the moral and ceremonial law since the old covenant in its entirety had been abolished at the Cross (2 Cor. 3:14). Paul insisted God had canceled the written code with its regulations, "nailing it to the cross" (Col. 2:14). Since we are free from the burden of the Law, there are no biblical grounds for imposing Sabbath-keeping on believers in the present church age (2:16). The author of Hebrews used the Hebrew Sabbath to illustrate "God's rest" into which a believer will enter when he "rests from his own work" (Heb. 4:9–10). He didn't challenge his readers to keep the Sabbath. He exhorted them to "make every effort to enter that [spiritual] rest" (4:11), that is, to enjoy the peace and rest Christ gives each believer at salvation.   **—DKC**

***

Thank God for a Sabbath rest from human effort for salvation.

SACRIFICE

The Scriptures frequently mention sacrifices and offerings. The Bible often uses these terms interchangeably. When a distinction applies, an offering was completely presented to God while a sacrifice might be divided between God and the priests who served at the altar. Some scholars hold that Israel borrowed the religious practices of surrounding nations to create her system of sacrifices. Archaeologists have excavated temple sites with altars and bones from animal sacrifices in Mesopotamia, Syria, Palestine, Egypt, Asia Minor, and the Aegean region. That only means that animal sacrifices occurred outside as well as inside Israel. The Old Testament asserts that Israel's sacrifices came about in response to a revelation from God.

In pagan cultures animal sacrifice provided food for the gods. Israel's sacrifices pleased God, but they did not feed Him. The emphasis of biblical sacrifices, rather, was on the blood. The Lord declared, "The life of a creature is in the blood, and I have given it to you to make atonement for yourselves on the altar; it is the blood that makes atonement for one's life" (Lev. 17:11). Worshipers deserved death because of their sins, but God allowed them to substitute slain animals in their place.

Before the Mosaic Law, various individuals offered sacrifices. God Himself killed the first animals that died on our behalf. They provided skins to cover Adam and Eve's nakedness after the Fall (Gen. 3:21). The Cain and Abel story (Gen. 4) reveals that God had somehow told the first family the proper way to approach Him. Abel responded to that revelation with faith and offered "a better sacrifice" than

Cain. Faith is always the right response to revelation (Heb. 11:4). In addition Noah, Abraham, Isaac, Jacob, and Job all offered sacrifices long before the Mosaic Law was given (Gen. 8:20; 12:7–8; 13:18; 15:9–17; 22:2–14; 26:25; 33:20; 35:3; Job 1:5; 42:7–9).

The Mosaic Law established a complex and well-defined system of sacrifice. It minutely prescribed both the animals and other foodstuffs to be sacrificed and the ceremonies connected with offering them.

The major biblical passage about the Mosaic sacrificial ritual is Leviticus 1—7, which describes five offerings. These offerings fall into two categories. Three offerings result in "an aroma pleasing to the LORD." These are burnt offerings (1:3–17), cereal offerings (2:1–16), and fellowship or peace offerings (3:1–17). The other two offerings atone for sins. They are sin offerings (4:1—5:13) and guilt or trespass offerings (5:14—6:7).

Numbers 28—29 presents a sacred calendar for Israel that records the relative frequency of these offerings. The priests offered a morning and evening sacrifice every day (28:3–8). They doubled the daily offerings on the Sabbath (28:9). Sacrifices were prescribed for every new moon (28:11–15). In addition Israel's year featured seven religious assemblies during which priests and worshipers presented numerous required and voluntary sacrifices and offerings to the Lord. The seven convocations included: the Passover that memorialized Israel's redemption from Egypt (Ex. 12; Lev. 23:5; Num. 28:16); the Feast of Unleavened Bread that symbolized the removal of sin (Ex. 12:15–20; Lev. 23:6–8; Num. 28:17–25); the Feast of Firstfruits that expressed thanksgiving to God for the barley harvest (Lev. 23:10–14); the Feast of Weeks that celebrated the wheat harvest (23:15–21); the Feast of Trumpets, a solemn gathering to prepare for the Day of Atonement (23:23–25); the Day of Atonement, an annual assembly for national repentance and atonement for sins (Lev. 16; 23:26–32); and the Feast of Tabernacles, that both thanked God for the harvest of fruit, olive oil, and wine and remembered Israel's wilderness experience (23:33–44).

The meaning of Israel's sacrifices and offerings went beyond their function in worship and atonement. They all prophetically pictured some aspect of the person and work of Christ. The Passover lamb prefigured "Christ, our Passover lamb" (1 Cor. 5:7). The burnt offering pictured Christ offering Himself to God in a substitutionary death for sinners (Eph. 5:2; Heb. 9:14; 10:5–7). The cereal or grain offering typified Christ offering to God His perfect life (Matt. 3:15; John 17:4). The peace offering foreshadowed Christ "making peace through his blood, shed on the cross" (Col. 1:20). The sin offering pictured Christ suffering "outside the camp" to provide redemption for sinners (Heb. 13:12). He was made "sin for us" (2 Cor. 5:21). The guilt or trespass offering typified Christ, who atoned not only for sin's guilt but also for the damage or injury of sin (Ps. 51:4; Is. 53:10).

How effective were the Levitical sacrifices in atoning for sin? Did they provide full and complete forgiveness? Did they achieve only partial forgiveness or temporary forgiveness? Theologians give various answers to those questions. (1) The Levitical sacrifices cleansed ceremonial impurity but left the guilt of sin to be removed by the sacrifice of Christ. This has been referred to as "the law with its incomplete atonement." (2) The Levitical sacrifices only covered the sin. There was no real forgiveness until Christ died. (3) Animal sacrifices provided atonement for a limited period of time, such as from one sin offering to another or from one Day of Atonement to another. (4) The best view is this: Old Testament sacrifices, offered in faith, provided a covering for unintentional transgressions (Lev. 4:1–2, 13, 22, 27; 5:14–15, 17–18) and a temporary stay of divine wrath in anticipation of the Cross.

The Gospels record shows Jesus participating in the Mosaic sacrificial system. He did not try to abolish it (Matt. 5:23–24). He told lepers whom He had cleansed to make the offerings required by the Mosaic Law (8:4; Luke 17:14). However, He did tell a teacher of the Law that love of God and neighbor is more important than burnt offerings and sacrifices (Mark 12:33–34). Jesus referred to His imminent death as a sacrifice (Mark 10:45 and Matt. 20:28; Mark 14:24 and Luke 22:20; Matt. 26:28).

The Pauline Epistles emphasize that Christ's death on the cross was a sacrifice to remove sin (Rom. 3:25; 5:9; 1 Cor. 10:16; Eph. 1:7; 2:13; Col. 1:20). Paul used the "pleasing-aroma" sacrifices, especially the burnt offering, as the basis for his appeal to us to offer our bodies "as living sacrifices, holy and pleasing to God" (Rom. 12:1).

Peter affirmed that the blood of Christ redeems us (1 Pet. 1:18–19; see also 1:2; 3:18). John wrote that Christ's death provides us with cleansing and propitiation (1 John 1:7; 2:2; 5:6, 8; Rev. 1:5). Hebrews 8—10 shows how the Old Testament sanctuary and sacrifices all pointed to Christ and were all fulfilled in Him.

Ezekiel prophesied that animal sacrifices will be offered once again in the Jerusalem temple during the millennial kingdom (Ezek. 43:13–27). The prophet described the prominent place the altar will occupy in the millennial temple and the animal sacrifices to be made on it. How can we reconcile Ezekiel's prophecies with the New Testament assertion that Christ "offered one sacrifice for sins forever" (Heb. 10:12, NKJV)? We recognize that just as the Old Testament sacrifices looked forward to the death of Christ, the millennial sacrifices will look back to the Cross. They will serve as memorials of His death, as the Lord's Supper does today. No animal sacrifice, past or future, ever could take away sin (10:4).

—DKC

***

Give thanks to God the Father,
Son, and Holy Spirit for
the sacrifice of Christ
on the cross.

SALVATION

Salvation is the work of God by which He provides a way to deliver humans from their sinful condition. He achieved this salvation through the sacrificial death of Christ and His resurrection from the dead. We can only receive this salvation and new life by faith apart from any merit or work on our part (Eph. 2:8–9). The primary Old Testament word for salvation is the Hebrew verb *yāšaʿ*, "to save, deliver, rescue." In the New Testament the Greek words are the verb *sōzō*, "to save, preserve, rescue" and the noun *sōtēria*, "salvation, deliverance."

When we stop and think about what God did to save us from our sins, we can only marvel at His love and grace. When Paul wrote about salvation, he ended up using phrases such as God's "incomparably great power" (Eph. 1:19), "the riches of God's grace that he lavished on us" (1:7–8), "his glorious inheritance" (1:18), "his great love for us" (2:4), and "the incomparable riches of his grace" (2:7). The writer of the Book of Hebrews called it "a great salvation" and warned us not to ignore it (Heb. 2:3). Jude ascribed "glory, majesty, power, and authority" to the Savior (Jude 25). In fact, salvation from sin fascinates the angelic world (1 Pet. 1:12).

John wrote that someday all heaven will resound with praise to the Savior for His great salvation (Rev. 5:9–14; 19:1). Salvation will always cause people to rejoice in song. Moses and the people of Israel sang about God's salvation when they were rescued from Egypt (Ex. 15:1–18). The Lord gave Moses a song of deliverance to teach the people so they could sing it after they conquered the Promised Land (Deut. 31:19; 32:1–43). David and other psalmists sang of God's national or personal deliverance (1 Chr. 16:23; Pss. 32:7; 95:1; 96:2; 98:1). Isaiah and Jonah put their thoughts about God's salvation into song (Is.12:2; Jon. 2:9). We will sing songs of redemption throughout all eternity (Rev. 5:9; 14:3; 15:3–4).

The Old Testament presents God's deliverance of Israel from Egyptian slavery as a great demonstration of His ability to save (Ex. 14:13–14). Because of the Exodus, Israel acknowledged God as the Source of salvation. The Exodus proved that what is impossible from a human perspective provides God an opportunity to display His grace and power for those He loves. From the time Israel entered the Promised Land (Josh. 5:14; 10:14), God fought for their deliverance. In the future God will again fight for Israel (Zech. 14:3), and the whole nation will experience salvation as prophesied by Isaiah (Is. 59:20) and Paul (Rom. 11:26).

God did not limit His Old Testament saving work to the nation of Israel. He delighted to save individuals who put their faith in Him. Hebrews 11:1–40 highlights a number of people in the Old Testament who trusted in God and experienced personal salvation. The psalms record the testimonies of individuals who enjoyed salvation from the Lord (for example, Pss. 18:2; 37:39–40; 62:1; 118:14). The prophets also spoke of personal salvation (Is. 12:2; Jon. 2:9).

The New Testament reports that when the Lord Jesus came to earth, angels announced that a Savior had been born (Luke 2:11). John the Baptist declared that Jesus is the "Lamb of God, who takes away the sin of the world" (John 1:29). Jesus Himself stated that He came to give His life as a ransom for sin (Matt. 20:28; Mark 10:45) and that He came to seek and save the lost (Luke 19:10). John's Gospel clearly states that the way of salvation is by faith in Christ (John 3:16; 10:9–10). The night before His crucifixion Jesus explained to His disciples that His death was a sacrifice for the forgiveness of sin (Matt. 26:28), but it wasn't until after His resurrection that they fully understood this truth (Luke 24:45–47).

The Epistles overflow with doctrine about our salvation. When we look at this multifaceted doctrine in the Epistles, we discover a kaleidoscope of theological terms. Each word adds another facet to the jewel. Some of these are "redemption" (Rom. 3:24; 1 Cor. 1:30; Heb. 9:12), "reconciliation" (2 Cor. 5:18–19; Rom. 5:11), "propitiation" (1 John 2:2, NASB), "regeneration" (Titus 3:5, NASB), "eternal life" (Rom. 5:21; 1 Tim. 1:16; 1 John 2:25), "delivered" (2 Cor. 1:10), "freedom" (Gal. 5:1; Eph. 3:12), "justification" (Rom. 4:25; 5:16), "grace" (3:24; Eph. 1:7; 2 Tim. 1:9), "victory" (1 Cor. 15:54, 57) "peace" (Eph. 2:15, 17; Col. 1:20), "forgiveness" (Eph. 1:7; Col. 1:14), "hope" (Rom. 5:2; Col. 1:23; 1 Pet. 1:3), "chosen" (Eph. 1:11; 1 Pet. 1:2), "adoption" (Rom. 8:15, NASB; 8:23), "sanctified" (1 Cor. 1:2; 6:11; Heb. 10:29), "glorified" (Rom. 8:30), "fellowship" (1 Cor. 1:9; 1 John 1:7), "inheritance" (Col. 1:12; 1 Pet. 1:4), and "blessed" (Rom. 4:7–8; Eph. 1:3).

The grace of God that saves sinners will remain active even after the church

S

has been raptured. During the Great Tribulation, God will save multitudes from every nation on the face of the earth (Rev. 7:9–17). During the Millennium children will be born and they will have sin natures (Is. 65:20, 23). We can assume that in the Millennium people will be saved as they are now by faith in Christ's sacrificial death for sin. Perhaps the reason animal sacrifices will be reinstituted (Ezek. 40:38–47) will be to remind everyone graphically that salvation is possible only through faith in Christ who offered Himself as the Sacrifice for sins. Throughout eternity salvation will never lose its significance because the Lamb who was slain will always be present (Rev. 22:3).

—WGJ

* * *

Each day think of at least one aspect of salvation that is meaningful to you and share it with a friend.

SANCTIFICATION

The word *sanctification* can refer either to the process or the result of being set apart for God's purposes. The noun *sanctification* does not occur in the New International Version, but variations of the verb "to sanctify" occur frequently in the New Testament. Variations of the verb "to consecrate" occur numerous times in the Old Testament. These words are used

in relation to persons or things set apart to God, "the Holy One of Israel" (Ps. 71:22; Is. 10:20; see Prov. 9:10), so they could be correctly translated "to sanctify" (John 17:17) or "to make holy" (Gen. 2:2–3).

You can see the fundamental idea of setting someone apart to God by looking at God's claim on the firstborn of Israel. God said, "Consecrate to me every firstborn male . . . whether man or animal" (Ex. 13:2; see also 13:12–13, 15; 22:29–30). Later God directed Israel to set apart the Levites in place of all firstborn sons to acts as priests and tabernacle servants (Num. 3:12–13, 45–48; 8:14–18). Israel also consecrated inanimate objects, such as the tabernacle, the altar of sacrifice, the ark of the covenant, and all the articles of furniture in the tabernacle (Ex. 29:44; 30:26–29). Fundamentally sanctification means dedicated to God (Gen. 2:3). By logical extension, it came to imply that people set apart to God should reflect His holiness (1 Pet. 1:15–16).

The Lord sanctified Israel by separating them to Himself as His people. When He said to Abram, "Leave your country, your people and your father's household and go to the land I will show you" (12:1), He promised to bless him and his descendants. After God brought Israel out of Egypt, He told them, "You will be for me a kingdom of priests and a holy nation" (Ex.

19:6; see also 22:31) and "You are a people holy to the LORD your God" (Deut. 7:6; 14:2, 21; see 26:19; 28:9). God is infinitely holy in the moral sense (Lev. 11:44, 45; 19:2; 20:7; Is. 6:3; 1 Pet. 1:15–16; Rev. 4:8). His call to Israel in the past and to us in the present to be holy includes moral sanctification as well as separation to Him (2 Cor. 6:17).

We will experience moral sanctification in three ways. First, we received positional sanctification the moment we trusted Jesus Christ for salvation. Jesus Christ lived a completely sinless life and provided a perfect, sinless sacrifice for sin in His death on the cross. God the Father views each of us who have identified with Christ by faith as participating in Christ's righteousness. For this reason God calls His people, whether in the Old or New Testament, "saints" (Rom. 1:7, literal translation; Eph. 1:1; Phil. 1:1). Paul even said the Corinthians were "sanctified in Christ Jesus and called saints" (1 Cor. 1:2, literal translation), even though they fell far short of being saintly in their conduct.

Second, God tells us to "be holy in all you do" (1 Pet. 1:15; see also 2 Cor. 7:1; 1 John 3:3). Each of us is "a temple of the Holy Spirit" (1 Cor. 6:19), and the Holy Spirit works to express His holy nature more and more in our lives as He indwells us (Rom. 8:4–5, 14; Gal. 5:16, 25). Progressive sanctification happens in fits and starts—three steps forward and two steps back. "The sanctifying work of the Spirit" (1 Pet. 1:2; see also 1 Thess. 4:7; 2 Thess. 2:13) will not reach completion during our earthly lives. However, the Holy Spirit of God will transform us into the image of Christ to the extent that we submit to Him and cooperate with Him.

The third level of sanctification will occur in the presence of the Lord. There we will experience complete sanctification. Complete sanctification will bring us into full conformity with the position God gave us when He justified us. We will achieve compete sanctification either at our death or at the rapture of the church. Jesus "loved the church and gave himself up for her to make her holy, cleansing her by the washing with water through the word . . . to present her to himself as a radiant church, without stain or wrinkle or any other blemish, but holy and blameless" (Eph. 5:25–27). God promises us that "when he [Jesus] appears, we shall be like him, for we shall see him as he is" (1 John 3:2). Therefore "everyone who has this hope in him [Jesus] purifies himself, just as he [Jesus] is pure" (3:3).   **—JAW**

***

Strive to manifest your position in Christ as a saint in your daily life, to God's glory.

S

SATAN

The Bible describes Satan as a fallen angel and the head of the demon world. Satan has various titles in the Bible, including devil, serpent (2 Cor. 11:3), dragon (Rev. 12:9), angel of the abyss (9:11), ruler of this world (John 12:31; 16:11, NASB), prince of the power of the air (Eph. 2:2, NASB), god of this world (2 Cor. 4:4, NASB), tempter (Matt. 4:3), Beelzebul (Matt. 12:24, NASB), and the evil one (Matt. 13:19; John 17:15; 1 John 5:18–19). Two Old Testament passages (Is. 14:12–17; Ezek. 28:11–19) reveal that God originally created Satan as a holy angel along with the other angels. He sinned against God and became the head of the fallen angels who joined him in rebellion against God. Together they form the demonic world.

Before he fell, Satan was described as the "morning star, son of the dawn" (Is. 14:12), but he proudly thought, "I will make myself like the Most High" (14:14). Ezekiel 28 speaks of a wicked king of Tyre, but the description reaches beyond the human tyrant to the spirit-being who motivated him. Satan had been "the model of perfection, full of perfection and perfect in beauty" (28:12). He had been "in Eden, the garden of God" and had been "anointed as a guardian cherub" (28:13–14). The Lord reminded Satan, "You were on the holy mount of God . . . blameless in your ways from the day you were created till wickedness was found in you" (28:14–15).

The first mention of Satan by name occurs in the Book of Job (Job 1:6–12; 2:1–7). Satan acted as an accuser of God's followers. In that capacity he accused Job of serving God simply because God had blessed him so richly. The Scriptures frequently refer to Satan as the opponent of the work of God who does all he can to interfere with God's purposes. Like a lion he aggressively sets out to pull believers away from God (1 Pet. 5:8), to hinder us (1 Thess. 2:18), and to deceive us (Gen. 3:13; 2 Cor. 11:3). In the Garden of Eden he appeared in the form of a serpent and tempted Eve (Gen. 3:1–5; see Rev. 12:9). Jesus, therefore, called Satan a murderer (John 8:44).

The devil denies the Word of God (Matt. 13:19, 39). He put treason in the heart of Judas (John 13:2). He blinds unbelievers to the gospel (2 Cor. 4:4). He hates Jesus Christ (John 13:27; see also 6:70; Luke 22:53). Jesus said Satan has already been judged and condemned (John 16:11). Nevertheless he will remain very active up to the time God casts him out of heaven (Rev. 12). Then Satan will be bound during the millennial kingdom. He and the demonic world will be totally inactive while Christ reigns on the earth. He will be loosed to lead a brief, intense rebellion at the close of the Millennium.

Then God will cast Satan into the lake of fire (20:1–3, 7–10).　　　**—JFW**

***

Be sensitive to the reality of the adversary's desire to thwart God's purpose for your life and submit to the Lord's guidance through His Spirit.

SCRIPTURE

The word *scripture* simply means "a writing." Moses identified the two tablets of stone with the Ten Commandments as "the writing of God" (Ex. 32:16). Second Chronicles 30:5 uses the expression "what was written" to indicate the holy Scriptures. "The holy Scriptures" (2 Tim. 3:15) specifically refer to the sixty-six books of the Bible. They are "holy" because they are inspired by God. "All Scripture is God-breathed and useful for teaching, rebuking, correcting and training in righteousness, so that the man of God may be thoroughly equipped for every good work" (3:16–17).

God directly dictated some portions of the Bible, but He inspired most of the Bible by working through the personalities, vocabularies, and styles of the human authors. Regardless of how God superintended its composition, the Bible claims to have the authority of God, even though fallible men penned its truths. Christ stated that His Father would fulfill the writ-

ten Scriptures down to the smallest letter (the Hebrew *yôd*) and the smallest part of a letter (Matt. 5:18).

The original manuscripts of the various books of the Bible no longer exist. What we have in museums and university libraries are handmade copies of them. Yet the hundreds of manuscripts of the Old and New Testaments, even though copies, agree remarkably with one another. Variations in the text of the Bible, though numerous, seldom matter theologically. When a theologically important passage is not clear in one manuscript, it is clear in others.

Scholars call the science of comparing manuscripts and determining the original reading lower criticism. Centuries of practice have refined lower criticism to a precise system. For all practical purposes we can accept the text of the Bible as we have it now as if it were the original.

In determining the correct reading of a passage, scholars consider the age of manuscripts containing it and the number of manuscripts that agree on the reading. New Testament manuscripts group into "families" depending on where they were copied and which master manuscript they were copied from. Time shows that some manuscript families are superior to others. The science of lower criticism is a complicated process, involving hundreds of manuscripts, but the findings

S

of careful scholars support the authenticity of the Bible as we have it.

Consider the Book of Daniel. In our Bibles, Daniel translates a manuscript from about A.D. 900. Among the Dead Sea Scrolls, however, a manuscript was found dating from 100 B.C., about one thousand years earlier than the previous existing manuscripts. The two manuscripts are practically identical. No important differences between them exist.   **—JFW**

***

Consistently memorize passages from the Bible that will assist you in living the Christian life.

SECURITY

Paul wrote, "For I am convinced that neither death nor life, neither angels nor demons, neither the present nor the future, nor any powers, neither height nor depth, nor anything else in all creation, will be able to separate us from the love of God that is in Christ Jesus our Lord" (Rom. 8:38–39): He believed his salvation was secure. "Security" is the belief that when God grants salvation through faith in Christ, it can never be lost because it is eternal.

Jesus taught throughout His earthly ministry that those who believe in Him have eternal life (John 3:15, 36; 5:24; 6:47). On one occasion Jesus stressed that it was the Father's will that no believer be lost (6:38–40). He said that those who believe in Him will never perish and no one can pluck them out of His hand (10:28). He then added that believers are also in the hands of His Father who is "greater than all." He sealed His case by asserting that "no one can snatch them out of my Father's hand" (10:29). The subject of security was one of the major themes in Jesus' extended prayer to the Father the night before He was crucified. He prayed specifically that God the Father would protect all believers from the evil one (17:11, 15), just as He (Jesus) had protected them during His earthly ministry (17:12). He prayed for the Father's protection of those of us who have believed down through the ages (17:20). In that prayer Jesus claimed that we have a union with Him like the one He has with the Father (17:21). Finally, He prayed that we would be with Him to behold His glory (17:24). We have no reason to believe that this prayer of the Lord has gone unanswered.

The apostle Paul taught the doctrine of security in his writings. He proclaimed that through the death of Christ, we have been justified and saved from God's wrath (Rom. 5:9). He taught that the resurrection of Christ implies that all who belong to Him will live as long as He lives (5:10). Because the risen Christ sits at the right hand of God interceding for us, no one can separate us from Christ's love (8:34–35). Paul also taught that God has sealed every believer with His Holy Spirit until the day of redemption (Eph. 1:13–14; 4:30). Since all of us are indwelt by and sealed with the Holy Spirit, we are permanent members of the body of Christ.

The author of the Book of Hebrews wrote his epistle to remind us of the present ministry of Christ as our Great High Priest. Because His priesthood is permanent, He is able to save completely (forever) since He continues to live and intercede for those He saves (Heb. 7:24–25). Because of His ministry on behalf of God's children, those who trust Him can have confidence and assurance that their salvation is secure (10:19–23).

Some people claim the concept of eternal security seems arrogant. They feel those who believe it think they're better than others. They think we might use the teaching to excuse sinful living. In reality, the doctrine of security must be seen as an outworking of God's grace. Salvation is the supernatural work of God. From the beginning to the end the whole process comes from Him. The character of God and the nature of salvation demand security.

Some New Testament verses seem to say that salvation is dependent on our faithfulness (for example, 2 Tim. 2:12; Heb. 6:4–8). These passages need to be read in their immediate context and in the larger context of the whole Bible. Of course the Christian life does challenge us to obey. We dare not drift through life, sinning casually as through it doesn't matter. Certainly we will sin in this life (Phil. 3:12; 1 John 1:8). But all of us need to make it our goal to be like Christ. We must not allow sin to master us.

If Christ's death was not sufficient to pay for every sin, there is no way He can be crucified again (Heb. 6:6). The biblical evidence is strong in affirming that His death is completely adequate and we are absolutely secure.

—WGJ

***

Praise the Lord daily for the certainty of your salvation and the security you have in Christ.

SERVANT

We may think being a servant seems like a degrading or inferior role, but God calls those whom He holds in highest esteem servants. In the Book of Isaiah God called His Son the Servant of the Lord (Is. 42:1; 49:6; 52:13). In the Bible the word *servant* has a range of meanings, spanning the spectrum from bondslave to highly trusted associate. In the ancient world prominent people could be called servants. In the Bible Abraham (Gen. 26:24),

S

Moses (Num. 12:7), David (Is. 37:35), and Daniel (Dan. 6:20) all are called servants of God or servants of a more prominent person.

A servant is one who obeys a master, seeks no personal recognition (Luke 17:7–10), and cares for others. Service may be menial or it may involve great responsibility such as that which Old Testament priests or church deacons exercised. Most of the time servants in the Bible literally were slaves owned by their masters (Gen. 47:18–21).

Israelites who could afford them had servants in their households. The Mosaic Law protected Israelites who became servants to other Israelites. They were to be treated as hired workers and not as slaves (Lev. 25:39–43). They were set freed at the next sabbatical year (Deut. 15:12). The Law required that non-Hebrew servants be treated with respect and dignity. Trusted servants might be treated almost as part of the family. God commanded Israelite masters to treat their servants generously because He had redeemed Israel out of slavery from the hands of the Egyptians (15:13–15, 18). Freed servants could opt to stay with their masters and become servants for life if they served in an exceptionally good setting (15:16–17).

God uniquely called Israel as a nation to be His servant (Is. 41:8–9). Israel was to bear witness of the power and greatness of God to all the nations of the world (43:10–13). In return God promised to protect and care for Israel in every way (44:1–5). How tragic, though, that the nation proved spiritually blind and unfaithful to its Master, the Holy One of Israel (42:19–20).

The prophet Isaiah wrote about another servant who was totally distinct from all others. This servant was the Messiah, the Servant of the Lord. Isaiah pictured Him as gentle, one who would not raise His voice in the streets or bruise a reed (42:2–3). Yet the power of the Spirit would be on Him and ultimately He would establish peace on the earth (11:2–5). Through Him the Gentile world would have opportunity for salvation, and the light of His salvation would shine to the ends of the earth (49:6). In Isaiah 50:5–7, the prophet pictured some of the physical abuse the Servant of the Lord would endure on behalf of God's people. The climax of Isaiah's prophecies about the Servant of the Lord occurs in chapter 53. The Servant of the Lord would bear the sins of the world as He died. He would be stricken for the transgressions of Israel (53:4–8). The prophet even foresaw that Israel would reject the message of salvation (53:1–3).

Matthew indicated that the miraculous ministry of Jesus fulfilled Isaiah's words about the Servant of the Lord (Matt. 12:17–21; see Is. 42:1–4). Jesus called Himself a servant when

He taught His disciples who would be considered great in the kingdom. He stated that the Son of Man came to serve and not to be served (Mark 10:45). In the hours before His crucifixion Jesus noted that He was fulfilling the words of Isaiah 53:12, which referred to the suffering Servant (Luke 22:37). The apostle John told how Jesus took a towel and a basin of water to wash the feet of His disciples (John 13:1–15). By doing so, Jesus dramatically portrayed Himself as the servant of His followers. Years later Paul reflected on the crucifixion of Christ and highlighted the servant attitude of Jesus, who obeyed the will of the Father, even to death (Phil. 2:6–11).

The apostles followed Christ, so it is not surprising that they identified themselves as servants of the Lord (Rom. 1:1; James 1:1; 2 Pet. 1:1; Jude 1; Rev. 1:1). Jesus had said that serving was the pathway of blessing (John 13:15–17). When Paul wrote in Romans 6:15–23 about the power of the death and resurrection of Christ, he emphasized that we had been in bondage to sin. He called us to choose to be servants of righteousness rather than slaves to sin.

The Epistles speak of ministry as an act of servanthood. The Greek word *diakonos* (servant) describes someone who carries out an appointed task. This term came to apply to the work of a deacon (1 Tim. 3:10, 13). The New Testament calls us servants of the New Covenant (2 Cor. 3:6), servants of righteousness (11:15), servants of Christ (1 Tim. 4:6), and servants of the gospel (Eph. 3:7). There are different kinds of spiritual gifts and different ways of serving, but there is only one Holy Spirit, one Lord, and one God who enable us to serve (1 Cor. 12:46). Since we are all servants, we stand equally before the Lord. No matter what task God has assigned to us as servants, we are totally dependent on Him for success. All glory and honor belongs to Him (3:5–9).   **—WGJ**

***

Exemplify the qualities of the Lord Jesus, especially a servant's heart like His, and always consider the needs of others.

SIN

One of the more intriguing issues in theology is the study of sin and its effect on every one of us. The Bible tells how sin entered the world, how sin has devastated human experience, how God's grace provides forgiveness of sin, and how God will one day wipe out all sin from the universe forever.

The story of Adam and Eve reports how sin entered the human history. "The serpent," who appears in Genesis 3:1 without any introduction, is identified in the Book of the Revelation as the devil (Rev. 12:9). In his adversarial position Satan questioned the truthfulness of God and His Word and persuaded Eve to listen to him. We learn the character of sin by analyzing the way Satan toyed with Adam and Eve. Satan questioned God's goodness and integrity, so sin is anything contrary to God's character (Gen. 3:5). God had told Adam and Eve not to eat from the tree of the knowledge of good and evil, so sin is anything disobedient to His commands (2:17; 3:6). Therefore sin consists of thoughts, attitudes, and actions contrary to the character or Word of God.

We can learn other lessons about sin by examining Cain's experience (4:3–6). The Hebrew term for "sin" in that passage means "to miss the mark." Sin is word or deed that comes short of God's perfection. Cain sinned by killing his brother Abel, who was in God's image. David acknowledged this spiritual reality when he confessed his adultery with Bathsheba: "Against you, you only, have I sinned and done what is evil in your sight" (Ps. 51:4). The ramifications of sin may reach far and wide among our network of human relationships, but what makes sin so detestable is that it opposes the character and Word of the holy, righteous, loving God.

The Book of Leviticus details the sacrificial requirements of the Law to atone for sin. All this ritual underscores the truth that sin is essentially wrongdoing that offends and angers God. Thus people are guilty, and redemption and restoration are mandatory. Sin drives people from God and excludes them from fellowship with Him (Lev. 1:4).

The prophets spoke repeatedly about sin as rebellion against God and His Law (for example, Is. 1:2; 43:27; Jer. 2:29; Ezek. 2:3–4). Amos indicted the nations around Israel for their transgressions (Amos 1:3—2:4). Then he added Judah and Israel to his list (2:4—3:15). God's judgment eventually fell on Israel and Judah because of their transgressions. Another term the prophets used to describe sin was "going astray" (see Is. 53:6; Ezek. 44:10). Many were led astray by false prophets (Jer. 23:32; Ezek. 13:10).

We can create a composite picture of sin from these Old Testament examples and teachings. Sin involves straying from God's path and missing the mark of His righteousness. Sin can be called rebellion, transgression, opposing God, and nonconformity to God's character or laws.

The New Testament teaching about sin builds directly on what the Old Testament says. First-century Jews knew what the Law and the Prophets declared about sin and its consequences. That is why the announcement by John the Baptist about Jesus was both timely and significant. John identified

Jesus as "the Lamb of God who takes away the sin of the world" (John 1:29). The singular word *sin* emphasizes the inherent sin nature of humankind rather than the sinful acts of individual people. Jesus came to deliver us from our sinful state and to give us eternal life (3:16).

We can learn a great deal about sin from what Jesus taught and from the way He treated sinners. Jesus taught that sin is "missing the mark" (Matt. 5:30; 26:28; John 8:21, 24). He regarded sin as "evil," namely something morally corrupt (Matt. 5:11; Luke 6:45; John 5:29). He treated sin as unrighteousness (Matt. 5:45); "lawlessness" or hostility toward God (1 John 3:4); and "transgression" or deviation from the truth (Mark 11:25, NASB; Matt. 6:14–15). The rest of the Bible leaves no doubt about the universality of sin (Eccl. 7:20; Rom. 3:23; 5:12). Jesus affirmed this too when He said sin comes from within and resides in the heart (Matt. 15:19; Mark 7:20–23). Jesus taught that sin results in condemnation (John 5:29; 3:18) and death (8:24; Rom. 6:23). Before He was crucified He explained that His death would be for the forgiveness of sins (Matt. 26:28).

The Epistles amplify the teachings of Christ and of the Old Testament concerning sin. In Romans 1—3 Paul skillfully developed an argument that proves both Gentiles and Jews are all condemned by sin. He cited numerous Old Testament passages to substantiate his charges (3:9–18). Paul reasoned that only the death and resurrection of Christ could break the power of sin in the lives of those who believe in Him (6:5–14). In Christ we have been set free from the penalty and power of sin to serve righteousness (6:18). The Law could never deliver anyone from sin. In fact the Law only made us more aware of sin's presence and power to bind us (7:7–8, 13).

Paul was convinced that sin in our lives is destructive and will keep us from living for Christ. Most of his Epistles address this issue in some detail. Sin affects the way we treat each other (Rom. 12:17, 21; 14:6, 23). It is the reason we get a bad attitude toward governing authorities (13:4), Sin diverts our attention from the real purpose of our Christian life (15:11–14). Sin in the church displeases the Lord and we need to remove it (1 Cor. 5:13). If we bring a sinful attitude into worship, we may experience personal discipline from God (11:27–32). Sin can destroy both our freedom in Christ (Gal. 5:13) and the unity of believers (Eph. 4:1–6). Sin hinders our walk with the Lord (Col. 3:5–10). It corrupts our personal purity (1 Thess. 4:3–8); and causes greed and hunger for power to take root in our hearts (1 Tim. 6:10).

Because of all these individual and corporate problems caused by sin, Paul issued several exhortations about it.

S

Flee from sin, put off every form of evil, and pursue righteousness (Col. 3:5–11; 1 Tim. 6:11; 2 Tim. 2:22). Study and apply the Scriptures, because they provide training in righteousness (3:16). Put on the total armor God has provided (Eph. 6:11–18; 1 Thess. 5:8). Live under the control of the Holy Spirit and put on all the gracious qualities He wants to produce in you (Rom. 8:9; Gal. 5:16, 22–23; Col. 3:12). Follow the example of godly leaders (Phil. 3:17–19). Consider yourself dead to sin but alive to God (Rom. 6:11), and yield your body to the Lord as an instrument of righteousness (6:13).

James echoed many of the teachings of his half-brother Jesus about sin. He emphasized that sins of the tongue corrupt the whole person (James 3:6), bring disunity to the church (4:1–2), cause Christians to slander one another (4:11–12), and even cause physical sickness (5:14–16). Peter exposed the sinful practices of false teachers and pointed out their devastating effect on the church (2 Pet. 2:1–22). The apostle John explained how sin affects our fellowship with a holy and righteous God (1 John 1:5–6). We must confess our individual sins because God "is faithful and just to forgive us our sins" in response to confession (1:9). John declared that genuine believers are not characterized by sin. Persistent, characteristic sin distinguishes the unrighteous from the righteous (3:7–10). John called sin lawlessness, and said we who are indwelt by Christ should not continue to sin in a lawless manner (3:4–6). When Christ returns to the earth, He will triumph over sin, Satan, and death (Rev. 20:1–15). God promises that in the city of God there will be no more death or evil or anything impure (21:4, 8, 27).

—WGJ

***

Keep in mind that sin does not have to enslave Christians because of the many God-given provisions and promises.

SLEEP

The word "sleep" describes the normal periodic state of suspended consciousness during which the human body rests and restores its powers. Most passages in the Bible that mention "sleep" refer to this normal physical activity. However, "sleep" readily suggests some metaphorical uses. The context of a given Bible passage makes clear whether the term is used in a normal or a figurative sense.

The Scriptures often use the imagery of sleep to convey the concept of death. *Sleep* as a metaphor for death must not be confused with the expression "soul sleep." Some theologians believe that the souls of dead people currently are unconscious until the resurrection of their bodies. They call this "soul sleep." However, the Bible clearly depicts the consciousness of those who die (Luke 23:43; 2 Cor. 5:8; Phil. 1:23). When the Bible uses *sleep* as a metaphor for death, it imagines the body waiting for the resurrection when it will be "awakened."

When King David died, he "slept with his fathers" (1 Kin. 2:10, NASB). The Bible uses the same language in reference to Solomon (11:43, NASB) and other kings. Job used the word *sleep* when he talked about death (Job 14:12). David called out to God for deliverance; otherwise, he said, he would "sleep in death" (Ps. 13:3). Moses declared that God would "sweep men away in the sleep of death" (90:5), and Jeremiah described the wicked as sleeping (Jer. 51:39, 57).

The New Testament also uses the metaphor of sleep to describe death. Jesus said that Jarius's daughter, who had died, was asleep (Matt. 9:24), and the Lord told His disciples that Lazarus, who had died, had fallen asleep (John 11:11). Luke wrote that Stephen, the first Christian martyr, "fell asleep" (Acts 7:60). Paul stated that Christians who were dead had "fallen asleep" (1 Cor. 11:30). Peter mentioned that scoffers doubted the Lord would keep His promise to return because their ancestors had already fallen asleep (2 Pet. 3:4, NASB).

When Paul discussed the resurrection, He used the term *sleep* to describe Christians who had died (1 Cor. 15:18, 20, 51). He also called those who had fallen asleep (1 Thess. 4:13–15) "the dead in Christ" (4:16). Paul told the Corinthians that not every Christian will sleep (die). The bodies of those who are alive when Christ returns will be changed to match the resurrection bodies of those who were asleep in Christ (1 Cor. 15:51–52). First Thessalonians 4:13–18 calls this event a "catching up" (the Rapture) of believers. It includes both those who had fallen asleep in Christ and those who will be alive at that time. No teaching in the Bible provides greater hope to Christians, especially those of us who have lost loved ones.

The Bible uses *sleep* to refer to other conditions than death. Sometimes God put people in trance-like states. The Bible says they fell into a "deep sleep." This happened to Adam (Gen. 2:21), Abraham (15:12), Jacob (28:12), and others. While these people were in "deep sleep" God did something special or sent a revelatory vision.

The term *sleep* occasionally functioned in the Bible as a euphemism for sexual relations (16:2; 30:3, 15; 38:16). Solomon also used the word to describe lazy people who would not work (Prov. 6:9–11). On one occasion a psalmist tried to rouse God from sleep because it seemed to him that the Lord

S

had hidden His face from him (Ps. 44:23–24).

Paul compared spiritual indifference to sleep. He then issued a "wake-up call" urging us to be spiritually alert (Rom. 13:11) and to put off sin (13:12–14). He also charged that spiritually ignorant believers were "asleep" (1 Thess. 5:6–7), unconscious of the darkness surrounding them (5:4–5). —**WGJ**

* * *

*Rejoice in the hope that all who
have died in Christ are asleep
in Jesus and will be
awakened to take part
in the resurrection.*

SOUL AND SPIRIT

We are considering these two words together because it's difficult to tell whether they mean different things or the same thing in the Bible. Some think *soul* and *spirit* both identify the immaterial part of human nature. Others think *soul* and *spirit* are separate parts of our immaterial being. The word *soul* translates *nepeš* (Hebrew) and *psychē* (Greek), and the word *spirit* translates *rûaḥ* (Hebrew) and *pneuma* (Greek). The Hebrew and Greek words for "spirit" also mean "air," "breath," and "wind."

People have a material component— a body—and an immaterial component. "The LORD God formed man from the dust of the ground and breathed into his nostrils the breath of life, and the man became a living being [literally, 'a living soul']" (Gen. 2:7). We are aware of our body. We sense the function of our immaterial nature (our conscience, mind, and will). But we don't sense a distinction between our soul and our spirit. Does this mean there is no distinction? Not necessarily. Let's examine the biblical evidence.

Scripture sometimes assigns the same qualities and the same actions to both soul and spirit. In parallel lines, Job spoke of "the anguish of my spirit" and "the bitterness of my soul" (Job 7:11). David wrote, "My soul is in anguish" (Ps. 6:3), but Asaph described his spirit as "embittered" (73:21). The pharaoh's "mind [literally, 'spirit'] was troubled" (Gen. 41:8), but the psalmist wrote, "My soul is downcast within me" (Ps. 42:6). Jesus said that He came "to give his life [literally, 'soul'] as a ransom for many" (Matt. 20:28), but Matthew wrote that Jesus "gave up his spirit" (27:50; see also Luke 23:46; John 19:30). Jesus said, "Now my heart [literally, 'soul'] is troubled" (John 12:27), but John reported that "Jesus was troubled in spirit" (13:21). References such as these suggest the words *soul* and *spirit* are interchangeable references to the immaterial nature of man.

Other Scripture verses, particularly in the Pauline Epistles, distinguish soul and spirit. Paul prayed for the Thessalonian believers, "May your whole spirit, soul and body be kept blameless at the coming of our Lord Jesus Christ" (1 Thess. 5:23). In 1 Corinthians 2:14—3:3 he wrote of the fleshly man, the soulish man, and the spiritual man, with apparent distinctions between them. Similarly in 15:44–47, he drew a distinction between "a natural [literally, 'soulish'] body" and "a spiritual body." Hebrews 4:12 states that "the word of God is living and active. Sharper than any double-edged sword, it penetrates even to dividing soul and spirit." Such passages make a distinction between soul and spirit.

On this basis many Bible students theorize a three-part structure to human nature (body, soul, and spirit). This model makes human nature a trichotomy instead of a dichotomy (material and immaterial aspects). Other theologians, however, point out that the Scriptures also speak of the human heart (Gen. 6:5; 1 Sam. 1:13; Ps. 111:1, Matt. 5:8), conscience (Gen. 20:6; Job 27:6; 1 Cor. 4:4; 1 Pet. 3:16), and mind (Deut. 28:28, 65; Ps. 26:2; Matt. 22:37; 2 Cor. 2:13) as important aspects of our being. No one, however, suggests that the immaterial part of people consists of five parts—soul, spirit, heart, conscience, and mind—as if they were all distinguishable. As a result many Bible students accept the twofold division (material and immaterial).

Both dichotomists and trichotomists recognize some kind of distinction between the words *soul* and *spirit* in many Scripture texts. The Bible tends to prefer *soul* when speaking of our immaterial nature in relation to creation (Job 33:22; Ps. 63:5; Prov. 2:10; 19:8) and other people (Job 30:25; Prov. 22:5). It tends to prefer *spirit* when speaking of our immaterial nature in relation to God (Ps. 51:10; Prov. 20:27; John 4:23) and to spiritual things (Ps. 31:5; Rom. 8:10; 1 Cor. 5:5). As a matter of statistical fact, the word *soul* occurs more frequently in the Old Testament, while the word *spirit* is used more frequently in the New Testament. In conclusion, it seems better to consider ourselves dichotomous, while keeping in mind that *soul* and *spirit* can describe different functions of our immaterial nature.   **—JAW**

* * *

Determine to serve God with your whole being, whether or not you can distinguish between your soul and spirit.

SPIRITUAL GIFTS

On the Day of Pentecost God launched a movement that has grown from a handful of frightened Galileans to a worldwide church encompassing millions of people. From heaven the risen Christ has given gifts and gifted people to stimulate the growth of His church. These gifts have played a major role in God's strategy to call out a people who would glorify His name (1 Pet. 2:9–10).

Four primary New Testament passages discuss the gifts of the Spirit: Romans 12:3–8; 1 Corinthians 12—14; Ephesians 4:7–13; and 1 Peter 4:10–11. In 1 Corinthians 12—14 Paul corrected the misuse of gifts by providing guidelines the Corinthian Christians could follow to use their gifts effectively. In Romans 12:3–8 Paul explained how the gifts are to be exercised. Ephesians 4:7–13 focuses on the people who receive gifts. First Peter 4:10–11 exhorts us to use gifts of speaking and serving in a manner that glorifies God.

These four Scripture passages do not describe the various gifts in detail, nor do they define the expression *spiritual gift*. But it is clear that spiritual gifts refer to abilities that go beyond our natural capacities. In the church, however, every believer has been given a spiritual gift (a supernatural enabling or ability) so that everyone in the body of Christ can participate in the Lord's work in a particular way (1 Cor. 12:7, 11).

The spiritual gifts of the New Testament are distinct from the gifts God gave people in earlier times. In Old Testament times the Lord gave gifts to a small number of people to accom-plish tasks of limited duration. He gave some people wisdom and skill to prepare garments for the priests (Ex. 28:3). He gave Bezalel and Oholiab wisdom and ability in all kinds of crafts so they could teach others to do the work on the tabernacle according to God's standards (31:3–6; 35:30–35; 36:1–2).

The Holy Spirit gives spiritual gifts to build up and serve the church, the body of Christ (Eph. 4:12; 1 Pet. 4:10). The Spirit sovereignly decides how to distribute these gifts (1 Cor. 12:4–6). The complexity of the human body illustrates the diversity of gifts (12:12–27). The human body analogy suggests each of us has a primary function in the body of Christ (12:27). Of course, we may have other talents apart from our spiritual gifts.

Since gifts are given sovereignly by God's Spirit at salvation (12:11), our desires are not the reason we receive a particular gift. Paul did say, "But eagerly desire the greater gifts" (12:31). However, the word "desire" is a plural verb and may be a command. This means the church *as a whole* should be more concerned about the greater gifts—apostles, prophets, teachers—because people with those gifts minister to the entire church. Some Corinthians were wanting the attention-getting spiritual gifts but should not have been doing so. The whole church should have been desiring the gifts that would benefit everyone and not the gifts that would benefit just a few people.

When Paul suggested that those speaking in tongues pray for ability to interpret the tongues, he was not saying they should pray for the "gift" of interpretation (14:13). He was saying they should ask for God's help in the same way they would ask for His assistance in preaching, teaching, witnessing, or giving. Praying to receive a particular spiritual gift has no biblical support. Paul wanted the Corinthians to stop exalting the more spectacular gifts. He prioritized the gifts in 1 Corinthians 12:27–28 to help the Corinthians get them back in proper perspective.

Some spiritual gifts served a foundational function, such as the gifts of apostles and prophets (Eph. 2:20). These gifts involved receiving direct revelation from the Lord for the whole church. We don't reproduce the foundation of the church now. We build on that foundation. Such foundational gifts were no longer needed after the church was established.

The four lists of spiritual gifts in the New Testament are not identical. This suggests that these are representative lists and not exhaustive catalogs of all possible gifts. If there were particular gifts necessary for the founding of the church, could not other specific gifts be needed at various times in the history of the church? God's sovereignty may dictate that some gifts cease, and new gifts appear to accomplish His purposes and plans for His church.

Some people at Corinth misused, copied, or counterfeited a few spiritual gifts (1 Cor. 12:1–3). That's why Paul wrote extensively to them about the gift of tongues. Understandably the gift of tongues might exhilarate the one who used it. However, the gifts were to edify the whole congregation and not just the individual (14:4, 12, 13–17, 19). The gift of tongues brought "some revelation or knowledge or prophecy or word of instruction" (14:6) to the church. It's reasonable to question whether this gift existed beyond the first century, since biblical revelation ceased when John wrote Revelation, the last book of the New Testament. Paul's personal illustration about discarding childish things as he grew to manhood suggests that some gifts would not be necessary once the church passed its infancy (13:8–11) and reached "perfection" (13:10). Here as elsewhere Paul used the word *perfect* (Greek, *teleion*) to mean "mature" (Eph. 4:13; Phil. 3:12, 15).

Spiritual gifts are important to the church. We need to serve others and glorify the Lord by exercising our gifts. The presence of gifted people who do God's work by His grace distinguishes the church from other merely social

S

or civic groups (1 Cor. 1:7). Congregational leadership should help church members discern their gifts. Timothy provides us a good example of this. The elders and Paul recognized that Timothy had the pastoral gift, so they ordained him for the work of the Lord (1 Tim. 4:14; 2 Tim. 1:6). If you are not sure what your spiritual gift might be, engage in various church ministries. People often discover their gifts by that process.   **—WGJ**

* * *

Realize God has graciously gifted you, and seek opportunities to serve Him.

SPIRITUALITY

Being a Christian and being truly spiritual are not the same thing, although salvation and spirituality share a common starting point. Every relationship with God begins with salvation, or what the Bible calls the new birth (John 3:3). Even in the Old Testament, saints were those who believed God and had a relationship with Him through the Holy Spirit. The Holy Spirit did not indwell Old Testament saints, but His presence still formed the basis for a close walk with the Lord (Ps. 51:10–12). New Testament spirituality involves walking in the Spirit so that He bears fruit in our lives and conforms our character to the image of Christ.

We can learn about spirituality by examining what the apostle Paul had to say about the spiritual person in 1 Corinthians 2:11–16. Paul taught that we cannot understand the things of God unless we possesses the Spirit of God. In fact, spiritual truths appear to be foolishness to an unregenerate person (2:14). True spirituality begins with salvation through faith in Christ and develops through the ministry of the indwelling Holy Spirit. Spirituality should distinguish those of us who are Christians from those who are not.

Since every redeemed person has a relationship with the Spirit, does this mean we are all spiritual? No. Some Christians are not spiritual (3:1). Spirituality results from cooperating with the Holy Spirit as He transforms our character through sanctification.

The Holy Spirit develops discernment in the hearts and minds of spiritual believers (2:15–16). As we submit our lives to the Word of Goad and the Spirit of God, the Spirit fills us to serve Christ (Eph. 5:18). The indwelling and filling of the Spirit enables us to know the mind of Christ (1 Cor. 2:16). When we make decisions, the Spirit gives us wisdom and discernment that reflect the Lord's mind.

The indwelling Holy Spirit helps us make decisions that please the Lord. This does not happen automatically, nor does it mean that every decision or judgment we make will always be what the Spirit desires. But when the

Holy Spirit controls our thoughts and actions, we live more consistently within the boundaries of the will of God, and the fruit of the Spirit more regularly characterizes our lives (Gal. 5:22–23).

When we fail to let the Spirit guide our thoughts, either because of neglect or disregard for His presence, we act just like people without Christ. That's what the Corinthians Christians did. They did not reflect the qualities of the Spirit. They behaved in a "worldly" manner, just as infant Christians might, but not as mature believers should (1 Cor. 3:1). As a result their church divided into special interest groups led by strong personalities with private agendas (3:4).

Paul compared the nonspiritual Corinthians to babies who had not grown. Spirituality can only result from a process of growth under the control of the Holy Spirit. New believers often make proper decisions when they yield to the Spirit, but sheer inexperience limits their capacity for deep spirituality. They aren't ready for the rugged challenges they will face later in their Christian experiences. Spirituality results from intentional, disciplined pursuit of knowledge of God's Word and obedience to God's Spirit.

Peter gave us insight into the process that leads to spirituality when he exhorted us to rid ourselves of everything malicious and devote ourselves to growth in holiness (1 Pet. 2:1–2). He emphasized the role of the Word of God, which he called "spiritual milk" (2:2). The Scriptures provide the foundation for our spirituality. We can live like Christ only as we meet the challenges of everyday life as He did. He is our example to follow (2:21).

Paul added another image to our growing picture of spirituality by comparing the Christian life to a journey. He had a destination in mind, and he wanted to make progress along the way. He wanted to know Christ (Phil. 3:12). Knowing Christ was not an intellectual process to Paul. He hurried down the road toward the destination of being like Him (3:14). If we are "spiritual," we too will set out down the road toward being like Christ in every way.

We've seen several truths so far. Christ sets the standard for spirituality. We set out to be like Him. We know that only the indwelling Holy Spirit can conform us to His image. How will spirituality express itself in our lives? Spiritual people love God and others in the body of Christ without reservation. They even love their enemies (Rom. 12:9, 20–21). Spiritual people want to study and obey the Word of God (2 Tim. 2:15; 3:14–17; Heb. 4:12; 5:11–14; 1 Pet. 2:2). They want to worship God privately and with other believers (Heb. 10:22–25). Spirituality unites families and produces harmonious homes

S

(Eph. 5:22—6:4; 1 Pet. 3:3–7). Spiritual people make good citizens who respect civil authority and promote peace (1 Pet. 2:13–17). Spiritual people respond to persecution and hatred as Jesus did (3:13–17).

The Bible emphasizes the positive traits of spirituality, but it does warn us against worldliness. If we want to walk in the Spirit, we must develop His loathing of sinful desires (Gal. 5:16–21). Paul warned us to put off sinful desires that characterize life apart from the Spirit (Eph. 4:22). He went so far as to tell us to put to death whatever relates to evil desires and sexual immorality (Col. 3:5; see also 1 Pet. 4:2–3). Sometimes we have to flee the kinds of temptations that can entangle us and trap us, such as the love of money (1 Tim. 6:11) and sexual immorality (1 Cor. 6:18). We need to reject emphatically ungodliness of every kind (Titus 2:11).

Usually a corresponding list of positive actions accompanies these lists of negative aspects of spirituality. Don't think of spirituality simply as things you don't do. Think of spirituality as the glorious result of the Spirit's work to make you like Christ.   **—WGJ**

***

Ask the Spirit of God to reproduce in you the beautiful qualities of Christ that will make you a truly spiritual person.

STEWARDSHIP

Responsibility and accountability have been integral parts of human experience since God created the world. God gave Adam and Eve authority to subdue the earth and rule over it (Gen. 1:28). He gave our first parents and all their descendants responsibility to manage the physical resources of the earth. He gave us this authority because He made us in His image. Everything belongs to God (Ps. 24:1). We are not owners. We are stewards accountable to God.

Jesus taught several principles of good stewardship in an unusual parable starring a crooked estate manager (Luke 16:1–13). Jesus concluded that we should use worldly wealth (money) to accomplish eternal results (16:9). In contrast to the steward in the story, the quantity of our possessions is less important than the quality of our character. If we prove faithful in handling little responsibilities, God will trust us with bigger ones (16:10; 19:11–27). For reasons like these, Jesus on another occasion said the widow who put two small copper coins in the temple treasury gave more than anyone else. She gave out of her poverty and from her heart (21:1–4). God often gauges our readiness to handle spiritual responsibility by how we use our money and possessions (16:11). God holds us accountable for how we handle everything He has entrusted to us (16:13).

Paul identified faithfulness as the hallmark of a good steward (1 Cor. 4:1–2). The New International Version interprets the word *steward* in this passage with the phrase "those who have been given a trust." Good stewardship is not restricted to how we manage our material possessions. Paul said the message of the gospel was a trust committed to him, and he felt compelled to proclaim it (9:15–18). Paul tried to be a good steward of the revelation God gave him about the development of the church, the body of Christ (Eph. 3:2–6). He felt a stewardship responsibility to preach the Word of God in its fullness (Col. 1:25). Paul wrote his second letter to the Corinthian church about giving an offering to the poverty-stricken church at Jerusalem. In it he concluded that we should give generously to those in need because of how generously God has poured His grace on us (2 Cor. 9:6–11).

Peter urged us to be good stewards of the spiritual gifts God has given us (1 Pet. 4:10, NASB). God has given each of us gifts, and He expects us to exercise these gifts to serve others (4:11).

In today's society we focus almost exclusively on our stewardship of earthly possessions. That is a very important subject, but we must not lose sight of what the New Testament emphasizes—the stewardship of our spiritual responsibilities. **—WGJ**

***

*Make a covenant with the Lord
to give generously of the
resources He has given you;
plan to spend time each
week in some ministry
for Christ.*

SUBSTITUTION

When Jesus Christ was nailed to the cross at Calvary, a transaction took place between the Father and the Son that we have struggled ever since to describe. The death of Christ is unique in history. He did not deserve to die, because He had no sin of His own (2 Cor. 5:21). God had planned Jesus' death in eternity past (Is. 53:10; Eph. 1:8–9; 1 Pet. 1:18–20, NASB). He died in the place of every person in the world. He was our substitute. He died for every sinner, so that everyone who believes in Him receives eternal salvation and will not come under condemnation (Rom. 8:1).

The substitutionary death of Christ is well-documented in the Bible. Jesus Himself taught that His death was substitutional. He said He gave His life "a ransom for many" (Matt. 20:28; Mark 10:45). The Greek preposition *anti,* translated "for," means "in the place of." When Caiaphas, the high priest, referred to one man dying "for the people" (John 11:50), he unknowingly spoke of Jesus' substitutionary death (11:51).

Paul's epistles teach that Christ's death was substitutional. When he wrote that Christ "died for all" (2 Cor. 5:14–15), he used the preposition *hyper. Hyper* conveys not only the idea of "on behalf of" but also "in place of." In Galatians 3:13 Paul stated that believers have been redeemed from the curse of the Law because Christ became a curse "for" (*hyper*) them. Paul also wrote that Jesus "gave himself as a ransom [*antilytron*, literally, 'a ransom in place of'] for [*hyper*] all men" (1 Tim. 2:6). The writer of Hebrews wrote that Jesus experienced "death for [*hyper*] everyone" (Heb. 2:9). Peter also taught the substitutionary atonement of Christ when he wrote that "Christ died for sins once for all, the righteous for [*hyper*] the unrighteous" (1 Pet. 3:18).

The Old Testament supports the doctrine of a substitutionary death. The sacrificial system under the Law of Moses required the death of an animal when an Israelite sinned unintentionally (Lev. 4:4–5). The slain animal took the place of the offender. Though these substitutionary deaths could not remove sin permanently, they did satisfy the demands of our holy God until Christ offered Himself as the once-for-all Sacrifice for the sins of the world (Heb. 10:11–14).   **—WGJ**

***

Accept the truth that Jesus Christ died in your place, and rejoice in the realization that God is pleased with the sacrifice of His Son.

SUFFERING

Every form of suffering—physical, emotional, mental, psychological, and spiritual—entered human experience when Adam and Eve sinned in the Garden of Eden. God had commanded Adam not to "eat from the tree of the knowledge of good and evil" (Gen. 2:17). He warned him that if he ate he would "surely die." A consequence of sin for women is the excruciating pain of childbirth (3:16). A consequence of sin for men is the constant "painful toil" necessary to coax a living out of the ground (3:17). Whether that living comes from a farm, a factory, or an office, it requires "the sweat of your brow" (3:19). In the final analysis all suffering, even the suffering of Jesus Christ, springs from that original sin and its punishment.

Like Adam and Eve, many people bring suffering on themselves, either in the form of natural consequences of their actions or in the form of God's judgment on them. Solomon warned his son against drunkenness and gluttony, saying, "Drunkards and gluttons become poor, and drowsiness clothes them in rags" (Prov. 23:21, see also

23:29–30). He also observed that "a companion of fools suffers harm" (13:20) and that "the simple keep going" in the face of danger "and suffer for it" (22:3; 27:12). Likewise, "Laziness brings on deep sleep, and the shiftless man goes hungry" (19:15); and the stingy person, who "withholds unduly . . . comes to poverty" (11:24).

Suffering can result from punishment by God for refusing to trust Him or for rebelling against Him. Israel suffered in the wilderness for refusing to enter the land (Num. 14:34–35). Later generations (14:33) during the times of the judges failed to drive out the Canaanites (Judg. 2:10–19). Eventually both the northern kingdom of Israel and the southern kingdom of Judah suffered conquest and captivity because of their idolatry (Lam. 1:12, 18). Concerning those who break His commandments, God said, "I will punish their sin with the rod" (Ps. 89:32). Paul wrote about the sexually immoral: "The Lord will punish men for all such sins" (1 Thess. 4:6).

Through the ages many people have jumped to the conclusion that all suffering is punishment from God for sin. Job's friends thought this about his suffering (Job 4:7–8, 17; 8:3–4). The disciples assumed that either the "man blind from birth" or his parents had sinned (John 9:1–2). Job, however, suffered at the hands of Satan to prove he didn't serve the Lord simply because God blessed him so much (Job 1:8–12; 2:3–6). While Job suffered, no one could possibly have known that. Jesus told his disciples that the blind man suffered "so that the work of God might be displayed in his life" (John 9:3). We usually have no idea what someone's suffering means.

Because of the sin of Adam, we all, as Eliphaz said, are "born to trouble as surely as sparks fly upward" (Job 5:7). Christian should never think they are exempt from suffering. Suffering can be punishment for sin or God's way of getting our attention so we respond to Him. Suffering can be a method God uses to prepare us for life (Heb. 12:4–12), or suffering may be the only way He can prepare us for special spiritual service. God may permit suffering to come through a direct attack by Satan or an indirect attack through his human agents. Whatever the case, we can glorify God by enduring our suffering faithfully in reliance on God's Spirit and strength.

The Lord Jesus Christ gives us the supreme example of faithfully enduring suffering to the glory of God. He "endured . . . opposition from sinful men" (Heb. 12:3). Jesus told the disciples that "he must go to Jerusalem and suffer many things . . . and that he must be killed" (Matt. 16:21; see also 17:12). His physical suffering climaxed in His death on the cross of Calvary (27:33–44).

S

Excruciating as it was, Jesus' physical suffering on the cross paled in comparison to His spiritual suffering. "God made him who had no sin to be sin for us" (2 Cor. 5:21; see also Rom. 4:25; 8:3; Gal. 3:13). Jesus agonized because of the sins of every person of all times to be the substitutionary Sacrifice for our sins. Jesus' prayer in the Garden of Gethsemane shows His anticipation of this spiritual suffering (Matt. 26:37–39, 42). His loud cry *Eloi, Eloi, lama sabachthani?*—which means, "My God, my God, why have you forsaken me?" (27:46)—sprang from the depths of that suffering. The darkness "from the sixth hour until the ninth hour . . . over all the land" (27:45) indicates the Father's response to His Son's suffering.

We are called on to share in the sufferings of Christ. Paul wrote, "I fill up . . . what is still lacking in regard to Christ's afflictions, for the sake of his body, which is the church" (Col. 1:24). Since all of us are members of Christ's body, the church (Rom. 12:5; 1 Cor. 12:12–13, 27), when "one part suffers, every part suffers with it" (12:26). Paul also wrote that "the sufferings of Christ flow over into our lives . . . which produces in you patient endurance of the same sufferings we suffer" (2 Cor. 1:5–6).

Peter pointed out that there is nothing particularly commendable about enduring punishment that is deserved. But he wrote, "If you suffer for doing good and you endure it, this is commendable before God. To this you were called, because Christ suffered for you, leaving you an example, that you should follow in his steps" (1 Pet. 2:20–23). Later he wrote, "But even if you should suffer for what is right, you are blessed. . . . It is better, if it is God's will, to suffer for doing good than for doing evil" (3:14, 17).

—**JAW**

***

*Through prayer and
self-examination seek God's
purpose in any suffering
you experience.*

Tt

TABERNACLE

The tabernacle was a portable shrine made of wood, cloth, skins, and precious metals where God met with the Israelites after the Exodus from Egypt. The Egyptians had worshiped at many sanctuaries or temples, whose remains can be seen at Karnak, Luxor, and other places. God instructed Israel to build only one worship center, the tabernacle, and later the temple. Scripture reveals four purposes for the tabernacle: (1) It provided a way for God to dwell in the midst of His people (Ex. 25:8). (2) It provided a way whereby God could reveal His glory (40:34–35). (3) It made it possible for a sinful people to approach a holy God. (4) It provided a picture of our redemption in Christ. According to Hebrews 8—10 the tabernacle illustrated both the earthly and heavenly ministries of Christ. Christ therefore is the fulfillment of all that the tabernacle prophesied by means of its furniture, priests, altar, and sacrifices.

The Old Testament refers to three tent structures used for sacred purposes that can be called tabernacles. (1) The provisional tabernacle erected by Moses outside the camp after the sin of the golden calf. It was called the "tabernacle of meeting" (Ex. 33:7, NKJV). There God met and talked with Moses. (2) The Mosaic tabernacle built according to detailed instructions the Lord gave Moses (Ex. 25—27; 30—31; 35—40; Num. 3—4; 7). (3) The Davidic tabernacle (2 Sam. 6:17, NKJV) erected by David in Jerusalem to house the ark of the covenant (6:12) until the temple was built.

The ground plan of the Mosaic tabernacle consisted of an outer court and the tabernacle itself. The court was formed by curtains hung from pillars that attached to bronze bases. The altar of burnt offering stood in the court inside the entrance gate (Ex. 27:1–8) to remind worshipers that sacrifice was an absolute requirement

for approaching God. The court also contained the bronze laver (30:13–21) where priests washed their hands and feet after offering sacrifices and before entering the holy place. As the psalmist later declared, clean hands and a pure heart are essential to draw near to God (Ps. 24:3–4).

The tabernacle proper stood within the court. It consisted of curtains draped over a framework (Ex. 26). The interior of the tabernacle contained two compartments, the Holy Place and the Most Holy Place. A veil divided the Most Holy Place from the Holy Place. The veil symbolized the barrier that separates sinners from God.

The Holy Place, which only the priests could enter, contained three pieces of furniture. The altar of incense stood before the veil (Ex. 30:1–7). Priests offered incense every morning and evening to symbolize prayers ascending to God at the beginning and end of each day. To one side of the Holy Place stood a table on which priests placed twelve loaves of showbread, called "bread of the Presence" (25:23–30). The priests ate and replaced the bread once a week to thank God for sustaining Israel's life. On the other side of the Holy Place stood the golden lampstand (25:31–40) that provided light for the priests to serve in the windowless room. It represented Israel as God's channel of light in the world (Zech. 4).

The only piece of furniture in the

Most Holy Place was the boxlike ark of the covenant (Ex. 25:10–15). The ark contained a jar of manna, Aaron's rod, and the stone tablets on which God had written the Ten Commandments (25:16). They represented the whole Mosaic Covenant God had made with Israel. A lid of solid gold, called the atonement cover, the mercy seat, or the propitiatory, covered the ark and its contents. On the Day of Atonement the high priest sprinkled blood on the mercy seat. The high priest in his annual visit was the only person in Israel who ever entered the Most Holy Place (Lev. 16:11–17). God's Shekinah glory rested between two crafted cherubim on the ends of the blood-sprinkled lid (Ex. 25:22; 40:34–35; Lev. 16:2). The blood of those sacrifices made it possible for God to dwell with His people.

Moses and the Levites erected the tabernacle for the first time at Mount Sinai on the anniversary of the Exodus (Ex. 40:2, 17). When Israel left Sinai and journeyed toward Canaan, they followed the ark of the covenant which led the people on the next stage of their journey (Num. 10:33–36). For nearly thirty-eight years they wandered in the wilderness, but their headquarters were at Kadesh. After Israel crossed the Jordan River into Canaan, Joshua temporarily set up the tabernacle at Gilgal, army headquarters during the conquest (Josh. 4:19; 5:10; 9:6; 10:6, 43). Eventually Shiloh in Ephraim was selected as the permanent location for the tabernacle. Shiloh's central location made it convenient for the men to attend the three annual pilgrimage feasts (18:1). During the time of the judges, the Philistines captured the ark in battle and destroyed Shiloh (1 Sam. 4). The Philistines soon returned the ark, which stayed at Kiriath Jearim for several years (6:21—7:1). At various times the tabernacle was located at Nob (21:1–6) and Gibeon (1 Chr. 16:39; 21:29). When David captured Jerusalem, he erected a tabernacle and brought the ark from Kiriath Jearim (2 Sam. 6:17; 1 Chr. 16:1). So for a time there were two tabernacles, one in Gibeon and one in Jerusalem. The original tabernacle and altar were ultimately transported six miles from Gibeon to Jerusalem and kept in the temple as a relic (1 Kin. 8:4). The tabernacle, according to 1 Kings 6:1, served as Israel's center of worship for nearly five hundred years.

As noted earlier, the tabernacle in both its furnishings and priestly ritual foreshadowed Christ in both His earthly and heavenly spheres of ministry. The brazen altar pictured the Cross of Christ on which He offered Himself without spot to God (Eph. 5:2). The laver represented Christ cleansing the believer from sin's defilement (John 13:2–10). The golden lampstand spoke of Christ as our Light, the One who enlightens our hearts and enables us to carry His light to a dark world (1:9; 8:12; Eph. 5:8). The showbread or bread of presence pictured Christ as He nourishes and sustains His believer-priests (1 Pet. 2:9; Rev. 1:6). The manna represented the life-giving Christ; the showbread stood for the life-sustaining Christ. The altar of incense represented Christ as the believer's Intercessor (John 17; Heb. 7:25). The veil that separated the Holy Place from the Most Holy Place spoke of the human body of Christ given in sacrifice to provide an unobstructed way to God (Matt. 26:26; 27:50; Heb. 10:20). As the Crucifixion drew to an end, the temple veil was supernaturally torn in two. God intervened to declare symbolically that the death of His Son had made possible instant and open access to His presence. The ark of the covenant with its blood-sprinkled mercy seat declared that the throne of judgment has become a throne of grace because of the shed blood of Christ (Heb. 4:14–16; 9:24–26; 10:19–22).

When God directed Moses to build the tabernacle, He started by describing the ark of the covenant in the Most Holy Place (Ex. 25:10–22). God in His grace wants to be among His people. He initiates contact with us. He is the One who reaches out to the

lost on the basis of His sacrifice. On the other hand, when the Israelites wanted to approach God, they had to start at the brazen altar. Sinners always have to start with a sacrifice for sin. For us that sacrifice is Christ, and the altar represents the Cross where atonement for sin was made.

—DKC

***

Study with care the Old Testament tabernacle, since it gives us a picture book of our redemption.

TEMPLE

One of the master strokes of military history was David's capture of Jerusalem, which he turned into the political and religious capital of Israel (2 Sam. 6). There David dreamed of building a worship center for Israel's God, a permanent building of stone to supplant the portable tabernacle. God would not let David build Him a temple because the king had shed a great deal of blood in battle. David did, however, purchase the temple site (24:18–24), collect most of the finances and materials for the project, and draw up the temple plans (1 Chr. 22:3–5, 14; 28:2, 11–19). David credited the Spirit of the Lord with guiding him in all these matters. Yet God committed the task of building the temple to David's son, Solomon.

The temple reproduced the general plan of the tabernacle on a grander scale. All dimensions were doubled, except for the height, which was tripled. The temple walls were built of stone and were overlaid with gold on the inside (1 Kin. 6:22). The veil between the Most Holy Place and the Holy Place was replaced with a double door of olive wood whose carvings were covered with gold (6:31–32). The ark of the covenant rested in the Most Holy Place. No idol stood in the sanctuary, which made the temple (and before that, the tabernacle) distinct from the pagan temples of the ancient world. In the Holy Place were ten golden lampstands, five on each side, and ten tables for utensils and accessories, five on each side (2 Chr. 4:8). Also in this room was a table for the "bread of the Presence." On the porch on the front of the building stood two hollow bronze pillars, named Jakin and Boaz (1 Kin. 7:15–22). Freestanding columns of this sort characterized ancient Near Eastern temples.

Two courts ran around the temple, the inner one exclusively for the priests and the outer one, called the "large court," for the use of the general populace (2 Chr. 4:9). The most striking object in the inner court was the molten sea, a huge, round tank of bronze provided for priestly washings (4:2–5). In addition, ten tables and ten lavers for the cutting and washing of the sacrifices occupied the inner court (4:6). The altar of burnt offering, made after the pattern of the altar for the tabernacle, also stood in the inner court (1 Kin. 8:64).

Construction of the temple took seven years and six months (6:37–38; 2 Chr. 3:1). Solomon dedicated the temple with a weeklong ceremony, which climaxed when fire fell from heaven and consumed the burnt offering (6:13—7:1). The Shekinah glory of God filled the temple and signified His approval and acceptance of the temple.

In addition to being Israel's worship center, the temple served as a depository of national wealth. This made the temple a target of foreign attack. Kings of the northern kingdom of Israel also plundered the temple to get funds to buy off oppressors (1 Kin. 14:25–28; 15:16–19; 2 Kin. 12:17–18; 14:8–14; 16:7–9). Temple worship sometimes nearly ceased. Reformer kings such as Joash (2 Kin. 12; 2 Chr. 24:1–16), Hezekiah (2 Kin. 18:1–6), and Josiah (2 Kin. 22—23; 2 Chr. 34) each restored the temple and its rituals. Judah's last king, Zedekiah, rebelled against the Babylonian emperor Nebuchednezzar, who attacked Jerusalem, took the king captive, and burned the city and temple to the ground (586 B.C.). Solomon's temple stood roughly 380 years. Its destruction fulfilled Jeremiah's somber prophecies regarding the destruction of Jerusalem, the temple, and the people on account of their sins (Jer. 25).

When the Jews returned from captivity (538 B.C.), they began erecting what has been called Zerubbabel's temple or the second temple. They quickly rebuilt the altar of sacrifice and reestablished the prescribed pattern of offerings (Ezra 3:1–6). But the initial enthusiasm died, and it was not until 520 B.C. that the prodding of the prophets Haggai and Zechariah got the actual construction under way. It took four years for the exiles to complete and dedicate the restored temple (6:15). The Bible gives a few dimensions of the second temple, but they are incomplete. We really have little idea of this temple's appearance. We assume it occupied the same location and followed the same general plan as the Solomonic temple, though without its splendor.

According to the Jewish Talmud, the rebuilt temple lacked five items that had been part of Solomon's temple: the ark of the covenant, the fire that consumed the initial sacrifices, the Shekinah glory, the Holy Spirit, and the Urim and Thummim. Josephus, a first-century A.D. Jewish historian, stated that the Most Holy Place was empty except for a stone

where the high priest sprinkled the atoning blood on the Day of Atonement. In the Holy Place there were one golden lampstand, one table of showbread, and the altar of incense. In front of the temple building stood an altar of unhewn stones the same size as Solomon's bronze altar (2 Chr. 4:1). In the intertestamental period the Syrian ruler Antiochus Epiphanes (175–164 B.C.) plundered and defiled the temple, but Judas Maccabeus restored and cleansed it. The annual Jewish Feast of Dedication (John 10:22), known today as Hanukkah, memorializes the cleansing of the second temple.

In 37 B.C. Herod gained control of Jerusalem with Roman help. Herod prided himself as a builder, and in about 21 B.C. he began to dismantle the second temple in preparation for the construction of a grand structure that would subsequently be known as Herod's temple. The Bible gives little information about this temple, but Josephus described it in detail. Herod thought he could placate his Jewish subjects by building a sanctuary as magnificent as Solomon's. The new structure had the same dimensions as the first temple and housed the same furniture except that the Most Holy Place was left empty. Four concentric courts surrounded the temple: the inner court for the priests, the next one for Jewish men, the next for Jewish women, and the outer court for interested Gentiles.

Jesus showed respect for the temple and frequently visited it. At age twelve He conversed with the rabbis in the temple courts and called the temple His Father's house (Luke 2:41–50). Twice He cleansed it in righteous indignation (Matt. 21:12–13; John 2:13–16). Jesus wept over the impending destruction of Jerusalem (Luke 19:41–44) and predicted the razing of the temple (Matt. 24:1–2). The Romans fulfilled these prophecies in A.D. 70. The early church used the temple courts for a time after Pentecost as its meeting place (Acts 5:12, 21, 42).

The crucifixion, resurrection, and ascension of Christ rendered the physical temple obsolete. Believers in Christ, indwelt by the Holy Spirit, in this age are each temples of God (1 Cor. 3:16–17; 6:19; 2 Cor. 6:16). The same is true of the body of believers, the church (1 Pet. 2:5; Eph. 2:22).

In the end times, following the rapture of the church, the Jews will build a temple in Jerusalem and restore their ancient sacrifices. The Antichrist, however, will disrupt the Jewish worship and take control of this temple, arrogantly exalting himself as God (Dan. 9:27; 2 Thess. 2:4).

Another temple will be erected in Jerusalem after Christ's return to earth, and during His millennial kingdom this temple will be the center for worship. The millennial temple is described in detail in Ezekiel 40:2—47:2. (See also Is. 11:1–16; 35:1–10; 60:1–22; Zech. 14:8–20.)

The Bible closes with a glorious description of heaven. John had a vision of the "Holy City, the New Jerusalem, coming down out of heaven from God" (Rev. 21:2). He looked in vain for a temple in the New Jerusalem, "because the Lord God Almighty and the Lamb are its temple."   —**DKC**

***

Realize how important it is to treat your body with care, since it is the temple of the Holy Spirit.

TEMPTATION

The Hebrew and Greek words translated *tempt* and *temptation* mean not only enticement of a person to sin but also testing by God of a person's worth and character. The context of a given passage determines which meaning is in view. In James 1:12, for instance, the noun *peirasmos* indicates testing by God, but in 1:13–14 the verb *peirazō* refers to temptation to sin. James specified that temptation comes from our own evil desires, and never from God.

Both the Old and New Testaments make it clear that the ultimate personal source of temptation to sin is Satan. He acted through the serpent to deceive Eve and cause the Fall that leaves all humans in bondage to sin (Gen. 3). When Satan afflicted Job, he demonstrated his role as the accuser of the saints (1:6—2:10). Various New Testament passages note Satan's role as tempter of believers (1 Cor. 7:5; 1 Thess. 3:5; 1 Pet. 5:8–9; Rev. 2:10). We also enter temptation through our love of the world. This includes "the cravings of sinful man, the lust of his eyes and the boasting of what he has and does" (1 John 2:16). Sensuality, covetousness, and pride have seduced even the best of people. Paul warned, "So, if you think you are standing firm, be careful that you don't fall" (1 Cor. 10:12). A third source of temptation, as noted earlier, comes from the desires of our sinful nature. James wrote, "Each one is tempted when, by his own evil desire, he is dragged away and enticed" (James 1:14). Our temptation may come from the devil, from the world, or from our evil desires, but "When tempted, no one should say, 'God is tempting me.' For God cannot be tempted by evil, nor does he tempt anyone" (1:13).

God never tempts, but He does test the reality of our trust in Him. For instance, He tested Abraham (Gen. 22:1), Israel (Ex. 15:25; 16:4), the tribe of Levi (Deut. 33:8), Hezekiah (2 Chr. 32:31), David (Ps. 26:2), and Philip (John 6:5–6). He may test us too (1 Pet. 1:7). We aren't promised exemption from testing, but God does promise

grace and strength to endure it (1 Cor. 10:13; 2 Cor. 12:7–8; 1 Pet. 4:12–16; 2 Pet. 2:9). God doesn't test us in an attempt to break our faith. He tests us for the same purpose an assayer tests ore samples: to reveal the true value of what is being tested.

The Old Testament refers to Israel testing God in the wilderness (Ex. 17:7; Num. 14:22; Ps. 95:8–9). The New Testament says the Pharisees and Sadducees tested Jesus with the hope that He would make self-incriminating statements (Matt. 16:1; 19:3; 22:35; Mark 8:11; 10:2; Luke 20:23). Ananias and Sapphira tested the Holy Spirit by lying (Acts 5:9). Paul admonished the Corinthian believers not to "test the Lord" as Israel had done (1 Cor. 10:9; see Num. 21:4–9). We must not test God in any of these ways.

Christ's temptation by Satan in the wilderness of Judea after His baptism demands special attention. No doubt Jesus experienced temptation throughout His ministry (Luke 4:13), but the crucial temptation is the one described in Matthew 4, Mark 1, and Luke 4. This temptation presents some theologically important questions: (1) Could Jesus Christ sin? (2) If not, could He be tempted? (3) If He couldn't sin, what was the purpose of the temptation?

Theologians debate whether Christ could have sinned. Some argue that Christ *could have sinned* but did not. Others maintain that Christ was able

T

not to sin. Still others declare that Christ was *not able* to sin. To solve this apparent dilemma we must recognize that Christ possessed (and still possesses) both a human and a divine nature. Christ's human nature was not a fallen, sin nature, but He was fully human. His human nature was able to sin (Heb. 4:15). But Christ's human nature never operated apart from His divine nature. He was, however, not a man with a divine nature tacked on. Rather, He was God who took on a human nature at the Incarnation. At that point He became the totally and forever unique God-Man. Christ, the divine-human person, could not sin. A wire is bendable or flexible when it stands alone, but it is absolutely unbendable when welded to a bar of steel.

But if Christ could not sin, could He be tempted? Though difficult to understand, we can answer that question from the details of the Gospel accounts and from the observation by the author of the Book of Hebrews, "We have one who has been tempted in every way, just as we are—yet was without sin" (Heb. 4:15). His temptations were real, but that doesn't mean He was capable of giving in to them. A tugboat may attack a battleship, but that doesn't mean the ship could be sunk by the tugboat.

What possible purpose did Christ's temptations serve if He couldn't sin?

God let His Son suffer temptation, not to see if He would sin, but to demonstrate His sinlessness. In addition, enduring temptation enabled Christ to become "a merciful and faithful high priest." As the writer of Hebrews explained, "Because he himself suffered when he was tempted, he is able to help those who are being tempted" (Heb. 2:17–18).

So the question remains: how should we deal with temptation? The following seven principles can serve as guidelines for this important area of your Christian life. (1) Recognize that temptation may come from the world, the flesh, or the devil (1 John 2:15–17). Temptation is "common to man" (1 Cor. 10:13). (2) Temptation tends to be periodic rather than constant. The lives of Joseph (Gen. 39), David (2 Sam. 11), and Jesus (Luke 4:13) all illustrate this. (3) Scripture is our best defense against satanic temptation. Jesus defeated the devil by quoting three times from the Book of Deuteronomy. John stated, "I write to you, young men, because you are strong, and the word of God lives in you, and you have overcome the evil one" (1 John 2:14).

(4) Peter gave us a corollary to the third principle. He said we should resist the devil, "standing firm in the faith" (1 Pet. 5:9). Peter urged us to defend ourselves. The apostle Paul enlarged on "standing firm in the faith" by urging us to "put on the full armor of

God" (Eph. 6:11–17). (5) When tempted, we should take the "way out" God promises to provide (1 Cor. 10:13). Joseph did (Gen. 39:12), while David did not (2 Sam. 11:1–4). (6) In Gethsemane Jesus strongly cautioned His disciples: "Watch and pray so that you will not fall into temptation" (Matt. 26:41). We must not let ourselves get into situations where we feel we have the freedom or privacy to yield to temptation. (7) We need to remind ourselves that God has given us three main resources to rely on when we are tempted. These are the Word of God (1 John 2:14), the indwelling Holy Spirit (4:4), and the interceding Son of God (Luke 22:32). With God's help we can be victors and not victims when we battle temptation.

—**DKC**

***

"Yield not to temptation,
for yielding is sin."

THEOPHANY

The word *theophany* is a theological term. It doesn't appear in the Bible. *Theophany* is a compound word formed from the Greek noun for God (*theos*) and the Greek verb "to appear" (*phaneō*). A theophany is a temporary, visible appearance of God. Theologians needed a term to describe the instances in the Old Testament when God showed up in visible form, either as a figure or a symbolic object. Theophanies were temporary revelatory acts. They stand in sharp contrast to the Incarnation, through which God permanently reveals Himself in Jesus Christ.

God most frequently appeared in human form during Old Testament times as the Angel of the Lord. This extraordinary angel who represents Himself as deity appeared to Hagar (Gen. 16:7), Abraham (18; 22:11–12), Lot (19), Jacob (32:29–31; Hos. 12:4–5), Moses (Ex. 3:2–6), Balaam (Num. 22:22), Joshua (Josh. 5:14–15), Gideon (Judg. 6:11–14), Manoah and his wife (Judg. 13:1–21), and David (1 Chr. 21:15, 18, 27). The Angel of the Lord led the Hebrews out of Egypt (Ex. 13:21; 14:19), and He reproached the Israelites for disobedience after they settled in Canaan (Judg. 2:1–4).

In the passages cited, the Angel of the Lord called Himself God, received worship, and spoke with divine authority. Others spoke of Him or reacted to Him as God. Some of these references distinguish the Angel of the Lord from God the Father. These must refer to preincarnate appearances of God the Son and technically should be called Christophanies.

God revealed Himself in symbolic form as well as personal form. When He made a covenant with Abraham, God appeared as "a smoking firepot with a blazing torch" (Gen. 15:17). He spoke to Moses from a burning bush (Ex. 3:2–6). The pillar of cloud and fire represented God's presence with His people. The cloud guided them on their journey during the day, and the fire provided light and protection at night (13:21–22; 14:19, 24; Num. 14:14). God made His presence known at Sinai by thunder, lightning, fire, smoke, and a thick cloud (Ex. 19:16, 18; 24:15–18). The Lord dwelt among Israel in the form of a shining light called the Shekinah glory. When Moses completed the tabernacle, the glory of God descended. "Then the cloud covered the Tent of Meeting, and the glory of the LORD filled the tabernacle. Moses could not enter the Tent of Meeting because the cloud had settled upon it, and the glory of the LORD filled the tabernacle" (40:34–35). Centuries later, when Solomon completed his temple, "the cloud filled the temple of the LORD. And the priests could not perform their service because of the cloud, for the glory of the LORD filled his temple" (1 Kin. 8:10–11). At the time of the Babylonian exile Ezekiel watched in a vision as the Shekinah glory abandoned the temple, the city, and the people (Ezek. 11:22–23). This departure signaled that judgment would soon fall on Jerusalem. Jerusalem will be devoid of God's presence until the Lord Jesus returns to establish God's millennial kingdom on earth. Then His glory will once again fill the temple, and He will dwell with His people forever (43:1–5).

Theologically, theophanies provided Old Testament glimpses into the triune nature of the Godhead, and they anticipated the New Testament doctrine of the Incarnation of Christ (John 1:14; 8:56).   **—DKC**

***

Read the Old Testament carefully, looking for theophanies, evidences that even before the Incarnation God pursued humanity, revealing Himself to people in human or symbolic form.

TIMES OF THE GENTILES

In Genesis 10, Moses gave an account of the origin of the races from the three sons of Noah. He made special note of the descendants of Noah's son Shem. God had selected one of Shem's descendants, Abram, to found a new racial line, later called Israel. Israel did not include all of Abram's descendants. Ishmael, son of Sarah's servant Hagar (16:15), and the children of Keturah (25:1–4) all founded other non-Israelite people groups. Only the descendants of Jacob's twelve sons make up Israel. The other descendants of Abram were Gentiles.

The great empires of the historical books of the Old Testament were made up of Gentiles, including Egypt and Assyria. Daniel prophesied of four Gentile world empires: Babylon, Medo-Persia, Greece, and Rome (Dan. 2; 7).

Ethnoi, the common Greek word translated "Gentiles," normally means "peoples" and thus refers to humankind (regardless of race). In the Bible *ethnoi* refers to all nations other than Israel. But the Bible occasionally uses the singular noun *ethnos* to indicate Israel as a specific ethnic group (for example, John 11:51–52). The New Testament regularly uses the word "Greeks" (*hellēnoi*) as a catch-all category for all Gentiles or non-Jews (as in Acts 21:28; Rom. 1:14; 1 Cor. 1:22).

Biblical prophecy for the most part concerns Israel. When prophecies address Gentile nations, it's usually because they have something to do with Israel. Israelites wrote the Old Testament. Jesus, the apostles, and most of the other New Testament writers also were Jews. The Bible is a very Jewish book.

Thus it is important to distinguish between God's prophetic plan for Israel and His prophetic plan for Gentiles. Premillennialism especially distinguishes Israel and the Gentiles with regard to the millennial kingdom. The Lord Jesus will rule from Jerusalem over Israel on David's throne as her Messiah.

The expression "the times of the Gentiles" identifies a period of history in prophecy that began in 605 B.C. when the Gentile Babylonians overran Jerusalem. This Gentile "abomination" will continue until the Second Coming of Christ. Luke 21:24 states, "They [Israel] will fall by the sword and will be taken as prisoners to all the nations. Jerusalem will be trampled on by the Gentiles until the times of the Gentiles are fulfilled." The times of the Gentiles spans the era of the four kingdoms predicted in Daniel 2 and 7. The fourth kingdom will be the restored Roman Empire, over which the Antichrist will rule for three and a half years just before the Second Coming of Christ.

Do not confuse "the times of the Gentiles" with the expression "the fullness of the Gentiles." "The fullness of the Gentiles" refers to the more limited church age during which Gentiles receive the gospel. Paul said, "I do not want you to be ignorant of this mystery, brothers, so that you may not be conceited: Israel has experienced a hardening in part until the full number of the Gentiles has come in" (Rom. 11:25). "The fullness of the Gentiles" began on the Day of Pentecost and will end with the Rapture. "The times of the Gentiles" won't end until Christ returns to the earth just before the Millennium. **—JFW**

***

Study the scriptural teachings about future events, and pray that the coming of Christ will be soon.

TONGUES

The word *tongue* refers to the organ of speech in our mouths. The Bible doesn't use the word often in its literal sense. James used the word "tongue" as a metaphor for speech that originates from a sinful heart. He began talking about our literal tongues but quickly turned to the topic of destructive speech. James said, "The tongue is a small part of the body, but it makes great boasts" (3:5), and it is "a fire, a world of evil among the parts of the body" (3:6). He added, "With the tongue we praise our Lord and Father, and with it we curse men who have been made in God's likeness. Out of the same mouth come praise and cursing." He concluded, "My brothers, this should not be" (3:9–10).

Other times "tongues" refers to languages. After the Flood "the whole world had one language [literally, 'tongue'] and a common speech" (Gen. 11:1). In time sinful people desired to "make a name" for themselves (11:4) by building a city and tower. This provoked God to "go down and confuse their language" so that they did not understand each other (11:7). God also "scattered them over the face of the whole earth" (11:9).

Jews from a dozen different countries were in Jerusalem on the Day of Pentecost when the Holy Spirit came on the disciples gathered in the Upper Room. All these people reported that they heard the Galilean disciples "declaring the wonders of God in [their] own tongues!" (Acts 2:11). Here the word *tongues* identified spoken languages. On the Day of Pentecost the disciples had the miraculous, God-given "ability to speak in different kinds of tongues" (1 Cor. 12:10, 28) without having learned those languages.

The Holy Spirit gave the disciples miraculous ability to speak in the various languages of these foreign visitors to Jerusalem. They "began to speak in other tongues as the Spirit enabled them" (Acts 2:4). Many believe the disciples spoke in ecstatic utterances, and the foreigners miraculously understood them as if they spoke in their individual languages. However, Luke said the Holy Spirit's miracle applied to the disciples who spoke (2:4), not to the listeners who heard. Luke also wrote that the apostles spoke in the "languages" of the people (2:6, 8).

The next incident of "speaking in tongues" in response to "the gift of the Holy Spirit" occurred in the house of the Gentile centurion Cornelius (10:45–46). Peter told his Jewish companions that these Gentiles had "received the Holy Spirit just as we have" (10:47). If at Pentecost the disciples miraculously spoke in actual languages they had not learned, the believing Gentiles at Caesarea must have done the same thing. They did not do something radically different, such as speak in ecstatic utterances.

The third incident of speaking in tongues in the Book of Acts parallels the second one. Paul met some "disciples" who had received "John's baptism" but did not know about the Holy Spirit (19:1–3). Paul "baptized [them] into the name of the Lord Jesus" and placed "his hands on them. The Holy Spirit came on them, and they spoke in tongues and prophesied" (19:5–6). On these three occasions in Acts, speaking in tongues followed the descent of the Holy Spirit and validated the message and ministry concerning Jesus Christ to a new group that needed to accept the gospel.

In 1 Corinthians 12 and 14 Paul discussed spiritual gifts, including "the ability to speak in different kinds of tongues" and "the interpretation of tongues" (1 Cor. 12:10, 28, 30). He labeled tongues and interpretation as gifts and manifestations of the Holy Spirit (12:4, 7). It seems best to conclude that Paul had in mind the skillful proclamation of the gospel in foreign languages known to the speaker when he alluded to "speaking in tongues" (14:6–13). Paul wrote, "I speak in tongues more than all of you" (14:18), a claim undoubtedly true in light of his extensive missionary travels.

On the one hand Paul explained, "Tongues, then, are a sign, not for believers but for unbelievers" (14:21–22). To support that he quoted Isaiah 28:11–12, a statement illustrated by the incidents in Acts. As a sign to unbelievers tongues-speaking authenticated the apostles' message (see 2 Cor. 12:12; Heb. 2:3). On the other hand, if "everyone [in the church] is speaking in tongues" (1 Cor. 14:23, literal translation)—apparently without interpretation—unlearned and unbelievers in the church assembly would say, "you are out of your mind" (14:23).

To prevent that, Paul set out some regulations for speaking in a tongue in church: "two—or at the most three—should speak, one at a time, and someone must interpret. If there is no interpreter, the speaker should keep quiet in the church and speak to himself and to God" (14:27–28). He concluded, however, "do not forbid speaking in tongues. But everything should be done in a fitting and orderly way" (14:39–40).

Apparently the Christians in Corinth were speaking repeatedly in tongues without interpretation, mimicking the Grecian pagan oracles of the time. Such speech, also frequently without interpretation or other regulations, characterized the tongues movement that gained widespread acceptance and attention in the twentieth century. If all churches had observed Paul's regulations, much of that movement would have disappeared.   **—JAW**

T

* * *

*Avoid the excesses of
emotionalism so common in
many churches today, seeking
instead to "live by the Spirit"
(Gal. 5:16).*

TRANSFIGURATION

Each of the synoptic gospels reports the transfiguration of Christ (Matt. 17:1–8; Mark 9:2–8; Luke 9:28–36). Peter, James, and John glimpsed the glory of Christ on a "high mountain" a few days after Peter confessed Jesus as Messiah at Caesarea Philippi. Scholars have suggested various locations for the Transfiguration, such as the Mount of Olives, Mount Carmel, Mount Tabor, and Mount Hermon. A southern ridge of Mount Hermon seems to be the best choice because of its elevation (over nine thousand feet) and its proximity to Caesarea Philippi (twelve miles northeast).

Three things took place at the Transfiguration. First, Jesus' "face shone like the sun, and his clothes became as white as the light" (Matt. 17:2). This was not merely a change in outward appearance; the divine glory of the Son of God shone through His body and transformed its appearance from within. For a brief time the rightful glory of the Son of God returned (see John 17:5). Peter, James, and John saw Christ as He presently appears in His ascended glory (Rev. 1:14–16) and as

He will appear when He returns at His Second Coming in power and glory (Matt. 24:30).

Second, Moses and Elijah appeared and spoke with Jesus about His death (literally, His "exodus," Luke 9:31). These two figures represented the Law and the Prophets of the Old Testament. They talked with Christ about His forthcoming death, burial, and resurrection. It is noteworthy that Moses and Elijah each had a vision of God on a mountain (Ex. 24; 1 Kin. 19); both are mentioned in the last verses of Malachi (Mal. 4:4–6); and, according to some, both will appear on earth during the Tribulation (Rev. 11).

Third, a heavenly voice said, "This is my Son, whom I love. Listen to him!" (Mark 9:7; see also Matt. 17:5; Luke 9:35). God spoke in response to Peter's impulsive suggestion that he build three shelters, one each for Jesus, Moses, and Elijah. No doubt Peter wanted to prolong this amazing experience. He may also have thought the kingdom had come and that he ought to build booths for the Feast of Tabernacles (Lev. 23:33–43; Zech. 14:16). At any rate, God rebuked Peter for placing Jesus on the same level as Moses and Elijah. The Father identified His Son as the Prophet of Deuteronomy 18:15–18, and as the Messiah who must suffer death as He had recently announced in Caesarea Philippi (Matt. 16:21). That was the message Peter (and the others) needed to hear and accept. What Jesus had said about dying on the cross aligned with the will of the Father.

Each of the Gospel accounts of the Transfiguration follows Jesus' cryptic words, "I tell you the truth, some who are standing here will not taste death before they see the Son of Man coming in his kingdom" (Matt. 16:28; see also Mark 9:1; Luke 9:27). Jesus had been proclaiming the coming of the kingdom of God. Soon the nation would reject Him as Messiah and kill their King. Jesus wanted to assure His disciples that the messianic kingdom would indeed be established in fulfillment of promises made to Israel— later if not immediately. The Transfiguration provided this assurance by giving Peter, James, and John a glimpse of the glory of the messianic kingdom before they died. Later Peter would explicitly connect Jesus' glory displayed at the Transfiguration with the future glory of Christ when He comes again to establish His earthly kingdom (2 Pet. 1:16–18).

The word "transfigure" (*metamorpheō*) is also used twice in the New Testament to describe the change the Holy Spirit wants to make in us. In Romans 12:2 Paul exhorted, "Do not conform any longer to the pattern of this world, but be transformed by the renewing of your mind." This transformation can only be described as a "metamorphosis," a total change

from the inside out. This metamorphosis starts in our minds which can be renewed by the spiritual disciplines of prayer, Scripture reading, Christian fellowship, and others. Paul compared our inner transformation to the outward transformation of Moses caused by being with God. "And we, who with unveiled faces all reflect the Lord's glory, are being transformed into his likeness with ever-increasing glory, which comes from the Lord, who is the Spirit" (2 Cor. 3:18; see Ex. 33:18–23; 34:29–35). As we yield ourselves to the Holy Spirit, He will produce in us the fruit of the Spirit (Gal. 5:22–23). The result will be a gradual transformation into Christlikeness, the ultimate goal of our Christian lives.

—DKC

***

Imagine what it was like to look on the glorious Christ on the Mount of Transfiguration, and then remember that when He returns we too will behold His glory.

TRIBULATION

The Scriptures confirm that trials and tribulations are universal elements of human experience. All of us face trouble in one form or another. Jesus said, "In this world you will have trouble" (John 16:33). And Eliphaz told Job, "Man is born to trouble as surely as sparks fly upward" (Job 5:7). James wrote that we face "trials of many kinds" (James 1:2). While troubles are inevitable, God always enables us to endure them.

In addition to the ordinary tribulations of life in a sin-cursed world, the Bible identifies a particular future era as a time particularly characterized by tribulation. Revelation 7:14 calls this "the great tribulation." This particular period of trouble lasts three and a half years and occurs immediately prior to the Second Coming of Christ. Daniel 12:1 refers to the Great Tribulation as "a time of distress such as has not happened from the beginning of nations until then." Jesus said it will be a time of "great distress, unequaled from the beginning of the world" and will "never . . . be equaled again" (Matt. 24:21). Obviously this special period of tribulation differs from troubles in general.

During the Great Tribulation, God's wrath will be poured out on the unbelieving world in an unprecedented way. It will begin when the Antichrist desecrates the Jewish temple (which is yet to be rebuilt) and designates the temple as the place where he must be worshiped (2 Thess. 2:4). He will perform "counterfeit miracles" (2:9). This will occur forty-two months (three and a half years) before Christ's second coming. It will happen in the middle of the seven-year period of Daniel 9:24–27, a time commonly called "the seventieth week of Daniel." (Each "seven" or "week" refers to seven years.) Revelation 13:5 confirms this scenario. It states that the world ruler ("the beast" or Antichrist) will exercise authority over the world for forty-two months. Daniel called this "time, times and half a time" (Dan. 7:25; 12:7; Rev. 12:14) and 1,260 days (12:6). Twelve hundred sixty days equals forty-two months of thirty days each.

Jeremiah 30:7 called the Great Tribulation a terrible "time of trouble for Jacob." He also prophesied that "Jacob" (the nation Israel) will be saved out of it (30:10–11) when Christ returns to establish His kingdom. Many Jews and Gentiles will turn to Christ as their Savior in the seven-year period after the Rapture, and many of them will be martyred for their faith. Revelation 7:9–17 calls them a great multitude "who have come out of the great tribulation" (7:14), that is, they will be delivered from the horrors of the Great Tribulation by death and into the safety of heaven. According to 20:4–6, the bodies of Tribulation martyrs will be resurrected after the Second Coming of Christ. Tribulation saints along with church-age believers will then reign with Christ for a thousand years.

During the Great Tribulation the Antichrist (1 John 2:18; 4:3) will reign over the entire world (Rev. 13:7) for three and a half years prior to the Second Coming. At Christ's return to earth, He will capture the beast and cast him into the lake of fire (19:20; 20:10). The Antichrist is the one whom "Jesus will overthrow with the breath of his mouth and destroy by the splendor of his coming" (2 Thess. 2:8).

The Book of Revelation characterizes the Great Tribulation as a time of divine judgment. God will pour out His wrath on unbelieving Gentiles and Jews in the form of seven "seal" judgments (Rev. 6), seven "trumpet" judgments (Rev. 8—9), and seven "bowl" judgments (Rev. 15—16).   **—JFW**

***

Be grateful to the Lord that the church will be raptured before the terrible "seventieth week of Daniel."

TRINITY

The word *Trinity* does not occur in the Bible. Nevertheless the Trinity is a primary biblical truth. Christians believe that the one God subsists in a tri-unity of coequal, coeternal, co-extensive persons—Father, Son, and Holy Spirit. This doctrine arises from multiple strands of evidence in God's Word. The Trinity logically represents the biblical testimony, but ultimately the Trinity is a revealed truth, not just a proposition of logic.

The strongest single passage of Scripture that supports the doctrine of the Trinity is the baptismal formula, "baptizing them in the name of the Father and of the Son and of the Holy Spirit" (Matt. 28:19). Christian baptism is administered in "the name," not "the names" of God. God is one. However, "the name" is that "of the Father and of the Son and of the Holy Spirit." This one God consists of three distinct persons, and not just different modes of expression of the one God.

In the New Testament the Incarnation sets the stage for the doctrine of the Trinity. The Gospel writers calls the One who entered human flesh the eternal Word of God (John 1:1–2) and the Son of God (1:14, 18) as well as Jesus (Matt. 1:20–25; Luke 1:30–38). The Gospels present Jesus Christ as the God-Man. A third divine being entered the stage of history on the Day of Pentecost in Acts 2. The Holy Spirit indwells believers in Christ, baptizes them into the body of Christ, transforms their lives, and empowers their ministry. Evidence for the Trinity multiplies in number and strength in the New Testament as compared to the Old.

The Old Testament, however, does contain evidence for God's existence as a plurality of persons. That evidence is not as clear and specific as New Testament teaching. Israel functioned in a world characterized by polytheistic idolatry. Accordingly the Old Testament emphasizes the unity of God. "The LORD our God, the LORD is one" (Deut. 6:4), and He alone is to be worshiped and served (4:35, 39). The Bible didn't need to reveal clear Trinitarian evidence until the second person of the Trinity entered human flesh as Jesus Christ.

Old Testament evidence for the Trinity can be compared to furniture in a dark room. It's there, but you can't see it until someone turns on the light. Even the statement "The LORD is one," allows for a plurality of persons. The Hebrew word rendered "one" is a term of unity rather than singularity. If Moses had wanted to stress the absolute singularity of God, he would have used the Hebrew word *yaḥîd* (as in Gen. 22:2, "your only son") Instead he used *>eḥād* (as in 2:24, "they will become one flesh"). The plural noun translated "God" (*>ĕlōhîm*) is a plural of majesty. It appears regularly with singular verbs (for example, "created," 1:1). But *>ĕlōhîm* also appears with plural verbs and plural pronouns— "let us make man in our image, in our likeness" (1:26). Ecclesiastes 12:1 reads literally, "Remember your Creators in the days of your youth." These plural references to God in the Old Testament are consistent with the doctrine of the Trinity.

The threefold benediction of Numbers 6:24–26 and the threefold ascription of holiness to "the LORD Almighty" by the seraphs in Isaiah 6:3 (see also Rev. 4:8) may also allude to the Trinity. The Old Testament includes a few instances in which God seems to be two distinct persons talking about one another (Pss. 45:6–7; 110:1; Hos. 1:6–7). The Old Testament occasionally personifies the Word of God (Pss. 33:6; 107:20; 147:15–18), and the Spirit of God (Gen. 1:2; Is. 63:10; Ezek. 2:2; 8:3; Zech. 7:12) in ways that make them seem like members of the Trinity.

The Angel of the Lord provides the clearest Old Testament evidence of plurality of persons in God. The Angel of the Lord regularly behaved as though He were the Lord Himself (Gen. 16:7–13; 22:11–18; 31:11–13; Ex. 3:2–10; Judg. 6:11–26; 13:3–23). The Lord has said, "I am the LORD, that is my name! I will not give my glory to another or my praise to idols" (Is. 42:8). Accordingly, theologians regularly identify the Angel of the Lord with the preincarnate Son of God, the Second Person of the Trinity.

In the New Testament the Trinity may be observed at the baptism of Jesus, when "the Holy Spirit descended on him in bodily form like a dove. And a voice came from heaven: 'You are my Son, whom I love; with you I am well pleased'" (Luke 3:22; see also Matt. 3:16–17; Mark 1:10–11; John 1:32–34). Paul linked the three persons of the Godhead in his appeal for Christian unity in Ephesians 4:3–6. The Lord Jesus taught that when He departed, the Holy Spirit would come to His disciples from God the Father (John 14:16–20, 23, 26; 15:26; 16:7, 12–15).

The New Testament regards Christ as fully divine. When Jesus Christ claimed, "I and the Father are one" (John 10:30; see also 5:16–18), the Jewish leaders recognized this as a claim of equality with God in person, not just in purpose (10:33). The writers of the New Testament called the Lord Jesus "the image of the invisible God" (Col. 1:15; see also 2 Cor. 4:4) and "the radiance of God's glory and the exact representation of his being" (Heb. 1:3). Paul also wrote that "God was pleased to have all his fullness dwell in him" (Col. 1:19). He said that Christ, "being in very nature God, did not consider equality with God something to be grasped" (Phil. 2:6).

New Testament evidence for the deity of the Holy Spirit is not as clear or as complete as the evidence concerning Jesus Christ. This is understandable since the Spirit's ministry, as Jesus told the disciples, is to "testify about me" (John 15:26) and to "bring glory to me by taking from what is mine and making it known to you" (16:14). Jesus implied the deity of the Holy Spirit by stating that "blasphemy against the Spirit will not be forgiven" (Matt. 12:31–32). Peter equated lying to the Holy Spirit with lying to God (Acts 5:3–4).

The three persons of the Godhead—Father, Son, and Spirit—cooperate in the major works of God. In creation God the Father (James 1:17; Gen. 1:14), Jesus Christ (John 1:3; Col. 1:16; Heb. 1:2, 10–12), and the Holy Spirit (Gen. 1:2; Job 33:4; Ps. 104:30) all participated. All three played a role in the Incarnation—Father (Luke 1:28, 32), Jesus Christ (Matt. 1:21, 23), and the Holy Spirit (1:20; Luke 1:35). All three Persons make critical contributions to the salvation of believers. God the Father chooses who will be saved (Eph. 1:3–6). Jesus the Son redeems them (1:7–12). The Holy Spirit indwells and seals them (1:13–14). Other New Testament passages that link the members of the Trinity in the work of salvation include Ephesians 2:18; 3:2–5; and Titus 3:4–7. The Persons of the Trinity cooperate to equip believers with spiritual gifts for the building up of the church, the body of Christ (1 Cor. 12:4–6).

As the members of the Trinity work together, they exhibit an administrative order. The Father formulates the plan, the Son executes the plan, and the Spirit implements the plan. So we call the Father the First Person, the Son the Second Person, and the Holy Spirit the Third Person of the Trinity. This order does not designate rank. It's just the way God functions. So, for instance, the Father sent the Son (John 3:17; Rom. 8:3). Jesus Christ, the Son, in turn, came to do the will of God the Father (John 4:34) and does "only what he sees his Father doing" (5:19; see also 5:30; 8:28; 12:49; 14:10). The Holy Spirit then glorifies Jesus Christ and God the Father (16:14–15) by testifying concerning them (14:26; 15:26; 16:7, 13). The work of the triune God is from the Father, through the Son, and by the power of the Holy Spirit.

Presently the Father exalts the Lord Jesus Christ through the church (Eph. 1:20–23; Phil. 2:9–11; 2 Thess. 1:12; 1 Pet. 1:21). In the end, however, after all things have been subjected to Christ, "then the Son himself will be made subject to him who put everything under him, so that God may be all in all" (1 Cor. 15:28).

—JAW

***

Focus your eyes of faith on Jesus, for in seeing Him you see God the Father and God the Holy Spirit (John 14:9–10).

TRUTH

In the final analysis "truth" corresponds to reality. "Truth" describes the way things actually are. Truth is found in God's person, His character, and His work of salvation provided through Jesus Christ. The frustrating philosophical search for truth finds its solution in theology—in God Himself.

God is the self-existent One, the Creator of all that exists. Therefore God is truth, and all truth is God's truth. The Bible calls Him "the God of truth" (Ps. 31:5; Is. 65:16). God declares, "I, the LORD, speak the truth; I declare what is right" (Is. 45:19). The Son "who came from the Father" was "full of grace and truth" (John 1:14). "Grace and truth came through Jesus Christ" (1:17). Jesus claimed, "I am the way and the truth and the life" (14:6). Jesus often began to teach by saying, "I tell you the truth" (for example, Matt. 5:18, 26). Jesus called the Holy Spirit "the Spirit of truth" (John 14:17; 15:26; 16:13). The apostle John added that "the Spirit is the truth" (1 John 5:6).

Truth resides in God, so His revelation to us is called "the truth" (John 17:17; see also Pss. 19:7–11; 119:89–92). The angel who appeared to Daniel called the Scriptures "the Book of Truth" (Dan. 10:21). Jesus told Pilate, "For this reason I was born, and for this I came into the world, to testify to the truth. Everyone on the side of truth listens to me" (John 18:37). When Christ returns to Jerusalem, it "will be called the City of Truth" (Zech. 8:3).

The Bible calls the gospel message concerning Jesus Christ "truth" (Gal. 2:5, 14; Col. 1:5). The apostles proclaimed the "truth" of Christ (2 Cor. 4:1–4; Eph. 1:13; 4:15–16, 20–21; 5:8–10; 3 John 1:8). "The church of the living God" is "the pillar and foundation of the truth" (1 Tim. 3:15). Each believer is commanded, "Stand firm then, with the belt of truth buckled around your waist" (Eph. 6:14).

—**JAW**

***

Pray with David, "Guide me in your truth and teach me, for you are God my Savior" (Ps. 25:5).

TYPES

The English word *type* derives from the Greek word *typos*. "Type" is a term used in identifying a special kind of prophetic symbol. The New Testament uses the Greek word *typos* to mean such various things as "print" (John 20:25, NKJV), "pattern" (Heb. 8:5), "form" (Rom. 6:17), and "example" (1 Cor. 10:6, 11; Titus 2:7). Other Greek words found in the New Testament related to prophetic typology are *skia* ("shadow," Heb. 8:4–5); *parabolē* ("figure" or "symbol," 9:9, KJV); *hypodeigma* ("copy" or "pattern," 9:23); and *antitypos* ("antitype").

A prophetic type is an Old Testament institution, event, person, object, or ceremony that had reality and purpose in biblical history, but which God also meant to foreshadow something yet future. The term *antitype* describes the fulfillment of the type in the New Testament or in the prophetic future.

A type is similar to, but not the same as, a prophecy. Both point to the fu-

ture, but a prophecy is more specific and *teaches* doctrine. A type only *illustrates* a doctrine taught elsewhere. A type differs from a symbol in that a symbol is a timeless image. For example, a dove symbolizes peace, whether in the past, present, or future. A type, on the other hand, had a historical meaning in the past and a predictive meaning for the future. For example, Israel's high priest directed Old Testament worship then and "typified" the future high priestly ministry of Jesus Christ.

A type is not an allegory. Allegorical interpretation looks for hidden, deeper meaning in the biblical text. Origen (around A.D. 185–254) and others in the early church carried allegorical interpretation to exaggerated lengths. The study of types in the Old Testament arises from the spiritual unity of the two Testaments and the way the New Testament interprets the Old. Types are not hidden meanings or fanciful meanings but revealed meanings of certain features of the Old Testament.

How much of the Old Testament is "typical" of the New? That isn't easy to answer. The early church fathers were as fanciful in typology as they were in allegorizing Old Testament history. The scholastic theologians of the Middle Ages weren't much better. The Reformers showed caution in typology, though they gave little attention to the subject. Bishop Herbert Marsh of England (1757–1839) formalized an approach to interpreting types that came to be known as Marsh's Principle. He said interpreters should call nothing in the Old Testament a type unless the New Testament treated it as a type.

Through the centuries since Marsh, many students of Scripture have relied on this interpretive standard because it's simple and cautious. Others think Marsh's Principle unduly limits the field of typology. They argue that we don't know that all the types in the Old Testament were identified by the New Testament writers. They suggest that the types described in the New Testament are only samples taken from a storehouse where still others can be found.

But if that's so, how can we identify other Old Testament types and their New Testament or future antitypes? Since "only God can make types," how can the interpreter determine what God designed? First, the New Testament identifies some Old Testament features as types. For example, Paul identified Adam as a type of Christ (Rom. 5:14, NKJV). Second, the New Testament may apply Old Testament labels to something without specifically calling it a type. For example, Paul called Christ "our Passover lamb" (1 Cor. 5:7). Third, where a clear, extended analogy exists between an Old Testament feature and a future truth,

we may cautiously infer a type exists. For instance, we may conclude Joseph functions as a type of Christ because of the many clear analogies between his life and Christ's earthly life.

We need to follow certain guiding principles when interpreting types. (1) Thoroughly understand the historical event, person, or institution before exploring its typical meaning. If an interpreter ignores the historical dimension, he or she may end up allegorizing the biblical text. (2) Unity must exist between a type and its antitype. A common theological principle must bind them together. One writer, for example, claimed the stone Jacob used for a pillow at Bethel was a type of Christ, the foundation stone of the church. But no common spiritual principle unites those two "stones." (3) Nothing forbidden or sinful should be considered a type of something good. For example, Isaac blessed Jacob while he was dressed in Esau's garments. This has been improperly called a type of God blessing believers who wear Christ's garment of righteousness. Someone even suggested that Samson and the prostitute from Gaza typify Christ and Israel during the Tribulation. Those examples show how far-fetched typology borders on allegorizing the Old Testament. (4) Don't try to make every detail of a type mean something prophetic. Distinguish what is essential in a type from what is peripheral. Moses was a type of Christ as a deliverer, a prophet, an advocate, and a lawgiver. It would be wrong to force a meaning onto every known details of Moses' life and ministry. The Book of Hebrews identified the typical meaning of the tabernacle in the functions of its furnishings and its priests with their sacrifices, but not in its boards and bars or its tent pins and tarpaulins.

A disciplined and enlightened typology can enrich your study of Scripture by giving you one more tool to make you a student "who correctly handles the word of truth" (2 Tim. 2:15). **—DKC**

***

Do not neglect the study of Old Testament types, because they provide wonderful illustrations of New Testament truths.

Uu

UNBELIEF

"Unbelief" refers to the state of denial that what God has revealed about Himself and eternal life are true. To describe unbelief, New Testament writers looked back to how people acted in the Old Testament. The Old Testament didn't employ a specific word for unbelief, but it reports many instances of it. Unbelief and rebellion characterized people in Noah's day (Gen. 6:5–7), so God destroyed them by the Flood. Peter called these unbelievers "ungodly" (2 Pet. 2:5). The writer of Hebrews attributed unbelief to the Israelites when they hardened their hearts and rebelled against God shortly after He had delivered them from Egypt (Heb. 3:19). They did not respond in faith to what they saw God do on their behalf (3:9; Ps. 95:9). Jude said God took the lives of those Israelites who did not believe (Jude 5). At the root of their problem was an unbelieving heart (Heb. 3:12).

Everyone without Christ lives in unbelief. They ignore or refuse the salvation Christ provided through His death on the cross (John 3:36). Unbelief blinds them to the light of the gospel (2 Cor. 4:4). Unbelief need not be permanent, as illustrated in the life of Paul. However, he did not overcome unbelief by his own efforts. God through His grace and mercy opened Paul's heart to receive the message about Christ (1 Tim. 1:13–16). Later Paul reminded the Roman church that the unbelief of Israel also is not permanent (Rom. 11:20–23).

People rejected Christ's miracles during His earthly ministry because of unbelief (Matt. 13:58; Mark 6:6). Mark tells of a father whose son was tormented by a demon. The man asked the Lord to help him overcome his unbelief (9:24). Obviously that man did not have a rebellious spirit, but he sensed a need for divine assistance to believe. Maybe he had watched the power of Satan operate in his son's life for so long that he doubted God's ability to help the boy. At any rate, he humbled himself in the presence of the Lord and asked for help to believe. We too will face all sorts of difficult challenges in life, but God promises victory because of our faith in Christ (1 John 5:4–5). **—WGJ**

***

Don't doubt the ability of the Lord to help you in the most difficult circumstances because your faith is "the victory that overcomes the world."

UNION WITH CHRIST

Paul repeatedly wrote that we are "in Christ." We have an indestructible relationship with Him characterized by unity. We are the bride of Christ. That marriage metaphor im-

plies our oneness with Christ. God has given us eternal life, so we have that in common with Christ too. The Holy Spirit baptized us into the body of Christ at the moment of our salvation. Christ is the Head of the body, so we are joined to Him as much as the members of our body are a part of us. We are justified by faith (Rom. 5:1), so God sees us clothed in the righteousness of Christ. Our faith unites us with Him (Eph. 4:13).

Salvation so unites us to Christ that it is as if we had experienced death, burial, and resurrection with Him (Rom. 6:3–5). We have union with Christ because we have passed from death to life (John 5:24) and from being in Adam to being in Him. Not only are we "in Christ," but Christ indwells each of us. As Paul wrote, He is "Christ in you, the hope of glory" (Col. 1:27). **—JFW**

***

Thank the Lord regularly because of the wonderful personal relationship Christians have with the risen Christ.

Vv

VINE

Vineyards were everywhere in the Middle East during Bible times, so the vine made an excellent metaphor for several abstract truths. The Old Tes-

tament employs vine language in a greater variety of ways than the New Testament does. Jacob told Joseph his inheritance would be abundant like "a fruitful vine" (Gen. 49:22). If Israel obeyed God's laws, He would bless them with abundant grape harvests (Lev. 26:3–5). Moses evoked images of the fertility of the Promised Land by describing it as a land of "vines and fig trees" (Deut. 8:8). The vine symbolized both Israel's national wealth and its ideal of a satisfying life (1 Kin. 4:25). The psalmist used imagery of a vine to describe a godly wife in a home that honored the Lord (Ps. 128:3). When the prophets wanted to say Israel would one day be a place of blessing and enjoyment, they said everyone would sit under his own vine (Mic. 4:4; Zech. 3:10). When a vine failed to produce fruit, it indicated God's judgment (Jer. 8:13). Amos reminded the Israelites that the Lord had struck their gardens and vineyards because they had neglected Him (Amos 4:9). When people planted vineyards, their neighbors assumed they meant to live there permanently, because it takes a long time and a lot of effort to maintain grapevines (Jer. 29:5).

The Old Testament writers often spoke of Israel as a vine. The psalmist called Israel a vine out of Egypt that had grown and flourished (Ps. 80:8–11). In the Song of the Vineyard (Is. 5:1–7), Isaiah portrayed Israel as God's choice vine planted on a fertile hillside. God Himself cared for the vineyard and expected the nation to bear fruit. When Israel did not bear fruit, God judged His "vineyard." To describe Israel's future the prophet pictured the nation as a vine planted once more in her own land never again to be uprooted (65:21–22; Amos 9:14–15).

The most significant biblical vine imagery appears in the New Testament where the Lord pictured His relationship to His disciples (John 15:1–17). He called Himself the true Vine, God the Father the Gardener (15:1), and His followers the branches. He called our work for the Lord fruit (15:5). The vine metaphor captures the intimate, living relationship Jesus wants to have with us. This unique relationship assures us that we can have a productive and meaningful life if we maintain our fellowship with Him. **—WGJ**

***

Stay in constant fellowship with Christ, since He is the Vine and since you as a branch cannot bear fruit without Him.

VOWS

A vow in Scripture is a formal promise someone made to God, usually in expectation of some divine favor in return. Sometimes a person made a vow simply as a solemn act of worship. We find vows more frequently in the Old Testament, especially in Psalms, than in the New Testament.

Some biblical vows were a type of bargain with God. Jacob at Bethel vowed to make that place a shrine and to give God a tithe if He would protect him and bless him on his journey

V

(Gen. 28:20–22). Jephthah vowed to sacrifice to God the first thing that came out of his house in exchange for victory over the Ammonites (Judg. 11:30–31). Hannah vowed that if God would give her a son, she would return the child to Him for a lifetime of service. Absalom vowed to worship the Lord in Hebron if He enabled him to return to Jerusalem from exile (2 Sam. 15:7–8).

The vows that abound in the psalms are primarily vows of praise—promises to worship God in special ways (Pss. 22:25; 50:14; 56:12; 61:8; 65:1–2; 76:11; 116:14, 18).

One special vow encoded in the Law of Moses was the Nazirite vow. Those who made Nazirite vows committed themselves to special service to God for a specified period of time (Num. 6:1–8). A Nazirite pledged to abstain from wine or grapes, to leave his or her hair uncut, and to have no contact with dead bodies for the life of the vow. Usually an adult made this vow for a short period of his or her life. The Bible reports three instances of children whose parents dedicated them to be Nazirites for life: Samson (Judg. 13), Samuel (1 Sam. 1:9–11), and John the Baptist (Luke 1:15, 80).

The Old Testament did not command Israelites to make vows. The Law did not consider refraining from making a vow to be sin (Deut. 23:22). However, once someone made a vow, he or she had to keep it (23:21, 23; Num.

30:2; Eccl. 5:4). The Bible warns against rash vows (Prov. 20:25; Eccl. 5:5–6). A father could cancel a rash or irresponsible vow made by an unmarried daughter (Num. 30:5), and a husband could cancel a similar vow made by his wife (30:8).

The New Testament uses the term *vow* only twice. Both involve the apostle Paul in the Book of Acts. Near the beginning of his ministry in Corinth, Paul took a Nazirite vow and let his hair grow for eighteen months. When he left Corinth, he cut his hair because the time of the vow was over (Acts 18:18). Later, in Jerusalem Paul joined four other men in purification rites at the temple. The four men seem to have taken a Nazirite vow that required some costly sacrifices when it was over. They could not afford to pay for their sacrifices, so Paul picked up their tab to show Jewish believers that he respected the Law (21:22–24). Some people criticize Paul for engaging in a temple ritual, but he could later say that he did not violate his own conscience (23:1). He operated according to a settled principle of his ministry. He became like a Jew to win the Jews and like one under the Law so as to win those under the Law (1 Cor. 9:20). Paul did participate in sacrifices at the temple to mark the end of the Nazirite vows (Num. 6:13–17). Presumably he looked on them as memorials of Christ's sacrifice.

The Gospels report that the Pharisees and teachers of the Law seriously misused vows (Matt. 15:3–6; Mark 7:9–11). Jesus charged them with substituting their own traditions for God's commands. He specifically cited their violation of the fifth commandment regarding the honoring of one's parents. They escaped their immediate obligations to care for aged parents by vowing their resources to God's temple when they died. Jesus sharply denounced such hypocrisy: "Thus you nullify the word of God by your tradition that you have handed down. And you do many things like that" (7:13).

In the Old Testament vows represent a major expression of devotion to God. Vows may not be what God expects of us, but the New Testament often urges us to demonstrate devotion to the Lord because He has blessed us so richly in Christ. Paul declared, "For you were bought at a price; therefore glorify God in your body" (1 Cor. 6:20, NKJV; see also Rom. 12:1–2). —**DKC**

***

Be careful to keep any vow or commitment you make to the Lord or to any person.

Ww

WALK

"Walk" is an ordinary word that occurs hundreds of times in the Scriptures. Most of the time "walk" refers to moving about on foot. Examples of this include Mark 1:16 ("As Jesus walked beside the Sea of Galilee, he saw Simon and his brother Andrew casting a net into the lake"); Luke 4:30 ("But he [Jesus] walked right through the crowd and went on his way"); and John 5:9 ("At once the man was cured; he picked up his mat and walked"). That kind of usage wouldn't rate an article in a book of important Bible words.

The idea of "walking" lends itself to several metaphorical meanings. "Walk" becomes a way of describing a believ-er's conduct or spiritual condition. For example, Enoch and Noah both "walked with God" (Gen. 5:24; 6:9), and God commanded Abraham, "Walk before me and be blameless" (17:1). Before crossing the Jordan River into Canaan Moses exhorted the Israelites, "Observe the commands of the LORD your God, walking in his ways and revering him" (Deut. 8:6).

In the New Testament John tells us that we lie if we claim to be in fellowship with God and yet "walk in the darkness" (1 John 1:6). On the other hand, "if we walk in the light, as he is in the light, we have fellowship with one another" (1:7). The Bible exhorts us to walk by faith (2 Cor. 5:7), "to walk in obedience to his commands" (2 John

W

6), "to walk worthy of the calling with which you were called" (Eph. 4:1, NKJV), to "walk in love" (5:2, NKJV), and to "walk as Jesus did" (1 John 2:6).

The most significant of these New Testament admonitions occurs in Galatians 5:16, "I say then: Walk in the Spirit, and you shall not fulfill the lust of the flesh" (NKJV). The Greek term for "walk" in this verse is *peripateō*, a compound word meaning "to walk around." We derive the English adjective "peripatetic" from this verb. "Peripatetic" describes a person who walks from place to place. In ancient Greece the Peripatetic School of Philosophy was named after Aristotle, who walked about in the Lyceum of Athens as he taught his students. In the New Testament, this Greek verb is usually used in the figurative sense to refer to a person's "walk of life" (lifestyle). In Galatians 5:16 the word "walk" refers to how we go about our daily duties, how we work at our usual tasks, and how we handle the inevitable temptations, victories, defeats, joys, and sorrows of life. Paul tells us we should live our entire life under the guidance and direction of the Holy Spirit. J. B. Phillips paraphrased Galatians 5:16, "Live your whole life in the Spirit."

If we do walk by the Spirit and depend on Him to give us both the desire and the power to do the will of God, we will not carry out the evil impulses of our fallen nature. Instead, we will resist them and conquer them. That doesn't mean we will be sinless, but it certainly does mean we will sin less! We who believe in Christ and are indwelt by the Holy Spirit have a responsibility to say "no" to the flesh and "yes" to the Holy Spirit.

The remaining verses of Galatians 5 develop the command and promise of verse 16. Negatively, if we do not "walk in the Spirit" but walk according to the flesh" (Rom. 8:4, NKJV), we will display the "works of the flesh." Paul listed a startling catalog of sins we will get tangled up in if we say "no" to the Spirit and "yes" to the flesh (Gal. 5:19–21). Positively, if we do depend on God's Spirit, our lives will exhibit the fruit of the Spirit (5:22–23), a catalog of graces supremely manifested in Jesus Christ. The Spirit wants to make them ours too.

We call flexible social services adapted to the changing needs of senior citizens "assisted living." In the spiritual realm Jesus has offered His disciples "assisted living" from the time He began His earthly ministry. Jesus told the Twelve, "Apart from me you can do nothing" (John 15:5). Paul reinforced this truth by insisting that we can live our Christian lives in one of two styles: We can "walk by the Spirit" and succeed in His power, or we can walk by the flesh and fail miserably. Rejoice that the Holy Spirit wants to produce His fruit in you. He wants to make you Christlike. That's God's ultimate purpose for each of His children (Rom. 8:29).   **—DKC**

***

Strive with God's help to walk in a manner worthy of your Christian calling.

WAR

Wars reached global proportions in the twentieth century. At the same time the development of nuclear weapons gave nations the capability of destroying all life on planet earth. The need to eliminate wars grew in urgency. In spite of all efforts to end war, smaller conflicts and police actions by international "peace-keeping" agencies proliferate. Jesus predicted concerning "the end of the age" (Matt. 24:3): "You will hear of wars and rumors of wars. . . . Nation will rise against nation, and kingdom against kingdom" (24:6–7; see also Mark 13:7–8; Luke 21:9–10). Unfortunately, as long as sinful human beings determine the policies of the world's nations, wars will continue. All conflicts, whether between individuals or nations, arise from sinful "desires that battle within you" (James 4:1–2).

In the Sermon on the Mount Jesus said, "Blessed are the peacemakers, for they will be called sons of God" (Matt. 5:9). Because of Jesus' teaching, some early church fathers were pacifists. After the Christianization of the Roman Empire under Constantine and the invasion of the empire by barbarians from the north, the church recognized the legitimacy of defensive wars. Most church leaders today agree that governments need to maintain standing armies for protection and for engagement in just wars as necessary. At the same time the number of strict pacifists is also increasing.

In the Old Testament God supported His people Israel in warfare. Most of these were just wars, such as Abram's rescue of his nephew Lot from Kedorlaomer and his allies (Gen. 14:1–16). Others were "holy wars," as when Israel drove out the inhabitants of Canaan because of their idolatry and wickedness (Gen. 15:16; Ex. 23:20–24, 27–33; Lev. 18:24–28). Many were defensive wars, such as those against Assyria (2 Kin. 15:29; 17:3–6) and Babylon (25:1–11).

The land of Canaan occupied a land bridge linking Egypt at the southern end of the Fertile Crescent with Assyria and Babylon farther north and east along the crescent. Wars ebbed and flowed between these ancient superpowers, and their armies marched back and forth through Canaan along the Mediterranean coast. Israel faced constant threats from these empires, and God desired to help His people. In Moses' song of victory after God

W

drowned the Egyptian army in the Red Sea, he said, "The LORD is a warrior" (Ex. 15:3). Jeremiah claimed, "The LORD is with me like a mighty warrior" (Jer. 20:11). During the time of the judges God used surrounding nations to invade and conquer Israel as a means of punishing His people for their rebellion and to restore her to Himself (Judg. 3:10; 11:4). Only during the reign of Solomon was Israel free of war (1 Kin. 4:25), in part because of his large and effective army (1:26; 10:26; 2 Chr. 1:14).

It is important to notice that in Bible times people held in high regard careers in military service. Elijah healed Naaman of leprosy (2 Kin. 5:9–15). It never occurred to the prophet to rebuke the "commander of the army of the king of Aram" (5:1) for his military life. Jesus healed the servant of a centurion (Matt. 8:5–13; Luke 7:1–10), and Peter preached the gospel to another centurion named Cornelius (Acts 10:3–48). Neither Jesus nor Peter questioned the legitimacy of the careers these men pursued.

When Jesus Christ establishes His millennial kingdom of righteousness and peace, "He will judge between the nations and will settle disputes for many peoples" (Is. 2:4). At that time, "they will beat their swords into plowshares and their spears into pruning hooks. Nation will not take up sword against nation, nor will they train for war anymore" (Mic. 4:3). Unfortunately until that time war will continue.   **—JAW**

***

In personal as well as national matters, remember that "wisdom is better than weapons of war" (Eccl. 9:18) and "a gentle answer turns away wrath" (Prov. 15:1).

WEALTH

The Bible assumes that God is the Creator, Owner, and Distributor of wealth. Scripture doesn't condemn the possession of riches. In fact, some of the great stalwarts of the faith were men of wealth, such as Abraham, Isaac, Job, Solomon, Joseph of Arimathea, Barnabas, and Philemon. Wealth is an abundance of possessions or resources. Early in Old Testament times, wealth consisted of vast herds of livestock. As Israel became a settled society, land and precious metals played a greater role in wealth. By New Testament times, coined money meant merchants no longer had to weigh pieces of gold and silver.

In Old Testament times people assumed riches indicated God's blessing on their owner (1 Sam. 2:7; Eccl. 5:19). In the Law God promised material prosperity to Israel as a reward for her obedience (Deut. 7:12–15). He repeated and expanded this pledge in Deuteronomy 28. Moses declared to the people, "If you fully obey the LORD your God and carefully follow all his commands I give you today, the LORD your God will set you high above all the nations on earth. . . . The LORD will grant you abundant prosperity—in the fruit of your womb, the young of your livestock and the crops of your ground. . . . However, if you do not obey the LORD your God and do not carefully follow all his commands and decrees I am giving you today, all these curses will come upon you and overtake you. . . . The LORD will send on you curses, confusion and rebuke in everything you put your hand to, until you are destroyed and come to sudden ruin because of the evil you have done in forsaking him" (28:1, 11, 15, 20). God also promised material blessing to individual Israelites who obeyed His commands. The psalmist declared, "Blessed is the man who fears the LORD, who finds great delight in his commands. . . . Wealth and riches are in his house, and his righteousness endures forever" (Ps. 112:1, 3).

At the same time, the Old Testament warned of the dangers that accompany great wealth. Wealth can war against the soul. It can cause a person to trust in his riches rather than in God. Some of the biblical warnings about trusting wealth instead of God are found in Deuteronomy 8:13–14; Psalms 49:6–7; 52:7; 62:10; and Proverbs 18:11.

Jesus taught a great deal about wealth. The basic principle of His teaching is that "a man's life does not consist in the abundance of his possessions" (Luke 12:15). Jesus warned us not to amass riches on earth but rather in heaven, because "where your treasure is, there your heart will be also" (Matt. 6:21). He said that the deceitfulness of wealth stifles the Word of God and makes it unfruitful in our hearts (13:22). After a conversation with a wealthy young man who loved his wealth more than God, Jesus told His disciples, "It is hard for a rich man to enter the kingdom of heaven" (19:23). Wealth can even imperil one's salvation! After giving the parable of the shrewd manager, Jesus warned, "No servant can serve two masters. Either he will hate the one and love the other, or he will be devoted to the one and despise the other. You cannot serve both God and Money" (Luke 16:13).

The Book of Acts records positive and negative illustrations of how early Christians used wealth in the church at Jerusalem. To meet the material needs of poor believers, Barnabas and others sold their lands and houses and gave the money to the apostles who distributed it to the needy (Acts 4:32–37). Ananias and Sapphira, however, lied to God and the apostles about the amount of money they brought, and that deceit led to their deaths (5:1–11).

W

The Epistles say less about money than the Gospels, but Paul and James both addressed the subject. Paul sharply warned that people who pursue wealth may fall into a trap that leads to destruction. He said, "The love of money is a root of all kinds of evil. Some people, eager for money, have wandered from the faith and pierced themselves with many griefs" (1 Tim. 6:10). The apostle urged the wealthy to be generous and share their riches. In this way they would "lay up treasure for themselves as a firm foundation for the coming age" (6:18–19). James admonished us not to show favoritism to the rich when we gather as the church (James 2:1–13). He also denounced wealthy people who accumulate riches by defrauding the helpless and the poor (5:1–6).

The Epistles of Paul say a lot about another kind of wealth—spiritual wealth. Paul spoke of "the riches of his [God's] kindness, tolerance and patience" (Rom. 2:4), the "riches of his glory" (9:23), the great spiritual riches to be enjoyed by Gentiles after the conversion of Israel at Christ's Second Coming (11:12), "the depth of the riches of the wisdom and knowledge of God" (11:33), "the riches of God's grace that he lavished on us with all wisdom and understanding" (Eph. 1:7–8), "the incomparable riches of his grace, expressed in his kindness to us in Christ Jesus" (2:7), and

"the glorious riches of this mystery, which is Christ in you, the hope of glory" (Col. 1:27). Second Corinthians 8:9 summarizes well our spiritual wealth: "For you know the grace of our Lord Jesus Christ, that though he was rich, yet for your sakes he became poor, so that you through his poverty might become rich." **—DKC**

***

Determine not to allow your possessions to war against your soul.

WILL OF GOD

The Bible frequently speaks of God's purposes and plans as His "will." God's will usually refers to what He has decreed, but occasionally God's will refers to what He desires but has not decreed. For example, it is His will (desire) that no one perish (2 Pet. 3:9), but He has not decreed that everyone be saved. Nor does God desire that any children be unsaved (Matt. 18:14).

Many acts of God, however, are His will in the sense that He planned them and will carry (or has carried) them out. God's will included creating "all things" (Rev. 4:11). Even birds do not fall to the ground apart from His will (Matt. 10:29). God willed that Christ be crucified to provide salvation. Isaiah wrote, "It was the LORD's will to crush him [the Messiah] and cause him to suffer" (Is. 53:10). When the people crucified Him, they did what God's "power and will had decided beforehand should happen" (Acts 4:28). Jesus was handed over to them "by God's set purpose" (2:23).

Jesus said that He came "to do the will of him who sent me" (John 4:34; 6:38). When He prayed in Gethsemane, Jesus said He would go to the cross because He knew that was the Father's will (Luke 22:42). Psalm 40:8 anticipated Christ's desire to do the Father's will, as explained in Hebrews 10:7, 9.

Jesus said the Father willed that everyone who believes in Christ should have eternal life (John 6:40). Paul wrote that those who believe in Christ are saved "because of [God's] own purpose and grace" (2 Tim. 1:9). They are "called according to his purpose" (Rom. 8:28). God's plan also includes that we be adopted as His children "in accordance with his pleasure and will" (Eph. 1:5).

By His will God also gives us spiritual gifts (Heb. 2:4). In five of his epistles Paul acknowledged that the only reason he was an apostle was because God willed it (1 Cor. 1:1; 2 Cor. 1:1; Eph. 1:1; Col. 1:1; 2 Tim. 1:1).

God also willed (planned) that believing Jews and Gentiles would be united in the body of Christ (Eph. 2:15; 3:11).

We should seek to know or understand God's will (Acts 22:14; Eph. 5:17; Col. 1:9), and we should "do" it. We should see that His desires are carried out in their lives. We should pray with David: "Teach me to do your will" (Ps. 143:10). The Bible does not give us a specific formula for finding God's will for the details of daily life, but the Scriptures do give us general commands that express His will. It is God's will (desire) that we be holy (1 Thess. 4:3), that we be grateful (5:18), that we dedicate ourselves to the Lord (2 Cor. 8:5), that we do good (1 Pet. 2:15), and that we suffer, if necessary, for doing good (3:17; 4:19). We should live not to gratify our own desires but to fulfill God's will (4:2).

God wants us to make wise decisions, based on circumstances, wise counsel, the leading of the Spirit, and biblical principles. When we follow God's will, we experience greater intimacy with Christ (Matt. 12:50), and we are assured of rewards in heaven (Heb. 10:36). Unlike the world, which will pass away, we will live forever if we follow the will of God (1 John 2:17).

God will equip us to do His will (Heb. 13:21). On our part, we should stand firm in His will (Col. 4:12). God listens to our prayers when we do His will (John 9:31), and He answers the prayers of those who desire that His will be done (1 John 5:14; see also Rom. 1:10; 15:32; James 4:15).

When we do the will of God, we

pursue a course of life that is "righteous" (Deut. 33:21) as well as "good, pleasing, and perfect" (Rom. 12:2).

—**JFW**

***

Rejoice in the fact that God "works out everything in conformity with the purpose of his will" (Eph. 1:11).

WISDOM

The Book of Proverbs teaches us about wisdom by using contrasts. In Proverbs 8—9 Solomon introduces us to two women. One is a virtuous lady, named Wisdom, who is concerned about others (8:1–5). She speaks words that are worthy, right, just, and true (8:6–9). What she has to offer is more precious than gold or rubies (8:10–11). Her ways help people know and understand God (9:10), and those who follow her enjoy many happy and long years (9:11). In stark contrast is the woman named Folly (9:13). She cares only for her own enjoyment. She is seductive, and what she says is untrue (9:17–18). Her ways do not lead to God; in fact, they lead to destruction. The rest of the Book of Proverbs continues to use contrasts to show us the characteristics and actions of wise people and foolish people.

Jesus also used contrast at many points in His teaching ministry. He taught the difference between a wise person and a foolish person by contrasting a man who built his house on a rock with one who built on sand. Jesus said that if we hear His word and put it into practice we are like the wise man, but if we disregard His teaching we are like the fool (Matt. 7:24–27). At a later time Jesus noted, "Wisdom is proved right by her actions" (11:19).

Paul employed a striking contrast to explain true wisdom. In order to explain why so many people reject the gospel of Christ, Paul contrasted the wisdom of the world and the wisdom of God (1 Cor. 1:20–31). In God's wisdom He chooses the weak things of the world. The wisdom of the Greek world exalted personal strength and discipline. It despised weak things. Greek thought would never have devised a plan of salvation that involved humility and self-sacrifice on the part of the Savior. Greek wisdom scoffed at Jesus, who was rejected by His people and crucified. The world's wisdom *seems* superior because of its eloquent words and complex philosophy (1:20). It has the illusion of cleverness and is bold and persuasive (2:4). But worldly thinking that has no room for God will perish and come to nothing (2:6).

James contrasted earthly wisdom and heavenly wisdom. He stated that true wisdom, which comes down from heaven (James 3:17) reflects the very characteristics of the Lord. It brings heavenly characteristics into our lives. The world's so-called wisdom, however, contains nothing heavenly. It is "earthly, unspiritual, of the devil" (3:15). Earthly wisdom will cause our lives to degenerate into "disorder and every evil practices" (3:16).

In a general sense wisdom refers to a faculty for successful, moral living. A wise person exercises understanding and good judgment. Inwardly, wisdom is characterized by discernment and skill. Outwardly it's marked by ability to apply knowledge to both the major dilemmas and the ordinary choices of life. Worldly-wise people may possess expertise that make them successful in their careers. Nebuchadnezzar, for example, administered an empire with the assistance of wise men in his cabinet, but they did not know God (Dan. 4:18). God has given human beings amazing ability to think, learn, create, and develop skills that lead to success in many areas. Individuals with no relationship to God can be "wise" in this one-dimensional way. They can function well in this world system. But "task wisdom" often is "relationship foolish." God's wisdom begins with a relationship with Him (Prov. 1:7) and leads to successful relationships with those around us. Human wisdom, no matter how intellectually brilliant, fails to produce intimacy with God and other people.

Eventually it leads to despair (Eccl. 1:18; Eph. 4:17–19).

True wisdom finds its source in God. Daniel said all wisdom belongs to "the God of heaven." He gives wisdom to the wise and reveals the unknown things to human understanding (Dan. 2:19–23). The Bible states that God gave wisdom to the craftsmen who built the tabernacle (Ex. 31:3–11) and to the workers who made the priestly garments (28:3–5). Their skills transcended normal craftsmanship.

God gave Solomon unusual wisdom so he could govern the people of Israel (1 Kin. 4:29–31; 2 Chr. 1:11–12). Government leaders of other nations realized that Solomon possessed a wisdom superior to anything they had seen (1 Kin. 10:6–9). The wisdom from God is so distinct even pagans recognize it (Dan. 5:14).

The ultimate truth about God's wisdom appears in the New Testament teaching that all treasures of wisdom and knowledge reside in Christ (Col. 2:2–3). When the apostle John saw visions of heaven, he witnessed one scene in which thousands of angels in heaven praised Jesus Christ. They said, "Worthy is the Lamb, who was slain, to receive power and wealth and wisdom and strength and honor and glory and praise!" (Rev. 5:12). In another scene he saw a great multitude of people from every nation, tribe, people, and language offering

W

praise to God for His wisdom, power, and strength (7:9–12).   **—WGJ**

* * *

Ask the Lord for wisdom to understand His Word and discern truth, and then be consistent in applying what you know to be right.

WOMAN

God completed His work of creation by making Adam and Eve. While the man and the woman individually reflected the image of God, they more fully expressed His image when they were in relationship with one another (Gen. 1:26–27). The Hebrew word ʾādām referred to humanity as expressed by both man and woman. It also functioned as the proper name for the first man (2:20).

After the general creation account of Genesis 1, Genesis 2 provides a detailed account of the creation of Adam and Eve. God formed Adam "from the dust of the ground" (2:7). "The man became a living being" when God "breathed into his nostrils the breath of life." Some time later the man named all the animals and birds without finding a "suitable helper" for him (2:19–20). God then anesthetized Adam, took one of his ribs, and "made a woman from the rib he had taken out of the man" (2:21–22). When Adam saw the woman he said, "She shall be called 'woman,' for she was taken out of man" (2:23). "For this reason," God said, "a man will leave his father and mother and be united to his wife, and they will become one flesh" (2:24). These accounts reveal the basic equality of male and female as well as the order of relationship between them.

Paul described this order of relationship when he wrote, "For Adam was formed first, then Eve" (1 Tim. 2:13), and, "For man did not come from woman, but woman from man; neither was man created for woman, but woman for man" (1 Cor. 11:8–9). As a result "the head of the woman is man" (11:3). This relationship arises from the order of creation, not from a difference in personal value or ability. "In the Lord, however, woman is not independent of man, nor is man independent of woman. For as woman came from man, so also man is born of woman. But everything comes from God" (11:11–12).

Because "the husband is the head of the wife as Christ is the head of the church, his body" (Eph. 5:23), wives are to "submit to [their] husbands as to the Lord" (5:22). "As the church submits to Christ, so also wives should submit to their husbands in everything" (5:24; see also Col. 3:18; Titus 2:5; 1 Pet. 3:1). This follows the statement advising all believers to "submit to one another out of reverence for Christ" (Eph. 5:21) and precedes the command that husbands must love their wives "just as Christ loved the church" (5:25) and "as their own bodies" (5:28).

To some degree the position assigned women in the family and in the church results from Eve's yielding to temptation in the Garden of Eden and leading Adam into sin (Gen. 3:1–8). Male headship derives from Adam's responsibility for sin entering the human race (Rom. 5:12, 14–18). Still "Adam was not the one deceived; it was the woman who was deceived and became a sinner" (1 Tim. 2:14; see also 2 Cor. 11:3). As a result Paul wrote, "I do not permit a woman to teach or to have authority over a man; she must be silent" (1 Tim. 2:12). Paul assigned men the responsibility for teaching and leading church congregations. Yet he envisioned all sorts of ministries for women, since he gave directions for women who were "praying or prophesying" (1 Cor. 11:5, 13).

The Ten Commandments afford men and women equal treatment. The fifth commandment states, "Honor your father and your mother" (Ex. 20:12; Lev. 19:3; Deut. 5:16; 27:16; Matt. 15:5; 19:19; Mark 7:10; 10:19; Luke 18:20; Eph. 6:2). Several Old Testament women held positions of prominence in Israel. Miriam, sister of Aaron and Moses (Num. 26:59), was a prophetess, who led the women in a song of victory after the defeat of the Egyptian army in the Red Sea (Ex. 15:20–21). She was a leader in Israel with her brothers (Mic. 6:4). Deborah, another prophetess, led Israel as a judge (Judg. 4:4). She and Barak delivered Israel from Sisera (4:6–24). Together they sang a song of deliverance and victory (5:2–31). Also Huldah (2 Kin. 22:14–20; 2 Chr. 34:22–29) and Isaiah's wife (Is. 8:3) prophesied. Rahab (Josh. 6:17–25; Heb. 11:31; James 2:25), Ruth (Ruth 1—4), and Hannah (1 Sam. 1—2) enriched Israel's history with their spiritual heroism.

The epilogue to the Book of Proverbs highlights a married woman's vital importance and significance as a wife, mother, and businesswoman (31:10–31). Proverbs 31 opens with the statement, "A wife of noble character . . . is worth far more than rubies," and closes with the admonition, "Give her the reward she has earned, and let her works bring her praise at the city gate." This woman is described as industrious, talented, generous, and wise. She serves as a good investor, manager, and merchant. She proves to be a source of benefit and blessing to her husband and her children. She epitomizes what God intended a woman and wife to be when He created her to be "a helper suitable" for man (Gen. 2:18; see also 2:22).

Women figured prominently in the life and ministry of the Lord Jesus Christ. Mary the mother of Jesus played

W

a role in her Son's life at various points. She stood by the cross as He died (John 19:25). Jesus ignored His anguish long enough to commit His mother to the care of "the disciple whom he loved" (19:26–27). Mary also met with the believers in Jerusalem after the Lord's ascension (Acts 1:14).

Other women who figured prominently in Jesus' ministry were Martha and Mary, the sisters of Lazarus (Luke 10:38–42; John 11:1–45; 12:1–8), and "Mary (called Magdalene) . . . Joanna . . . Susanna; and many others" (Luke 8:2–3). As Luke explained, "These women were helping to support them [Jesus and the disciples] out of their own means" (8:3). Some of the women witnessed Jesus' crucifixion (Matt. 27:55–56). "Mary Magdalene and the other Mary were sitting there opposite the tomb" (Matt. 27:61), intending to return after the Sabbath to prepare Jesus' body for proper burial (28:1). As a result Mary Magdalene saw the resurrected Christ before anyone else (John 20:14–18). In the course of His life Jesus met and ministered to the woman at the well at Sychar (4:4–42), the widow of Nain (Luke 7:11–17), and the woman "subject to bleeding for twelve years" (Mark 5:25–34).

Women played significant roles in the apostolic church and the ministry of the apostles. Several other women met with Jesus' mother and the male disciples in the Upper Room after Jesus' ascension (Acts 1:14). Peter restored Tabitha to life (9:36–42). The disciples gathered in the house of "Mary the mother of John, also called Mark" to pray for Peter's release from prison (12:5, 12–17). Paul spoke highly of Lois and Eunice, Timothy's grandmother and mother (2 Tim. 1:5; 3:14–15). Lydia helped found the church at Philippi (Acts 16:13–15, 40).

Paul called Priscilla and her husband Aquila "my fellow workers in Christ Jesus" (Rom. 16:3). They met him and provided employment for him in Corinth (Acts 18:2–4). When he traveled to Antioch in Syria, they accompanied him as far as Ephesus (18:18–19). There they led Apollos into a more accurate knowledge of the gospel (18:26). Apparently they remained and ministered in Ephesus (1 Cor. 16:19; 2 Tim. 4:19). Paul spoke highly of Phoebe (Rom. 16:1–2), Mary (16:6), Tryphena and Tryphosa (16:12), Persis (16:12), Rufus's mother (16:13), Julia, and the sister of Nereus (16:15). Paul's letters place limits on the ministry of women in church services, but he fully accepted and appreciated their faithful ministry for Christ.

Women filled various ministries in the apostolic church. They served as prophetesses (Acts 21:8–9) and deaconesses (Rom. 16:1). The church provided aid to widows in need (Acts 6:1). Churches enrolled and cared for widows over sixty years of age whose families could not care for them (1 Tim. 5:5–11).

In today's churches women have many opportunities for ministry that do not violate Paul's restrictions. The woman is still a helper suitable for the man. Together they share in the image of God.   **—JAW**

***

Respect and submit to each other, man and woman, out of reverence for Christ.

WORD

In the Bible, the English noun *word* translates the Hebrew noun *dābār* and the two Greek nouns *logos* and *rhēma*. These Hebrew and Greek terms refer to the shortest unit of speech that names an object or conveys a concept. "Word" becomes an important theological term because God reveals Himself through words, and "word" becomes a synonym for revelation.

The ultimate biblical use of *word* appears in the opening statement of the apostle John's Gospel: "In the beginning was the Word, and the Word was with God, and the Word was God" (John 1:1). Amazingly, "the Word became flesh, and made his dwelling among us. We have seen his glory, the glory of the One and Only, who came from the Father, full of grace and truth" (1:14). This Word, who became incarnate as Jesus Christ, previously had visibly expressed God as the Angel of the Lord (Gen. 16:9–13; 22:11–18; Josh. 5:14–15; Judg. 6:11–27; 13:3–23; 1 Chr. 21:15, 18). The Angel of the Lord had claimed to be God and had been treated as God (Ex. 3:2–17).

In the Old Testament God spoke His "word" directly to the patriarchs (Gen. 3:9, 11, 13–14, 16–17; 4:6, 9–10, 15; 6:13; 7:1; 8:15; 9:1, 8, 12, 17; 12:1; 13:14). He appeared to them in visions (15:1; 26:2; 46:2; Num. 24:4, 16) or dreams (Gen. 15:12-13; 20:3; 28:12; 31:10–13, 24). God also communicated to His prophets through visions and dreams. Examples include Moses and Miriam (Num. 12:6), Samuel (1 Sam. 3:1, 15), Solomon (1 Kin. 3:5, 15), Isaiah (Is. 1:1), Micah (Mic. 1:1), Nahum (Nah. 1:1), and Zechariah (Zech. 1:8).

Abram had a vision in which "the word of the LORD came to [him]" (Gen. 15:1; see also 15:4). This "vision" apparently had an audible as well as visual component to its message. In His rebuke of Aaron and Miriam, God explained that with Moses, "I speak face to face, clearly and not in riddles" (Num. 12:8; see also Ex. 33:7–11, 18–23; Deut. 34:10). As a result Moses acted "as he was commanded by the word of the LORD" (Num. 3:16, 51).

The Old Testament regularly identified the messages received by the prophets, whether for the present or

W

the future, as "the word of God." This practice began with Samuel (1 Sam. 15:10) and continued with the speaking prophets Nathan (2 Sam. 7:4), Gad (24:11), Solomon (1 Kin. 6:11), Shemaiah (12:22), Jehu (16:1), Elijah (17:2, 8), and Elisha (2 Kin. 7:1). Most of the writing prophets also referred to their oracles as "the word of God."

Luke said "the word of God came to John" the Baptist (Luke 3:2). This expression linked John to the Old Testament prophetic tradition (1:76; see also Matt. 11:9–15; Luke 7:24–27). Jesus was the Word of God, but the Gospel writers never said He received the "word of God." In fact, no one else in the New Testament is described as receiving "the word of God." This is because, although "in the past God spoke to our forefathers through the prophets at many times and in various ways . . . in these last days he has spoken to us by his Son" (Heb. 1:1–2). The message of the apostles explained the person and work of the Lord Jesus Christ.

In the New Testament the phrases "the word of God" and "the word of the Lord" refer to the gospel message (Acts 8:14, 25; 11:1; 13:5, 44, 46, 49; 19:20; Phil. 1:14; 1 Thess. 2:13; 1 Pet. 1:23). Because the message of the gospel quoted extensively from the Old Testament, these two phrases soon became identified with the Scriptures. Paul exhorted the Ephesians to take

"the sword of the Spirit, which is the word of God" (6:17). Because "the word of God is living and active" (Heb. 4:12; see also 1 Pet. 1:23), Paul charged Timothy, "Preach the Word" (2 Tim. 4:2). "Word" is capitalized in that verse in the New International Version because it applies to Jesus Christ as well as to the Scriptures.

The word of God, whether personal, spoken, or written, is "perfect" and has many other admirable qualities (Ps. 19:7–9). Jesus declared, "Heaven and earth will pass away, but my words will never pass away" (Matt. 24:35; Mark 13:31; Luke 21:33). Peter wrote, "The word of the Lord stands forever. And this is the word that was preached to you" (1 Pet. 1:25).

—JAW

***

By life and witness fulfill Paul's charge to Timothy, "Preach the Word; be prepared in season and out of season" (2 Tim. 4:2).

WORK

The primary Hebrew word translated "work" (*ʿāsâ*) means "to construct, make, produce." It can also refer to the results of such activity. The primary Greek word for "work" (*ergon*) influences the English term *energy* which speaks of the power it takes to work. We will discuss the theme of "work" in the Bible in two parts: first, the work of God that involves all three Persons of the Trinity—Father, Son, and Holy Spirit—and, second, our work as human beings. Both discussions consider physical and spiritual work.

In the Bible the physical work of God began when He created "the heavens and the earth" (Gen. 1:1), all the plants (1:11–13), the animals (1:20–25), and, finally, man and woman (1:26–27). The Bible assigns a role in creation to each person of the Godhead: the Word of God, that is, the preincarnate Lord Jesus Christ (John 1:3; Col. 1:16; Heb. 1:2, 10), the Holy Spirit (Gen. 1:2; Ps. 104:30), and God the Father (James 1:17). After God finished creation, He "rested from all his work" (Gen. 2:2–3). He rested because He was satisfied with all He had done, not because He was tired.

God continues to work within His creation. His work sustains the physical universe. The active power of God is the cohesive principle of the universe, not gravity or some mysterious quantum energy of the subatomic world (Rom. 11:36; Eph. 4:6). The Second Person of the Trinity takes personal responsibility for carrying out the will of God the Father as the sustainer of the material world (Col. 1:17; Heb. 1:3). Whenever He desires, God can suspend natural laws and act in ways we call miraculous.

After the Fall of men and women, God launched His spiritual work project. He set out to provide salvation for all human beings who would respond by faith to Him. God based our salvation on the sacrificial, substitutionary death of His Son, Jesus Christ, on the cross of Calvary. God the Father decreed this provision in eternity past (Eph. 1:11; 3:11) and administered it through various dispensations down to the present church age (3:9; Rom. 16:25; Col. 1:26). Through much of the Old Testament, God worked through Israel, His "own possession among all the peoples . . . a kingdom of priests and a holy nation" (Ex. 19:5–6, NASB; see also Deut. 7:6). God has temporarily set aside Israel because of her rebellion and sin, and so God has extended salvation to the Gentiles and has established the church, the body of Christ (Rom. 11:1–24). When Christ returns to the earth, Israel will be restored to God's favor and regenerated (Deut. 30:1–6, 8; Jer. 23:5–8). Meanwhile the triune God works to build the church.

The Lord Jesus Christ implemented the plan of God the Father relative to the work of salvation. He became incarnate, ministered on earth, provided the substitutionary sacrifice for sin, and now serves as "head over everything for the church, which is his body" (Eph. 1:22; see also 5:23). Jesus told His disciples that He came "to do the will of him who sent me and to finish

W

his work" (John 4:34). He told the Jews, "My father is always at his work to this very day, and I, too, am working" (5:17), and, "The very work that the Father has given me to finish, and which I am doing, testifies that the Father has sent me" (5:36).

Jesus once said that a blind man's condition "happened so that the work of God might be displayed in his life. As long as it is day, we must do the work of him who sent me" (9:3–4). In the Upper Room Jesus told the apostles, "It is the Father, living in me, who is doing his work" (14:10). As Jesus looked back on His ministry and ahead to His death on the cross, He prayed to God the Father, "I have brought you glory on earth by completing the work you gave me to do" (17:4). On the cross His final words were, "It is finished" (19:30).

Turning from God's work to our physical work, we need to look briefly at God's judgment on Adam for his sin. God told Adam, "Cursed is the ground because of you; through painful toil you will eat of it. . . . By the sweat of your brow you will eat your food" (Gen. 3:17, 19). All human work has an arduous unpleasant dimension to it. Thorns and thistles, real ones or metaphorical ones, spring up and frustrate us in every "field" of human endeavor. Before the Fall, Adam and Eve worked. "The LORD God took the man and put him in the Garden of Eden to work it and take care of it" (2:15). Nothing ever frustrated their efforts. Work led invariably to accomplishment and satisfaction. In our hearts we know that's the way it should be. A job well done is incredibly satisfying. But since the Fall, work is both pleasure and pain. Sin turned work into toil.

Human spiritual work can be looked at negatively and positively. Negatively, God does not want us to try to work for His acceptance and approval. Salvation can never be obtained through human "works." Salvation, as seen earlier, is the work of God. We can only be "justified by faith apart from observing the law [literally, 'works of the law']" (Rom. 3:28). Salvation is "the gift of God, not by works, so that no one can boast" (Eph. 2:8–9; see also 2 Tim. 1:9; Titus 3:5).

Positively, we can express our gratitude to God for the gift of salvation through works of service. We were "created in Christ Jesus to do good works, which God prepared in advance for us to do" (Eph. 2:10; see Titus 2:14). The Holy Spirit instructed the church at Antioch, "Set apart for me Barnabas and Saul for the work to which I have called them" (Acts 13:2). Paul recognized his own spiritual work (1 Cor. 9:1; 16:9) and mentioned the spiritual work of Tryphena, Tryphosa, Persis (Rom. 16:12), Timothy (1 Cor. 16:16), and Epaphroditus

(Phil. 2:25). He also challenged and encouraged Corinthian believers (1 Cor. 15:58; 2 Cor. 9:8), Archippus (Col. 4:17) and Timothy (2 Tim. 4:5) to work for the Lord.

Paul admonished the Philippian Christians to "continue to work out [their] salvation with fear and trembling" (Phil. 2:12), because their selfishness had divided the church into competing factions (2:2–5). He urged them to express their salvation through the quality of their lives. We all should work *out* our salvation, that is, to put it into practice. We never work *for* our salvation. In Philippians 2:12, the pronoun "your" is plural. Paul wanted the whole church to work toward humility and unity.   **—JAW**

***

Through Bible study and prayer seek to discover and to carry out the work God has prepared for you to do (Eph. 2:10).

WORLD

The biblical concept of the "world" did not envision planet earth orbiting the sun as part of a constellation in a vast universe. Modern astronomy has produced that model. The ancients thought of the world in terms of what they observed every day. The primary Hebrew words translated "world" (ʾereṣ and tēbēl) can as easily mean "land" (the ground beneath our feet, as in Ex. 3:8) as "earth" (the sum total of all "ground,"as in Gen. 1:1; 2:1; Pss. 91:2; 93:1). The primary Greek word for "world" is *kosmos,* which identifies the world as an orderly system. A less frequently used word is *aiōn* (from which we get *aeon*) which describes the world in terms of time. Another Greek word is *oikoumenē* (from which we get *ecumenical*) which identifies the inhabited world. In biblical times people thought and spoke of the world in terms of what they saw and knew, much as the average person does today.

The first thing the Bible says about the world is that God created it. The psalmist wrote, "The heavens are yours, and yours also the earth; you founded the world and all that is in it" (Ps. 89:11; see also Gen. 1:1; Pss. 24:1; 50:12; 90:2; John 1:3; Col. 1:16; Heb. 1:2). Furthermore God created the world according to a divine plan (Is. 14:26–27). God "founded the world by his wisdom" (Jer. 10:12; 51:15; see also Prov. 8:22–31). Therefore, David concluded, "The heavens declare the glory of God; the skies proclaim the work of his hands. . . . Their voice goes out into all the earth, their words to the ends of the world" (Ps. 19:1–4; see also Job 12:7–10; Is. 41:19–20; Rom. 1:20).

When sin entered human experience in the Garden of Eden (Gen. 3:1–8), Satan gained control of the fallen human race (Eph. 2:1–2) and the entire

W

world system (1 John 5:19). As a result, the devil truly could offer the Lord Jesus "all the kingdoms of the world" if He would "bow down and worship" him (Matt. 4:8–9). Since the Fall, God has worked to let people know that He is the One to worship. He did this in the Old Testament through miracles and through His interaction with His chosen people Israel (Ex. 34:10).

After providing salvation for all through the sacrificial death of His Son on the cross (John 3:16), God sent the gospel message to all the world. Jesus commanded the apostles, "Go into all the world and preach the good news to all creation" (Mark 16:15; see also Matt. 28:19; Acts 1:8). God called Paul to be an apostle to the Gentiles (9:15; 22:21) and sent him to carry the gospel throughout Asia Minor, the Grecian peninsula, and as far as Rome (and possibly on to Spain).

Satan usurped control of the world by deceiving the human race. Consequently the people of the world stand condemned and will be judged in the future by God. David wrote that God "will judge the world in righteousness" (Pss. 9:8; 98:9). The Gospel of John reports a time when God spoke from heaven as Jesus was resolving to face His looming death. Jesus explained the significance of God's utterance this way: "Now is the time for judgment on this world; now the prince of this world will be driven out" (John 12:31). The Holy Spirit has ministered since the Day of Pentecost to "convict the world of guilt in regard to . . . judgment, . . . because the prince of this world now stands condemned" (John 16:8, 11). Paul told the Athenians that God "has set a day when he will judge the world with justice by the man he has appointed" (Acts 17:31), namely, the resurrected Jesus Christ.

Since Satan now controls the world system (1 John 5:19; see also 2 Cor. 4:4; Eph. 2:2), the Bible commands, "Do not love the world or anything in the world" (1 John 2:15) because "everything in the world . . . comes not from the Father" (2:16). Eventually "the world and its desires pass away" (2:17).

In a sense God postpones judgment on the present world because He "desires all men to be saved and to come to the knowledge of the truth" (1 Tim. 2:4, NASB; see 2 Pet. 3:9). Meanwhile we live and minister in the world (2 Cor. 10:3). We face the hatred of the world (1 John 3:13) and do battle against the devil and "the powers of this dark world" (Eph. 6:12). We may "use the things of the world" (1 Cor. 7:31), but we need constantly to remember that "friendship with the world is hatred toward God" and that "anyone who chooses to be a friend of the world becomes an enemy of God" (James 4:4). When God's time of judgment comes, believers "will judge the world" (1 Cor. 6:2) and angels (6:3).   **—JAW**

***

While here on the earth we are to be a light in the world (Matt. 5:14) and a witness for Christ as we look for His return.

WORSHIP

One of the reasons God created the human race was so He could reveal Himself to His creatures. In turn God wanted us to recognize Him and respond to Him in fellowship. He placed in the human heart the need to worship Him. Genesis doesn't say that God commanded Cain and Abel to worship Him, but they felt compelled to bring an offering to Him. The need was in their hearts, and God expected them to worship Him wholeheartedly. Abel offered his sacrifice with a sincere heart, but Cain didn't (Gen. 4:3–7). Noah built an altar (8:20), even though the early chapters of Genesis do not contain any instruction about altars. Abram built an altar when the Lord appeared to him, as though that were the natural thing to do (12:7). When Abraham prepared to offer Isaac as a sacrifice in obedience to the Lord's command, he was preparing to worship God (22:5). Some five centuries later God gave Moses the Law, which prescribed how Israel should worship the Lord.

We can begin to define worship in the Bible by looking at the Hebrew and Greek words used to describe it. One Hebrew word means "to bow down" or "to prostrate oneself on the ground." This implies that worship involves respect, adoration, and recognition that God is highly exalted. The corresponding Greek term is *proskyneō*, "to fall down before." These words tell us that inwardly our heart should humbly adore God.

Another Hebrew word, *ʾābad*, and its Greek counterpart, *latreuō*, convey the concept of service. These words describe the outward aspect of worship. Worship serves God and honors Him. Our service, to be sure, must grow out of our inner attitude of humble adoration toward the Lord. Only worship from the heart pleases God.

The psalms were composed as personal expressions of worship, so they provide insight into the meaning of Old Testament worship. The psalms express worship in a variety of ways, including praise, petition, and thanksgiving. They confess sins and admit frustration and uncertainty. Some psalmists wrote beautiful descriptions of God and His greatness. In fact, every aspect of God's character can be seen in the psalms. Worship centers around the Lord. It extols His virtues and thanks Him for His salvation and blessing.

The Old Testament prophets often wrote about the dangers of superficial worship—ritualistic words and actions void of meaning. Many of the prophets ministered during times when Israel had turned her back on God. For

W

example, Jeremiah urged the people of Judah to stop worshiping the Lord with empty words and phrases (Jer. 7:2–7). He accused the people of worshiping other gods and reaching greater depths of wickedness than any of their ancestors (16:11). Because the residents of Jerusalem worshiped pagan gods, God allowed the Babylonians to destroy the city and its temple (22:9).

God always held out hope to Israel in her darkest hours. The prophets predicted a future when people from all nations will go to Jerusalem and worship the Lord (Is. 66:22; Zech. 14:16). The nation Israel has a glorious future that centers on worshiping the Lord.

The definitive biblical passage about worship falls in the portion of the Gospel of John that records Jesus' conversation with the Samaritan woman by the well at Sychar. When the woman realized Jesus knew about her immorality, she tried to change the subject by starting an argument about whether Jews or Samaritans worshiped the right way. Jesus ignored the woman's smoke screen and went to the heart of true worship (John 4:4–26).

Jesus explained a number of things about worship in this brief passage. He confirmed that God created man to worship Him (4:23). He affirmed that God had revealed Himself to Israel and had chosen her to be the channel of salvation to the world. He affirmed that worship of false gods is meaningless (4:22). Then Jesus dropped a bombshell when He asserted that true worship was about to change (4:21, 23). In fact, Jesus said that change "has now come" (4:23). God remains the focus of worship, but worshipers can have a much more intimate relationship with Him. True worshipers can go directly to God. In fact, God seeks worshipers who want that kind of relationship with Him.

We can summarize Jesus' message about worship in one statement with two emphases. True worshipers worship God "in spirit and in truth" (4:24). These two concepts align perfectly with the character of God. First, God is "spirit," so the best way to reach Him is in the spiritual realm. We worship from our innermost being. We exercise faith in the Lord, because without faith it is impossible to please Him (Heb. 11:6). Second, God is "truth," so we revere all He has revealed. Jesus Himself is the truth (John 14:6). The Holy Spirit is the Spirit of truth who leads us into all truth (16:13). The Spirit does this by illumining the Scriptures so we can grasp the truth of God.

Until the time of Jesus, Jerusalem served as the center of worship for the Jews. Since our Lord's death, resurrection, and ascension, the place of worship no longer matters. Christ serves as our Great High Priest in heaven, and His throne of grace is available to everyone who comes to Him in faith (Heb. 4:14–16). We no longer need animal sacrifices or an earthly priesthood.

The Book of Acts narrates how important worship was to the early church. Acts 2:42–47 gives us our first picture of a worshiping congregation. Paul's epistles give us glimpses of the early church worshiping through prayer, singing, Scripture reading, giving to the needy, and praising God. The churches gathered on the first day of the week to worship God and celebrate their faith in the Lord.

Interestingly the Book of Revelation refers to worship as often as the rest of the New Testament all together. The apostle John's description in Revelation 4—5 of the scene in heaven is unparalleled in all of Scripture. Angels and all the redeemed fall down in worship before God the Father and His Son, Jesus Christ. They praise the Father and Son by reciting a litany of their glorious qualities. In Revelation 21 John recorded his vision of the new heavens and the new earth, the eternal state. Those of us whom Jesus redeemed by His precious blood will eternally worship and serve the Lord God.   **—WGJ**

***

Take time every day to reflect on the majesty of the Lord and allow your heart to respond in praise and adoration.

WRATH

God is holy and absolutely righteous. God's purity makes Him a "consuming fire" (Heb. 12:29) to anything impure that enters His presence. Evil people need to fear Him (Is. 8:13–14; Heb. 10:31) because He hates sin. Sin revolts God because it offends His holiness. From the standpoint of sinful humanity, this aspect of God's character is frightening.

God is a God of wrath (Rev. 6:16–17). Wrath is not an attribute of God's character. Wrath is the necessary response of God's holiness to sin. The prophet Habakkuk declared that the eyes of God are too pure to look on evil (Hab. 1:13). Sin provokes God's wrath. Those who fail to submit to God, even though the creation clearly reveals Him, deserve His wrath (Rom. 1:32). When people reject God's love, they end up with His wrath (John 3:16, 36).

God directs His wrath against all ungodliness and wickedness. The earliest recorded expression of God's wrath occurred in heaven in response to the rebellion of Satan and his angels (Luke 10:18; 2 Pet. 2:4). The Old Testament includes many illustrations of God's wrath. The Flood covered the entire world and wiped out every living creature except those in the ark because of human wickedness God could not tolerate (Gen. 6:7). He destroyed Sodom and Gomorrah because

W

their sin grieved Him so (18:20). God struck Egypt with plagues to judges Pharaoh, the Egyptian nation, and their gods (Ex. 12:12; 15:7). Before Israel ever set foot in the Promised Land, God warned her that disobedience to the Mosaic Law would bring His severe judgment on her (Deut. 28:58–63). The Assyrian captivity was a result of God's wrath against Israel's sins (Is. 9:18–21). Jeremiah warned the people of Judah that God's wrath would come on them unless they had a change of heart (Jer. 4:3–4). The Babylonian captivity happened because of Judah's sin (7:20). Scores of times the prophets warned of God's wrath.

The New Testament also contains various warnings about God's wrath. These warnings point forward to an unprecedented time of judgment that will fall on the world before the Lord returns to establish His millennial kingdom. Jesus taught this to His disciples (Matt. 24:15, 21) in fulfillment of the prophecies of Jeremiah and Daniel (Jer. 30:7; Dan. 9:27; 11:31; 12:1). Revelation 6—18 records this devastating series of events that make up the seven-year Tribulation. This period of time will be characterized by "the wrath of the Lamb" (6:16). At least two-thirds of the people living on the earth will die in the Tribulation (6:8; 8:11; 13:15; 16:18–21). People will seek death in an effort to escape God's wrath (6:16–17; 9:6). The coming of the Lord with His saints will mark the end of this terrible tribulation period (19:11–16).

Only faith in the Lord Jesus Christ saves us from the wrath of God (John 3:36; Eph. 2:3–4). His death paid for the sins of the world, and we are justified by His blood and "saved from God's wrath through him" (Rom. 5:9). All who reject Christ will ultimately suffer the wrath of God and be cast into the lake of fire (Rev. 20:14–15). Believers will be delivered from eternal wrath (John 3:16; Rom. 6:23). They also will be saved by the Rapture from the wrath known as the Tribulation (1 Thess. 1:10; 5:9; Rev. 3:10).

—**WGJ**

***

Be sensitive to those who are in danger of experiencing the wrath of God, and pray fervently for their salvation.

Scripture Index

Mark

John